EIGHTH EDITION

Literature
for Children
A SHORT INTRODUCTION

David L. Russell
Ferris State University

PEARSON

Boston • Columbus • Indianapolis • New York • San Francisco • Upper Saddle River
Amsterdam • Cape Town • Dubai • London • Madrid • Milan • Munich • Paris • Montréal • Toronto
Delhi • Mexico City • São Paulo • Sydney • Hong Kong • Seoul • Singapore • Taipei • Tokyo

Vice President and Editorial Director: Jeffery Johnston
Acquisitions Editor: Kathryn Boice
Editorial Assistant: Carolyn Schweitzer
Marketing Manager: Christopher Barry and Krista Clark
Production Editor: Mary Beth Finch
Full-Service Vendor: Jouve
Manufacturing Buyer: Linda Sager
Cover Designer: Diane Lorenzo
Cover Image: Draco77/iStock Vectors/Getty Images

Credits and acknowledgments borrowed from other sources and reproduced, with permission, in this textbook appear on the appropriate page within text or on page 318.

Many of the designations by manufacturers and sellers to distinguish their products are claimed as trademarks. Where those designations appear in this book, and the publisher was aware of a trademark claim, the designations have been printed in initial caps or all caps.

Library of Congress Cataloging-in-Publication Data
Russell, David L.
   Literature for children: a short introduction / David L. Russell. — 8th edition.
      pages cm
   Includes bibliographical references and index.
   ISBN-13: 978-0-13-352226-6
   ISBN-10: 0-13-352226-1
   1. Children's literature—History and criticism.   2. Children—Books and reading.   I. Title.
   PN1009.A1R87 2014
   809'.89282—dc23
                                                                    2013043624

10   9   8   7   6   5   4   3   2   1

ISBN 10: 0-13-352226-1
ISBN 13: 978-0-13-352226-6

This for my grandchildren
Mason, Mariya, Emily, Sarah, Lily, and *Ella*
And to the memory of
Tookie Brian Woods (2008)
and
William Brian Woods, Jr. (1977–2009)

About the Author

David L. Russell is a professor of languages and literature in Michigan where he teaches children's literature and folk literature. He is the author of *Patricia MacLachlan* and *Scott O'Dell*, both published by Twayne, as well as *Stuart Academic Drama: An Edition of Three University Plays*, published by Garland. Additionally, he has published numerous scholarly articles on children's literature and was a contributor to *The Oxford Encyclopedia of Children's Literature*, *The Continuum Encyclopedia of Children's Literature*, and *The Cambridge Guide to Children's Books in English*. He is currently co-editor of *The Lion and the Unicorn*.

Contents

Preface   xvii

CHAPTER **1**   The History of Children's Literature:
How We Got Here   1

Introduction   1

The Earliest Children's Literature   1

The Middle Ages   2

The Renaissance   3

The Eighteenth-Century Moral Writers   7

The Rise of Folktales   8

The Victorian Golden Age   8

The Early Twentieth Century   12

The Late Twentieth Century and Beyond   13

Children's Literature around the World   15

Summary   16

For Reflection and Discussion   17

Works Cited   18

Recommended Resources   18

CHAPTER **2**   Literature and the Child:
Growing through Reading   21

Introduction   21

Language Acquisition   22

Modern Theories of Child Development   22

Jean Piaget and Cognitive Development   23

Erik Erikson and Psychosocial Development   25

Lawrence Kohlberg and Moral Development   26

Child Development and Reading   28

Sexuality   28

Death and Dying   29

War and Violence   31

Bibliotherapy   31

Intellectual Freedom   33

Summary   35

For Reflection and Discussion   35

Works Cited   36

Recommended Resources   36

CHAPTER 3   The Literature Experience:
Reading, Writing, Talking, and Doing   39

Introduction   39

Educational Theories   39

Lev Vygotsky and Social Interaction   40

Louise Rosenblatt and Reader Response   41

The Common Core Curriculum   42

Using Literature in the Classroom   44

Reading Experiences   44

Writing Experiences   47

Dramatic Experiences   50

Artistic Experiences   51

Technology in the Classroom   52

Summary   55

For Reflection and Discussion   55

Works Cited   56

Recommended Resources   56

CHAPTER 4   Diversity and Inclusion:
Reading the World   59

Introduction   59

Definition of Culturally Diverse Literature   60

Types of American Cultural Diversity   61

African Americans   61

Latinos/as   64

American Indians   65

Asian Americans   66

Other Cultures   67

Types of Social Diversity   68

Gender Awareness   69

Alternative Families   70

The Physically, Emotionally, and Intellectually Challenged   70

Summary   71

For Reflection and Discussion   72

Works Cited   72

Recommended Resources   73

Books Dealing with Cultural Diversity: A Selected and Annotated Booklist   74

CHAPTER 5   Beginning Books:
Knowledge through Delight   81

Introduction   81

Mother Goose Rhymes   81

Definition and Origin   81

Mother Goose and Child Development   83

Choosing Mother Goose Books   87

Alphabet and Counting Books   87

Alphabet Books   89

Counting Books   90

Perceptual Concept Books   91

Wordless Picture Books   92

Tactile Book and Movable Books   94

Easy Readers   95

Summary   96

For Reflection and Discussion   97

Works Cited   97

Recommended Resources   97

Books for Beginners: A Selected and Annotated Booklist   98

CHAPTER **6**   Picture Storybooks:
The Collaboration of Story and Art   103

Introduction   103

Picture-Book Characteristics   103

Picture-Book Stories   105

    Plot   105

    Character   106

    Language   106

Elements of Picture-Book Art   107

    Line   107

    Shape   107

    Space   107

    Texture   109

    Composition   110

    Perspective   111

    Color/Black and White   111

Artistic Media   112

    Painterly Techniques   112

    Graphic Techniques   113

    Photography and Digital Art   114

    Collage   114

Artistic Styles   114
   Realism   115
   Cartoon Art   115
   Folk Art   115
   Naïve Art   116
   Art Nouveau   116
   Expressionism   116
   Surrealism   116

Design and Meaning in Picture Books   117
   Rhythm and Movement   117
   Tension   118
   Page Layout   118

Picture Book Layout: Three Examples   120

Graphic Novels   122

Summary   122

For Reflection and Discussion   123

Works Cited   124

Recommended Resources   124

Picture Storybooks: A Selected and Annotated Booklist   125

CHAPTER 7   Poetry:
For the Love of Language   131

Introduction   131

Definition of Poetry   131

Sounds in Poetry   132
   Rhyme   132
   Rhythm   133

Pictures in Poetry   135
   Sensory Description   135
   Comparative Description   136

Kinds of Poetry   138
   Narrative Poetry and Ballads   138
   Lyric Poetry   139

Found Poetry   142

Sharing Poetry with Children   146

Summary   148

For Reflection and Discussion   148

Works Cited   149

Recommended Resources   149

Poetry for Children: A Selected Booklist   150

CHAPTER **8**   Folk Narratives:
The Oldest Stories   155

Introduction   155

The Elements of the Folk Narrative   156

Setting and Plot   156

Character   157

Language and Style   158

Images and Symbols   159

Motifs   159

Taboos   162

Types of Folktales   163

Talking Animal Tales   163

Fables   163

Wonder Tales   164

Merry Tales   164

Cumulative Tales   166

Tall Tales and Local Legends   166

Ghost Stories and Jump Tales   167

Trickster Tales   168

Pourquoi Tales   168

Myths and Traditional Epics   169

Folktales in the Classroom   171

Summary   172

For Reflection and Discussion   172

Works Cited   173

Recommended Resources   173

Folk Narratives: A Selected and Annotated Booklist   174

CHAPTER **9** The Elements of Story:
Reading Fiction   179

Introduction   179

Narrative Point of View   179
    First-Person Narrator   179
    Limited Narrator   180
    Omniscient Narrator   180

Setting   181

Characters   181
    Character Types   181
    Character Traits and Development   182
    Character Revelation   182

Plot   183
    Dramatic Plot   183
    Episodic Plot   183
    Parallel Plot   184
    The Journey   185

Conflict   185
    Protagonist against Another   186
    Protagonist against Society   186
    Protagonist against Nature   187
    Protagonist against Self   187

Style   189
    Exposition and Dialogue   189
    Foreshadowing and Flashback   189

Tone   190
    Didacticism   190
    Sentimentalism   191
    Humor   191
    Parody   192
    Irony   193

Theme   193

Ways of Reading Literature   195
   Formal Approach   195
   Archetypal Approach   196
   Historical Approach   197
   Psychoanalytical Approach   198
   Feminist Approach   199
   Ecocriticism   199

Summary   200

For Reflection and Discussion   201

Works Cited   201

Recommended Resources   202

CHAPTER **10** Fantasy:
The World of Make-Believe   203

Introduction   203

Fantasy Fiction Characteristics   204

The Qualities of Fantasy   205
   The Fantasy World   206
   The Fantasy Rules   206
   The Fantasy Characters   207

Types of Fantasy Fiction   207
   Animal Fantasy   209
   Toy Fantasy   210
   Magical Fantasy   211
   Tall Tales   212
   The Enchanted Journey   212
   Epic Fantasy   212
   Miniature Fantasy   213
   Supernatural and Time-Shift Fantasy   214
   Science Fiction and Speculative Fiction   215
   Dystopias   215

Summary   216

For Reflection and Discussion   217

Works Cited   218

Recommended Resources   218

Fantasy Fiction: A Selected and Annotated Booklist   219

CHAPTER 11 Realistic Fiction:
The Days of Our Lives   225

Introduction   225

Historical Realism   225
    Definition and Background   225
    Capturing the Period   227

Contemporary Realism   228
    Definition and Background   228
    New Realism and the Problem Novel   229

Topics in Realistic Fiction—Historical and Contemporary   230
    Family Relationships   231
    Friendship   233
    Adventure and Survival   235
    Social Outcasts   236
    Sexuality   237
    Death and Dying   237
    Mysteries and Puzzlers   238
    Sports   239
    Animals   239

A Word about Verse Novels   240

Summary   240

For Reflection and Discussion   241

Works Cited   242

Recommended Resources   242

Historical Realism: A Selected and Annotated Booklist   242

Contemporary Realism: A Selected and Annotated Booklist   245

CHAPTER **12** Nonfiction:
Telling It Like It Is   251

Introduction   **251**

Characteristics of Nonfiction   **251**

Purpose and Audience   252

Factual Information   252

Style   254

Format   254

Illustrations   255

Types of Nonfiction   **256**

Science and Nature   258

Arts and Leisure   260

Human Growth and Development   261

History, Society, and Culture   262

Biography and Autobiography   262

Nonfiction and the Common Core Curriculum   **265**

Summary   **266**

For Reflection and Discussion   **266**

Works Cited   **267**

Recommended Resources   **267**

Nonfiction: A Selected and Annotated Booklist   **268**

Appendix Children's Book Awards   281

American Awards   **281**

The Newbery Medal   281

The Caldecott Medal   284

The Mildred L. Batchelder Award   287

The Laura Ingalls Wilder Award   288

The Coretta Scott King Award   289

National Council of Teachers of English Award for Excellence
in Poetry for Children   291

The Scott O'Dell Award for Historical Fiction   291
NCTE Orbis Pictus Award for Outstanding Nonfiction for Children   292
Robert F. Sibert Informational Book Award   293

International Awards   **293**
The Carnegie Medal   293
The Kate Greenaway Medal   295
The Hans Christian Andersen Award   297
The Astrid Lindgren Memorial Award   298

Glossary   299

Children's Literature Resources   303

Index   305

Credits   318

Preface

Katherine Paterson famously said, "I love revision. Where else can spilled milk be turned into ice cream?" It is with this spirit that I have entered into this eighth edition. Certainly, being asked to do a revision is both an honor and an opportunity—and I have tried to make the most of that opportunity. In doing so, I hope to have preserved the features that faithful users have liked, and to have made changes that will improve the text for everyone.

As frequently happens, this revision turned out to be more dramatic than I had originally envisioned. Large portions have been rewritten in the interest of clarity and economy. More examples have been included, which has often permitted a streamlining of the text. I have always believed one of the virtues of this book is its adaptability to a wide variety of course designs. The chapters have been reorganized—always a dangerous thing to do for loyal users. But it seems to me that moving the chapter on literary elements to the place just before the chapters on fantasy, realism and nonfiction makes a great deal of sense. And I have found that in my own classes, I used the elements chapter in conjunction with the genre chapters. Naturally, every instructor has to adapt the text to his or her own needs and goals.

New to This Edition

- All chapters have been rewritten and some have been reorganized to accommodate new research and material.
- All resource lists have been updated resources.
- The booklists following Chapters 4, 5, 6, 10, 11, and 12 now provide a brief annotation for each entry, which should make the lists more useful to prospective teachers and to general readers.
- A brief discussion of world literature around the world has been restored to Chapter 1. acknowledging the increasingly international flavor of children's literature.
- Chapter 3 (The Literature Experience) now includes a brief discussion of the Common Core Curriculum and a discussion of the use of technology in the classroom.
- A list of 25 Things to Do with Poetry has been included in Chapter 7 (Poetry).
- Chapter 8 (Folk Narratives) now includes a section on using folktales in the classroom.
- Chapter 9 (The Elements of Story) now includes a brief discussion of critical approaches to literature as applied to children's literature.

- Chapter 12 (Nonfiction) now includes guidelines for evaluating nonfiction texts.
- The Orbis Pictus Award has been added to the Book Awards Appendix

Literature for Children: A Short Introduction was originally written as a supplement to primary texts used in the classroom. My own students spend most of their time reading the primary material—the picture books, the poetry, the folktales, the fantasies, the realistic fiction, the nonfiction. This book is but a guide—and I hope a friendly one. Finally, I offer no apology for my approach, which is decidedly literary, reflecting my own background as a teacher of English literature. My hope is that all who use this book come away with more than just ideas about how to make reading fun in the classroom (however important that is). Children's literature provides an excellent opportunity for us to develop an appreciation for the art of literature and an understanding of how literature reflects our world and ourselves.

I would like to thanks the reviewers of this book for their comments: Gail Ditchman, Moraine Valley Community College; Brenda Dales, Miami University; Lee Edward Allen, University of Memphis; Christine Warren, Southeast Missouri State University; Olga H. Fischer, University of Texas at Tyler.

As always, I close with a quotation from *Ecclesiasticus,* a question that goes to the heart of education:

If thou hast gathered nothing in thy youth, how canst thou find anything in thine age?

CHAPTER 1

The History of Children's Literature

How We Got Here

Introduction

It is popular to date the history of children's books from the mid-eighteenth century, when the English publisher John Newbery began selling books for children in his shop near St. Paul's Cathedral in London. But children, just like adults, have always enjoyed good stories, and the true origins of children's literature can be traced back thousands of years (see Jonathan Gottschall's *The Storytelling Animal* and Brian Boyd's *On the Origin of Stories* on the importance of storytelling in human life and history). Humanity's earliest storytelling experiences were both oral and communal, stories told aloud to an entire community—men, women, and children—a practice still found in many places around the world. At first, little distinction was made between stories for children and stories for adults; everyone enjoyed the same stories, and some stories were simply diluted for the very young (just as today). But over time, and for a variety of reasons, children's literature began to be separated from adult literature, until children's literature finally came to occupy its own niche in the literary canon. Let's see how that happened.

The Earliest Children's Literature

The earliest European literature we know of is that of the ancient Greeks (ca. 850 BCE–150 BCE) and the ancient Romans (ca. 150 BCE–476 CE). Sometime in the eighth century BCE, the Greek poet Homer wrote *The Iliad*, the story of the Trojan War, and *The Odyssey*, the story of Odysseus's travels back home to Ithaka following the war. Even though Homer clearly had adults in mind, these stories have long been popular with children. After all, they contain exotic adventures, wondrous creatures with magical powers, and some of the world's first superheroes—the forerunners of Superman, Batman, and Wonder Woman. These tales are still being told for children, as in Padraic Colum's *The Children's Homer*

(1918), Marcia Williams's *Greek Myths* (1992), and Jeanne Steig's somewhat daring *A Gift from Zeus: Sixteen Favorite Myths* (2001).

The Greeks also gave us Aesop's *Fables*, brief talking animal stories, each with a pointed moral. These include such famous tales as "The Wolf in Sheep's Clothing" (its moral being "Things aren't always what them seem"), "The Tortoise and the Hare" ("Slow and steady wins the race"), and "The Ant and the Grasshopper" ("Always be prepared"). Tradition has it that they were written by a teacher named Aesop in Greece around 600 BCE, presumably as lessons for his students. Printed editions date back to the fifteenth century (William Caxton's *The Fables of Aesop*, 1484), and they remain a staple on children's bookshelves, with modern versions illustrated by Arnold Lobel (1983), Don Daily (1999), Jerry Pinckney (2000), and Brad Sneed (2003), for readers from about 4 years and older.

The Roman poet Ovid (ca. 43 BCE–17/18 CE) wrote down many of the ancient Greek and Roman myths and legends in his book *Metamorphoses*. He retells, among others, the tales of Hercules, of the famed lovers Pyramus and Thisbe (an inspiration for *Romeo and Juliet*), and of Pygmalion, who sculpted a statue of a woman so beautiful he fell in love with it. Adrian Mitchell's *Shapeshifters: Tales from Ovid's Metamorphoses* (2010) is a recent retelling for children. Also for young children are Ursula Dubosarsky's dramatic versions (2012), which are available electronically for classroom use. The ancient myths have also inspired modern variations, notably Rick Riordan's popular Percy Jackson series, including the books *Percy Jackson and the Olympians* and *The Heroes of Olympus*. So you see, children are not immune to ancient tales; in fact, these oldest of stories remain among the most powerful and most popular.

The Middle Ages

The Middle Ages (approximately the period from the fall of the Roman Empire in 476 to around 1450) was a rather rough-and-tumble period that was kept civilized through the efforts of the Roman Catholic Church. Although education declined during this period, and few people could read, the oral tradition was kept alive. Naturally, all children would have been familiar with the biblical stories—Adam, Eve, and the forbidden fruit; Noah and the flood; Jonah and the great fish; Moses and the parting of the Red Sea; David and Goliath. But a wealth of other adventure stories and hero tales existed as well. Favorites included the adventures of King Arthur, Charlemagne, Roland, and Beowulf. The epic of *Beowulf*, composed sometime between 900 and 1100, tells of the struggles between a great king and a dreadful monster, Grendel, and his even more dreadful mother. It is rather a grizzly tale, as monster stories usually are, but dozens of versions of this story for children are in print, including James Rumford's recent *Beowulf*, from 2007.

For modern children's versions of these medieval tales, see Michael Morpurgo's *Sir Gawain and the Green Knight* (2004), illustrated by Michael Foreman; *Sir Gawain and the Loathly Lady*, by Selina Hastings and illustrated by Juan Wijngaard (1987); Benedict Flynn's *King Arthur and the Knights of the Round Table* (2008), which comes with an audio CD; and Gerald Morris's *Sir Gawain the True* (2011), one of a series of books containing loose, but lively, adaptations of Arthurian legends.

The Renaissance

The predominately oral culture of the Middle Ages gradually gave way to the more literate culture of the Renaissance (beginning roughly around 1400, and earlier in some places, like Italy). The Renaissance is usually seen as a flowering of European culture, and people began to look to the sophisticated cultures of ancient Greece and Rome for inspiration (the term *Renaissance* means "rebirth"—a reference to this return to classical ideals).

Perhaps the most important development of the entire era was the perfection, around 1440, of the movable-type printing press, attributed to Johannes Gutenberg (although the Chinese had actually invented it long before that). No longer did books have to be laboriously copied by hand, but they could be mass produced. Books became cheaper and more plentiful, literacy increased, and learning advanced. In short, the printing press was one of the most influential inventions of the past 1,000 years.

Still, the Renaissance produced very few books specifically for children. Among the earliest were hornbooks (see Figure 1.1), which were not really books but sheets of parchment attached to wooden slabs and covered with transparent horn (from cattle, sheep, and goats), an early form of lamination to make them durable. Hornbooks were used by very young children in school and usually contained simple language lessons (the alphabet, numbers, the Lord's Prayer). One of the first true books for children was John Comenius's *Orbis Sensualium Pictus* (see Figure 1.2), which appeared in 1658. It is not a storybook but a textbook designed to teach Latin vocabulary—a sort of Latin through pictures. (Every educated person in Europe knew Latin in those days; professors even delivered college lectures in Latin.) One of the most famous schoolbooks of the period was the *New England Primer*, which first appeared sometime around 1690 and continued in print in some form or another until 1886. It introduced young Puritan children to the alphabet through rhymes ("In Adam's fall/We Sinned all" for the letter *A*) and moved to increasingly sophisticated reading material—all with a religious intent (see Figure 1.3).

But when literate children wanted to read books for pleasure, they had to turn to adult books, like John Bunyan's *The Pilgrim's Progress* (1678). Although it is a serious religious allegory about human salvation, it is filled with thrilling adventures and terrifying monsters (much as in *Beowulf*). These features appealed to young readers from the very beginning. Today hundreds of editions remain in print, including many retold for children, such as that by Geraldine McCaughrean. Equally popular was Daniel Defoe's *Robinson*

FIGURE 1.1 ■ This typical hornbook from the time of Shakespeare illustrates the religious nature of education at that time. It is simply parchment fastened to a wooden paddle and laminated with animal horn for durability. Very young students in the sixteenth and seventeenth centuries would have learned to read using such a teaching device.

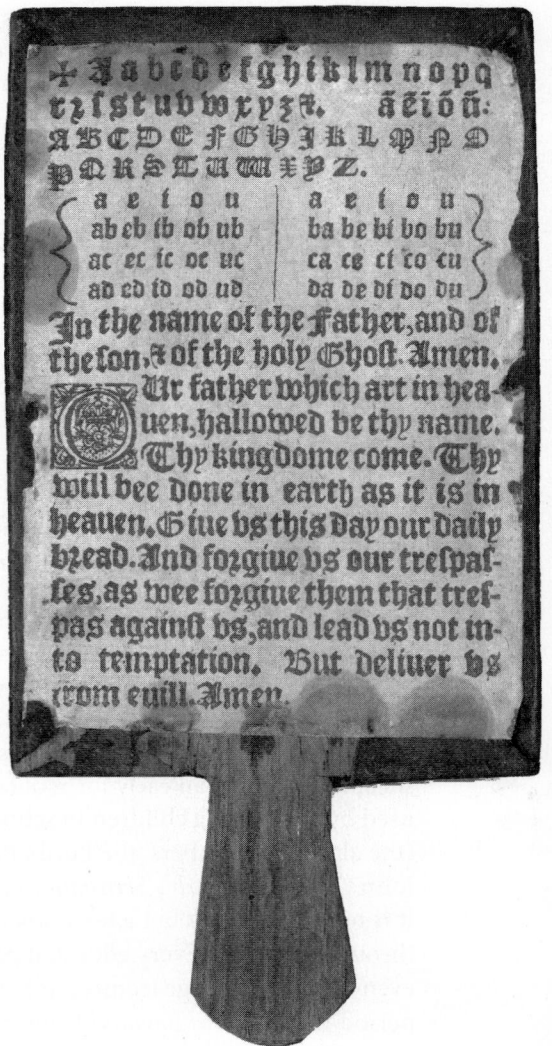

Crusoe (1719), about a man surviving on a strange deserted island. Defoe's story is still to be found in many modern children's versions, including one beautifully illustrated by N. C. Wyeth. It has become the prototype for modern survival stories (such as Scott O'Dell's *Island of the Blue Dolphins* and Jean Craighead George's *Julie of the Wolves*). Survival stories involving young heroes and heroines remain enormously popular with children. Jonathan Swift's *Gulliver's Travels* (1726) is also a journey tale, one that visits several wildly fanciful lands filled with extraordinary adventures. Gulliver's story remains available to children in many adapted versions (such as the "Classic Starts" edition of 2006) and has found its way into several film adaptations.

CXXXVI.

Ludi Pueriles.

Boyes-Sport

Boys used to play either with *Bowling-stones* 1. or throwing a *Bowl*, 2. at *Nine-pins*, 3. or striking a *Ball*, through a *Ring*, 5. with a *Bandy*, 4. or scourging a *Top*, 6. with a *Whip*, 7. or shooting with a *Trunk*, 8. and a *Bow*, 9. or going upon *Stilts*, 10. or tossing and swinging themselves upon a *Merry-totter*, 11.

Pueri solent ludere vel *Globis fictilibus*, 1. vel jactantes *Globum*, 2. ad *Conas*, 3. vel *mittentes* Sphærulam per *Annulum*, 5. *Clava*, 4. versantes *Turbinem*, 6. *Flagello*, 7. vel jaculantes *Sclopo*, 8. & *Arcu*, 9. vel incidentes *Grallis*, 10. vel super *Petaurum*, 11. se agitantes & oscillantes.

FIGURE 1.2 ■ John Comenius's *Orbis Sensualium Pictus* is often considered the first children's picture book. It first appeared in 1658 as a German/Latin textbook and was an immediate success. It revolutionized Latin instruction, a necessity in a society in which Latin was still the language of scholarship. The English/Latin version, from which this illustration is taken, appeared in 1659. Although the woodcut illustrations are crude, they provide a wealth of information about seventeenth-century European life.

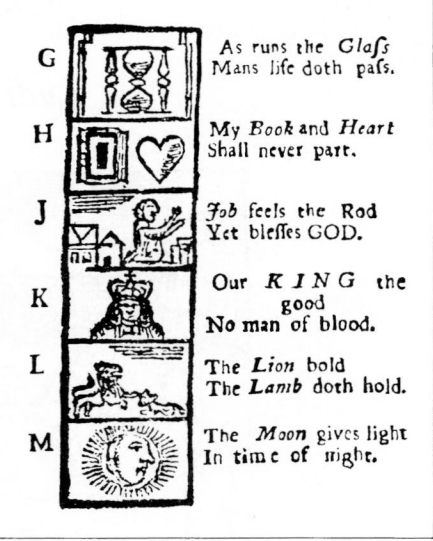

FIGURE 1.3 ■ The *New England Primer* was one of the longest-lived school texts in American history, flourishing from approximately 1690 to 1830. The earliest surviving copy is from 1727, from which these illustrations are taken. Intended to teach the children of the early Puritans how to live a godly life, the book is unabashedly didactic, which is evident even in its rhyming alphabet, recalling a time when church and state were not as separate as they are now.

The Eighteenth-Century Moral Writers

Three men had an extraordinary influence on children's reading in the eighteenth century—John Locke, John Newbery, and Jean-Jacques Rousseau. In 1693, the English philosopher John Locke (1632–1704) wrote a famous essay called *Thoughts Concerning Education*. Here, he described the minds of young children as blank slates (or in Latin, *tabula rasa*) waiting to be written upon. All children, he argued, had equal capabilities to learn, and adults needed to provide the proper learning environment and suitable material to fill the youthful minds. For Locke, heredity was unimportant, since everyone, he believed, began life on an equal footing, with the same capacity to learn and understand. Thus began the perennial argument over the relative influence of heredity and the environment (that is, nature versus nurture). Today, Locke's ideas have been seriously challenged by human genetic studies (see Chapter 2; let's face it, we are not all born with equal abilities), but his belief in the importance of education still drives our schools and universities.

John Newbery (1713–1778) was not a philosopher or a writer. Instead, he was a businessman who hit upon the idea of marketing books especially written for children. His *A Little Pretty Pocket Book* (1744) is considered a landmark in children's book publishing. It was one of the first children's books found on sale in a bookshop. Newbery wrote and compiled other books for children—none of them very good—but more importantly, he provided a market for other writers. Now there was a place where children's books could be purchased, and writing books for children could be lucrative. Without Newbery's idea, children's literature as we know it today could never have come about. Newbery was immortalized when the American Library Association established, in 1922, the famous medal that bears his name and is given to what is judged the best children's book published in the United States.

The third influence was French philosopher Jean-Jacques Rousseau (1712–1778), who wrote a book called *Emile* (1762). This work describes Rousseau's notion of an ideal education, which he believed should emphasize moral development through a simple lifestyle, preferably lived in the country, away from the corrupting influence of the city. Curiously, Rousseau did not encourage reading, which he believed could have a corrupting influence—a belief rather unfortunately held by some people yet today (see "Intellectual Freedom" in Chapter 2). However, he did admire *Robinson Crusoe* and its argument for self-sufficiency. Rousseau inspired many followers who wrote didactic and moralistic books to teach children how to be good and proper human beings.

Among Rousseau's English followers was Maria Edgeworth (1744–1817), who wrote a popular book titled *Simple Susan* (1796), about a country girl whose goodness helps her to triumph over an ill-intentioned city lawyer. Another disciple of Rousseau was Sarah Trimmer (1741–1810), who wrote *The Story of the Robins* (originally called *Fabulous Histories*, 1786), about a family of robins living side-by-side with a human family who learn from the robins the virtue of kindness. The story was unusual in a time that frowned on tales of talking animals. (The eighteenth-century rationalists thought it was illogical, and religious zealots thought it unholy.) Mrs. Trimmer carefully pointed out to her young readers that her story is a fable and that animals cannot really talk. She is also famous for condemning fairy stories for children because they were sacrilegious and lacked moral purpose. Mrs. Sherwood (1775–1851), another of the moral writers, wrote *The History of the Fairchild Family* (1818), which includes frighteningly vivid stories about the souls of impious children moldering in cold graves or being consigned to the fires of hell. This was serious moral stuff.

The Rise of Folktales

Alongside the moralistic tales came something rather refreshing—the revival of the old folktales from the quickly fading oral tradition. Actually, folktales were printed in England as early as 1729. At that time, *Tales of Mother Goose*, originally retold by the Frenchman Charles Perrault (1628–1703), was first translated and published in English. Although they were not originally for children, these tales, which included "Cinderella," "Little Red Riding Hood," and "Sleeping Beauty in the Wood," soon became staples in English nurseries. John Newbery's successor, Elizabeth Newbery, published the first children's edition of the Middle Eastern *Tales from the Arabian Nights*, featuring Sinbad the Sailor, Aladdin and his lamp, and others, in about 1791.

At the beginning of the nineteenth century, two German brothers, Jacob (1785–1863) and Wilhelm (1786–1859) Grimm, collected and published a great number of folktales, and the Grimms' tales are still the most famous of all collections. The Grimms also inspired a number of folktale collectors throughout Europe, including Hans Christian Andersen in Denmark (who also wrote many of his own original tales) and Asbjörnsen and Moe in Norway, and Joseph Jacobs (*English Fairy Tales*) and Andrew Lang (*The Blue Fairy Book*, *The Red Fairy Book*, and so on) in Great Britain. Folk rhyme collections, variously called Mother Goose rhymes or nursery rhymes, became equally popular (see Figure 1.4).

The Victorian Golden Age

In 1865, Lewis Carroll (pseudonym for Charles Dodgson) published *Alice's Adventures in Wonderland*, usually considered the first English children's story written purely for entertainment with no thought toward moral rectitude. The sequel, *Through the Looking-Glass*, appeared in 1871–1872. These wild fantasies continue to fascinate children (and moviegoers) today, and its unforgettable characters (Alice, the Mad Hatter, the Cheshire Cat,

9

The man in the moon came down too soon
To inquire the way to Norridge;
The man in the south, he burnt his mouth
With eating cold plum-porridge.

FIGURE 1.4 ■ Abel Bowen's woodcut illustration of "The Man in the Moon," from *Mother Goose's Melodies*, dramatically depicts the contrast between the ridiculous and the sublime that underlies much of children's literature. On the left side, with grace and elegance, a youth descends from the crescent moon; on the right side, a buffoonish character is engaged in a nonsensical act. Dating from 1833, this illustration is among the earliest American children's books designed purely for the pleasure of young readers.

the Jabberwock, Tweedledum and Tweedledee, the Red Queen, the White Knight, and many others) are indelibly fixed in English-speaking culture. Carroll's works helped to establish the trend away from eighteenth-century didacticism in children's literature. No longer were children's books viewed as merely vehicles for lessons in living or moral and religious guides. Children's literature was beginning to be seen as entertainment rather than moral and spiritual education.

Alice's Adventures in Wonderland heralded things to come. Encouraged by increasing prosperity, a rising middle class, the broadening of public education, and the development of technology, children's literature began to flourish in the later nineteenth century. Soon, high-quality books were appearing chiefly in Great Britain but increasingly in the United States. They covered a broad literary spectrum, including

- *Adventure stories* (R. M. Ballantyne's *The Coral Island*, 1857, and Mark Twain's *The Adventures of Tom Sawyer*, 1876)—often set in exotic places in the far-flung British Empire or in the vastness of America;

- *Series books* (Oliver Optic's *Outward Bound; or, Young America Afloat*, 1867, and Horatio Alger, Jr., *Ragged Dick; or, Street Life in New York*, 1867)—also adventure stories for boys, but usually with an educational or moral purpose, which were very popular in America;

- *Historical novels* (Robert Louis Stevenson's *Kidnapped*, 1886, and Howard Pyle's *Otto of the Silver Hand*, 1888)—usually adventure stories, but set in some romantic or exotic past;

- *Domestic and family stories* (Charlotte Yonge's *The Daisy Chain*, 1856, and Louisa May Alcott's *Little Women*, 1868)—usually intended as fare for girls, about the joys, trials, and tribulations of family life;

- *School stories* (Thomas Hughes's *Tom Brown's School Days*, 1857, and Edward Eggleston's *The Hoosier Schoolmaster*, 1871)—a counterpart to domestic and family stories but for boys and with a school setting where boys could have adventures beyond the watchful eyes of their parents (many of these stories take place in boarding schools);

- *Fantasies* (George MacDonald's *The Princess and the Goblin*, 1872, and L. Frank Baum's *The Wonderful Wizard of Oz*, 1900)—following in the path of *Alice's Adventures in Wonderland*, stories set in magical lands or about magical interventions in our own world;

- *Poetry* (Edward Lear's *A Book of Nonsense*, 1846, and Robert Louis Stevenson's *A Child's Garden of Verses*, 1885)—some delightfully nonsensical (Lear), others charming and sentimental (Stevenson); and

- *Folktales* (Andrew Lang's *The Blue Fairy Book*, 1889, and Joseph Jacobs's *English Fairy Tales*, 1890)—following in the tradition of the brothers Grimm.

FIGURE 1.5 ■ Walter Crane's sophisticated use of line and composition can be seen in his portrayal of Jack and Jill carrying the bucket of water down the hill, from *The Baby's Opera* (1877).

In addition, by the mid-1800s, printing technology had perfected color printing, and this attracted many fine illustrators to the field of children's books. Walter Crane (see Figure 1.5) and George Cruikshank were among the pioneers in this arena. Randolph Caldecott (1846–1886) brought a lively humor to his illustrations (see Figure 1.6). Kate Greenaway (1846–1901) depicted a charming and carefree Victorian childhood in her illustrations of popular nursery rhymes and poems (see Figure 5.4). Their illustrations set the standard for the age and are admired today. A little later, Beatrix Potter became a sensation with *The Tale of Peter Rabbit* (1901), which she both wrote and illustrated (see Chapter 6, Color Plate A). Her books are still in print and much loved, perhaps in part because Potter followed her own advice: "I think the great point in writing for children is to have something to say and to say it in simple, direct language" (quoted in Hunt, *An Introduction to Children's Literature*, 88). The later nineteenth century is widely regarded as the Golden Age of children's literature—and certainly it was the period during which children's literature came into its own.

FIGURE 1.6 ■ Randolph Caldecott, the great nineteenth-century English illustrator, was one of the pioneers of children's book illustration. His art is characterized by an economy of line and a playfulness of manner that make his work appealing today, more than a century after his death. The American Library Association annually awards the Caldecott Medal, named in his honor, to what it judges the most distinguished picture book published in the United States. This illustration from *The Frog He Would A-Wooing Go* (1883) depicts Caldecott's lively sense of humor.

The Early Twentieth Century

The early twentieth century continued the rich tradition of the nineteenth and gave us such classic fantasies as J. M. Barrie's *Peter Pan* (1904), about the boy who would not grow up; Kenneth Grahame's *The Wind in the Willows* (1908), about the irrepressible Rat, Mole, Badger, and Mr. Toad of Toad Hall; and A. A. Milne's ever-popular *Winnie-the-Pooh* (1926).

Realistic novels continued to gain a foothold. Frances Hodgson Burnett's *The Secret Garden* (1911) is the story of Mary Lennox, initially a rather unappealing heroine, who ultimately finds her redemption on the bleak English moors. The book, which continues to be popular, is rich in Gothic atmosphere and mysterious characters.

If children's literature was no longer so didactic as in the eighteenth century, much of it nevertheless remained conservative, particularly the realistic fiction. In America we find the much-loved semi-autobiographical series by Laura Ingalls Wilder, beginning with *The Little House in the Big Woods* (1932). The celebration of the pioneer spirit has a distinctly patriotic ring to it, and the attitude toward Native Americans seems a bit uncomfortable to some modern readers, although the books themselves are rather less preachy than the 1970s television adaptations.

Wilder's works were among many of the first half of the twentieth century that celebrated the family. Carol Ryrie Brink's *Caddie Woodlawn* (1935) is, in the Wilder vein, also a frontier/family story. And Eleanor Estes's *The Moffats* (1941), the first of a series, is set just after World War I.

Fantasy has always been quick to challenge the status quo. P. L. Travers's *Mary Poppins* (1934), a collection of wildly fanciful stories about an eccentric nanny, has raised many an adult eyebrow because of the title character's outrageous behavior. (Indeed, her nature was dramatically softened in the 1964 Disney movie.) And we find another challenge to the status quo when Theodore Geisel began writing unorthodox picture books under the pseudonym Dr. Seuss. J. R. R. Tolkien's fantasy, *The Hobbit; or, There and Back Again* (1937), is the prequel to his great trilogy, *The Lord of the Rings*, a fantasy for young adults and adults. But *The Hobbit* is quite suitable for children, with its lovable, self-deprecating hero, Bilbo Baggins. The story is high fantasy, featuring dramatic battles, fanciful creatures, very real dangers, and just a touch of humor.

The Late Twentieth Century and Beyond

World War II changed the world dramatically—and it changed children's literature. The collapse of totalitarian regimes at the end of World War II spelled the end of the old class systems; socialism was on the rise, and education was seen as the means of overcoming the ignorance and prejudice that had contributed to the war. Studies in child psychology, especially those by Jean Piaget, and advances in early childhood education, such as those made by Maria Montessori (whose work actually began in the early 1900s), helped to refocus concerns on the development of the child as an individual. Then, in 1946, Dr. Benjamin Spock published *The Common Sense Book of Baby and Child Care*, which revolutionized how society as a whole looked at children. Spock's influence was widespread, and he used it to advocate for the personal needs of the child over the requirements of society, which in turn nurtured such movements as the empowerment of children in the classroom, the advocacy of children's rights in the legal system, and, indeed, the entire "youth culture" that has dominated Western society for the past half century. In such an atmosphere, children's literature was bound to flourish, but it would be a literature that would thrive on bold, independent-minded young heroes and heroines. And it would explore all facets of childhood and young-adulthood—the good, the bad, and the ugly, as they say.

In fantasy, a number of series have appeared in the past 50 years that have remained favorites of children. These include C. S. Lewis's Chronicles of Narnia (*The Lion, the Witch and the Wardrobe*, 1950, and sequels); Mary Norton's *The Borrowers* (1952) and sequels; Lucy Boston's *The Children of Green Knowe* (1954) and sequels; Lloyd Alexander's Prydain chronicles (*The Book of Three*, 1965, and sequels); and Ursula Le Guin's Earthsea series (beginning with *A Wizard of Earthsea*, 1967). Books such as E. B. White's *Charlotte's Web* (1952) and Natalie Babbitt's *Tuck Everlasting* (1975) have been accorded status as modern fantasy classics. And, of course, J. K. Rowling's Harry Potter series (beginning with *Harry Potter and the Sorcerer's Stone*, 1998) has been nothing short of a publishing and cinematic phenomenon. Suzanne Collins's *The Hunger Games* (2008) and its sequels are enjoying a similarly enthusiastic reception, and, in their depiction of a frightening and impersonal future world, they show us how fantasy can be both compelling and thought provoking.

Similarly, in realistic fiction, the trend has been toward greater realism in children's books. Beverly Cleary, whose Ramona books remain immensely popular, have perpetuated the traditional family story. But others have given us a less romanticized vision of the family: the broken family, the troubled family, the dysfunctional family. Judy Blume and others helped to introduce the so-called *problem novel*, which focuses on some crisis of childhood or adolescence; for example, Cleary addressed the trauma of divorce in her Newbery Award–winning *Dear Mr. Henshaw*.

The other notable trend in modern realism is what has come to be known as the *new realism*, characterized by a franker and more open approach to subjects once thought taboo in children's books: sexuality, violence, drugs, war, and so on. It was perhaps J. D. Salinger's *Catcher in the Rye* (1951), a book for adolescents rather than children, that signaled the trend toward greater realism, harsher language, and a willingness to face head-on the problems of growing up. Through the 1950s it was virtually impossible to find a children's book that included any but white children. African American writers such as Virginia Hamilton, Mildred Taylor, Walter Dean Myers, and Christopher Paul Curtis have sought to correct the cultural disparity that once prevailed in children's literature. The disparity is still apparent, but at least it is now possible to find books about African Americans, Hispanic Americans, Native Americans, and Asian Americans. Among the most popular children's writers in America today is Grace Lin, daughter of Taiwanese immigrants, whose novels for young readers (*The Year of the Dog* (2006) and others) capture the true multicultural experience in very positive, and humorous, ways.

In another arena, children's and young adult books are being addressed to the LGBTQ (lesbian, gay, bisexual, transgender, and questioning) community as society continues to become more inclusive and tolerant. A surprising number of these books are actually picture books for very young readers, perhaps the most famous being Michael Willhoite's

Daddy's Roommate, which first appeared in 1991. For older readers, Alex Sanchez, author of the Rainbow Boys series; M. E. Kerr, author of *Deliver Us from Evie*; and Francesca Lia Block, author of the quirky Weetzie Bat books, are just some of the writers bringing this conversation into the mainstream.

Modern children's poetry has grown widely diverse. It includes those heirs of Edward Lear's wonderfully outrageous *Book of Nonsense*, such as Dr. Seuss and Shel Silverstein. And there are more serious poets, including David McCord, Myra Cohn Livingston, Jack Prelutsky, Valerie Worth, JoArno Lawson and many others, who share their joy of language with children of all ages.

And finally, in the field of children's illustration, the postwar era has seen some stunning work. Consummate artists like Maurice Sendak, Michael Foreman, David Macaulay, Barbara Cooney, Chris Van Allsburg, Margot Zemach, John Burningham, Ashley Bryan, Lauren Child, and Mo Willems, to name just a few, have given children some of the most imaginative and beautiful picture books that have ever been created. Of particular note are the so-called postmodern picture books (such as the imaginative work of David Wiesner and Emily Gravett), which experiment with the traditional linear plot, play with literary devices, and are aware of themselves as books.

In the past 100 years, the field of children's literature had gained considerably in prestige. This has been most notably marked by the creation of numerous children's book awards. In the United States came the Newbery Medal in 1922, for the best American children's book of the year, and, in 1938, its counterpart for best illustration, the Caldecott Medal (named for Randolph Caldecott). In Great Britain came the Carnegie Medal for literature and the Greenaway Medal for illustration. Lifetime achievement awards have been added, such as the Laura Ingalls Wilder Award, named for the beloved author of the Little House books. And on the international level are the Hans Christian Andersen Award and the Astrid Lindgren Award. (The latter two are international awards open to children's writers everywhere.) The world over, we can find hundreds of medals, awards, citations, and other recognitions now showered upon talented children's authors and illustrations—a sure sign that the field has come of age.

Children's Literature around the World

Indeed, the field of children's literature has grown worldwide, and many of the best works have been translated into English. We have room to mention only some of the most famous and influential works of the past two centuries.

The Adventures of Pinocchio (1883), by the Italian author Carlo Collodi, is the world's most famous puppet story, with its familiar theme of a toy wishing to be alive. France has given us Jean de Brunhoff, the creator of *The Story of Babar, the Little Elephant* (1931), the first of a series of picture books (seven in all) about a little elephant who becomes a wise and benevolent ruler. And Antoine de Saint-Exupéry's *The Little Prince* (1943), also French, remains a fantasy classic for all ages. Germany, in addition to the brothers Grimm, also boasts Heinrich Hoffmann, who wrote *Struwwelpeter* (1845), a collection of cautionary tales that some view as hilarious and others as horrifying. Felix Salten's *Bambi* (1923) and Erich Kästen's *Emil and the Detectives* (1929) are two modern German works that have become classics. Sweden's Selma Lagerlöf, who won the Nobel Prize for Literature in 1909, wrote *The Wonderful Adventures of Nils* (in two volumes, 1906–1907), a highly imaginative work of fantasy. In 1945 Astrid Lindgren, the best-known Swedish children's author, wrote *Pippi Longstocking*, the fanciful story of a remarkable girl with superhuman strength, unconventional values, and complete independence—in other words, every child's hero. The Finnish writer Tove Jansson created the Moomin family in a popular series of books beginning with *Comet in Moominland* (1946). These books about the gentle Moomins and their eccentric friends contain a healthy dose of philosophy as their adventures and misadventures unfold in a delightfully amorphous way.

Canada, Australia, and New Zealand have all made significant contributions to children's literature, particularly in the twentieth century. Among the early Canadian writers are the naturalists Ernest Thompson Seton (*Wild Animals I Have Known*, 1898) and Charles G. D. Roberts (*Red Fox*, 1905), who are usually credited with inventing the realistic animal story. Perhaps the most famous Canadian writer, Lucy Maud Montgomery (*Anne of Green Gables*, 1908), wrote domestic stories about life on Prince Edward Island. Modern trends include literature by and about the native peoples of Canada (Basil Johnston's *Tales the Elders Told: Ojibway Legends*, 1981). One of the most famous contemporary Canadians in children's literature is author/illustrator Jon Klassen, who has won the Canadian Governor General's Award for illustration (for *Cat's Night Out* by Carolyn Stutson, 2010) and the Caldecott Medal for *This Is Not My Hat*, 2012).

Kate Langloh Parker's *Australian Legendary Tales* (1896) was one of the first books to explore aboriginal legends. Among the best-known modern Australian children's writers are Patricia Wrightson, much of whose work is based on aboriginal traditions (*The Ice Is Coming*, 1977), and Ivan Southall, a writer of vivid survival stories, often with bleak endings (*Ash Road*, 1965), and more recently Mem Fox and illustrator Bob Graham. And New Zealand's most celebrated children's author, Margaret Mahy, twice won the prestigious Carnegie Medal (for *The Haunting*, 1981, and *The Changeover*, 1983).

Summary

Children's literature has been around for a long time and has enjoyed a wide variety of influences, from the ancient Greeks, whose wondrous mythological tales still enthrall us, to the rich diversity of the twenty-first century. We have also seen that the good stories never grow old and, significantly, children do not seem to care how old a story is—they just know a good one when they hear it. But, of course, we have seen decided changes as well, particularly from the day when John Newbery was selling children's books from his

London shop in the eighteenth century. Beginning in the mid-nineteenth century, children's literature started to become far broader in its interests and more inclusive in its appeal, as well as more experimental. It was then that truly talented writers and illustrators turned to creating books for children.

One of the most satisfying developments of the past 50 years has been the increasing diversity—racial, ethnic, gender, social, and so on—in children's books and children's writers. Another important development has been the broadening scope of children's books. We now see books for children on virtually every subject—including some very controversial ones, such as war, abuse, and sexuality. Children's illustrators continue to explore new artistic styles and media, and children's picture books have achieved a new depth and sophistication. This is not to say, though, that the field is not still crowded with the mediocre, the cheap, and the tawdry. Such books are found in great abundance. But we do have choices. Treasures are out there, but we have to know what we are looking for.

As we move through the twenty-first century, we trust that the demand for excellence in children's literature continues, for without reading, our civilization would disintegrate in a single generation. The ideas of our past would be lost forever, forcing humanity once again naked into the world. As students of children's literature, our great purpose is to bring the joy of reading to the next generation, giving them the tools they will need to build a better world than their parents have known.

For Reflection and Discussion

1. Choose a Greek or Roman myth or tale that has been retold for children (versions by Padraic Colum, Ingri and Edgar Parin d'Aulaire, Jeanne Steig, Marcia Williams and others). Compare this version with an account taken from Ovid or some other adult reference source from ancient times. How has the adaptation changed the story?

2. Compare two or more versions of an ancient Greek, Roman, or medieval hero story. What seem to be the messages? What are the major differences?

3. Identify what specific influences John Locke, Jean-Jacques Rousseau, and John Newbery had on children's literature. Do you find yourself agreeing with the ideas of one over another? Explain.

4. Choose a prominent eighteenth-century author of children's books. (Use the chapter or explore on your own to find names.) Research the author's background. Read one or more works by the same authors and compare the style and content to that of modern children's books.

5. Make a list of the major changes in books for children from the eighteenth century to today—consider such things as the subject matter, the treatment, and the

physical layout. Explain what specifically brought about these changes. Choose any modern picture storybook or children's novel that you know well. How would the story and the book have been different if it had appeared in the eighteenth century? In the nineteenth century? In the early twentieth century?

Works Cited

Dubosarsky, Ursula. Plays, Based on Ovid's Metamorphoses, ursuladubosarsky.squarespace. com, 2012.
- Including "Arachne," "Echo and Narcissus," "Icarus," "Pygmalion," and others.

Wooden, Warren W. *Children's Literature of the English Renaissance*. Lexington: University of Kentucky Press, 1986.

Recommended Resources

Aries, Philippe. *Centuries of Childhood: A Social History of Family Life*. New York: Knopf, 1962.

Boyd, Brian. *On the Origin of Stories: Evolution, Cognition, and Fiction*. Cambridge, MA: Harvard University Press, 2009.

Carpenter, Humphrey. *Secret Gardens: A Study of the Golden Age of Children's Literature*. Boston: Houghton Mifflin, 1985.

Carpenter, Humphrey, and Mari Prichard. *The Oxford Companion to Children's Literature*. Oxford: Oxford University Press, 1984.

Cullinan, Bernice, and Diane G. Person, eds. *The Continuum Encyclopedia of Children's Literature*. New York: Continuum, 2001.

Darton, F. J. Harvey. *Children's Books in England: Five Centuries of Social Life*. Cambridge: Cambridge University Press, 1982.

Demers, Patricia. *Heaven Upon Earth: The Form of Moral and Religious Children's Literature, to 1850*. Knoxville: University of Tennessee Press, 1993.

Demers, Patricia, and Gordon Moyles, eds. *From Instruction to Delight*. Toronto: Oxford University Press, 1982.

Gottschall, Jonathan. *The Storytelling Animal: How Stories Make Us Human*. New York: Houghton Mifflin Harcourt, 2012.

Hunt, Peter, ed. *Children's Literature: An Illustrated History*. Oxford: Oxford University Press, 1995.

——. *An Introduction to Children's Literature*. Oxford: Oxford University Press, 1994.

Jackson, Mary V. *Engines of Instruction, Mischief, and Magic: Children's Literature in England from Its Beginnings to 1839*. Omaha: University of Nebraska, 1990.

Lerer, Seth. *Children's Literature: A Reader's History from Aesop to Harry Potter*. Chicago: University of Chicago Press, 2009.

Lystad, Mary. *From Dr. Mather to Dr. Seuss: 200 Years of American Books for Children*. Cambridge, MA: Harvard University Press, 1980.

MacDonald, Ruth. *Literature for Children in England and America from 1646 to 1774*. Troy, NY: Whitston, 1982.

MacLeod, Anne Scott. *A Moral Tale: Children's Fiction and American Culture, 1820–1860*. Hamden, CT: Archon, 1975.

Marcus, Leonard. *Minders of Make-Believe: Idealists, Entrepreneurs, and the Shaping of American Children's Literature*. New York: Houghton Mifflin Harcourt, 2008.

Meigs, Cornelia, Elizabeth Nesbitt, Anne Thaxter Eaton, and Ruth Hill. *A Critical History of*

Children's Literature: A Survey of Children's Books in English. New York: Macmillan, 1969.

Nikolajeva, Maria, ed. *Aspects and Issues in the History of Children's Literature*. Westport, CT: Greenwood, 1995.

Pickering, Samuel F., Jr. *John Locke and Children's Books in Eighteenth-Century England*. Knoxville: University of Tennessee Press, 1981.

——. *Moral Instruction and Fiction for Children, 1749–1820*. Athens: University of Georgia Press, 1993.

Pinker, Steven. *The Blank Slate: The Modern Denial of Human Nature*. New York: Viking, 2002.

Schorsch, Anita. *Images of Childhood: An Illustrated Social History*. New York: Mayflower, 1979.

Summerfield, Geoffrey. *Fantasy and Reason: Children's Literature in the Eighteenth Century*. Athens: University of Georgia Press, 1983.

Thwaite, Mary F. *From Primer to Pleasure in Reading: An Introduction to the History of Children's Books in England*. Boston: The Horn Book, 1972.

Townsend, John Rowe. *Trade and Plum-Cake for Ever, Huzza! The Life and Work of John Newbery, 1713–1769*. Cambridge, UK: Colt, 1994.

——. *Written for Children: An Outline of English-Language Children's Literature*, 5th rev. ed. London: Kestrel, 1990.

Tucker, Nicholas. *The Child and the Book: A Psychological and Literary Exploration*. Cambridge: Cambridge University Press, 1981.

Watson, Victor, ed. *The Cambridge Guide to Children's Books in English*. Cambridge: Cambridge University Press, 2001.

Wooden, Warren W. *Children's Literature of the English Renaissance*. Lexington: University of Kentucky Press, 1986.

Zipes, Jack, ed. *The Oxford Encyclopedia of Children's Literature*. Oxford: Oxford University Press, 2006.

2 Literature and the Child

Growing through Reading

Introduction

The eminent psychologist Carl Gustav Jung wrote, "In studying the history of the human mind one is impressed again and again by the fact that the growth of the mind is the widening of the range of consciousness, and that each step forward has been a most painful and laborious achievement" (*Contributions to Analytical Psychology* 340). It is commonplace to regard childhood as an idyllic and carefree time, but, as Jung suggests, childhood and adolescence are perhaps the most difficult, the most challenging, years of our lives. We are born completely helpless, unable to walk, talk, or feed ourselves. With each day, we are confronted with something new, something that causes us to reevaluate our ideas of the world around us, and we are forced continually to adapt to that world. All things considered, we might wonder how many adults could cope with the dramatic transformations that infants and toddlers experience on a daily basis. The child's ability to adapt and to absorb so much in so short a time is a marvel.

In this chapter, we will take a brief look at the various ways children develop, especially in the formative years between birth and the age of 6 or 7, and we will consider specifically how that development impacts their reading habits and tastes. As adults, we often underestimate children. It is good to remind ourselves how keen their perceptions are, how quickly they grasp concepts, and how sharply their imaginations work—for these are issues that directly influence the types of books they enjoy (or could be enjoying). Also in this chapter, we will consider issues tangentially related to child development and reading: the introduction of sensitive topics into children's books, the use of bibliotherapy, and the concept of intellectual freedom. In one way or another, all these issues are connected to children's intellectual, emotional, and social development.

Language Acquisition

Before we look at the developmental theories, it might be helpful if we consider the one human ability that makes literature itself possible: the ability to use language to communicate. One area in which children seem to excel beyond the expectations of adults is language acquisition. It is amazing that in five short years, children can master the abstract concept of attaching meanings to certain sounds (words) and to organize those sounds into intelligible patterns (sentences) to convey those meanings.

Russian psychologist Lev Vygotsky, whom we will examine more closely in Chapter 3, was interested in how children learn language. He argued that language is, in fact, a way of thinking about something—that our ability to formulate words, to put ideas into words, actually helps us to think and to understand. (Anyone who has talked through personal problems with a friend or therapist or used a diary or journal to help sort out personal conflicts will understand Vygotsky's point.)

Steven Pinker, a psychologist who has studied human thought and language, is convinced that language acquisition is innate. He argues that we are born with the ability to memorize the meanings of words and their various forms (such as verb tenses) and to assimilate the rules of grammar and syntax of the language that we hear on a daily basis. Very young children possess a linguistic plasticity, or malleability, that extends to their abilities to create sounds. Despite the popular notion that pronunciation is difficult for children, they often have a much easier time of it than do most adults. Indeed, the time for children to start learning a second language is when they're in preschool or the early elementary grades—when it's easier to memorize, to make new sounds, and to adapt to new language patterns. It is a pity that the U.S. educational system, with some notable exceptions, has neglected this opportunity.

All this research shows that as adults—and as teachers—we should build on children's language abilities and their natural curiosity about sound, sense, and language. The books they read or that we read to them should be expanding their vocabulary—not accommodating it. Most children love language and love practicing it. Even the simplest Mother Goose rhymes offer exciting and challenging vocabulary, with their nonsense words and archaisms. Difficult vocabulary rarely discourages a child. Take, for example, Old Mother Hubbard, who successively went to the joiner's, the fishmonger's, the cobbler's, and the hosier's; or the crooked man who went a crooked mile and "found a crooked six-pence against a crooked stile." In neither case do the obscure words spoil the child's pleasure in the rhyme. In fact, we might go so far as to say that a book without any challenging words is a book wasted.

Modern Theories of Child Development

If we are to help children find the best and most appropriate books, we need to have some knowledge of child development, and what follows here is only the briefest survey of three of the most influential modern theories of child development. Jean Piaget was concerned with intellectual or cognitive development, Erik Erikson with social development, and Lawrence Kohlberg with the development of moral judgment. All three individuals viewed human development as occurring in a series of stages through which children pass on their way to maturity. Progressing through these stages is like climbing a mountain: If we don't have sure footing or a firm grasp, we will slip back down. Likewise, we find backsliding in human development: The progress is not always forward. Also, the movement through stages is gradual, almost imperceptible, and different individuals develop at different rates. Consequently, the age spans mentioned here are only approximations.

We should note that these theories have been criticized for ignoring female development, which, some argue, is not the same as male development. Males, for example, generally value competition, self-assertiveness, individual rights, and social rules. Females, on the other hand, tend to value human relationships, responsibility to others, cooperation, community values, and tolerance for opposing viewpoints. In addition, some argue that females reach these developmental stages more quickly than males do. Another criticism of these theories is that they neglect minority groups, whose values are often quite different from those of the majority. Nevertheless, these theories are helpful as a general guide—so long as we remember their limitations.

Jean Piaget and Cognitive Development

The Swiss psychologist Jean Piaget (1896–1980) is famous for his theory of cognitive development, which attempts to explain how we comprehend the world around us. In the 1920s and 1930s, Piaget outlined four major periods of intellectual development, some of which he subdivided into stages. What follows is a very broad overview of these stages.

SENSORIMOTOR PERIOD: BIRTH TO 2 YEARS ■ During this earliest period, Piaget argues, children are entirely egocentric (they are unaware of the needs of others), and they experience the world entirely through their senses (what they can see, hear, taste, touch, and smell—they cannot be told about experiences). For them, books are objects to feel and manipulate with their hands—once they've learned that books are not objects to eat. For infants, durable cardboard and cloth books are great introductions to reading. And, naturally, it is chiefly through the pictures that very young children respond to books. Tactile books, such as Dorothy Kunhardt's classic, *Pat the Bunny*, allow them to touch and feel. Sounds fascinate them (even nonsense words), and so it is that they enjoy being read to, even if they don't always comprehend what a story is about. Very early, they respond to the sounds and rhythms of nursery rhymes ("Peter, Peter, Pumpkin Eater," "Hickory Dickory Dock," and others). Most important is that they are getting acquainted with books, learning to hold books, to turn pages, and to connect language and books.

PREOPERATIONAL PERIOD: 2 TO 7 YEARS ■ The second of Piaget's periods is the time when children acquire and refine their motor skills. They become less egocentric and start making friends. Although they still don't think logically, they can use symbols to represent ideas (after all, that's what written language is—a symbolic representation of ideas).

And, although children can grasp certain concepts—colors, shapes, opposites, the forms and sounds of letters of the alphabet, and counting objects—they still understand things only in concrete terms. In the early years of this period, children find alphabet, counting, and concept books fascinating. Most 3-year-olds can memorize letters of the alphabet or the numbers from 1 to 20 and beyond. In fact, because of their excellent recall, preschoolers often appear far more knowledgeable than they actually are. Also, they tend to give human qualities to everything (a concept known as *animism*), which helps explain their fondness for books about talking animals and animated toys and machines (such as folktales or stories like Virginia Lee Burton's *Mike Mulligan and His Steam Shovel*, Margaret Wise Brown's *The Runaway Bunny*, and Dorothy Cronin's *Click, Clack, Moo: Cows That Type*). Eventually, they no longer require pictures to help tell the stories. By the final years of this developmental period, when they reach about second grade, children have learned to read and comprehend the fundamental ideas of plot, conflict, and character. Now they are ready to move on to a new level of understanding.

PERIOD OF CONCRETE OPERATIONS: 7 TO 12 YEARS ■ Although they still have difficulty with abstract ideas, children in this third period are able to apply a kind of logic to their thinking. They are capable of understanding these basic concepts of logic:

- *Conservation*—understanding that quantity is unaffected by appearance (a tall, thin glass may hold just as much water as a short, chubby glass);
- *Reversibility*—understanding that some actions (such as a knot in a shoestring) can be undone;
- *Assimilation*—using what we already know to explain new information (a St. Bernard and a Chihuahua are both dogs); and
- *Accommodation*—revising what we already know to explain new information (not all creatures with four legs are dogs).

Children in this stage begin to lay aside the picture books, which they now see as "babyish." (But this doesn't mean they don't still enjoy some of them.) Now they begin reading chapter books. (That perennial favorite, E. B. White's *Charlotte's Web*, is typically read in second grade.) Children are now able to grasp the concept of history and the passage of time (and can therefore enjoy Laura Ingalls Wilder's Little House books). As they begin to seek their identity, they turn to books such as Judy Blume's *Blubber* and *Tales of a Fourth Grade Nothing* or Lois Lowry's Anastasia series, so they can read about children like themselves.

PERIOD OF FORMAL OPERATIONS: 12 TO 15 YEARS ■ Finally, the fourth period occurs between the ages of about 12 and 15 (when most children reach full cognitive maturity). In these early teen years, young people begin to use formal logic and engage in a true exchange of ideas, comprehending the viewpoints of others and understanding what it means to live in a society. Having entered adolescence, most are ready for more mature topics, such as love, sexuality, social issues, and even politics.

Erik Erikson and Psychosocial Development

Whereas Piaget was interested in how we develop intellectually, Erik Erikson (1902–1994) explored how we develop socially and psychologically. He classified the maturation process into a series of psychosocial conflicts, each of which must be resolved before one can move on to the next, in much the same way that Piaget saw successive levels in cognitive development. This is part of the "painful and laborious achievement" to which Jung was referring. Erikson's theory includes five principal stages of development throughout childhood, which complement, not compete with, Piaget's stages.

TRUST VERSUS MISTRUST: BIRTH TO 18 MONTHS ■ During this first stage, children have little option but to trust those who are their caregivers. However, at the same time, they must overcome fears such as abandonment when they are put to sleep in their own beds (which is why bedtime is often so difficult for some children). Books for this stage can provide both security and reassurance. Margaret Wise Brown's classic, *Goodnight Moon*, has long been popular with the very young. It exudes warmth and coziness, as we observe a little bunny saying goodnight to all his favorite possessions in his womb-like bedroom. The repetitive patterns in both text and illustration are comfortably reassuring. Children in this stage also like hearing familiar books read night after night; these books become like old, reliable friends, providing stability and a sense of security.

AUTONOMY VERSUS DOUBT: 18 MONTHS TO 3 YEARS ■ Now that they can walk and talk, children begin to experiment with their independence. At the same time, however, they are wary of their abilities. Crockett Johnson's imaginative story *Harold and the Purple Crayon*, about a boy who creates his own world with a magical crayon, charmingly portrays an autonomous child who proves capable of handling his newfound independence—and extricating himself from some interesting dilemmas. The story might appeal nicely to children who are exploring their own imaginative world—often with crayons (and not always on paper). At the same time, they are also beginning to grasp the concept of right and wrong and may feel guilt when they make the wrong choices.

INITIATIVE VERSUS GUILT: 3 TO 6 YEARS ■ At this stage, children first begin to realize they have responsibilities (potty training springs to mind). Children want to take the initiative to do things on their own and to decide what to do and when to do it. In Ezra Jack Keats's *Peter's Chair*, young Peter exhibits hostility when his parents decide to paint all his baby furniture pink for his new sister. Peter "runs away"—a common ploy at this stage exhibiting the child's attempt at independence—and camps outside their apartment. But he soon realizes that home is where he wants to be, baby sister and all, and offers his furniture to his sister. Peter has arrived at a higher stage of psychosocial development, which is shown by his willingness to change his attitude and behavior. Such a book both validates a child's feelings and shows at least one method of coping with them.

INDUSTRY VERSUS INFERIORITY: 7 TO 11 YEARS ■ At this stage, children desire to achieve success, often working in concert with others. At the same time, however, they have a tendency to measure themselves against their peers and often feel inferior. Books such as Beverly Cleary's *Henry Huggins* and *Ramona the Pest* help young readers explore these desires for both personal achievement and acceptance and friendship.

IDENTITY VERSUS ROLE CONFUSION: 11 YEARS AND BEYOND ■ As they move toward adolescence, young people begin to discover who they are (individually, socially, and culturally). They are torn between the familiar security of childhood and the natural, if uneasy, desire to become adults. Louise Fitzhugh's *Harriet the Spy* is a seriocomic story about a girl dealing with just these issues. In this book, Fitzhugh sugarcoats nothing and provides no easy solutions; in other words, she tells the readers exactly what they need to hear. Soon young people in this age group seek out books that show other young people struggling with identity. Judy Blume's popular *Are You There, God? It's Me Margaret*, the story of a girl facing her first menses along with a crisis in religious belief, is a perennial favorite for girls at this stage. Most readers at this stage crave openness and honesty, preferring stories about others like themselves (realism), but many also find pleasure in escapist tales (fantasy, science fiction, and so on).

Lawrence Kohlberg and Moral Development

Lawrence Kohlberg (1927–1987) studied the development of moral reasoning and moral judgment—that is, how individuals determine what is right and wrong. Also, like Piaget and Erickson, he saw development occurring in a series of stages through which an individual passes to moral maturity (at least, ideally). Kohlberg identifies three levels of development—Preconventional, Conventional, and Postconventional—each subdivided into two stages, which he called "orientations." The first two levels are most important for our purposes.

PRECONVENTIONAL LEVEL ■ The very youngest children are not aware of social conventions—being polite, using manners, and so on. Initially, right and wrong are simply a matter of what does and does not result in punishment or what pleases others. Children remain in the Preconventional Level throughout much of elementary school.

The first stage is *Punishment/Obedience Orientation*, when children obey rules because the rules come from some authority figure (a parent or a preschool teacher) or because they wish to avoid punishment. In Beatrix Potter's *The Tale of Peter Rabbit*, we see Peter's sisters obeying their mother and enjoying delicious currant buns at the end of the story, whereas Peter, who disobeyed the rules, suffers in bed with a cold. Obedience to authority has some obvious advantages.

The second stage is *Self-Interest Orientation*, when children believe that "right" behavior is any action that helps them. In other words, the first question is "What's in it for me?" Take Templeton the rat in E. B. White's *Charlotte's Web*, a thoroughly self-centered creature who helps out only if he is promised food—that is, only if there is something in it for him. The character of Templeton shows us that this selfishness is unattractive and potentially destructive. It is, of course, Wilbur whom we are to emulate, doing things to bring happiness to others.

CONVENTIONAL LEVEL ◼ The second level is generally not reached until adolescence, when individuals finally understand and observe social conventions. It is the stage in which most adults operate, and it also has two parts.

During the first stage, *Interpersonal Concordance* (or "*Good Boy/Good Girl*") *Orientation*, one's behavior is governed by a desire to have the approval of others. This usually occurs in the early teenage years, and the appearance of "cliques" and the need to conform are familiar aspects of adolescence. Many books for children in middle school and early high school focus on just these issues, such as Beverly Cleary's *Dear Mr. Henshaw*, about a young boy's difficulty dealing with his parents' divorce and his feeling like an outsider.

"Law and Order" Orientation involves individuals conforming in order to abide by the law and accept their obligations as members of society. People at this stage are aware of their place in the world and demonstrate concern for others—two important signs of maturity. Mildred Taylor's *Roll of Thunder, Hear My Cry*, about an African American girl coming of age in the 1930s in the Deep South where she encounters hateful racial discrimination, is a good example of this orientation. Robert Cormier's *The Chocolate War*, about unscrupulous behavior in a private school, explores the issue of maintaining personal integrity when it comes up against peer pressure and social conformity.

POSTCONVENTIONAL LEVEL ◼ Kohlberg felt that most people never reach this final level, in which individuals act in the interest of the welfare of others or of society as a whole; this is usually called the *Social Contract Orientation*. And the highest level, *Principled Conscience Orientation*, people act out of regard for ethical principles or their own conscience. (Those at this level are chiefly martyrs and saints.)

The best children's literature is in touch with the intellectual, psychological, and sociological interests of its intended audience. As children develop, they put aside certain books and move on to others that are both more challenging and better suited to their developmental needs. In very young children, these transitions occur rapidly, and in the course of a very few years, they outgrow the nursery rhymes and picture books and require more complex stories, more compelling characters, and more probing themes.

Child Development and Reading

Closely related to the concept of child development is the idea that a child's understanding of certain subjects is related to his or her intellectual and emotional development. But our notions about what very young children can or ought to understand have changed rather dramatically in the past several decades. Whereas adults once felt that children should be sheltered from any of life's unpleasantness, many now believe that we should be preparing them for these eventualities. Life, under the best of circumstances, is not easy, and children discover this all too soon, despite the concerted efforts of well-meaning adults to protect them from its harsh realities. Marriages end in divorce, loved ones die, violence disrupts cities, war disrupts society. Oftentimes, the very books that children need to be reading are the ones that adults want to keep from them—books about death, about divorce, about violence and war. Although, as adults, our first instinct is to protect and shelter our children from the hard facts of life, we should, instead, be preparing them. Now, this doesn't mean that we should go around bursting their bubbles of optimism and idealism. Preparing them for the hard facts of life can be done with sensitivity.

The conflicting ideas about what is and what is not suitable for young readers have resulted in some interesting controversies in the field of children's books, and we will now look briefly at some of these issues. Chapter 11 continues these discussions for older readers.

Sexuality

Sexuality has always been one of the most difficult issues for adults to broach with children. Some households avoid discussions of sex like the plague—apparently because the adults think that if they don't talk about it, it will go away. But in a world where eight-year-old girls are getting pregnant and deadly diseases are transmitted through sexual behavior, we cannot afford to stand on ceremony. Fortunately, a large number of honest and accurate books are now available to assist those diffident adults in getting the necessary information to children. Take, for example, the light-hearted (but effective) *Mommy Laid an Egg* by Babette Cole, or *It's Perfectly Normal: Changing Bodies, Growing Up, Sex, and Sexual Health* by Robie Harris (illustrated by Michael Emberley).

Books with LGBTQ (lesbian, gay, bisexual, transgender, and questioning) themes are more commonly intended for older children, but there are notable exceptions. Michael Willhoite's *Daddy's Roommate*, first published in 1991, is a picture book for preschoolers describing the weekends a young boy spends with his father and his father's male partner. You might wonder about the appropriateness of this subject for so young an audience. But today, in fact, many children are raised by gay couples. *Daddy's Roommate* provides honest, sensitive treatment of a subject many people find difficult to discuss. The simple illustrations and straightforward story told by a child narrator provide just the right amount of information for very young readers, and the book concludes with the statement that being gay is just "one more kind of love." It is never too early to begin the campaign to stamp out bigotry and prejudice. Leslea Newman and Diana Souza's *Heather Has Two Mommies* is a sort of counterpart to Willhoite's book, in which a lesbian couple is raising a child.

No one is suggesting that teachers should use these books in their classrooms; few of them were ever intended for that. But it is important for us to realize that these issues are not isolated, and they affect a broad spectrum of our population. Knowing about some of these titles, being aware that these subjects are dealt with in good children's books, will come in handy at some point—for everyone. Learning about the difficult issues of life through reputable books, sensitively written, and under the guidance of a caring and knowledgeable adult is surely preferable to picking up rumor and misinformation from the streets and playgrounds. See Chapter 11 for a discussion of sexuality in books for older readers.

Death and Dying

Death is often the first of life's hard hurdles that children must confront—the deaths of pets, grandparents, and even, sadly, parents, siblings, and friends. As much as we would like to shelter our children from this, perhaps life's greatest sorrow, it just is not possible—nor is it wise to try. Although they cannot provide the answers (nothing or no one can), good books on the subject can help the very young deal with these issues. The best books on dying deal in metaphors we can grasp and resist the temptation to offer simple platitudes.

It is important to remember that not everyone shares our own spiritual outlook and that there are many different ways to look at death. Not everyone is assuaged by a promise of an afterlife, as in Christianity or Islam. Some cultures, like Hinduism and Buddhism, embrace the concept of reincarnation. Other cultures, like Judaism, place the emphasis on this life and daily living—and not an afterlife. So when approaching the idea of death with children other than our own, it is wise for us to respect other beliefs and honor other cultures.

Regardless of one's personal convictions about death, such a loss is painful. The sorrow is difficult and necessary, but it is not permanent. And that is probably the best message for very youngest readers. Margaret Wise Brown's *The Dead Bird* is a simple picture book about a group of children who find a dead bird and proceed to give it a burial. After the obsequies, which are solemn and touching, the children soon find themselves engaged once again in play—back about the business of their lives, as they should be. Death is presented as part of the natural cycle of life, as *The Book of Common Prayer* correctly tells us, "In the midst of life, we are in death."

Sometimes, death is approached metaphorically—that is, the writer uses symbols to convey his or her ideas, which can help to make a complex idea more easily understood. An example is Oliver Jeffers's *The Heart and the Bottle*, in which a young girl's grief over the death of her father—which is only implied, never obliquely stated—causes her to "bottle up" her heart. But keeping her heart in the bottle also prevents her from moving on with her own life and experiencing other feelings, such as happiness or wonder. Only when she has accepted the loss and recognized that beauty and joy still exist in the world is she able to let her heart out of the bottle and once again embrace life—while still keeping the good memories.

Wolf Erlbruch's *Duck, Death and the Tulip* is, at first glance, a rather startling book (see Figure 2.1). It tells the story of Death, personified as a skeletal figure clad in a long plaid coat, who builds a relationship with the inquisitive Duck, who wants to know what death is like. At one point, we even see Duck attempting to comfort Death, who experiences a chill. When her own end approaches and Duck herself suddenly feels cold, she asks her

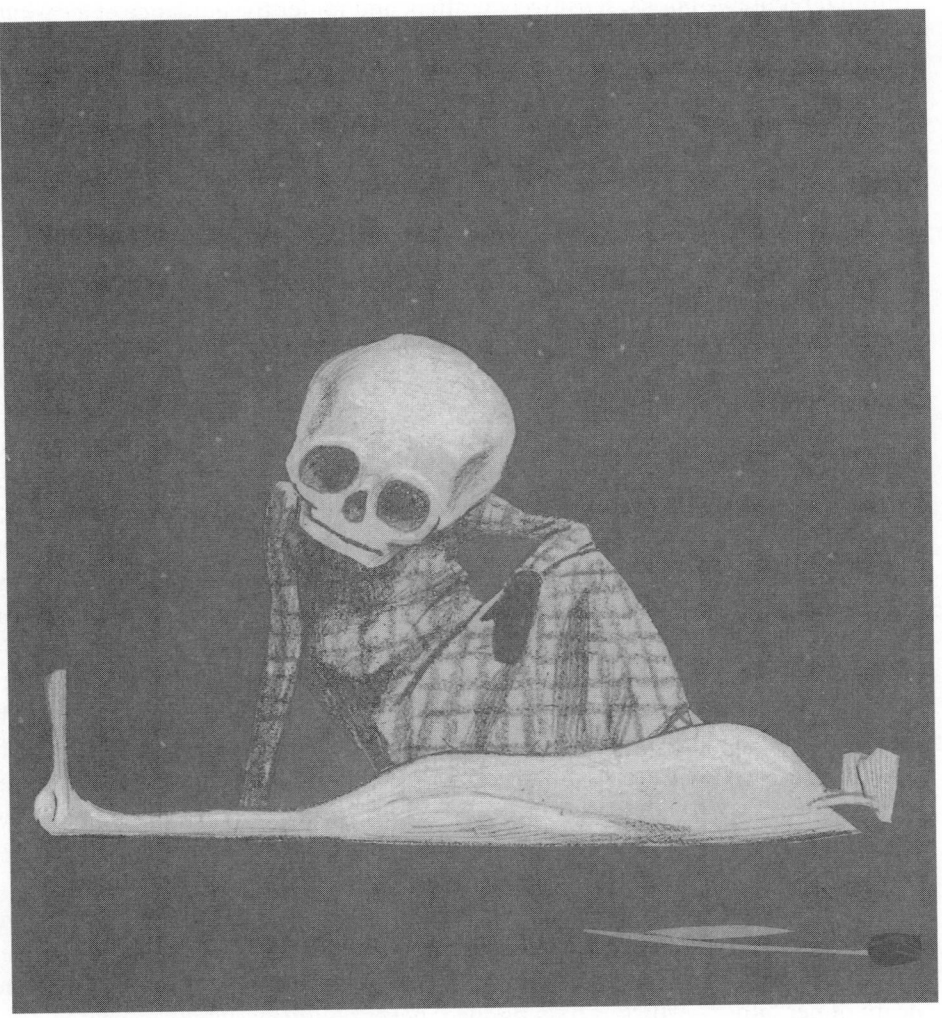

FIGURE 2.1 ▪ In this illustration from Wolf Erlbruch's *Duck, Death and the Tulip*, the figure of Death, with a skeletal face but dressed in comfortable plaid with warm mittens, gazes almost sympathetically upon Duck, who has just died.

friend, Death, to help keep her warm. Duck then dies quietly, and Death, after laying a tulip on her, gently places her lifeless body in the great river (the book does not broach the subject of an afterlife) and nudges her on her way. Death itself is almost moved by Duck's passing but then utters the final line: "But that's Life." With its message that we all walk with death and that death itself is part of life, as natural as birth, growth, and love, and not an enemy, this moving picture book presents life and death as seamless parts of a beautiful process (perhaps symbolized by the tulip, which is never actually referred to in the text). Without speculating on religious implications or diminishing the sense of loss, Erlbruch offers a simple, straightforward view of this inscrutable subject and makes it accessible for even very young children.

War and Violence

Surprisingly, we can find books for very young children on such unlikely subjects as war and its grim effects and even street violence. Why introduce such elements into a child's book? Sadly, we cannot shelter children from the effects of these dreadful experiences. Today in America, far too many children know the tragedy of losing a parent to war. We would not expect children to understand the politics of war, or its history, or its purpose (do we understand that ourselves?). Instead, children's books on war deal with its effects on society, on families, on individuals. One profoundly moving book is Roberto Innocenti and Christophe Gallaz's *Rose Blanche*, a story of a young German girl who discovers a Nazi concentration camp during World War II and, risking her own life, secretly brings food to the prisoners. The uncompromising ending in which the girl is killed during a battle is sensitively handled and, although very sad, is not without hope for a better world.

Toshi Maruki's *Hiroshima No Pika* (Boston: Lothrop, Lee, & Shepard, 1982) is a children's picture that describes the August morning in 1945 when the atomic bomb was dropped on Hiroshima. The simple but frank descriptions from a little girl's point of view, illustrated by stark, expressionistic paintings, provide a moving portrayal of an event children should not have to experience. But children did experience that, and many more children today experience the tragedies of disease, war, starvation, and neglect. And this is why these books and others like them, despite their horrifying subjects, remain appropriate for children. If told with the proper sensitivity—common sense must always be our guide—these stories might encourage a more humane world in the future. It is never too early for children to learn empathy for others.

Bibliotherapy

Many of the books mentioned above are used for what is called *bibliotherapy*, which refers to the use of books, poetry, or other written material to address emotional or psychological issues. The term itself goes back to the 1930s, but the idea that reading books can be part of the healing process for both mind and body is very old indeed. Above the entrance to the library at Thebes in ancient Greece was an inscription that announced: "A Healing Place for the Soul."

For very young children, some of the most famous examples of books used for bibliotherapy are the Berenstain Bears books by Stan and Jan Berenstain. The characters are a typical family—mother, father, daughter, son—except, of course, they are bears. Each book addresses a very specific childhood experience and shows typical responses from both children and parents to these situations (*The Berenstain Bears and the Bad Dream* and *The Berenstain Bears Go to the Doctor* are two examples). The Berenstains, who began writing in the 1960s and whose work has been continued by their son Mike, have evolved with society, writing stories about children who are physically challenged and children who encounter drug dealers. As with most other didactic literature, the plots of these books are predictable and contrived, and the characters a bit flat, since all else is sacrificed for the lesson being taught.

However, life lessons can be found in books that simply tell good and wise stories, without resorting to didacticism. Ezra Jack Keats wrote and illustrated a series of books about Peter, a young boy growing up in the inner city and dealing with bullies (*The Snowy Day*), a new baby sister (*Peter's Chair*), and a first "crush" on a girl (*A Letter to Amy*). Lucille Clifton wrote a series of picture books in poetry, describing the transitions in a young child's life, including the death of a parent (*Everett Anderson's Goodbye*), a mother's new boyfriend (*Everett Anderson's 1, 2, 3*), and, boldly, child abuse (*One of the Problems of Everett Anderson*)—all for children between the ages of about 4 and 6 years.

The problem with bibliotherapy is not whether it works—people have been assuaged and emboldened by books for centuries—but how it should be used. Do we wait until a grandparent dies to hunt down a children's book on death? And does the book have to be specifically about the death of a grandparent to do any good? Do we wait until a crisis occurs before sharing books about broken families? And does the book's crisis have to mirror our own? One librarian, Maeve Visser Knoth, has suggested that the best use of bibliotherapy is to encourage wide and deep reading that prepares children for life's eventualities—rather than to scramble for the perfect antidotal book when a difficult occasion arises. She writes:

> I would rather inoculate children than treat the symptoms of the emotional trauma. We give children vaccinations against measles. We can't vaccinate against divorce, but we can give children some emotional knowledge to use when their families, or other families they know, do go through a divorce. I advocate that we read picture books about death and divorce and new babies when no one is dying, when a marriage is strong, before anyone is pregnant. (273–274)

Reading is one of the most important ways we learn about life (our own experiences are rarely enough). When children read lots of good books, they learn about people and about their fears, their dreams, their failings, and their endurance; they learn how people cope with inevitable traumas of life. This is why it is vital that writers be honest in their writing, that the human feelings they describe be genuine, and that the characters they invent be emotionally real. It is also vital for children to read books that tell of life's sorrows as well as of life's joys, that describe our human weaknesses as well as our strengths. That is the best kind of bibliotherapy—the kind that prepares us for the curves life will surely throw us.

Intellectual Freedom

Finally, we should say a word about censorship—the act of determining what is and what is not objectionable for readers to read. Now it is true that parents act as censors when they choose not to read a particular book with a young child; however, this is merely personal preference. This sort of selection is different from some authority—political, social, or religious—forbidding the public to read certain books, see certain films, and so on. That is censorship.

In February 2007, a news item swept the nation when several librarians around the country announced that they were going to remove Susan Patron's Newbery Award–winning *The Higher Power of Lucky* from their libraries. And why? Because on the very first page, the book's female protagonist, 10-year-old Lucky Trimble, overhears a character describing a rattlesnake biting his dog on the "scrotum." Because they thought that term inappropriate in a book for 10-year-olds, or, more likely, they feared community backlash, some nervous librarians took the book off the shelves. Never mind that the book is the uplifting and beautifully told story of a young girl's finding her inner strength, her "higher power." We are reminded of that old saying about tossing out the baby with the bathwater. Fortunately, most professionals take a more reasonable approach to these matters and realize that attempts to shelter children from reality never work. Most feel it is better that children learn about sensitive and controversial topics from responsible adults rather than from their friends—or worse.

Censorship of children's books is rooted in society's desire to protect the "innocence" of childhood. Its goal is to guard against elements deemed inappropriate for young readers—harsh language, sexual innuendos, death and dying, violence, and "unapproved" religious beliefs or philosophies. But who makes these judgments? The following books have all been banned by some authority at one time or another: Mark Twain's *The Adventures of Huckleberry Finn*, Anne Frank's *Diary of a Young Girl*, Maurice Sendak's *In the Night Kitchen*, Shel Silverstein's *A Light in the Attic*, and all of J. K. Rowling's Harry Potter books, to name just a few. Indeed, a list of the most frequently banned books almost suggests that if a book has not been banned somewhere, it may not be any good at all.

In fact, censoring books almost always backfires. The quickest way to make a book popular is to ban it. All this is not to say that some subjects demand more mental and emotional maturity than others. It would be foolish to share a story about a teenage girl's first menstrual cycle with a preschooler. On the other hand, many preschoolers have had to

FIGURE 2.2 ■ A Brief Guide to Preserving Intellectual Freedom in the Classroom

1. **Know your rationale for using a book in the classroom. Answer these questions:**
   - Is the book appropriate for this age level?
   - Does the book meet your objectives in the class, and how?
   - Does the book appear on recommended lists, and what have been the reactions of critics?
   - What possible objections could be raised to the book—language, tone, theme, subject matter—and how can you best address these objections?
   - As a last resort, what alternative readings can you offer in place of this book?

2. **Have guidelines for handling community and parental objections. Carefully organized procedures can do much to stem the tide of emotionalism. Include the following:**
   - A complaint form on which specific objections are to be recorded
   - A clearly designated procedure for dealing with the complaint
   - A broad-based committee of teachers, administrators, and community representatives for hearing the complaints
   - A clear philosophical statement articulating the school's educational principles

3. **Join with other teachers and the administration to protect students' right to read (and the teachers' right to teach).**

4. **Actively support other teachers when they encounter censorship challenges.**

5. **Educate the community about the importance of intellectual freedom.**
   - Write letters or articles for the local newspaper.
   - Lobby the school board members and other community leaders.
   - Conduct or sponsor community workshops on censorship.

6. **Keep informed about censorship issues through professional journals, reports, association meetings, and new media.**

deal with deaths in the family, child abuse, divorce, and other traumas. So, well-written books on these topics may fill an important need for these children. Common sense is every educator's best asset. (See Figure 2.2 for a guide to combating censorship and preserving intellectual freedom in our schools.)

Perhaps most importantly, there is no real evidence that censorship protects anyone or makes society better. But there are plenty of examples throughout history of censorship being used to squelch ideas, to keep people enslaved, to stop progress. The purpose of a censor is to control ideas. And stopping the spread of new ideas is rarely good for a society. It is right that the fight against censorship is now usually referred to as the fight for intellectual freedom.

Summary

Human development is a complex process that occurs on many different levels—physical, intellectual, and emotional. A child's developmental level directly impacts his or her response to reading. As adults, we often underestimate the abilities of small children—especially their linguistic abilities, including their ability to imitate sounds, put together sentences, and acquire new vocabulary. In their first 7 years, children go through developmental changes more rapidly than they will throughout the rest of their lives. Consequently, it is important to keep in mind the process of child development when we help them choose their books. A 1-year-old enjoys simple cloth picture books, but by age 7 many children are ready for chapter books. Of course, children develop at different rates, and we, as adults, are challenged to tune in to each child's needs and abilities. Fortunately, today we can find children's books to meet virtually every requirement and satisfy every desire.

We sometimes mistakenly believe that issues such as human sexuality, death, war, and violence are inappropriate subjects for children's books. But children are not immune to life's tragedies, and the many beautifully and sensitively written books on these topics can provide ways for children to cope and understand. And we might be wise to share some of these books during the normal course of events rather than wait until a crisis occurs. Reading should broaden a child's view of the world—not obscure it. And this is the best argument against any form of censorship.

For Reflection and Discussion

1. Select a picture book for young children (such as one from the list at the end of Chapter 6) and analyze it from the standpoint of one or more of the development theories presented in the chapter. What age level does it seem to be addressing? What leads you to that conclusion? What specific issues of that age level does the book seem to be concerned with?

2. Locate and read two picture books on a similar theme—new babies (Ezra Jack Keats's *Peter's Chair* and Martha Alexander's *Nobody Asked Me if I Wanted a Baby Sister*), parental relationships (Margaret Wise Brown's *Runaway Bunny* and Jane Yolen's *Owl Moon*), or death and dying (Lucile Clifton's *Everett Anderson's Goodbye* and Tomie dePaola's *Nana Upstairs, Nana Downstairs*). What specific differences do you see in the way the writers and illustrators address the issue? Which, if either, is more effective? Why?

3. Locate three or four picture books that all focus on one social or personal issue (such as three or four books on human sexuality or on alternative family lifestyles

or on emotional or physical challenges). Determine the intended audience and note the publication date for each book. Now read the books carefully and evaluate them on their content and approach. Is the subject represented accurately and sensitively? What differences do you see in the treatment of the subject? Does one book stand out from the rest? Why?

4. Locate a children's picture book on a controversial issue (death, sex, war, violence, etc.) and read it carefully yourself. Then share it with several different people—children would be ideal, but you may also want to share it with some friends both male and female to get as many points of view as possible. What have you learned through this experience? Did your response to the book change over the course of the various readings? Explain.

Works Cited

Jung, Carl Gustav. *Contributions to Analytical Psychology.* London: Routledge & Kegan Paul, 1948.

Knoth, Maeve Visser. "What Ails Bibliotherapy?" *The Horn Book Magazine* (May/June 2006): 273–276.

Recommended Resources

American Library Association website, www.ala.org.
  • A good place to look for a list of recently censored books.

Erikson, Erik. *Childhood and Society.* New York: Norton, 1950.

Greven, Philip. *Spare the Child: The Religious Roots of Punishment and the Psychological Impact of Physical Abuse.* New York: Alfred A. Knopf, 1990.

Griswold, Jerry. *Feeling Like a Kid: Childhood and Children's Literature.* Baltimore, MD: The Johns Hopkins University Press, 2006.

Healy, Jane. *Your Child's Growing Mind: Brain Development and Learning from Birth to Adolescence.* New York: Three Rivers Press, 2004.

Kohlberg, Lawrence. *The Philosophy of Moral Development.* San Francisco: Harper & Row, 1981.

——. *Essays on Moral Development. Vol. II: The Psychology of Moral Development, the Nature and Validity of Moral Stages.* San Francisco: Harper & Row, 1985.

Kozulin, Alex, and others, eds. *Vygotsky's Educational Theory in Cultural Context.* Cambridge: Cambridge University Press, 2003.

Lane, Frederick S. *The Decency Wars: The Campaign to Cleanse American Culture.* Amherst, NY: Prometheus, 2006.

National Coalition Against Censorship, www.ncac.org.

Neubauer, John. *The Fin-De-Siecle Culture of Adolescence.* New Haven, CT: Yale University Press, 1992.

Piaget, Jean. *The Language and Thought of the Child.* New York: Harcourt, Brace, 1926.

——. "Piaget's Theory." In P. H. Mussen. *Handbook of Child Psychology. Book I: History, Theory, and Methods,* 4th ed. Ed. W. Kessen. New York: John Wiley & Sons, 1983.

Pinker, Steven. *The Blank Slate: The Modern Denial of Human Nature.* New York: Viking, 2002.

——. *How the Mind Works.* New York: Norton, 1998.

——. *The Language Instinct.* New York: HarperCollins, 2000.

Ravitch, Diane. *The Language Police: How Pressure Groups Restrict What Students Learn*. New York: Knopf, 2003.

Sugarman, Susan. *Piaget's Construction of the Child's Reality*. Cambridge: Cambridge University Press, 1987.

Vidal, Fernando. *Piaget before Piaget*. Cambridge, MA: Harvard University Press, 1994.

Vygotsky, L. S. *Mind in Society: Development of Higher Psychological Processes*, rev. ed. Cambridge, MA: Harvard University Press, 2006.

3 The Literature Experience

Reading, Writing, Talking, and Doing

Introduction

The great Greek philosopher Socrates said, "Education is the kindling of a flame, not the filling of a vessel." This is especially true of reading, for it is an attitude or a habit, rather than a block of knowledge or set of facts. In this chapter we will look at ways to help kindle that flame in children so that it will continue to burn throughout a lifetime.

One of the greatest gifts we can give to a child is a love for reading. This love is usually developed early in life. However, one of my college students once told me of a summer he spent, when he was 18, in a cabin in the Michigan woods, without electricity or running water. He had never been much of a reader, but, lacking electronic devices to help him pass the time, he turned to books. By the end of the summer, he found himself a devoted reader. "Now," he said, "I can't get enough to read!" It is never too late to acquire a love for reading, but we cannot count on young people isolating themselves in the woods to accomplish this. As adults, we have to do whatever we can to encourage reading and instill a passion for books.

With most lessons of life, example is the best teacher. Children are more likely to read if they see the adults around them reading and if books are readily available. Also, there are many exciting ways to promote good reading experiences for children, both at home and in the classroom. This chapter is directed primarily to educators, and most of the ideas are for use in the classroom.

Educational Theories

Modern education is still being influenced by two educational theories developed in the past century—those of Lev Vygotsky and Louise Rosenblatt. As with all useful theories, they have undergone many adaptations over the years, but many of the basic premises remain relevant. What follows is but a very brief overview.

Lev Vygotsky and Social Interaction

Lev Vygotsky (1896–1934) was a Russian psychologist whose ideas on child development sharply parted with those of Piaget and his followers (see Chapter 2). Vygotsky discarded the stage theory of development and, instead, believed that human development is a continuing and never-ending process—that we have no developmental "goals" to reach, only a series of lifelong transformations to experience. He also believed that human beings are essentially social creatures and that it is through our social interaction that we learn about ourselves and the world.

Vygotsky believed that learning fell into three categories: there are things we can learn on our own, things we can learn with the help of others, and things we just cannot learn (not all of us can learn to sing grand opera or write prize-winning novels or play professional hockey). Formal education deals with the second category: things we can learn with the help of others. Vygotsky developed a concept called the *zone of proximal development* (*ZPD*). The ZPD is that area between what we can learn on our own and what we can learn with the help of others (see Figure 3.1), and this, he believed, is what education must focus on. This idea may seem like a "no-brainer" to us today, but it revolutionized education because it suggest that learning is a reciprocal process in which the teacher and the students have a shared responsibility: Students learn from teachers, teachers learn from students, and students learn from each other.

Vygotsky's ideas reject the traditional classroom, in which the teacher delivers information to attentive students sitting quietly in neat rows. In its place is a room of clustered desks, workspaces for small groups, and specialized learning stations. This is a place where everyone is responsible for teaching as well as learning, and education is a matter of mutual give-and-take. Small group discussions replace lectures; team projects replace individual examinations. Students assume responsibility for helping each other. The

FIGURE 3.1 ■ Vygotsky's Zone of Proximal Development

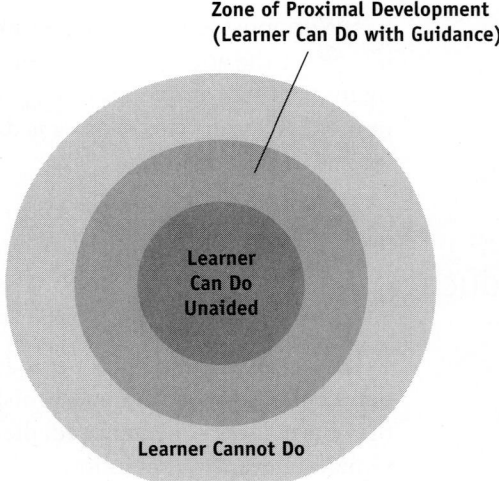

teacher relinquishes the authoritarian grip over the classroom in exchange for a cooperative community of learning. For many teachers, this switch requires a great deal of faith and a fair amount of risk. But for those able to make this leap, the teaching experience—if more challenging—is more enjoyable and more rewarding.

Louise Rosenblatt and Reader Response

Vygotsky was concerned with education in general. Louise Rosenblatt (1904–2005) looked more specifically at the teaching of reading and literature. She is most famous for two works, *Literature as Exploration* (1938) and *The Reader, the Text, the Poem: The Transactional Theory of the Literary Work* (1978). In these works she reacted against the prevailing notion of teaching literature, which seemed to suggest that there is a right way and there is a wrong way to interpret literature (and the teacher usually had the right way). Rosenblatt, instead, argued that reading literature is a process of give-and-take between the reader and the text and that no two readers interpret a text in the same way. Each of us comes from a unique set of experiences—personal, familial, psychological, social, educational, intellectual, religious, and so on—and these help determine how we react to a text.

One of the most famous results of Rosenblatt's ideas is what we call "reader-response theory." Reading a literary text is, according to this theory, part of a complex process that includes a collaboration of the writer (who has a message), the text (the symbols the writer uses to convey the message), and the reader (who receives the message and then interprets it according to his or her own experiences, thoughts, and beliefs). And, each time we reread a text, we may find our attitudes and interpretations changing, since our life experiences and knowledge are always changing. So the text acts on the reader, and the reader interacts with the text. (Some call this *transaction*, and hence this method is often referred to as *transactional analysis*.)

Let's use a simple example. The familiar folktale "Rumpelstiltskin," you will remember, is about a miller who lies to the king about his daughter's ability to spin straw into gold. The king agrees to marry the daughter if she spins a roomful of straw into gold each night for a year. Fortunately, a mysterious stranger appears, offering to help her if she promises him her firstborn child—and she agrees. Eventually the time comes for her to make good on her bargain, which she now regrets. So the stranger agrees to yet another bargain. She can keep her child if she can guess his name. She does so through the help of a spy, and, presumably, lives happily ever after.

If we ask readers to rank the main characters—Rumpelstiltskin, the miller, the daughter, the king—according to who acts most and least ethically, we find a wide range of attitudes and little general agreement. Sometimes readers cannot even agree on who is the hero and who is the villain. This discrepancy has to do with the readers' individual differences. For some, the miller's daughter is an innocent victim, a pawn of her greedy father and king. But others fault the daughter for bargaining with the life of her own child. Some readers see Rumpelstiltskin as villainous and opportunistic, but others believe he was only acting fairly, in accordance with the agreement. Some dislike the miller for his dishonesty, which puts his daughter's life in jeopardy. Others say he was simply trying to give his daughter a break in life. Many people regard the king as merely greedy, but others see him as a victim, deceived by the miller and his daughter, and a man of his word. So we see that reader response often points out the complexity of human behavior and the difficulty in determining right and wrong.

Reader-response theory opens up many doors for discussion. Rather than finding the one correct reading for a work of literature, it allows for a variety of simultaneous interpretations and encourages us to see the complexity and the richer fabric of the work. And it also explains why the reputations of books change over time. Some works lose their appeal, and others grow in popularity. However, reader-response theory is most helpful when we, as individual readers, are able to explain our responses (to ourselves and to others). In other words, we should try to discover why we feel the way we do about a novel, a poem, or a play.

The Common Core Curriculum

In 2014, a new set of educational standards in English Language Arts and Mathematics was implemented across the United States, and the overwhelming majority of the states have officially adopted them. These standards, prepared by the Common Core State Standards Initiative, are designed to provide consistent educational outcomes from state to state and, in the words of the initiative's mission statement, "to be robust and relevant to the real world, reflecting the knowledge and skills that our young people need for success in college and careers" (www.corestandards.org). Beginning in 2014, the standardized tests required by the No Child Left Behind Act of 2001 now assess student progress in attaining the goals of the Common Core.

Although most people agree with the idea that schools should be held accountable, the idea of standardized testing has long been controversial. Among the criticisms are that teachers will only "teach to the test," that the pressure to perform often results in cheating, and that students from poorer schools are at a disadvantage. And, indeed, the government has given waivers to "failing" schools across the country, based on their disproportionately large number of poor and/or minority students. Nevertheless, it seems likely that most of you who are hoping to be teachers will be required to address state and national standards in your classroom—and in most cases that will mean the Common Core Standards.

The documents outlining the Common Core Standards in English Language Arts (including reading, writing, speaking/listening, and language) are complex and detailed. But the most salient features, for our purposes, are these describing the reading component:

Children (in both elementary and high schools) should be able to

- Read closely (understand what they read, the vocabulary, the syntax, and the organization)
- Make logical inferences (draw conclusions from what they read, connect it to other texts they have read, and apply it to their personal lives)

- Cite specific textual evidence (use written material to support an argument or a point of view)
- Read complex literary and informational texts (comprehend a range of reading material—novels, plays, poetry, and the wide range of nonfiction, from science to history to business and beyond) (www.corestandards.org)

This last point is a significant one, since the goal is that the assigned reading for elementary school students should be at least 50 percent nonfiction (purely informational material) and in high school that percentage should increase to 70 percent. The argument for this is that most adults, from college students to people on the job, read primarily nonfiction—letters, memos, technical manuals, and reports. This element in the Common Core Standards has been a source of concern for some experts.

One concern is with the list of recommended (but not mandated) nonfiction. The suggested readings include the Preamble to the Constitution, George Washington's "Farewell Address," Lincoln's "Gettysburg Address," and Martin Luther King, Jr.'s "Letter from Birmingham Jail"—all relatively short works. (It is interesting that only the Constitution's Preamble is cited—and not the whole Constitution.) The problem is that all of these works were written in a specific historical context and can be fully understood only within that framework. One critic notes:

> The New Common Core Standards are meant to prepare our students to think deeply on subjects they know practically nothing about, because instead of reading a lot about anything, they will have been exercising their critical cognitive analytical faculties on little excerpts amputated from their context. So they can think "deeply," for example, about Abraham Lincoln's Second Inaugural Address, while knowing nothing about the nation's Founding, or Slavery, or the new Republican Party, or, of course, the American Civil War. (Fitzhugh, n.p.)

We should also keep in mind that reading excerpts from historical documents is not the same as reading an entire book of history, in which an argument is supported (if the book is good) by reliable facts that lead to a reasonable conclusion. So if nonfiction is to be emphasized in high school, for example, wouldn't it make sense that students read *good* nonfiction? And wouldn't it make sense that they read entire books of nonfiction and not just bits and pieces? Good nonfiction authors, such as Russell Freedman (*Lincoln: A Photobiography*), Jim Murphy (*An American Plague: The True and Terrifying Story of the Yellow Fever Epidemic of 1793*), and Seymour Simon (the author of some 200 science books), capture readers' interest and encourage them to want to read more. It seems unlikely that reading mundane memos, reports, and encyclopedia articles will stimulate the same interest in reading.

A second concern is that the Common Core Standards seem to undervalue fiction (novels, short stories, plays, and poems). Indeed, as noted earlier, by the senior year of high school, the standards recommend that 70 percent of students' reading be nonfiction. Now, admittedly, this includes reading material from all disciplines, so theoretically, the English classroom need not be affected. But, since the English teachers are the ones being held accountable for the reading standards, some critics fear that the literary classics will be replaced in the classrooms by mundane informational texts.

Further this approach to reading devalues the intellectual challenges that good literature offers readers. In other words, teaching reading should go beyond simple reading competency. The best literature—from Shakespeare to Jane Austen to Mark Twain to George Orwell (all of whom have been traditionally taught in high school)—offers a cultural and intellectual broadening that readers will not get from snippets in the daily news, memos from the boss, and how-to manuals. The role of the language arts teacher is not only to teach competence in reading but also to teach the accompanying thinking and reasoning skills that great books require of us.

Toddlers are enticed to read by their love of language and love of story. And we all know that our favorite books from childhood are the great fictional stories—*Charlotte's Web, The Secret Garden, Charlie and the Chocolate Factory, The Lion, the Witch and the Wardrobe, Treasure Island, The Adventures of Huckleberry Finn, Island of the Blue Dolphins.* These are the stories young readers fall in love with, and these are the stories that encourage them to read more. Moreover, recent scholarship suggests that storytelling fosters learning, cooperation, and creativity. Storytelling is fundamental to human nature—even our dreams come in the form of stories, complete with characters, plots and settings. (See Boyd, *On the Origin of Story*, and Gottschall, *The Storytelling Animal*, cited in Chapter 1.) English and language arts teachers should build on these early successes and direct students to the very best literature. These are the works that will turn young readers into lifelong readers and, more importantly, into critical thinkers with cultural awareness and intellectual insight, and into creative thinkers.

At the end of the day, yes, we want our students to be able to read on-the-job materials. But education should aspire to something more than job training. Education should open doors, broaden vistas, and (to paraphrase Socrates) kindle flames.

Using Literature in the Classroom

Reading Experiences

Following are some ideas for bringing about a connection between children and the books they read—and, we hope, to nurture a love of reading in all children. This list of suggestions is certainly not exhaustive—so always be on the lookout for fresh ideas.

READING ALOUD ■ From a parent's gentle singing of a lullaby while rocking an infant to sleep to the reading of such childhood classics as *Alice's Adventures in Wonderland* or *Pinocchio*, sharing literature orally with children can be one of the most fulfilling human experiences. The relaxing moments of story time with young children are among the most cherished memories of parenthood. And the times are equally magical when young children want to read the stories to us. However, we should not think that only small children like being read to. Even college students enjoy it. Effective reading aloud can be modeled by observing a few guidelines:

- Read stories you enjoy (unless you are a very good actor and can pretend to like the story). Your own enthusiasm will be contagious.
- Choose stories that fit the children's intellectual, emotional, and social developmental levels (see Chapter 2). Don't be afraid of a few challenging words—they never bother children—but make sure you know how to pronounce the words and what they mean. (Young children don't let you get away with much.)
- If the book is a picture book, make sure everyone can see the pictures. This is easy when you're reading to a single child but trickier when reading to a class of 25. Remember that it is most effective if your audience can see the pictures as you are reading—not before or afterward.
- Keep the reading experience an interactive one. Depart from the text when doing so seems necessary. Allow for questions and comments as you read—and you should feel free to ask questions as well.
- Rehearse your reading and be sure to use the proper inflections, the appropriate cadence, and the right tone (some books are "quiet" books; some are "noisy"). If there is dialogue, try reading in different voices. Children love this.

The reward for you is a grateful and delighted audience—and that is well worth the effort you put into reading aloud.

STORYTELLING ■ Storytelling, the art of narrating a tale from memory rather than reading it, involves two elements: selection and delivery. First, you need to choose good stories—ones with interesting characters, lively action, perhaps an unusual twist at the end. Pick your personal favorites and prepare a repertoire of stories to draw on. To be a good storyteller, you must also be a performer (and, admittedly, this is not for everyone). Practice your delivery. Assume voices for the various characters. Remember that timing is everything—speeding up, slowing down, and pausing at the right times. And most importantly, rehearse, rehearse, rehearse.

Folktales are natural fodder for storytellers. They include easily memorized patterns and ample dialogue to enliven the story, and they are brief enough to be relayed in a single sitting. Also, they lend themselves well to adaptation, so you can adjust the tale to the audience. Some storytellers like to create their own tales, sometimes from their own experiences or from their imaginations. All stories work best when they gradually build to a climax and quickly end while the audience's interest is still at a peak.

Of course, a rich and beautiful voice is an asset to any would-be storyteller. However, if you don't have such a voice, don't worry. Develop some other assets—effective body movement, facial expressions, eye contact, clear enunciation, meaningful inflection, and appropriate pauses—or maybe fancy dress. And, with practice, you can develop a greater vocal range and a voice that will project. Pacing and dynamics are crucial. You have to know when to slow down, when to speed up, when to talk in near whispers, when to shout, and so on. And do not overlook physical movement. Natural body gestures (and at times even exaggerated ones, depending on the story) and direct eye contact will help engage the audience. Finally, don't be afraid to ham it up. This is no time to be shy.

BOOK TALKS ■ A book talk, which should result in a free-flowing group discussion of a book, can work very well with older students (upper elementary and above). And it is a welcome replacement for those set questions from the teacher and the expected "correct" answers from the students.

A good book discussion requires serious preparation. Also, a good book discussion evolves and transforms as it proceeds. Be sure that you are well prepared before beginning a book discussion. This means not only reading the book carefully but also finding out what other readers (including critics) have said about it. (You can find a lot of information online. Just make sure your sources are reliable and consult the works listed in "Children's Literature Resources" at the back of this book.) You might want to include visual aids, photographs, a geographical map, a time line, a web, a story map, and anything else that might give readers some useful insight. Integral to most book discussions are the questions asked by the leader. The following types of questions progress from least to most sophisticated:

- *Memory questions* are the simplest type of questions and make good icebreakers. These questions ask readers to recall facts about the setting, plot, and characters. However, memory questions that dwell on insignificant details are a waste of time. In a discussion of E. B. White's *Charlotte's Web*, for example, questions like "What was Wilbur's favorite food?" or "What was Charlotte's oldest child's name?" seem a bit silly. Instead, ask questions like "Why was Wilbur's life in danger?" and "How did Fern save Wilbur?" In other words, your questions should have a good purpose and lead to further discussion.

- *Interpretation questions* ask the readers to draw conclusions from the facts in the story. Many readers are anxious to offer their own opinions; however, opinions ought to be based on facts from the text. For example, after a reading of *Charlotte's Web*, you might ask such questions as "How does the relationship between Fern and Wilbur change over the course of the book?" and "How does Wilbur's character change from the beginning to the end of the book?"

- *Application questions* ask the readers to apply knowledge received from a book to real-life situations or to other books. These questions help readers see the relationships between literature and life and require deeper thinking. A discussion of *Charlotte's Web* might include a question such as "In what ways do Templeton, Charlotte, and Wilbur remind you of people you know?"

- *Evaluation questions* ask the readers to judge the quality of a story. They ask readers to make comparisons between texts—for example, "Compare the treatment of death in Katherine Paterson's *Bridge to Terabithia* and Natalie Babbitt's *Tuck Everlasting*." These are the most sophisticated questions and are usually reserved for older readers. However, this does not mean we should not ask younger readers to make similar comparisons and evaluations of their books. It is never too early to begin.

All these questions attempt to help readers understand why they feel the way they do about a piece of literature.

Writing Experiences

As early as second grade, most children are capable of responding to literature through writing. Certainly by the time they reach the middle elementary grades, children should be writing as a regular part of their total curriculum. Several possibilities are available at all grade levels.

WEBBING AND MAPPING ■ Webbing is a visual means of demonstrating relationships between story elements or concepts. A web consists of a figure (the simplest resembles a spider's web, which is where the term comes from) on which labels are placed to show the connections between aspects of a literary work. For example, the web in Figure 3.2 illustrates the ways in which the principal characters in the folktale "Cinderella" are opposites. Almost any image can be a potential tool for webbing or mapping a story. The petals of a flower, the steps of a stairway, the points of a star, or the branches of a tree

FIGURE 3.2 ■ Web for "Cinderella"

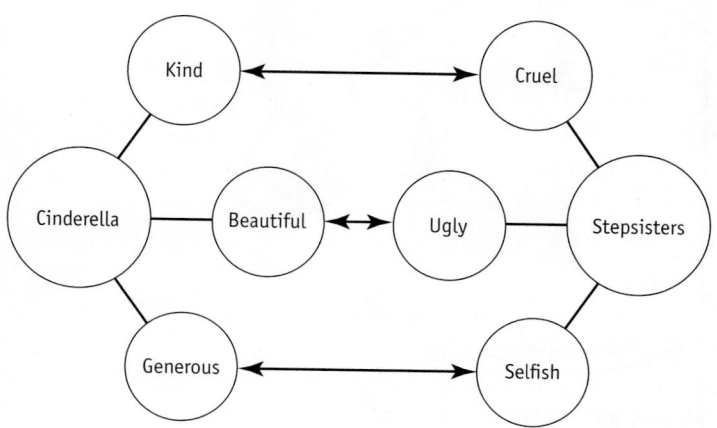

are just some of the images that can be used to demonstrate the connections in a work of literature. For example, we might label the petals of a flower with a character's personality traits to show how the individual grows (or "blossoms") throughout the course of a story. Since many people are visual learners and grasp ideas more quickly if they can see them illustrated, webbing is an effective tool for examining relationships in a poem, story, or play.

Very much like a web, a story map charts the progress of a book's plot in a visual manner. Figure 3.3 is a very simple story map that illustrates the circular journey of Hansel and Gretel from their home to the witch's cottage and back. The labels suggest possible character development that might occur in the main characters along the way. In addition to being educational, a webbing exercise can be fun for children.

RESPONSE JOURNALS ■ When we write down our thoughts, we usually think them through more thoroughly. Having young readers write in a response journal, in which they can freely record their feelings, is one way to get them to ponder their reading experiences. One approach to a useful response journal is to have students write a paragraph after completing each chapter of a book. In that paragraph they may express whatever they wish about the characters, the plot, the setting, the theme, and so on. A more directed approach is to give students a set of questions to respond to in their journals. (Review the various types of questions discussed above.) Sharing journals (with other students, with teachers, or with parents) can also be a rewarding experience. Of course, it goes without saying that

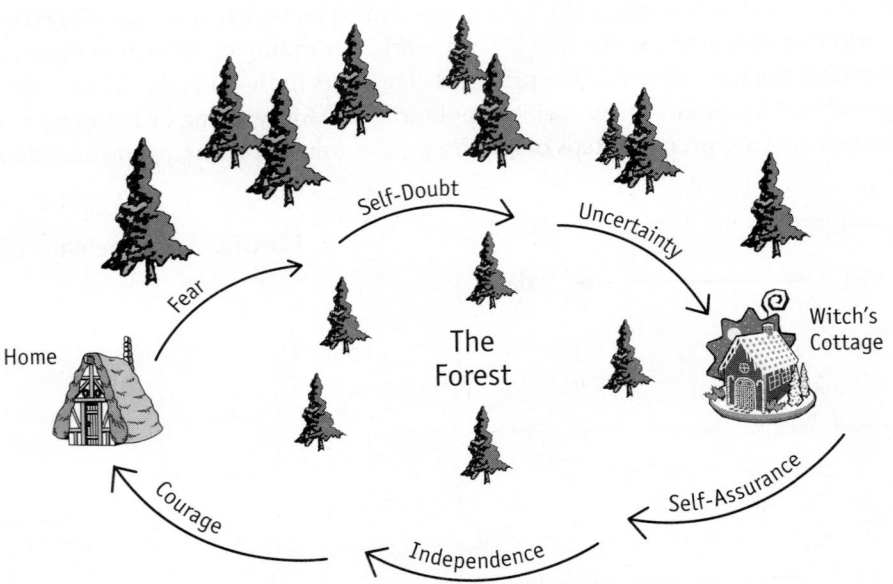

FIGURE 3.3 ■ Story Map for "Hansel and Gretel"

we should never share private journals with others without the writer's consent. (See Sharon Creech's novel, *Walk Two Moons*, in which a teacher publicly shares the students' private journals—and the grim consequences of such ill judgment.)

BOOK REPORT ALTERNATIVES ▪ For many, book reports conjure up dreary memories of dull and rambling plot summaries, often inflicted on an entire classroom of students on an appointed day. However, many interesting variations can actually be stimulating. See Figure 3.4 for some ideas.

FIGURE 3.4 ▪ Twenty-Five Things to Do with a Book

1. Create a story map for the book.
2. Prepare a two-minute radio spot promoting the book.
3. Write a biographical sketch of the author.
4. Turn one chapter into a child's picture book.
5. Create a collage or montage emphasizing the plot or theme.
6. Write a three- or four-paragraph book review for the local newspaper.
7. Create a dust jacket for the book.
8. Make a list of your 10 favorite things about the book.
9. Create a poster advertising the book.
10. Write a defense for the villain's actions.
11. Pick a favorite scene or chapter and prepare a dramatic reading.
12. Create a diorama of your favorite scene.
13. Create a mobile or stabile representing the theme or a character.
14. Make a cast list of well-known actors for a film of the book.
15. Create a geographical map of the setting based on evidence from the book.
16. Prepare a timeline for events in the story.
17. Write a news article reporting on an event in the story, as if it just happened.
18. Write a new episode for the book using the same characters.
19. Create a bulletin board display to entice others to read the book.
20. Rewrite an episode from a different point of view.
21. Write a poem about the book.
22. Create a web illustrating the interactions of the main characters.
23. Rewrite a scene to include yourself as a new character.
24. Write a fictional biographical sketch of your favorite character.
25. Rewrite one chapter as a one-act play.

Dramatic Experiences

Dramatic responses to literature offer opportunities for individual creativity and cooperative achievement. Most of the following dramatic exercises can be adapted to folktales or to chapters from favorite books.

STORY CIRCLE ■ A story circle is an experience in which participants sit in a circle (on chairs, on the floor, whatever works) and take turns reading or simply telling stories, poems, memories, and songs. This can be a nonthreatening and very rewarding experience. This could be a fine way to begin or end the school week. The secret is to keep everything informal and relaxed and not to force participation. You may have to make a few rules— you don't want the same handful of people doing all the talking, for example. But it may be best to keep things as fluid as possible, at least at the beginning. You might want to announce a theme—family, holidays, sports, hobbies, and so on. It will take time for some to become at ease with the process, but most will come around—and at the very least, even the observers will gain something from the experience.

STORY THEATER ■ Story theater is a pantomime accompanied by a narrator who reads or tells the story while others act out the plot. Since even inanimate objects (such as a tree) might be portrayed by an actor, story theater allows for a very flexible number of performers. (Some children may enjoy portraying objects like the moon or a door, for example.) The performance can be as simple or elaborate as the means and story dictate. Pantomime, because it does not require memorization, is one of the simpler dramatic forms for children. It does require one good reader, however, and some uninhibited actors. Often younger children have few inhibitions, so story theater is a good exercise to begin in the elementary years. The best tales for a story theater presentation are those with plenty of action; otherwise, the performers will be little more than furniture. Many folktales are good sources for story theater, particularly the farcical tales, such as "Clever Gretel," where action rather than dialogue dominates.

READER'S THEATER ■ True reader's theater is traditionally performed without any physical action whatsoever. Instead, the readers are usually seated, and each takes one of the speaking parts in a script. The old-time radio dramas were, in essence, reader's theater. All the audience's attention is directed to the language, so the readers must be expressive and read with clarity and precision. To avoid distraction from the reading, performers might want to wear uniform clothing—usually in black or black and white. But a reader's theater performance does not have to be a formal affair. It can be readily adapted to the classroom—even on an impromptu basis. It requires no memorization, physical movement, scenery, or props—just a lively script. The best stories are those with several speaking parts, ample dialogue, a fairly easy vocabulary but with expressive language, and, finally, a good conflict. "Hansel and Gretel," for example, would involve at least five characters (Hansel, Gretel, father, wicked stepmother, and witch) and a narrator. To increase the number of parts so more readers can participate, it is easy to divide the narrator's part among several readers. The real fun in reader's theater happens when the readers themselves become engaged in their roles and begin to read with feeling and conviction. (See Recommended Resources at the end of this chapter for a good website for reader's theater resources.)

PUPPET THEATER ■ Combining both dramatic and artistic responses to literature, puppet theater is a favorite medium of young (and sometimes old) children. Puppet making is an elaborate and time-honored art form, and it can easily be simplified. Puppets can be made from old socks, paper bags, construction paper and sticks, cardboard cylinders, vegetables (they make wonderful puppets, but don't wait too long to do the show), or, for the truly creative, string-operated marionettes with movable hands, feet, eyes, and mouths. The puppet theater itself can be as simple as a table draped with a sheet to hide the puppeteers. Large appliance boxes open up many possibilities. Once the puppet is made, the dramatic part of the experience begins. Stories with ample dialogue and action work best. And, since lines need not be memorized and the puppeteers are hidden from the audience's view, puppet theater can be an ideal form for beginning thespians. It is also perfect for shy children who, behind the mask of the puppet, may find an exhilarating outlet for their creativity.

Artistic Experiences

Another popular means of exploring literature is through art. As soon as they can handle a crayon or pencil, even the youngest children can be asked to draw pictures in response to a story. And for older children, the possibilities are limitless.

GRAPHIC ART ■ Children love working with paints, watercolors, crayons, and pencils. Drawings and paintings require the simplest of art supplies and minimal initial instruction, yet they allow for a great deal of originality. Having children draw pictures suggested by picture storybooks can be a means of getting them to explore different artistic styles, such as the Art Nouveau style of Kay Nielsen's illustrations for *East of the Sun, West of the Moon*, Beatrix Potter's delicate representational style in *The Tale of Peter Rabbit*, and Ludwig Bemelmans's expressionism in *Madeline*. (Illustrations from these and other works can be seen in Chapter 6.) Encouraging children to draw pictures after hearing stories read to them can result in some of the most highly individualistic creations, for they do not have another artist's work to imitate.

For those who have limited graphic skills, a collage or montage is a viable alternative. A collage is a picture created from various materials (cloth, wood, cotton, leaves, rocks, and so on) that can be fixed to a poster board or other surface to make a unified work. Quite similar is the montage, which is composed entirely of pictures (cut from magazines, newspapers, and so on). Creating a collage or a montage about a favorite story can be both enjoyable and enlightening, since it requires a certain amount of synthesis and analysis.

Posters can be made to represent a theme, a character, plot details, or even a mood, using the collage or montage method.

PLASTIC ART ■ The plastic arts include three-dimensional works (unlike graphic works, which generally are two-dimensional). Although sculpture and pottery can be unwieldy to create in a typical classroom, figures can be made from clay, paper, or wood to represent story characters or objects. Another artwork that can be accomplished in the classroom is a mobile, a free form usually cut from paper or cardboard and interconnected and suspended by string or wire so that when hung, the parts turn freely in the breeze. A mobile can demonstrate the relationships between plot elements or characters of a story. A diorama is a three-dimensional scene often created from a shoebox or another carton (an unused fish aquarium, with its glass sides, provides some interesting opportunities as well) and decorated with cardboard cutouts, plastic figures, or other suitable objects.

BOOK CREATION ■ Making their own books is a rewarding activity for children of all ages, and it is an activity that combines a variety of literary experiences. Very young children can create alphabet, counting, or concept books, or they can do takeoffs on favorite nursery rhymes or poems. Older children might want to experiment with ghost stories, adventure stories, family stories, or poetry. Books can be illustrated with a variety of media—crayon, watercolor, collage, montage, pencil, and so on. Binding the books can be as simple as fastening them in a loose-leaf folder or as elaborate as sewing the pages together and making cloth-covered cardboard covers. Not only does such a project give children first-hand experiences in designing books and laying out pages, but it can also result in an attractive finished product suitable for a gift or a keepsake. Creating a book is a rewarding way of bringing a writing exercise to a satisfying climax.

Regardless of the art project, it is important to remember that the art is an extension of the literature and not an end in itself. In other words, we are not reading *Pinocchio* for the purpose of making our own puppet when we are finished. And the art should not be simply gratuitous ("Now that we have read *Pinocchio*, let's all draw a picture of his nose"). The art project should become a meaningful part of the study of the literature, helping children to understand and appreciate the literature.

Technology in the Classroom

In this day and age, any discussion of instructional practices has to include some mention of technology. Although we always want to keep our focus on the literature itself—using technology can extend, deepen, and enliven the study of a literary work. Even preschool children regularly use computers for educational purposes (although perhaps too often for recreation). In some preschools, 3- and 4-year-olds are daily provided with Internet lessons in Spanish and Mandarin Chinese. And early elementary children are often quite well versed in the use of computer technology. Technology is a crucial part of the fabric of our society, and we should make the best use of it. We cannot begin to explore all the possibilities for using technology in the classroom, and many good resources are available to help you with that. What follows are only a few ideas for making technology a useful tool in the study of literature.

POWERPOINT ▪ This software, now quite commonplace in classrooms, allows classrooms to view visual presentations on a screen. Some teachers use it daily to identify and outline the day's objectives, remind students of assignments, and so on. But a PowerPoint presentation can be an effective way to introduce a book, an author, an illustrator, or, indeed, almost any educational concept. Unfortunately, if not prepared carefully, a presentation can be as deadly as a dull lecture. As with most other technology, a good PowerPoint presentation may take a great deal of time to prepare. But the results can be very satisfying. Here are some tips:

- Make sure you use plenty of illustrations—if you're just going to use words and sentences, you might as well prepare a written handout.
- Don't overload the slides. Keep them neat and uncluttered. (Try to follow the 6 × 6 rule: no more than 6 lines of text on a slide, and no more than 6 words to a line.)
- For text, use at least a 28-point typeface so the audience can easily read the slide.
- Prepare slides with animation, so, for example, the text or an illustration on a slide can be revealed when you are ready for it.
- Enhance a presentation by using the hyperlink options—connecting to online videos, for example.

WEBSITES ▪ For students in middle and upper elementary grades, the Internet will quickly become an indispensable tool in their research—although we can hope it will not be the only tool. Through search engines such as Google and Yahoo!, information can be found on virtually every topic under the sun. Fifth-grade students reading Lois Lowry's *Number the Stars*, a story set in Denmark during World War II, can quickly find a great deal of information on Denmark, the Nazis, the Danish Resistance Movement, King Christian X, Judaism, and countless other subjects mentioned in the book. However, the key is to be sure the information is reliable. And there's the rub: Computers may not create lazy students, but they do make it a lot easier to be lazy. Part of every teacher's instruction today should include the effective use of the Internet, including how to search for information, how to evaluate websites, and how to use the information accurately and honestly. Websites have made plagiarism very easy—through "cut and paste"—although it is equally easy to discover plagiarism, and an astute teacher is always on the lookout for it.

And, of course, a classroom might want to set up its own webpage, where the students can design the format and post their own research, presentations, daily classroom updates . . . the list is almost inexhaustible. It is easy to locate websites that provide directions and suggestions for projects like this.

BLOGS ■ A *blog* (derived from the term *Web log*) is a communication system that acts as an online personal journal. Here a student can record his or her personal responses to a book, poem, or story and then post it on a website for others to read. Then others may post their own responses. Using a blog can be a good way to get students thinking about and reacting to their reading, particularly if it is continued for a good period of time, allowing for the development of ideas.

CHAT ROOMS ■ Unlike the blog, a chat room allows for real-time conversations among several people online. A chat room is hosted by an Internet provider and allows people to post thoughts on a specific topic. This is a rather informal environment, and the messages are usually not permanent. For educational purposes, a teacher, using the school's server, can create a chat room for a class.

DISCUSSION BOARDS ■ Also called an Internet forum, a discussion board is similar to a chat room, except that is it more formally organized, and the messages do not disappear as quickly as with a chat room. A discussion board can be arranged so that everyone involved is online at the same time, or members can log in at their convenience. A discussion board also allows for "threads" or specific topics or subtopics on which members comment. The threads help keep the discussion organized. Discussion boards can be set up for an individual class as well.

WEBQUEST ■ The website WebQuest.org provides the tools to design "inquiry-oriented" lessons, in which students explore a topic through information provided online. Typically, students are given a problem to solve, and they proceed on a journey through preselected websites to reach the resolution, with questions and clues guiding them along the way. Students are then asked to complete a project, based on their research. As with many other technology tools, this is a bit time-consuming, but the payoff comes in enthusiastic students.

A word of caution, however. Before attempting any classroom project involving web postings (webpages, blogs, discussion boards, chat rooms, and so on), make sure you have considered the necessary privacy and safety issues, as well as the school's policy on such postings. Make sure you are aware of the school's policy on web use in the classroom. And remember, all postings on the Internet must be made judiciously—we have seen careers ruined by ill-considered Internet communications.

Perhaps the most important thing to remember about technology in the classroom is that it can provide a wealth of resources, but it cannot think for us. The hard work of learning—and it is hard work (anything that's worthwhile is)—must be accomplished by us alone.

Summary

As adults, we understand that we must attend to the physical and emotional well-being of children, but just as important is attending to their intellectual well-being. Today we live in a world beset by media—mostly visual, from computers to movies to television—all competing to see which can produce the wildest stimulation. This makes our encouragement of reading and of the love of books all the more important. Reading books, unlike watching television, requires us to think, to interact mentally. This is why reading is so vital to intellectual development.

Reading should be at the center of the learning experience. But we also should look for ways to keep children engaged in their reading. The reader-response approach to literature is a method that encourages children to go beyond merely reading the words in a book; it invites them to bring their own personal responses to the reading, to find in the reading what is meaningful to them, and to explore the responses of others.

Our goal in the classroom should be to enrich the reading experience and stimulate critical reading. Some ways to achieve these goals include reading aloud, storytelling, book discussions, writing experiences (including webbing, mapping, journal writing, and various written responses to books), dramatic experiences (including story circles, reader's theater, puppetry, and creative dramatics), artistic responses in both the graphic and plastic arts, creation of original books, and the extensive possibilities of today's technology. All these can broaden children's understanding, stimulate their imagination, and embolden their passion. A sign in one of my favorite local bookstores advises "Eat, Sleep, Read." It really is that important.

For Reflection and Discussion

1. Read (or reread) a favorite children's book and then write a personal response to it. Take into account what we have said about a reader's response to literature. What are the influences in your life that you think may have had an effect on your reading and interpretation?

2. Choose a favorite children's book and prepare a set of discussion questions that might be asked of elementary or middle school students. Make sure to include all four levels of questioning.

3. Choose a favorite children's story—a folktale or any other story—and prepare a web or a story map that might be useful in illustrating some important aspect of the work.

4. Choose one of your favorite folktales and prepare an oral reading—or, better yet, an oral storytelling in your own words. Practice your storytelling technique until you

feel completely comfortable and then seek an audience, preferably of young children. Enjoy your celebrity status!

5. Choose a favorite children's author or illustrator and explore the Internet to see what information you can find about that person. Compare the various websites and determine which are reputable and which are questionable. On what did you base your opinion?

6. Design a PowerPoint presentation on a favorite children's author or illustrator, making it suitable for either an elementary or secondary classroom. Experiment with the various capabilities available to you to create a polished work. Make sure you have substance as well as style.

Works Cited

Fitzhugh, Will. "Turnabout," educationviews.org, August 28, 2012.

Giannetti, Louis, and Scott Eyman. *Flashback: A Brief Film History*. Englewood Cliffs, NJ: Prentice Hall, 1986.

Recommended Resources

This list barely scratches the surface, but it is intended only to provide examples of some of the methods discussed in the chapter. There is no shortage of ideas. Hundreds and hundreds of education books are in print, and more are coming out each year. Thousands of websites provide instructional materials as well.

"Aaron Shepherd's RT Page: Scripts and Tips for Reader's Theater," www.aaronshep.com/rt/index.html.
  • A fine source for free reader's theater scripts for elementary and middle school use.

Bromley, Karen D'Angelo. *Webbing with Literature: Creating Story Maps with Children's Books*, 2nd ed. New York: Simon & Schuster, 1995.

"Carol Hurst's Children's Literature Site by Carol Otis Hurst and Rebecca Otis," www.carolhurst.com.
  • A compendium of book lists and classroom ideas on a wide range of subjects.

Engler, Larry, and Carol Fijan. *Making Puppets Come Alive: How to Learn and Teach Hand Puppetry*. New York: Dover, 1997.

Gottschall, Jonathan. *The Storytelling Animal: How Stories Made Us Human*. New York: Houghton Mifflin Harcourt, 2012.
  • Explores our need to tell stories.

Hobbs, Renee. *Digital and Media Literacy: Connecting Culture and Classroom*. Newbury Park, CA: Corwin, 2011.
  • For the secondary classroom.

Kennedy, John. *Puppet Planet: The Most Amazing Puppet-Making Book in the Universe*. Cincinnati, OH: North Light Books, 2006.

McCaslin, Nellie. *Creative Drama in the Classroom and Beyond*, 8th ed. Boston: Allyn & Bacon, 2006.

Mikkelsen, Nina. *Powerful Magic: Learning from Children's Responses to Literature*. New York: Teachers College Press, 2005.

Norfolk, Sherry, Jane Stenson, and Diane Williams. *The Storytelling Classroom: Applications across the Curriculum*. Westport, CT: Libraries Unlimited, 2006.

Pellowski, Ann. *The Storytelling Handbook: A Young People's Collection of Unusual Tales and Helpful*

Hints on How to Tell Them. New York: Simon & Schuster, 1995.

Pitler, Howard, Elizabeth R. Hubbell, and Matt Kuhn. *Using Technology with Classroom Instruction That Works,* 2nd ed. Alexandria, VA: Association for Supervision and Curriculum Development, 2012.

• For K–12 classrooms.

Purves, Alan, et al. *How Porcupines Make Love: Teaching a Response-Centered Literature Curriculum.* White Plains, NY: Longman, 1990.

Salem, Linda C. *Children's Literature Studies: Cases and Discussions.* Westport, CT: Libraries Unlimited, 2005.

Sawyer, Ruth. *The Way of the Storyteller.* New York: Penguin, 1942.

• A classic introduction to storytelling from a noted storyteller and author of children's books.

Schickedanz, J. A., and Renee Casberque. *Writing in Preschool: Learning to Orchestrate Meaning and Marks,* 2nd ed. Newark, DE: International Reading Association, 2009.

Shedlock, Marie. *The Art of the Storyteller.* New York: Dover, 1951.

• Advice on storytelling from a celebrated storyteller, a classic work.

Simon, Fran, and Karen Nemeth. *Digital Decisions: Choosing the Right Technology Tools for Early Childhood Education.* Lewisville, NC: Gryphon House, 2012.

Sloan, Glenna Davis. *The Child as Critic: Developing Literacy through Literature, K–8,* 4th ed. New York: Teachers College Press, 2003.

Trelease, Jim. *The Read-Aloud Handbook,* 7th ed. New York: Penguin, 2013.

Vasquez, Vivian Maria, and Carol Branigan Felderman. *Technology and Critical Literacy in Early Childhood.* New York: Routledge, 2012.

Yopp, Ruth Helen, and Hallie Kay Yopp. *Literature-Based Reading Activities,* 5th ed. Boston: Allyn & Bacon, 2009.

4 Diversity and Inclusion

Reading the World

Introduction

The famed sociobiologist Edward O. Wilson wrote, "Diversity is the way a parent hedges its bets against an unpredictably changing environment" (122). If we were all exactly alike, a single catastrophic event, such as an epidemic, could wipe us out. But because of our diversity, there is a good chance that some will possess the right genetic makeup to survive. Our differences make us stronger as a species; so sameness is not only dull, it is dangerous for humankind.

In an ideal world, we would celebrate our differences and be grateful for the advantages that our diversity provides us. Unfortunately, we live in a world where bigotry and prejudice still thrive. And how, we should ask, can we come to understand and accept human differences? Perhaps the best answer is education. We fear and mistrust what we don't understand. Usually, the greater our knowledge, the less our fear. Here is where books can help—especially children's books. One of the great benefits of children's literature is that it can broaden young minds and show children the fundamental humanity in all people, regardless of their color, religious beliefs, language, or customs. Literature can expand our horizons, deepen our understanding, and show us ultimately that we are all in this world together, sharing the same fears, hopes, and dreams. Stories and novels tend to focus on individuals—not types. And when we begin to see people as individuals, it is not so easy to harbor bigotry and prejudice. In this chapter we will be looking at books that can help raise our consciousness about other cultures and about people who face challenges different from our own. Reading their stories heightens our awareness and deepens our sensitivity.

Definition of Culturally Diverse Literature

Culturally diverse literature is simply literature that reflects the broad cultural makeup of a society. In the United States, that would have to include, in addition to stories about European Americans, African Americans, Latinos, American Indians, and Asian Americans, at the very least. Unfortunately, the appearance of heroes from minority cultural groups has been a belated one in children's literature. Only in the latter half of the twentieth century, beginning with the social movements of the 1960s, did we begin to see significant numbers of books about people outside the European American culture (or, for that matter, outside the Anglo American culture). The United States is one of the most culturally diverse nations on earth, and rather than let our diversity destroy us, we should embrace it. But we should not forget that the true goal of recognizing cultural diversity is to bring about the inclusion of those diverse cultures into the wider circle of humanity.

Rudine Sims Bishop has very clearly identified the necessity for culturally diverse literature, as well as the detriment in not having it:

> *If literature is a mirror that reflects human life, then all children who read or are read to need to see themselves reflected as part of humanity. If they are not, or if their reflections are distorted and ridiculous, there is the danger that they will absorb negative messages about themselves and people like them. Those who see only themselves or who are exposed to errors and misrepresentations are miseducated into a false sense of superiority, and the harm is doubly done.* (quoted in Harris 43)

In other words, culturally diverse literature enriches everyone. First, it provides members of minority groups with positive role models and bolsters cultural pride and individual dignity. Second, it provides the majority culture with exposure to the various minority cultures and thus helps break down old prejudices and dispel misunderstandings.

Some critics insist that only members of an ethnic group can honestly write about that group. August Wilson, an African American playwright, argues that "someone who does not share the specifics of a culture remains outside, no matter how astute a student or well meaning the intentions" (quoted in Harris 42). Thus, Wilson insists that only African Americans should write about African Americans, only American Indians about American Indians, and so on. However, another African American, the critic Henry Louis Gates, Jr., disagrees: "No human culture is so inaccessible to someone who makes the effort to understand, to learn, to inhabit another world" (Gates 30). In other words, Gates believes that a writer does not have to be African American to write about African Americans, but that writer does have to know a lot about them and has to be able to empathize with them, to walk in their shoes. Let us hope that Gates is correct, for that offers us the promise of a better world. (See Figure 4.1 for a guide to evaluating books for cultural sensitivity.)

What follows is a brief discussion of some of the major cultural groups in the United States and their treatment in modern children's literature.

FIGURE 4.1 ▪ Criteria for Culturally Diverse Children's Books

- *Cultural accuracy*—There are no sloppy or incorrect cultural facts.
- *Balance and authenticity*—The cultural aspects are genuine, true to life, and presented from various sides.
- *Sensitivity*—The culture is presented respectfully, without cultural stereotypes or biases.
- *Sympathy*—The culture is presented with a positive and intelligent understanding of the issues.
- *Genuine characters*—The characters are presented first and foremost as individual human beings, not types or representatives.
- *Accurate and sensitive illustrations*—Any illustrations respectfully represent the culture and are of high quality.
- *Engaging literary elements*—The work is good on its own literary merits—character, plot, language, and so on—and not simply because it happens to be about a certain ethnic group.

Types of American Cultural Diversity

African Americans

One of the most controversial children's books in history may be Helen Bannerman's *Little Black Sambo*, first published in 1899. It is actually a rather innocent story about a little boy from southern India who outwits four ferocious tigers who want to eat him. But Bannerman's rather crude illustrations (see Figure 4.2) and the use of the name "Sambo" would eventually come to signify American Black racism—even though Bannerman was Scottish, and her story was about an Indian. For many years in the mid-twentieth century, the book was effectively blacklisted (and even banned in some places). However, in 1996, a re-illustrated version by Fred Marcellino appeared (see Figure 4.3). This version retained Bannerman's original text, except that the names of the characters were changed (Little Black Sambo became Little Babaji), and the illustrations eliminated all hints of racial stereotyping. These changes revealed a charming tale of a heroic boy triumphing over tremendous odds. The point is that language and illustration do make a difference when it comes to cultural sensitivity.

Prior to the 1970s, few children's books featured African American characters. One notable exception is *Call Me Charley* by Jesse Jackson (not the minister/politician/activist). First published in 1945, it is the story of a young African American boy attempting to assimilate into a white, middle-class neighborhood. Jackson deals frankly with racial conflict, and his main character, Charley, sets the tone when he retorts to a boy who refers to him as "Sambo": "My name is Charles. . . . Sometimes I'm called Charley. Nobody calls

FIGURE 4.2 ■ An illustration from Helen Bannerman's 1899 book *The Story of Little Black Sambo*. Although unintended, Bannerman's artless portrait of her little hero would become the poster child for American racism.

THE STORY OF LITTLE BLACK SAMBO

me Sambo and gets away with it" (8). The story seems dated now. Charley is finally accepted by the white community, but only because he abandons his black identity and his cultural roots. The book reflects the American melting pot ideal of the 1940s. Cultural minorities, if they wanted to fit in, were expected to give up their distinctive habits, language, dress, and so on and adopt the ways of the dominant white culture.

The Civil Rights Movement would change that, and in the 1970s, books began to appear that celebrated African American values and cultural identity. Award-winning writers such as Virginia Hamilton (*The Planet of Junior Brown*), Rosa Guy (*Ruby*), Alice Childress (*A Hero Ain't Nothin' but a Sandwich*), and Mildred Taylor (*Roll of Thunder, Hear My Cry*) all captured the vitality of the African American culture, dispelling stereotypes and portraying genuine, flesh-and-blood characters engaged in the business of living. Today, many fine writers are producing books that present vivid and honest portraits of both modern-day African American culture (see Jacqueline Woodson's books) and its historical contexts (see Christopher Paul Curtis's books).

American picture books prior to the 1960s rarely depicted African American characters except as menials and objects of comic derision (see Inez Hogan's "Nicodemus" books from the 1930s and 40s or Sara Cone Bryant's *Epaminondas and His Auntie*). One of

THE·STORY·of·LITTLE·BABAJI

FIGURE 4.3 ■ Fred Marcellino's stylish re-illustrations for Bannerman's *Little Black Sambo* and a new name for the hero transform what has long been regarded as an icon of politically incorrect literature into the classic tale it really is.

the first picture books with a positive African American protagonist was *The Snowy Day*, which appeared in 1962. Written and illustrated by Ezra Jack Keats (who was, in fact, a white Jewish American), this Caldecott Medal–winning book describes a young, inner-city African American boy, Peter, enjoying the simple pleasures of the fresh snowfall one wintry day. Although the book lacks "cultural specificity"—that is, nothing except Peter's skin color identifies him as an African American—it remains an important groundbreaker and is still being enjoyed by children. The importance of books like Keats's is that they dispel the stereotypes. In Peter, we see a boy with the same joys, hopes, worries, and fears shared by all children.

However, it is also important for a book to acknowledge and celebrate cultural differences. Carolivia Herron's *Nappy Hair*, which appeared in 1997, describes a young black girl's unruly, nappy hair—a feature that was once a source of ridicule from racist whites. In Herron's story, the hair becomes a proud symbol of the girl's black heritage. And Herron deftly re-creates the joyous black dialect with its pattern of call and response, adding both flavor and authenticity to the story.

The establishment of the Coretta Scott King Award in 1970, honoring African American contributions to children's literature, has helped to encourage continued high quality in the field of African American literature.

Latinos/as

First, a word about terminology. Over the years, the cultural group now known as Latinos has been referred to as Mexican American, Chicano, and Hispanic. These terms are not interchangeable, and no single term captures the true diversity of this culture. *Hispanic*, for example, refers to individuals from the Spanish-speaking cultures of Mexico, Central America, and South America, whereas *Latino* includes all of Latin America, including Portuguese-speaking Brazilians. However, none of the terms really accommodates the indigenous people of these regions (such as the Zapotec in Mexico.) So, with these caveats, in this text we use the term Latino (Latina is the feminine form) because it is slightly more inclusive.

The Latino culture in the United States has been characterized by the Spanish language, the Roman Catholic Church (but not exclusively), and the folk traditions of Latin America (which includes Mexico, Central America, and South America). This group is still vastly underrepresented in children's books, and its portrayal has been controversial. Unfortunately, we still find in the modern media the unfair and negative stereotypes of the criminal alien or the helpless victim, the volatile Latin temperament, the male machismo, and so on. Although children's books usually avoid these stereotypes, earlier books portray an overabundance of poor migrant workers or other rural laborers. This image is quite contrary to the reality. Today, most Latinos are city dwellers, and they can be found in all walks of life.

We are now seeing more and more writers of Latino heritage producing some very fine works for young readers. One popular Latino author, Gary Soto, has distinguished himself as both a poet and a storyteller, with prose works like *Baseball in April* and *Buried Onions* and poetry collections including *A Fire in My Hands* and *Canto Familia*. His subjects are modern-day Latino children pursuing their hopes and dreams like all other children. Pat Mora has published several poetry collections, including *Borders*, *Chants*, and *Communion*, in addition to several family stories for young children, such as *A Birthday Basket for Tia*. Mora's poems for young children are filled with images of the Southwest and Latino culture, and throughout she scatters Spanish expressions, reminders that the Latino culture is often a bilingual culture. Sandra Cisneros gained fame for her book for older children, *The House on Mango Street*. All these writers focus on the importance of the family—especially the extended family—in the Latino community, which is key to Latinos' personal identity. The characters also tend to be bilingual, which allows them to hold onto their traditional heritage as well as function successfully in the English-speaking culture. The prevalence of the Spanish language in the United States has inspired a new trend in modern picture books—the dual-language book, such as Carmen Lomas Garza's *Family Picture/Cuadros de Familia*.

Like African Americans, Latinos have become a significant social and political force in American society. There has never been a greater need for sensitive, honest, and intelligent children's books representing Latino culture than there is today.

American Indians

Again, we need to start this section with a word about terminology. The argument over the terms *Native American* and *American Indian* has largely subsided. Most of the people grouped under these terms prefer to be identified by their tribal associations (Navajo, Cherokee, Ojibwe, and so on), just as "white" Americans might consider themselves English, German, or Italian rather than European. For general purposes, the terms *American Indian* and *Native American* are now used interchangeably, with the former, despite its geographic and cultural inaccuracies, often being preferred today—and that's the term we use here.

American Indians have long been the subject of a mythology that continues to cloud the general public's perception. Too often we lump together all American Indians into one vision of a beaded, feathered warrior in moccasins. For a long time, children's picture books either ignored the American Indian altogether or fell back on the stereotypes. Perhaps many still do. American Indians argue that even today's picture books rely on the old images and fail to portray the modern American Indian realistically. Indeed, by and large, picture books about American Indians still feature the traditional images and ignore the fact that currently about 2 million American Indians live in the United States—without teepees, headdresses, or bows and arrows. They have homes, cars, careers, and hobbies, and they also enjoy a rich and ancient heritage.

Some of the finest examples of American Indian literature are found in the folktales that have been collected over the years (including those by Joseph Bruchac, Craig Kee Strete, and others). The best of these children's versions of the folktales identify the specific American Indian tribal affiliations (e.g., Iroquois, Sioux, Ojibwe) and the Native tellers themselves. (For a fuller discussion of folktales, see Chapter 8.)

Two important and popular types of American Indian literature are historical fiction and nonfiction. Since about 1970, the predominant theme of this literature has been the correction of misconceptions (about the relationships between whites and American Indians, for example). Scott O'Dell, although not American Indian himself, was one of the earliest children's writers to offer the Indian point of view. His *Sing Down the Moon* is a fictionalized account of the brutal, forced relocation of the Navajo in the nineteenth century. Margaret Craven's *I Heard the Owl Call My Name* is the story of a priest sent to work in a First Nations parish on the coast of British Columbia. (In Canada, the native populations are referred to as First Nations.) This moving and beautiful story describes the priest's coming to terms with the traditional native culture, as well the difficulties facing that culture and its survival in the modern world.

True stories are every bit as compelling as fiction. Ignatia Broker's *Night Flying Woman: An Ojibway Narrative* describes the life of the author's great-great-grandmother and the uprooting of her people by nineteenth-century whites. For works with a modern setting, we have the compelling stories of Alexie Sherman, including *The Absolutely True Story of a Part-Time Indian*, describing life on a reservation, and *War Dances*, a collection of writings expressing the writer's keen observations on modern American Indian life. Sherman's works are acutely realistic, many based on the author's own experiences, with a healthy dose of humor.

Culturally conscious books include portraits of American Indians as individuals, sensitive descriptions of American Indian cultural traditions, and an awareness that each American Indian society is a distinctive cultural entity—that there are Creek, Iroquois, Sioux, and so on. These books reject demeaning vocabulary, artificial dialogue, and cruel and insensitive Indian stereotypes. Donnarae MacCann suggests that we ask ourselves "Is there anything in the book that would make a Native American child feel embarrassed or hurt to be what he or she is? Can the child look at the book and recognize and feel good about what he or she sees?" (quoted in Harris 161).

Asian Americans

The term *Asian American* is another catch-all word; it includes Chinese Americans, Japanese Americans, as well as those from other Asian nations—Korea, Cambodia, Thailand, and so on. Asian Americans, like the other groups we have discussed so far, have been subjected to unkind stereotypes—in this case, misogynistic males and submissive females, all speaking English very poorly and being reticent and docile. Claire Huchet Bishop's *The Five Chinese Brothers*, published first in 1938, is an example of what was thought to be an innocent folktale that took on racial overtones. The text tells us, for example, that the five brothers "all look alike," and Kurt Wiese's illustrations have been criticized for caricaturing Chinese stereotypes. (This story has also been criticized because of violent references in the text.) To be sure, we have to take into consideration the book's age and that it reflects the attitudes of an earlier era. But that argument will mean little to 5- and 6-year-old children (the presumed audience of *The Five Chinese Brothers*). When using a book that portrays another culture, our first concerns should be whether it could offend any member of the audience and whether it could create inaccurate or unfavorable views about the culture being represented.

Naturally, the most responsible modern writers and illustrators try to undo the deplorable stereotypes of Asian Americans, and this often begins with distinguishing between the various Asian cultures—many of which have little in common with each other. To lump people of Chinese, Japanese, Korean, Thai, and Vietnamese descent all together as if they were a single national/ethnic group is both inaccurate and insensitive. We can now find many books that reflect and celebrate the uniqueness of each individual culture.

Today, several writers and illustrators are producing beautiful picture books that accurately evoke Asian and Asian American cultures. Ed Young has written and illustrated children's books that display his passion for his native China, and his art reflects the influence of traditional Chinese painting. His *Lon Po Po: A Red-Riding Hood Story from China* won the 1990 Caldecott Medal. Allen Say's beautifully illustrated books—such as *Grandfather's Journey* (winner of the 1994 Caldecott Medal), which tells the story of Japanese American immigrants—are fine examples of culturally sensitive narratives. Asian culture too often overlooked is that of India. A good place to start is with Sandhya Rao's award-winning picture book, *My Mother's Sari*, or Kashmira Sheth's *Moonsoon Afternoon*, illustrated by the Japanese artist, Yoshiko Jaeggi (a truly international collaboration).

Laurence Yep's *Dragonwings*, a work for older children, describes life as it was lived in San Francisco's Chinatown in the early 1900s. In *Coolies*, Rosanna Yin describes the experiences of the earliest Chinese immigrants, the workers who helped lay the transcontinental railroad in the nineteenth century. *A Step from Heaven*, by An Na, describes the difficult experiences of a young Korean girl growing up in America. The harrowing story of the Japanese American internment during World War II has been the subject of several moving books, both fiction and nonfiction. Perhaps the most famous is the autobiographical *Farewell to Manzanar* by Jeanne Wakatsuki and James D. Houston.

Finally, Grace Lin, who built a reputation as a popular picture-book author/illustrator, has recently gained fame as a novelist. And her *The Year of the Dog* is the first of a popular series, the Pacy Lin series, about Pacy, the young daughter of Taiwanese immigrants growing up in America. These books, which are semi-autobiographical, have been celebrated for portraying the reality of living in a multicultural world, where each individual must find his or her place, far from ethnic stereotypes. Her recent Newbery Honor Book, *Where the Mountain Meets the Moon*, beautifully weaves Chinese folk legends into a magical adventure narrative.

Other Cultures

It is now possible to find children's books on a wide variety of world cultures, from virtually every continent. Among the most prominent, perhaps, are books on the Jewish experience. Judaism as a culture transcends national boundaries. Jewish Americans have long played crucial roles in American culture, in the arts, business, education, and politics. However, anti-Semitism has been a blot on Western civilization, in the United States as well as Europe. Of course, when we think of anti-Semitism, most of us see visions of the Holocaust and the slaughter of 6 million innocent victims of the Nazi regime. Indeed, when it comes to children's literature about Judaism, stories of the Holocaust dominate the list. Anne Frank's *The Diary of a Young Girl*, a teenager's firsthand account of the horrors of the Nazi occupation of the Netherlands, is the most famous. Other memoirs include Aranka Siegal's *Upon the Head of a Goat: A Childhood in Hungary, 1939–1944*, which describes the atrocities perpetrated in eastern Europe, and Judith Kerr's *When Hitler Stole Pink Rabbit*.

Aside from books about the Holocaust, books about Jewish culture tend to fall into three categories: folktales, informational books, and contemporary novels. Nobel Laureate Isaac Bashevis Singer recorded many tales of Jewish life, including *Shlemiel Went to Warsaw and Other Stories*, *Zlateh the Goat and Other Stories*, and *Mazel and Shlimazel*. These are partly his own original stories and partly retellings of traditional Jewish folktales that he heard as a child. They are filled with a rich sense of humanity and the warm humor often associated with Jewish culture. Informational books generally describe Jewish customs and religious rituals. Michele Lee Meyer's *My Daddy Is Jewish and My Mommy Is Christian* is a picture book that describes circumstances becoming increasingly familiar in U.S. society. Among the novelists, one of the most celebrated is Chaim Potok, whose *My Name Is Asher Lev* is the story of a young Hasidic Jew, an artist engaged in the conflict between his faith and his art, as well as tradition and modernity.

Not surprisingly, one culture that has attracted tremendous interest in the past few years is Islam. (We should perhaps say "cultures," though, since, like Christianity and Judaism, the Muslim faith consists of many variations.) Recent books about the Muslim culture reveal several tendencies. Demi's *Muhammad* is a picture book describing the life of the prophet who founded the faith in the seventh century. Joelle Stoltz's *The Shadows of Ghadames* is a novel set in Libya in the nineteenth century that provides some historical perspective on Islam. And Elizabeth Fama's *Overboard*, which is set in Indonesia (the world's most populous Muslim country), is a contemporary story that brings together Muslims and Western Christians.

The myths and legends of Hinduism are now being illustrated for young children. For a good example, see Sanjay Patel and Emily Haynes's *Ganesha's Sweet Tooth*, a brightly illustrated picture book, and Amy Novesky's *Elephant Prince: The Story of Ganesh*.

Naturally, it is impossible to cover all cultures and ethnic groups, and any omission here is not intended as a slight. Combing the Internet can produce some interesting results. Any good book about a culture or a place or a people we do not know can make us better world citizens—tolerant, understanding, and empathetic. Rosa Guy, a distinguished writer of books for young adults (*The Friends*, *Ruby*, and others) and a native of the former British colony of Trinidad, has issued this call to arms for all cultural groups:

> *I reject the young of each succeeding generation who dare to say: "I don't understand you people . . ." "I can't stand those people . . ." or, "Do you see the way they act . . .?" They are us! Created by us for a society which suits our ignorance.*
>
> *I insist that Every child understand this. I insist that Every child go out into the world with this knowledge: there are no good guys. There are no bad guys. We are all good guys. We are all bad guys. And we are all responsible for each other. (34)*

Types of Social Diversity

Social diversity refers to individual differences unrelated to a person's heritage—particularly gender, physical or mental or emotional disabilities, sexual orientation, and alternative lifestyles. Once largely ignored in children's books, these issues are now seen as important to a child's growth and development. Learning to accept individual differences is a first step toward achieving a society of tolerance, harmony, and compassion—an ambitious goal, perhaps, but one well worth working for. The treatments of sexuality, death and dying, and violence in children's books are dealt with in Chapter 2, since these are closely related to a child's emotional growth.

Gender Awareness

For thousands of years, most of human society has been male dominated, effectively relegating the woman's position to one of subservience. Society has come to value the so-called masculine traits of physical strength, assertiveness, independence, power, aggressiveness, and ambition, and to devalue the so-called feminine traits of passivity, docility, emotionalism, physical weakness, dependence, and accommodation. These stereotypes are both inaccurate and unfair—to both men and women. Traditionally, this bias has occurred in three distinct areas:

- *Gender-based language*—terms which imply that masculinity is superior to femininity, such as *chairman*, *mailman*, and *policeman*. These retain the stigma of the culture's male bias and remain offensive to many people. (What about *chair*, *mail carrier*, and *police officer?*)
- *Professional stereotypes*—the identification of certain jobs with males (physician, pilot, company president) and other jobs with females (nurse, secretary, teacher). These stereotypes are disappearing, and we now find male nurses and secretaries and female physicians and pilots. The liberation of women over the past half century has also resulted in the liberation of men.
- *Behavioral stereotypes*—identifying certain traits as masculine (physical strength, emotional insensitivity, social ineptitude) and others traits as feminine (physical delicacy, emotional vulnerability, tenderness). Traditionally, a male child was expected to be physically active, even mischievous, but a female child who showed such traits might be labeled a "tomboy," another disparaging term. These are dangerous generalizations, and all of us would probably rather be seen as individuals than as types.

The bottom line is simply that children need books that portray positive images of women and men, without the stereotyping of roles and behavior. We can find books with strong and clever heroines, such as Louise Fitzhugh's *Harriet the Spy*, Mildred Taylor's *Roll of Thunder, Hear My Cry*, and Ian Falconer's picture-book series about the fiercely independent pig, Olivia. And there are books with sensitive males, such as Beverly Cleary's *Dear Mr. Henshaw*.

However, it is important to remember that we can't fault the language or gender bias of earlier writers. If we rejected books from the past because they do not live up to our standards of gender decorum, we would have to eliminate virtually everything written before about 1970. That would be ridiculous. To use a well-worn saw, let's not toss the baby out with the bathwater.

Alternative Families

I grew up watching the sitcoms of the 1950s—*Father Knows Best*, *Leave It to Beaver*, *The Donna Reed Show*, and so on. And although I may have enjoyed them, I certainly did not identify with them. How different those families were from my own blended family of stepparents and step- and half-siblings, which, I concluded, made us outsiders. Today, few children grow up in homes in the suburbs with two parents, a sibling, and a dog. No longer do most mothers don their aprons in the morning and spend their days cleaning and cooking for their families, while the fathers head off to the office and bring home the bacon. Single-parent homes are commonplace, and the vast majority of women now work outside the home. Modern children's books are at last coming to reflect this reality. Children who have stepparents, stepsiblings, and half-siblings may find comfort in books depicting other families like theirs.

More than half of all American marriages end in divorce. Although many informational manuals abound to explain how children can cope through such a difficult time, for younger children a story is often better. Lucille Clifton's *Everett Anderson's 1-2-3* is a picture book about a young African American boy dealing with his parents' divorce. Other books in this series show him moving through a series of other family adjustments—coping with his mother's remarriage, a new sibling, and, eventually, his father's death. Unlike how-to manuals, which can be dull and preachy (although the best are very helpful), Clifton's stories are told in lovely poetic lines, and they portray children surviving in a world that is not always kind, not always joyful, not always fair—in other words, they show us real life.

Subjects that were once controversial are now fairly common in children's books. Norma Klein's *Mom, the Wolfman, and Me*, about an unwed mother, her boyfriend, and her daughter, reflects social trends. And Katherine Paterson's *The Great Gilly Hopkins*, about an unruly child in foster care, and Cynthia Voigt's *Homecoming*, about four children abandoned by their mother in a parking lot, are all too realistic in their portrayal of modern dysfunctional families.

Another family-related issue, child abuse—physical, emotional, and sexual—has come late to children's books, despite the fact that it is an issue that concerns children deeply. Among the recent offerings on the subject are Chris Crutcher's *Staying Fat for Sarah Byrnes*, James Howe's *The Watcher*, and Mirjam Pressler's *Halinka*. This subject, like so many other delicate issues, has been swept under society's carpet of respectability for too long. We do no service to young people by ignoring these problems, and, in the hands of a capable writer, much good can come of sharing both facts and feelings. These books do not endorse these lifestyles, but they do acknowledge the existence of these issues—and that alone may bring comfort to some readers and understanding to others.

The Physically, Emotionally, and Intellectually Challenged

Another change taking place in our society is a more receptive attitude toward individuals with special needs. These individuals were once virtually ignored in children's books, undoubtedly a holdover from the time when people with physical, emotional, or intellectual differences were largely hidden away from society—either institutionalized or secluded at home. Society is now more sensitive to the needs of these individuals. Our laws now recognize the existence of physically challenged individuals, and our schools seek to include and accommodate all children. Although this is a subject still not widely addressed in children's books, a few titles deserve mention. Perhaps the most famous of these books is Robert Kraus's *Leo the Late Bloomer*, about a young tiger who develops more slowly than others. Taro Yashima's *Crow Boy* is about a Japanese boy suffering from shyness; Lucille Clifton's *My Friend Jacob* describes the relationship between a young black boy and his older white friend who is intellectually challenged. Virginia Hamilton's *Sweet Whispers, Brother Rush* is about a family coping with an inherited mental disorder. And physical disabilities are featured in such books as Carolyn Meyer's *Killing the Kudu*, which tackles stereotypes about people in wheelchairs. It is fairly safe to say that there is virtually no disability—from autism to speech disorders—that is not addressed in some children's book. The best books present their subjects with sensitivity and emphasize the need for society to embrace all individuals. And many stories reveal that disabilities do not prevent one from becoming a good friend and productive member of society.

Summary

As human beings, our ability to flourish in the world has depended greatly on our diversity and our ability to adapt to changing environments. Wide reading can help make us more adaptable, for books enrich our personal experiences, enlarge our horizons, and nurture tolerance and understanding. Books about cultures different from ours and about people who worship different gods, practice different customs, hold different beliefs, and enjoy different lifestyles all help us widen our intellectual horizons. Reading such books may help us achieve one of society's most important goals—to acknowledge the tenet in the *Universal Declaration of Human Rights* that "All human beings are born free and equal in dignity and rights."

In addition to appreciating cultural diversity, we have come a long way toward recognizing other differences in the human family. The most basic is probably the gender difference, which has been explored extensively in the past 50 years, causing us to lay aside the old prejudices engendered by patriarchal societies the world over. We now want our sons and daughters to enjoy the same rights, privileges, and degree of respect in society. Perhaps no area of social concern has moved so quickly in the past decade as our understanding of sexual preference and orientation, which, despite what some may think, does impact even very young children. And, finally, society is becoming more sensitive to the needs of those living with emotional, intellectual, and physical challenges. The goal of celebrating diversity is really inclusion, and this is where intelligent and sensitive children's books can help, for they portray a rich and diverse world, extending the imagination of young readers to embrace life in its wondrous variety. The popular American poet Edwin Markham articulated the goal of diversity in his poem "Outwitted":

> He drew a circle that shut me out—
> Heretic, rebel, a thing to flout.
> But Love and I had the wit to win:
> We drew a circle that took him in.

For Reflection and Discussion

1. Locate three or four picture books that all focus on one social or personal issue (such as three or four books on African American or American Indian cultures or on alternative family lifestyles or on emotional or physical challenges, and so on). Determine the intended audience and note the publication date for each book. Now read the books carefully, and evaluate them on their content and approach. Is the subject represented accurately and sensitively? What differences do you see in the treatment of the subject? Does one book stand out from the rest? Why?

2. Locate and read a book intended for young readers that deals with a specific cultural group. Pay close attention to how the culture is portrayed. What is the author's attitude? Is the author objective? Do some research to determine whether the author presents the culture accurately.

3. Locate and read a book intended for young readers that deals with a special social issue with which you have some personal experience (gender, alternative family lifestyle, physical or emotional challenges, and so on). How do you feel the book deals with the issue? Is it fair, accurate, honest, and complete? Is it interestingly written?

4. Locate and read a book intended for young readers that deals with an ethnic or religious culture that you would like to learn more about. What did you learn about the culture? Does it seem to be represented accurately and sensitively? Do you see any evidence of stereotyping? When was the book published? How does that make a difference in your evaluation of the book?

Works Cited

Gates, Henry Louis, Jr. "'Authenticity,' or The Lesson of Little Tree." *The New York Times* 24 (November 1991): 1, 26–30.

Guy, Rosa. "Innocence, Betrayal, and History." *School Library Journal* (November 1985): 33–34.

Harris, Violet, ed. *Teaching Multicultural Literature in Grades K–8.* Norwood, MA: Christopher-Gordon, 1993.

Wilson, Edward O. *On Human Nature.* Cambridge, MA: Harvard University Press, 1978.

Recommended Resources

Belensky, Mary Field, and others. *Women's Ways of Knowing.* New York: Harper, 1986.

Benes, Rebecca C. *American Indian Picture Books of Change: The Art of Historic Children's Editions.* Santa Fe: Museum of New Mexico Press, 2004.

Botello, Maria José, and Masha Kabakow Rudman. *Critical Multicultural Analysis of Children's Literature: Mirrors, Windows, and Doors.* New York: Routledge, 2009.

Day, Frances A. *Lesbian and Gay Voices: An Annotated Bibliography and Guide to Literature for Children and Young Adults.* Westport, CT: Greenwood, 2000.

Derman-Sparks, Louise. "Revisiting Multicultural Education: What Children Need to Live in a Diverse Society." *Dimensions of Early Childhood* 22(1993): 6–10.

Dowd, F. S. "Evaluating Children's Books Portraying American Indian and Asian Cultures." *Childhood Education* 68, 4 (1992): 219–224.

Fox, Dana L., and Kathy G. Short, eds. *Stories Matter: The Complexity of Cultural Authenticity in Children's Literature.* Urbana, IL: NCTE, 2003.

Gebel, Doris. *Crossing Boundaries with Children's Books.* Lanham, MD: Scarecrow, 2006.

Giorgis, Cyndi, and Janelle Mathis. "Visions and Voices of American Indians in Children's Literature." *The New Advocate* 8, 2 (Spring 1995): 125–142.

Gopalakrishnan, Ambika G. *Multicultural Children's Literature: A Critical Issues Approach.* Washington, DC: SAGE Publications, 2010.

Harada, V. H. "Issues of Ethnicity, Authenticity, and Quality in Asian-American Picture Books, 1983–93." *Journal of Youth Services in Libraries* 8, 2 (1995): 135–149.

Harris, Violet J. "Continuing Dilemmas, Debates, and Delights in Multicultural Literature." *The New Advocate* 9, 2 (Spring 1996): 107–122.

Lindgren, Merri V. *The Multicultural Mirror: Cultural Substance in Literature for Children and Young Adults.* Fort Atkinson, WI: Highsmith Press, 1991.

Lo, Suzanne, and Ginny Lee. "Asian Images in Children's Books: What Stories Do We Tell Our Children?" *Emergency Librarian* 20, 5 (May–June 1993): 14–18.

Manna, Anthony L., and Carolyn S. Brodie, eds. *Many Faces, Many Voices: Multicultural Literary Experiences for Youth.* Fort Atkinson, WI: Highsmith, 1992.

McCann, Donnarae, and Gloria Woodard. *The Black American in Books for Children: Readings in Racism.* Metuchen, NJ: Scarecrow, 1985.

McIntosh, Peggy. "White Privilege: Unpacking the Invisible Knapsack." *Peace and Freedom* (July/August 1989): 10–12.

Norton, Donna E. *Multicultural Children's Literature: Through the Eyes of Many Children*, 3rd ed. Boston: Pearson, 2008.

Pang, V. O., C. Colvin, M. Tran, and R. H. Barba. "Beyond Chopsticks and Dragons: Selecting Asian-American Literature for Children." *The Reading Teacher* 46, 3 (1992): 216–224.

Pratt, Linda, and Janice J. Beaty. *Transcultural Children's Literature.* Upper Saddle River, NJ: Merrill/Prentice Hall, 1999.

Rochman, Hazel. *Against Borders: Promoting Books for a Multicultural World.* Chicago: American Library Association, 1993.

Sims, Rudine. *Shadow & Substance: Afro-American Experience in Contemporary Children's Fiction.* Urbana, IL: NCTE, 1982.

——. "Walk Tall in the World: African-American Literature for Today's Children." *Journal of Negro Education* 58 (1990): 556–565.

Smith, Katherine Capshaw. *Children's Literature of the Harlem Renaissance.* Bloomington, IN: Indiana University Press, 2004.

——. "Introduction: The Landscape of Ethnic American Children's Literature." *MELUS* 27.2 (Summer 2002): 3–8.

Books Dealing With Cultural Diversity: A Selected and Annotated Book List

This list includes only books focusing on culture and ethnicity. For additional books on diversity, see the booklists at the end of Chapter 11.

African American and African Heritage

Brooks, Gwendolyn. *Bronzeville Boys and Girls.* 1967. Illus. Faith Ringgold. New York: Amistad, 2006.
- Poems originally written by Pulitzer Prize winner Brooks in 1956, now newly illustrated.

Coles, Robert. *The Story of Ruby Bridges.* Illus. George Ford. New York: Scholastic, 1995.
- The story of a 6-year-old girl who becomes the first African American in an integrated New Orleans school in 1960.

Curtis, Christopher Paul. *Bud, Not Buddy.* New York: Delacorte, 1999.
- A Depression-era story of a young African American boy hoping to find his father.

——. *Elijah of Buxton.* New York: Scholastic, 2009.
- A narrative of a young Canadian black boy, son of former slaves, who learns about slavery in the United States in the mid-nineteenth century.

Duncan, Alice Faye. *Honey Baby Sugar Child.* Illus. Susan Keeter. New York: Simon & Schuster, 2005.
- A simple warm depiction of the bond between an African American mother and her child.

Feelings, Tom. *Soul Looks Back in Wonder.* New York: Dial, 1993.
- A collection of poems on black themes for all ages.

Fox, Paula. *The Slave Dancer.* New York: Bradbury, 1973.
- A heartbreaking tale of the eighteenth-century African slave trade.

Giovanni, Nikki. *Shimmy Shimmy Shimmy Like My Sister Kate: Looking at the Harlem Renaissance Through Poems.* New York: Holt, 1996.
- Poems for young people by a celebrated African American poet.

Guy, Rosa. *The Friends.* New York: Viking, 1973.
- The story of a difficult friendship between two girls of color—one from the West Indies and one from New York.

Hamilton, Virginia. *M. C. Higgins, the Great.* New York: Macmillan, 1974.
- A black teenager in the Appalachian Mountains must choose between tradition and change.

Herron, Carolivia. *Nappy Hair.* Illus. Joe Cepeda. New York: Knopf, 1997.
- A lively picture book celebrating a young black girl's wondrous hair.

King, Martin Luther, Jr. *I Have a Dream.* Illus. various artists. New York: Scholastic, 2007.
- One of the most inspiring speeches of the twentieth century, beautifully illustrated by award-winning artists.

Lester, Julius. *To Be a Slave.* Illus. Tom Feelings. New York: Dial, 1998.
- A celebrated nonfiction work, first published in 1968, that describes the life of a slave in the words of slaves themselves.

Levine, Ellen. *Henry's Freedom Box: A True Story from the Underground Railroad.* Illus. Kadir Nelson. New York: Scholastic, 2007.
- A slave in the early nineteenth century mails himself to freedom. A brief story, beautifully illustrated.

Long, Mark, and Jim Demonakos. *The Silence of Our Friends.* Illus. Nate Powell. New York: First Second, 2012.
- A graphic novel for teenage readers about a racial incident at a Texas university in 1968.

Mathis, Sharon Bell. *Teacup Full of Roses.* New York: Viking, 1972.
- The story of a troubled African American family with a child on drugs.

McKissack, Patricia. *Goin' Someplace Special.* Illus. Jerry Pinckney. New York: Atheneum, 2001.
- A touching picture book set in the segregated South in the 1950s.

Nelson, Kadir. *We Are the Ship: The Story of Negro League Baseball.* New York: Hyperion, 2008.
- A well-told and beautifully illustrated history of the Negro baseball leagues in the early twentieth century.

Raven, Margot Theis. *Circle Unbroken.* Illus. E. B. Lewis. New York: Farrar, Straus & Giroux, 2004.
- African American history told through a woman teaching her granddaughter the ancient art of basket weaving.

Rhodes, Jewell Parker. *Ninth Ward.* New York: Little Brown, 2010.
- A story of the tragedy of Hurricane Katrina in New Orleans and an African American girl's will to survive.

Rhuday-Perkovich, Olugbemisola. *Eighth-Grade Superzero.* New York: Arthur A. Levine, 2010.
- The trials and tribulations of a boy adjusting to a Brooklyn middle school.

Ringgold, Faith. *Tar Beach.* New York: Crown, 1991.
- A picture book with a Depression-era setting in Harlem. A magical tale with a comment on social injustice.

Robinson, Sharon. *Safe at Home.* New York: Scholastic, 2006.
- A story in which baseball helps to fill the void left when a young boy's father dies. Well-drawn characters by the daughter of baseball legend Jackie Robinson.

Scattergood, Augusta. *Glory Be.* New York: Scholastic, 2012.
- A story seen through the eyes of a 12-year-old girl, when the Civil Rights movement reaches a small Mississippi town in 1964.

Steptoe, John. *Mufaro's Beautiful Daughters.* New York: Lothrop, 1974.
- A beautifully illustrated picture-book version of a traditional Zimbabwean folktale.

Taylor, Mildred. *Roll of Thunder, Hear My Cry.* New York: Dial, 1976.
- A story of an African American family in the Deep South of the 1930s, facing brutal racial prejudice; the second of a five-book series, along with *The Land, Song of the Trees, Let the Circle Be Unbroken,* and *The Road to Memphis.*

Wiles, Deborah. *Freedom Summer.* Illus. Jerome Laguerrique. New York: Aladdin, 2005.
- A young white boy and black boy experience the beginnings of integration in 1964.

Woodson, Jacqueline. *If You Come Softly.* New York: Putnam, 1998.
- A moving teenage love story about an African American boy and a Jewish girl.

Williams-Garcia, Rita. *One Crazy Summer.* New York: Amistad, 2011.
- A powerful story of three black sisters who find themselves involved in the social upheaval of 1968.

American Indian and Native Heritage

Andrews, Jan. *Very Last First Time.* Illus. Ian Wallace. Vancouver, BC: Douglas & McIntyre, 2002.
- A picture book about an Inuit girl finding mussels on the ocean floor, under ice.

Broker, Ignatia. *Night Flying Woman: An Ojibwa Narrative.* St. Paul: Minnesota Historical Society Press, 1983.
- An account of the lives of several generations of Ojibwa people in Minnesota.

Bruchac, Joseph. *Squanto's Journey: The Story of the First Thanksgiving.* Illus. Greg Shed. New York: Harcourt, 2000.
- A familiar tale told from the American Indian perspective.

——. *Wabi*. New York: Dial, 2006.
- A shape-shifter tale woven into a novel of self-discovery and young love. Just one of many great books by the famed Abenaki writer.

Dorris, Michael. *Morning Girl*. Logan, IA: Perfection Learning, 1999.
- A historical novel set in The Bahamas in 1492, when a young girl sees Columbus arrive.

Erdrich, Louise. *The Game of Silence*. New York: HarperCollins, 2005.
- Sequel to *Birchbark House* (1999), a story about nineteenth-century Ojibwe people whose way of life is threatened by European settlers.

Highwater, Jamake. *Anpao: An American Indian Odyssey*. New York: Harper, 1977.
- A mystical tale of a young American Indian's journey across many time periods.

Lacapa, Michael. *The Flute Player*. Menomonie, WI: Northland, 1990.
- An Apache *pourquoi* tale about lost love. A picture book for early elementary children.

Manitonquat (Medicine Story), reteller. *The Children of the Morning Light: Wampanoag Tales*. New York: Macmillan, 1994.
- A collection of tales from the American Indians of New England.

McDermott, Gerald. *Arrow to the Sun: A Pueblo Indian Tale*. New York: Viking, 1974.
- A strikingly illustrated retelling of a cultural origins tale.

——. *Raven: A Trickster Tale from the Pacific Northwest*. New York: Harcourt, 1993.
- A beautifully illustrated tale about Raven's bringing light to the world.

Mikaelsen, Ben. *Touching Spirit Bear*. New York: HarperCollins, 2002.
- The wrenching story of a juvenile delinquent who is transformed by a traditional Native American custom, banishment to an isolated Alaskan island for one year.

Nelson, S. D. *Buffalo Bird Girl: A Hidatsa Story*. New York: Abrams, 2012.
- The true story of a Hidatsa Indian girl in the Dakotas in the nineteenth century.

O'Dell, Scott. *Sing Down the Moon*. Boston: Houghton Mifflin, 1970.
- The story of the cruel relocation of the Navajo in the nineteenth century.

Pearsall, Shelley. *Crooked River*. New York: Knopf, 2005.
- Set in 1812, the story of a young girl who befriends an Ojibwe Indian enslaved by her father. A moving tale of injustice and inhumanity.

Savageau, Cheryl. *Muskrat Will Be Swimming*. Illus. Robert Hynes. Menomonie, WI: Northland, 1996.
- A story of a young girl coming to appreciate her native heritage through the help of her grandfather and the art of storytelling. For early elementary children.

Sherman, Alexie. *The Absolutely True Diary of a Part-Time Indian*. New York: Little Brown, 2007.
- A story of a modern teenager from the Spokane Indian Reservation attending an all-white school. Wonderfully told and based on the author's life.

Speare, Elizabeth George. *The Sign of the Beaver*. Boston: Houghton Mifflin, 1983.
- A survival story of two eighteenth-century boys, one white and one Indian, who become reluctant friends.

Sneve, Virginia Driving Hawk. *The Christmas Coat: Memories of My Sioux Childhood*. Illus. Ellen Beier. New York: Holiday House, 2011.
- A charming tale from the author's own childhood in South Dakota.

Sneve, Virginia Driving Hawk, selector. *Dancing Teepees: Poems of American Indian Youth*. Illus. Stephen Gammell. New York: Holiday House, 1989.
- Poems from both the oral tradition and contemporary Indian poets.

Tingle, Tom. *Crossing Bok Chitto: A Choctaw Tale of Friendship and Freedom*. Illus. Jeanne Rorex Bridges. El Paso, TX: Cinco Puntos Press, 2006.
- A picture book that portrays a cross-cultural friendship in Mississippi in the 1800s.

Vaughan, Richard Lee. *Eagle Boy: A Pacific Northwest Native Tale.* Illus. Lee Christiansen. Seattle, WA: Sasquitch Books, 2000.

- A story of a young boy befriending an eagle and saving his people. A retelling of a tale told among several native peoples of the Pacific Northwest.

Wyss, Thelma Hatch. *Bear Dancer: The Story of a Ute Girl.* New York: Margaret K. McElderry, 2005.

- A tale of cultural clashes in which a nineteenth-century Ute girl encounters white people for the first time.

Yellow Robe, Rosebud. *Tonweya and the Eagles and Other Lakota Stories.* Illus. Jerry Pinkney. New York: Dial, 1979.

- A collection of animal tales from the Plains Indians.

Latinos/as and Latino Heritage

Alvarez, Julia. *Return to Sender.* New York: Knopf, 2009.

- A story about the struggle of illegal migrant workers in Vermont.

Anaya, Rudolfo. *Maya's Children: The Story of La Llorona.* Illus. Maria Baca. New York: Hyperion, 1997.

- Based on the tragic Hispanic folktale "Crying Woman," a strikingly illustrated version modified for younger readers.

Canales, Viola. *Tequila Worm.* New York: Paw Prints, 2008.

- A story in which a teenage Latina must fit in at an elite Texas boarding school.

Cisneros, Sandra. *Hairs/Pelitos.* Illus. Terry Ybánez. New York: Knopf, 1994.

- A bilingual picture book celebrating diversity.

——. *The House on Mango Street.* Houston: Arte Público, 1984.

- A coming-of-age story of a girl growing up in a Hispanic neighborhood in Chicago.

De Treviño, Elizabeth Borton. *I, Juan De Pareja.* New York: Bell Books, 1965.

- Set in seventeenth-century Spain, the story of a slave of the painter Velasquez who teaches himself painting.

Dorros, Arthur. *Abuela.* New York: Dutton, 1991.

- A picture-book story of a young girl's magical bond with her grandmother, her *abuela*.

Galarza, Ernesto. *Barrio Boy.* Notre Dame, IN: University of Notre Dame Press, 1971.

- An early-twentieth-century story of a boy from rural Mexico adjusting to city life in the United States.

Garza, Carmen Lomas. *Family Picture/Cuadros de Familia.* San Francisco: Children's Book Press, 1990.

- A celebration of the author's girlhood. A bilingual text with outstanding illustrations.

Griego, M. C., Betsy L. Bucks, Sharon S. Gilbert, and Laura H. Kimball. *Tortillitas para Mama and Other Nursery Rhymes, Spanish and English.* Illus. Barbara Cooney. New York: Square Fish, 1987.

- Latin American nursery rhymes in a bilingual edition with lovely illustrations.

Herrera, Juan Felipe. *Calling the Doves/El Canto de las Palomas.* Illus. Elly Simmons. 1990. San Francisco: Children's Book Press, 2001.

- A biographical account of a boy growing up as a migrant farm worker. Bilingual text beautifully illustrated.

Lopez, Diana. *Confetti Girl.* New York: Little Brown, 2009,

- The story of a Latina girl in a bilingual Texas community dealing with the tribulations of middle school, complete with sorrow, anger, and joy.

Marcantonio, Patricia Santos. *Red Ridin' in the Hood and Other Cuentas.* Illus. Renato Alarcão. New York: Farrar, Straus & Giroux, 2005.

- Retellings of familiar tales with a Latino twist. Great fun.

Martinez, Victor. *Parrot in the Oven: Mi Vida*. New York: HarperCollins, 1996.
  - The story of a Hispanic boy from a dysfunctional family coming of age in a small California town.

Mora, Pat. *Confetti: Poems for Children*. Illus. Enrique O. Sanchez. New York: Lee and Low, 1996.
  - Narrative poems about the culture of the American Southwest. Colorfully illustrated.

——. *Tomás and the Library Lady*. Illus. Raul Colón. New York: Knopf, 1997.
  - Based on the true story of the son of itinerant farm workers who learns to love reading.

Rice, David. *Crazy Loco*. New York: Dial, 2001.
  - A collection of short stories about life in a small south Texas town.

Ryan, Pam Muñoz. *The Dreamer*. New York: Scholastic, 2010.
  - A fictionalized portrait of the childhood of the great poet Pablo Neruda.

——. *Esperanza Rising*. St. Louis, MO: Turtleback, 2002.
  - The story of a 13-year-old girl from Mexico adjusting to a new way of life during the Depression of the 1930s.

Soto, Gary. *Chato's Kitchen*.
  - The story of Chato the cat, who lives in the barrio and invites the mice to dinner (as guests or meal?).

——. *A Fire in My Hands*. New York: Harcourt, 2006.
  - Poems for teenage readers inspired by the poet's own youth.

——. *Snapshots from the Wedding*. Illus. Stephanie Garcia. New York: Putnam, 1997.
  - A Mexican American wedding described with free verse and imaginative illustrations.

Tafolla, Carmen. *What Can You Do with a Paleta?* Illus. Magaly Morales. New York: Tricycle, 2009.
  - A playful picture book illustrating life in the barrio while celebrating the Mexican popsicle.

Torres, Leyla. *Subway Sparrow/Gorrión del Metro*. New York: Farrar, Straus & Giroux, 1993.
  - A story of four people who speak different languages coming together to help a trapped bird.

Asian American and Asian Heritage

Crew, Linda. *Children of the River*. New York: Bantam, 1989.
  - The story of a Cambodian refugee coping with haunting memories as she adjusts to life in America.

Fritz, Jean. *Homesick: My Own Story*. New York: Putnam, 1982.
  - The story of a famed American author recalling her childhood in China.

Houston, Jeanne Wakatsuki, and James D. Houston. *Farewell to Manzanar*. New York: Bantam, 1973.
  - Based on the true story of the Japanese American relocation during World War II.

Kadohata, Cynthia. *Weedflower*. New York: Atheneum, 2006.
  - The story of a Japanese American girl befriending a Mohave boy during World War II.

Lin, Grace. *Where the Mountain Meets the Moon*. New York: Little Brown, 2011.
  - A Newbery-Honor book about a girl's adventure to save her family. This enchanting tale is set in China and draws on Chinese folktales.

——. *Dim Sum for Everyone*. New York: Dragonfly, 2003.
  - A story about traditional Chinese food.

——. *The Year of the Dog*. New York: Little Brown, 2006.
  - A humorous coming-of-age story about the daughter of Taiwanese immigrants living in upstate New York. Followed by the sequels, *The Year of the Rat* and *Dumpling Days*.

Lord, Bette Bao. *In the Year of the Boar and Jackie Robinson*. New York: Harper, 1984.

- A very funny and ultimately uplifting story of a Chinese girl moving to America in 1947 and adapting to a new culture.

Louie, Ai-Ling. *Yeh-Shen: A Cinderella Story from China.* Illus. Ed Young. New York: Philomel, 1982.
  - A beautifully illustrated folktale.

Mahy, Margaret. *The Seven Chinese Brothers.* Illus. Jean and Mou-Sein Tseng. New York: Scholastic, 1990.
  - A retelling of an old Chinese folktale about brothers with extraordinary gifts.

Na, An. *A Step from Heaven.* Asheville, NC: Front Street, 2001.
  - The story of a Korean girl's acculturation after her move to America.

Say, Allen. *Grandfather's Journey.* Boston: Houghton Mifflin, 1994.
  - A picture-book portrait of the author's grandfather's immigration to America.

Uchida, Yoshiko. *A Jar of Dreams.* New York: Atheneum, 1991.
  - The story of a Japanese girl growing up in America during the Depression who learns the importance of her heritage.

Vaughan, Marcia K. *The Dancing Dragon.* Illus. Stanley Woo Hoo Foon. New York: Mondo, 1996.
  - The Chinese New Year, described in rhymed couplets and colorfully illustrated.

Wang, Rosalind C. *The Fourth Question.* Illus. Ju-Hong Chen. New York: Holiday House, 1991.
  - A retelling of a Chinese folktale in which a simple man seeks wisdom.

Wong, Janet S. *Good Luck Gold and Other Poems.* New York: Margaret K. McElderry, 1994.
  - A collection of poems about a young Chinese American girl's experiences.

Yacowitz, Caryn. *The Jade Stone.* Illus. Ju-Hong Chen. New York: Holiday House, 1992.
  - A retelling of a traditional Chinese tale about an artist and his devotion to art.

Yagawa, Sumiko. *The Crane Wife.* Tr. Katherine Paterson. Illus. Suekichi Akaba. New York: Mulberry, 1987.
  - A retelling of a traditional Japanese folktale of animal transformation.

Yep, Laurence. *Angelfish.* New York: Putnam, 2001.
  - The story of a young Chinese American ballet student uncovering the secret of an unpleasant man.

——. *Dragon Prince: A Chinese Beauty and the Beast Tale.* Illus. Kam Mak. New York: HarperCollins, 1997.
  - Lovely illustrations accompany the retelling of a traditional tale.

Yin Lau, Rosanna. *Coolies.* Illus. Chris Soentpiet. New York: Penguin, 2001.
  - A story of the Chinese railroad workers of the 1860s.

Young, Ed. *Lon Po Po: A Red-Riding Hood Story from China.* New York: Philomel, 1990.
  - A Chinese folktale beautifully illustrated by an award-winning artist.

Other Cultures

Boyne, John. *The Boy in the Striped Pajamas.* New York: David Fickling, 2006.
  - A narrative of the Holocaust, as viewed through the eyes of a 9-year-old boy.

Cohen, Barbara. *Molly's Pilgrim.* Illus. M. J. Deraney. New York: Lothrop, Lee, and Shepard, 1983.
  - The story of a young Russian Jewish immigrant showing her American classmates a new meaning of Thanksgiving.

Cunnane, Kelly. *For You Are a Kenyan Child.* Illus. Ana Juan. New York: Atheneum, 2006.
  - A picture book describing a day in the life of a Kenyan boy.

Demi. *Buddha.* New York: Henry Holt, 1996.
  - A beautifully illustrated picture book about the life and legends of the Buddha.

——. *Muhammad.* New York: Margaret K. McElderry, 2003.

- A picture-book narrative of the prophet's life, with an explanation of Islam.

Fama, Elizabeth. *Overboard*. Peru, IL: Cricket, 2002.
- The story of a shipwreck that leaves an American girl and an Indonesian boy struggling to survive in the ocean.

Frank, Anne. *The Diary of a Young Girl: The Definitive Edition*. New York: Doubleday, 1995.
- The famed diary of a young Jewish girl in hiding from the Nazis in World War II.

Innocenti, Roberto, and Christophe Gallaz. *Rose Blanche*. New York: Creative Education, 1985.
- A picture book about a young German girl aiding Jews in a concentration camp.

Katz, Karen. *My First Ramadan*. New York: Henry Holt, 2007.
- A picture book about a young boy observing the Muslim holy month with his family.

Kerr, Judith. *When Hitler Stole Pink Rabbit*. New York: Coward McCann & Geoghegan, 1971.
- The adventures of a Jewish girl forced to flee Hitler's Germany.

Kherdian, David. *The Road from Home: The Story of an Armenian Girlhood*. New York: Greenwillow, 1979.
- A powerful memoir of the Armenian holocaust.

Lasky, Kathryn. *The Night Journey*. New York: Warne, 1981.
- The story of a Jewish girl learning about her grandmother's experiences in Czarist Russia.

McCormick, Patricia. *Sold*. New York: Hyperion, 2006.
- The harrowing tale of a 13-year-old Nepalese girl whose father sells her into prostitution in India.

Naidoo, Beverley. *The Other Side of Truth*. New York: HarperCollins, 2001.
- The story of a young Nigerian girl caught up in the violence plaguing her country.

Novesky, Amy. *Elephant Prince: The Story of Ganesh*. Illus. Belgin K. Wedman. San Rafael, CA: Mandala, 2004.
- A picture book about one of Hinduism's most endearing gods.

Patel, Sanjay, and Emily Haynes. *Ganesha's Sweet Tooth*. Illus. Sanjay Patel. San Francisco: Chronicle, 2012.
- The story of how the beloved elephant god of Hinduism came to write one of India's most important epics.

Polacco, Patricia. *The Keeping Quilt*. New York: Simon & Schuster, 1988.
- A picture book about an immigrant Jewish family attempting to keep Russian traditions.

Potok, Chaim. *My Name Is Asher Lev*. New York: Knopf, 1972.
- The story of a Hasidic Jew struggling with his commitment to his faith and to his art.

Staples, Suzanne Fisher. *Shabanu: Daughter of the Wind*. New York: Knopf, 1989.
- The story of a modern Pakistani girl struggling with the conflict between tradition and modernity.

Stolz, Joelle. *The Shadows of the Ghadames*. New York: Delacorte, 2004.
- The story of a Muslim girl in nineteenth-century Libya being introduced to a changing world.

Wolk, Bernard. *Coming to America: A Muslim Family's Story*. New York: Lee & Low, 2003.
- A photo essay describing a Muslim family's immigration to America and the subsequent adjustment.

Yolen, Jane. *The Devil's Arithmetic*. New York: Perfection, 1990.
- The story of a girl being transported back through time to Poland in the 1940s, where she witnesses the horrors of the Holocaust.

Beginning Books

Knowledge through Delight

Introduction

From the lullabies of the nursery to the alphabet song set to Mozart's familiar melody to tuneful counting rhymes, there is no shortage of memorable songs, poems, and literary entertainments to share with the very youngest children. And how early should we begin introducing children to the miracle of language? Some parents begin reading to their unborn child still in the womb. It's not a bad idea, even if it is only good practice for the parents. Few things in life are more rewarding than sharing a good picture book with a young child who, curled up in your lap, can't wait to see what happens on the next page.

In this chapter we will examine Mother Goose books; alphabet, counting, and concept books; and tactile and movable books designed for the very youngest audiences—with an eye toward finding the very best. After all, childhood is too short to waste on mediocre books.

Mother Goose Rhymes

Definition and Origin

No one knows who Mother Goose was, or even where the name came from. In the seventeenth century, a Frenchman, Charles Perrault, named his collection of folktales *Tales from Mother Goose*, but it contains no nursery rhymes. Some speculate that the name may have been popularly given to the woman who, in earlier times, kept the village geese and who was the traditional community storyteller. Whatever her origins, by the end of the eighteenth century, books of nursery rhymes were being published in New England with the name Mother Goose on them, and since then, she has been inextricably tied to the poetry of the nursery.

These familiar rhymes are not only a child's first introduction to literature but are an indelible part of our cultural heritage. Who doesn't know about Humpty Dumpty's

FIGURE 5.1 ■ This primitive wood engraving from one of the earliest American editions of Mother Goose depicts the Sprats licking the platter clean. The illustration lacks a comic touch (see Figure 5.2), and the result is nearly grotesque.

catastrophe, Little Bo Peep's loss, Little Boy Blue's laziness, and Old Mother Hubbard's poverty? They find their way into a multitude of references in our daily lives. The lilting rhythms, the comical rhymes, the unusual sounds of these verses ("Mistress Mary, quite contrary," "Hey! diddle, diddle, the cat and the fiddle," "Hickory, dickory, dock," and so on) endear them to young children. These are often the first words they memorize. And these rhymes are often a child's first introduction to memorable fictional characters. In addition to those mentioned above, there are Jack Sprat (see Figures 5.1 and 5.2), Little Miss Muffet (see Figures 5.3 and 5.4), Little Jack Horner, Old King Cole, the Queen of Hearts, Georgie Porgie, Wee Willie Winkie, Simple Simon, Peter the Pumpkin Eater, and the Old Woman who lived in a shoe (to name but a few).

Nursery rhymes were always meant for fun and were frequently subversive. Curiously, many of them were not originally meant for children. Instead, they were derived from war songs, romantic lyrics, proverbs, riddles, political jingles, lampoons, and the cries of street vendors (an early version of the television commercial). Most of the best-known rhymes can be traced back to the sixteenth, seventeenth, and eighteenth centuries. "Three Blind Mice" was set to music as early as 1609, "Jack Sprat" may have ridiculed a certain Archdeacon Spratt in the mid-seventeenth century, and "Little Jack Horner" may have referred to a Thomas Horner of Mells, whose "plum" was the land he acquired from the monasteries dissolved by Henry VIII in 1536. The heroes of nursery rhymes typically come from the lower walks of life: Simple Simon, Tom the Piper's Son, Mother Hubbard, the Old Woman in the Shoe, and so on. Nursery rhymes that mention kings and queens ("Sing a Song of Six Pence" and "Old King Cole," for example) are often comical and irreverent. Scarcely hidden beneath the surface of these rhymes and jingles are the jibe and the barb.

FIGURE 5.2 ■ L. Leslie Brooke depicts a decidedly older couple and from an earlier time—the costumes are Renaissance. As always with Brooke, a close examination of his illustration reveals his wry humor: Notice the bovine fattened for market prominently displayed on the Sprats' coat of arms. Like many other Victorian children's artists, Brooke imbued his representational drawings with rich, subtle details.

J ACK SPRAT could eat no fat,
  His wife could eat no lean:

And so, betwixt them both, you see,
  They lick'd the platter clean.

Mother Goose and Child Development

In addition to their sheer joy, nursery rhymes can help infants and toddlers in some unexpected ways. They can assist in cognitive development, such as counting—"One potato, two potato, three potato, four" and "One, two, three, four, five/Once I caught a fish alive." Nursery rhymes broaden vocabularies. The crooked man who found a "crooked

FIGURE 5.3 ■ Kate Greenaway could not bring herself to include unsavory elements in her illustrations; consequently, she detracts from the drama by focusing all attention on the prim and proper Miss Muffet. The spider is barely noticeable off to the left.

Little Miss Muffet,
Sat on a tuffet,
Eating some curds and whey ;
There came a great spider,
And sat down beside her,
And frightened Miss Muffet away.

K.G

sixpence against a crooked stile," "Jack be nimble," and "Pease porridge hot" all include words not normally used by children. This is a great way to expand a child's language skills. And what about this famous riddle:

> As I was going to St. Ives
> I met a man with seven wives;
> Every wife had seven sacks,
> Every sack had seven cats,
> Every cat had seven kits,
> Kits, cats, sacks, and wives,
> How many were going to St. Ives?

(One, of course, just the speaker.) And here is a riddle that has stumped many a child:

> Elizabeth, Elspeth, Betsy, and Bess,
> They all went to together to seek a bird's nest,

FIGURE 5.4 ■ Arthur Rackham, in contrast to Greenaway, portrays a truly monstrous-looking, but not ungentlemanly, spider. The spider's appearance completely overwhelms the picture, and there is a wonderful contrast between the sedate Miss Muffet (somewhat more mature than Greenaway's), her lip daintily pursed, and the grotesque creature about to interrupt her. Rackham's surrealistic, frequently nightmarish quality is tempered here by a bit of wry humor as the spider gallantly doffs his hat.

> They found a bird's nest with five eggs in,
> They all took one and left four in.

And how could four eggs remain? Because Elspeth, Betsy, and Bess are nicknames for Elizabeth—there is only one girl. (It may be a little unfair, but aren't all riddles?)

Mother Goose rhymes can also help with a child's aesthetic development, or the appreciation for beauty, for much of the language is quite lovely (even if it does not make any sense). Nursery rhymes, with their lively meter, appeal to a child's natural sense of rhythm, perhaps hearkening back to the womb and the rhythmic beat of the mother's heart. The repeated refrains and insistent rhymes provide children with the pleasures of balance and structure in language. The playful sounds of nonsense words ("Hickory dickory dock," "Diddle, diddle dumpling, my son John," "Higgledy, piggledy, my black hen," "Eeny, meeny, miny, mo") appeal to the sheer joy in the sounds of words.

Many nursery rhymes are interactive and can contribute to a child's physical development. "Pat-a-Cake, Pat-a-Cake" calls for physical coordination and interpersonal contact; "Ring around the Rosey" and "London Bridge Is Falling Down" call for the exercise of large-motor skills as well as social interaction. Jump-rope rhymes are simply nursery rhymes gone to the playground, and they appear to be an almost worldwide childhood pastime (see Butler, *Skipping Around the World*). By extension, we could also argue that some of these jingles help children release aggression and hostility in acceptable ways. Take, for example, this popular jump-rope jingle:

> Fudge, fudge, tell the judge
> Mother has a newborn baby;
> It isn't a girl and it isn't a boy;
> It's just a fair young lady.
> Wrap it up in tissue paper
> And send it up the elevator:
> First floor, miss;
> Second floor, miss;
> Third floor, miss;
> Fourth floor,
> Kick it out the elevator door.

This brings us to one of the controversies surrounding many nursery rhymes—their often violent content. We find babies dropping from treetops, cradle and all; a farmer's wife chopping off the tails (or heads) of three blind mice; a beleaguered old woman living in a shoe with unruly children whom she whips soundly; a ladybug whose children (save for one) are apparently lost in a fire; a man who keeps his wife in a pumpkin shell; and more. Indeed, one assiduous critic, Geoffrey Handley-Taylor, discovered, in a collection of some 200 familiar nursery rhymes, at least 100 rhymes with "unsavory elements," including 8 allusions to murder, 2 cases of choking to death, 1 case of decapitation, 7 cases of severing of limbs, and the list goes on (Baring-Gould and Baring-Gould 20). Sylvia Long has produced a beautifully illustrated modern collection of nursery rhymes, titled *Sylvia Long's Mother Goose*, eliminating some of the more indelicate aspects of the verses. The baby who rocks in the treetop is a little bird who flies to safety when the bough breaks; the old woman who lives in shoe is a spider who doesn't spank her children but kisses them before putting them to bed. Such adaptations may be more for the adults than the children. The rhymes are certainly much less exciting and probably less memorable. Young readers are wise enough to realize that what occurs in a nonsense rhyme is not what ought to occur in real life. And it is safe to say that no child ever turned violent from reading nursery rhymes. Reading provides vicarious pleasure; this is no different for children than for adults. Even very young children know when something is "just a story" or "only make-believe."

Choosing Mother Goose Books

A good Mother Goose book should be a staple in every child's home. But there are so many to choose from, it is often difficult to tell which ones are the good ones. Below are some points to consider when choosing from the many collections available:

- Is the book attractive and well made? These books get a lot of use. A flimsy paperback may be, ultimately, a waste of money.
- Are there enough rhymes to justify the cost of the book? Usually, the larger collections are the best buy—and this is not a book to be read through in a single sitting.
- Is there a balance between the familiar rhymes and those that are less often anthologized? You want the old standbys, but it's good to have some fresh verses as well. In other words, try to get the most for your money.
- Are the illustrations examples of good art, both imaginative and well executed? (For more about this, see Chapter 6.) It is great if each rhyme has its own illustration; although if the collection is very large, some illustrations are often sacrificed.
- Are the pages uncluttered in appearance and are the rhymes juxtaposed with the proper pictures? The format should be clear enough for children to follow.
- Is there an index so that specific rhymes can be easily located? This is not essential, but an index is very helpful if you are trying to fill special requests.
- In newer collections, you might want to look for rhymes from other cultures—African, Asian, Native American, and so on. Of course, don't pass up such classic collections as Blanche Fisher Wright's *The Real Mother Goose* (see Figure 5.5) or Marguerite de Angeli's *Book of Nursery and Mother Goose Rhymes* or Raymond Briggs's *The Mother Goose Treasury* simply because they are not sufficiently multicultural. That would be a great loss.

Mother Goose rhymes hold tremendous possibilities for young children—and the children quickly figure that out. These rhymes need no defense; they are pure fun. Their delightful nonsense and eccentric characters remain with us long beyond childhood.

Alphabet and Counting Books

Also among the first books we share with small children are those introducing the letters of the alphabet and numbers. Books about letters and numbers provide authors and illustrators limitless creative possibilities, which is probably why there are so many of these books. Some

FIGURE 5.5 ■ Blanche Fisher Wright depicts an eighteenth-century husband and his solicitous mate. Typical of her illustrations for the popular collection *The Real Mother Goose*, the lines are clean and sharp, and her characters are well defined.

of the best selections go beyond simply supplying a picture next to a letter or number. Rather, they function as works of art unified by a subject (such as animals in Bert Kitchen's *Animal Alphabet*) or a specific design pattern (as in Suse MacDonald's *Alphabatics*, in which the letters transform into objects) or an idea or a theme (such as the alphabet drama in Chris Van Allsburg's *Z Was Zapped*). As with Mother Goose books, alphabet and counting books are far more complicated than we might first imagine—and they can also be very rewarding. We will first consider alphabet books and then briefly look at counting books.

Alphabet Books

Most alphabet books operate on the premise that children learn the sounds of the alphabet through words that begin with those letters. This is, in many ways, a false premise. For example, the letter *A* might be represented by "apple," even though we could just as well use "aardvark," "ape," or "automobile"—all of which have very different *A* sounds. The consonants are usually much easier. The sounds of *B*, *D*, and *F*, for example, are quite consistent, and Dr. Seuss's lively alphabet book, *Dr. Seuss's ABC*, can effectively demonstrate the sound of *F* with a nonsense word, the mythical creature called the "Fiffer Feffer Feff." However, the consonant *C* is another matter. Does it sound like the *C* in "ceiling" or in "cat" or in "church" or in "czar" or in "chute"? It can even be silent, as in "chthonic" (meaning something related to the underworld) or in "ctenoid" (meaning having teeth like structures, like a comb). And what about that troublesome *X*? It is interesting to see how many alphabet books resort to using "xylophone," which really starts with the sound for *Z*. We turn again to Dr. Seuss, who had a better idea, showing us that we can learn the sound of *X* by listening to such words as "ax" and "extra fox."

The point is that, at their best, alphabet books can offer only approximate associations of sounds and letters. Children learn early on that the associative sounds of letters frequently don't help them pronounce or spell words. (I still recall, as a child, mispronouncing the name Stephen as Step-hen whenever I saw it in print.) In the end, we have to accept that the erratic spelling of English requires that we memorize the spellings and sounds of hundreds and hundreds of words.

So, in light of all these difficulties with the quirkiness of the English language, the alphabet book is an imperfect tool. If it is designed to introduce letters and their sounds and shapes to children, its first goal should be clarity and simplicity. The design and the illustrations of an alphabet book require attention to detail. Most alphabet books juxtapose the letters and the pictures that represent them; that is, they are side by side on the same page or facing pages. (There are exceptions to this. In Chris Van Allsburg's *Z Was Zapped*, dramatic full-page illustrations depict some mysterious thing happening to each letter—the name of the action corresponding to the letter itself. So, for example, *B* is "badly bitten," and *K* is "kidnapped." We, as readers, are invited to guess the calamity that befalls each letter, with the answer found by turning the page.) It is helpful if the letters are set in a clear and easily recognizable typeface. Some books include both uppercase and lowercase letters.

The distinctions between uppercase letters are usually easier for very young children to spot, whereas certain lowercase letters (for example, *b*, *d*, *p*, and *q*) have more subtle variations and are more easily confused. But that doesn't mean they shouldn't appear in alphabet books; children have to learn lowercase letters at some point.

Also, if the goal is to teach preschoolers the sounds and shapes of letters, the objects associated with the letters should be concrete items. Remember, we are still talking about children in the preoperational period. However, this doesn't mean the objects need always be familiar. Bert Kitchen's dramatic alphabet book *Animal Alphabet* includes stunning paintings of such creatures as an ibex, a dodo, and a jerboa—unfamiliar animals to most of us, to be sure, but children (and adults) can quickly learn what they are by looking at the pictures. After all, one of the important objectives of any book should be to expand our understanding of the world. How else do we learn new things? On the other hand, Joan Walsh Anglund's *A Is for Always* uses abstract concepts far beyond cognitive skills of its intended readers—very young children. For example, *D* is for "determined," *E* is for "efficient," and *Y* is for "young-in-heart." Try explaining those terms to a 3-year-old.

Finally, we come to those alphabet books that really have no intention of teaching the alphabet—those for advanced readers (sometimes even grownups). Many of these books are really exercises in artistic creativity. Margaret Musgrove's *Ashanti to Zulu: African Traditions* is a rather sophisticated alphabet book for much older children (children in the period of concrete operations). It presents the alphabet through descriptions of traditional African cultures. Chris Van Allsburg's *Z Was Zapped*, mentioned previously, describes a series of alphabetical disasters befalling each letter in turn and is clearly meant for readers who already know the alphabet. Judith Viorst's *The Alphabet from Z to A (With Much Confusion on the Way)* even casts aside the traditional order of the letters. Graeme Base's *Animalia* is a lavishly illustrated book, using, as the title suggests, animals to introduce the letters of the alphabet. The full-color, double-page spreads abound with objects that help to reinforce the letter sounds, and throughout are hidden pictures of the artist as a child. The result is a visual feast that accompanies an imaginative, tongue-twisting text—a treat for adults as well as for children. And, in a classic alphabet book filled with dark humor for much older readers, Edward Gorey's *The Gashlycrumb Tinies* depicts the demise of 26 children in a series of morbid catastrophes (one falls down the stairs, one chokes on a peach, one is trampled in a brawl, one drinks too much gin). So, an alphabet book is not always an educational tool; it may just be an aesthetic treat for readers to enjoy.

Counting Books

Counting books or number books (both names are used) may be even less successful than alphabet books in achieving their goal. The concept of counting is something that children do not fully grasp until they reach Piaget's period of concrete operations, for they need to understand the concepts of conservation (some things remain the same even if their shape changes), reversibility (some things can be undone), and so on. In fact, many counting books are actually for readers who already understand the concept of numbers and are therefore not intended to teach counting at all.

Nevertheless, counting books offer opportunities for young children to practice their numbers and to count (and they offer opportunities for artists to showcase their talents). Alison Jay's *1, 2, 3: A Child's First Counting Book* is an example, with imaginative and colorful illustrations drawn from familiar folktales. Anthony Browne's *One Gorilla: A Counting Book* asks the reader to count various species of primates drawn in Browne's inimitable style. Tom and Muriel Feelings's very beautiful counting book, *Moja Means One: A Swahili Counting Book*, introduces cultural information along with counting concepts; it is clearly intended for readers who can count. Other variations include Molly Bang's award-winning *Ten, Nine, Eight*, which asks the reader to count backward. And Pat Hutchins's *The Doorbell Rang* includes the concepts of division and addition. Familiar counting rhymes, such as "Over in the Meadow," have inspired books by such noted illustrators as Feodor Rojankovsky and Ezra Jack Keats. The beautiful counting rhyme by S. T. Garne, *One White Sail*, takes the reader to the magic of the Caribbean with such evocative lines as "Five blue doors/in the baking hot sun/Six wooden windows/let the cool wind run."

Today, counting books have joined the ranks of the many very handsome picture books being produced for young children, and we no longer have to settle for the ordinary and the humdrum.

Perceptual Concept Books

In addition to alphabet and counting books, we can find many other types of concept books for toddlers and preschoolers, introducing ideas such as colors(Leo Lionni's *A Color of His Own*) or shapes (Suse MacDonald's *Shape by Shape*) or opposites (Laura Vacaro Seeger's *Black? White! Day? Night!*).

The format of most concept books generally appeals to a preschool audience—these books are short and rely chiefly on illustration to get their point across. They work best when they are kept simple and direct. *Eric Carle's Opposites* is an example that identifies very basic concepts—day/night, up/down—and additionally included tabs that young readers lift to reveal the opposite. This interactive book allows them to guess what the opposite is.

Again, we have to look to Piaget for guidance. For, as with numbers and counting, certain concepts are simply beyond the developmental stage of very young children. If the concepts can be easily classified, differentiated, and visually depicted—for example, the concepts of basic colors or shapes (square, circle, triangle)—most 3- and 4-year olds can grasp them. Relative size can also be explained to very young children, and Steve Jenkins's striking book *Biggest, Strongest, Fastest* shows us how a concept book can appeal to a variety of cognitive levels (see Figure 5.6). But many concepts are either too sophisticated for the very young or unsuited to a book format. For example, books describing sounds (such as sounds of bells, horns, drums, and so on) are seldom helpful—unless they contain, as many do now, actual recordings of the sounds being presented. Equally difficult is trying to explain movement—fast and slow, for example—in a book for a 3-year old. Some concepts are best taught through life experiences rather in the pages of a book.

The smallest bird is the bee hummingbird.

The bee hummingbird is an acrobatic flier that is only 3 inches long. It weighs 1/30 of an ounce — less than a dime.

FIGURE 5.6 ■ Steve Jenkins's collage depicting a hummingbird extracting nectar comes from the concept book *Biggest, Strongest, Fastest*, which illustrates superlatives. In the lower-right corner, notice how Jenkins illustrates the relative size of the hummingbird by comparing it with a human hand in silhouette.

Wordless Picture Books

Many alphabet and counting books are wordless, but so, too, are many storybooks. Books that set out to tell a story entirely through pictures present interesting challenges for both the illustrator and the reader. (See the essays by Cianciolo [1984] and Groff [1984] for two different viewpoints on the value of wordless picture books.)

The key to a successful wordless picture book is the storytelling quality of its illustrations; more will be said of this in Chapter 6. Indeed, some wordless picture books are quite sophisticated and intended for older readers. In Mitsumasa Anno's *Anno's Journey*, a lone traveler makes his way through Europe on horseback; moving from countryside to village to city, he travels across time as well. If we look closely, we will see, among other things, Little Red Riding Hood and the Big Bad Wolf, Don Quixote tilting at a windmill, Big Bird and Kermit the Frog from *Sesame Street*, a developing romance, an escaping prisoner, and so on. It is also a seek-and-find book in which we are invited to locate the traveler in each picture. (The most famous seek-and-find books are probably the Where's Wally? books, created by the British illustrator Martin Handford. First appearing in the 1980s, the series became an international phenomenon, with the character's name being adapted to different geographic regions—he is "Hetty" in India, "Hugo" in Sweden, and, of course, "Waldo" in the United States.)

Sometimes a little text is necessary. Eric Rohmann's Caldecott Award–winning *My Friend Rabbit* (see Figure 5.7) incorporates just enough text to let us know that

"Not to worry, Mouse,
I've got an idea."

FIGURE 5.7 ■ Eric Rohmann's Caldecott Award–winning *My Friend Rabbit* is virtually a wordless picture book, with only minimal text at the very beginning, in the middle, and at the end of the story. This illustration is the final one in the book. Rohmann has placed the characters in the upper-right corner, suggesting that they are high up in the tree. Note that he also uses artistic conventions to suggest movement, which will be discussed in Chapter 6.

well-meaning Rabbit is always getting into trouble; it is a delightful story in pictures, showing Rabbit's bizarre idea for retrieving Mouse's airplane from a treetop—stacking animals (from hippos to elephants) in order to reach the high branches. The book's appeal is in the bold and comical illustrations of the assortment of animals enlisted by Rabbit to help. Words would be superfluous; the body language and facial expressions say it all.

David Wiesner, a three-time Caldecott medalist, is a modern master of the wordless picture book whose works delight all ages. His *Tuesday* (see Chapter 6, Color Plate D) is a fanciful tale of what might happen if, for one night only, frogs could fly. The stunning full-color illustrations, with an unsettling surrealistic mood, depict a series of vignettes—a record of the occurrences on this magical night. The story is simple enough for very young children to grasp and clever enough and amusing enough to captivate adults.

The success of a wordless storybook depends on the narrative quality of the pictures (again, more on this in Chapter 6). Are the picture details adequate to replace the words? Does the sequence of the illustrations convey the plot development? Is the style of the illustrations suited to the tone and theme of the story? And, of course, most importantly of all, are the illustrations and the concept compelling?

Tactile Books and Movable Books

Extremely popular with very young children are cloth books, board books, and movable or pop-up books. Cloth books, made from fabric, are for the very young. The soft material makes it almost impossible for children to harm themselves—and there is no danger that they will eat the pages. Some are even washable. However, they lack the feel of books, and they do not store very easily—unless we put them in sock or underwear drawers. Children usually find board books more satisfactory. These are printed on very thick and glossy paperboard and are quite practical for 1- and 2-year olds. The tactile quality of both cloth and board books appeals to the sensorimotor period of development of children in these early years. Board books are durable, can be easily cleaned up, and will withstand rough treatment. They also work well for helping children learn how to properly handle books—the turning of pages, for instance. It is now common to see classic picture books converted into board books; Margaret Wise Brown's *Good Night Moon* and *Runaway Bunny* and many of Eric Carle's books are examples. Sometimes the text of a board-book version has to be shortened (or the board book would be too thick to hold comfortably in the hands).

Also popular with very young children (from about 1 to 3 years of age) are tactile books—books that contain something for the children to touch and feel. Some of these have become classics. Dorothy Kunhardt's *Pat the Bunny* contains textured surfaces (cotton to suggest the bunny's fur and sandpaper to represent Daddy's scratchy beard) and movable parts (drawers that pull out). These are great interactive books, asking the child to perform certain tasks during the reading of the story.

Movable books incorporate movable parts within the pages—anything from lift-the-flap or pull-the-tab devices to pop-up mechanisms of extraordinary refinement. There are examples of movable books from the Middle Ages and the Renaissance, although those were not for children. For example, in the Renaissance, pages with movable parts were used in anatomy books. The earliest movable books for children, dating from the eighteenth century, were of the lift-the-flap variety, inviting children to lift flaps to reveal a picture beneath—perhaps opening the shutter to a window or a door to a cabinet. Another early device, still widely used, is the pull-tab, which can be used to reveal a hidden picture or to operate several moving parts at once. Dorothy Kunhardt's *Pat the Bunny* uses both the lift-the-flap and pull-the-tab devices.

By Victorian times (the late nineteenth century), the movable book had approached high art. The Victorians used a technique we call scanimation, in which sliding paper gives the illusion of motion, which is wonderfully used in Rufus Butler Seder's 2007 book *Gallop!* But the nineteenth century also perfected the elaborate pop-up book that opened up to reveal dramatic three-dimensional scenes with several moving parts, included rotating paper discs called *volvelles*. The German illustrator Lothar Meggandorfer (1847–1925) became famous for his pop-up creations, and today the Movable Book Society annually awards the Meggandorfer Prize in his memory to honor a modern creator of pop-up and movable books.

In the United States, among the most celebrated of pop-up artists is Robert Sabuda. His lavish pop-up books include a dazzling version of L. Frank Baum's *The Wonderful Wizard of Oz*, Lewis Carroll's *Alice's Adventures in Wonderland*, his own *Winter's Tale*, and many more. Every page opens to an elaborate set piece with many movable parts, resulting in some very thick books. Equally accomplished is Matthew Reinhart, who has collaborated with Sabuda on several books, including *Encyclopedia Prehistorica: Dinosaurs*, a masterful work appealing to the fascination so many young children have with those awesome creatures. On his own, Reinhart has created works such as the intriguing concept books *Animal Popposites: A Pop-up Book of Opposites* and *Cinderella: A Pop-up Fairy Tale*. All these books have raised the bar for future pop-up and movable books.

It goes without saying that when a work of literature is transformed into a movable book, plot details, character, and language are usually replaced by moving figures and three-dimensional scenery. A pop-up book should never be considered a substitute for the story itself. Movable books are, after all, more visual art than literature.

Easy Readers

In 1957, Dr. Seuss, acting on a wager with his publisher, brought out *The Cat in the Hat*, a book written with a vocabulary of just 236 words—and the easy reader book was born. In the same year, Else Holmelund Minarik came out with the first of her Little Bear series, illustrated by Maurice Sendak, and in 1970, Arnold Lobel's Frog and Toad series was launched. These are all beginning books for readers. They all have in common a controlled vocabulary aimed at giving children in the early elementary grades good stories with which they can practice reading.

The texts of some of these books are highly acclaimed. Two of Lobel's books, *Frog and Toad Are Friends* and *Frog and Toad Together*, received Newbery Honor citations. The Henry and Mudge books, by Newbery Award–winning author Cynthia Rylant and illustrated by Suçie Stevenson, make up another popular easy-reading series. Henry is a little boy, Mudge is his dog, and they engage in a series of often-ingenious adventures that now runs to some 25 books that move through various reading levels. Other series include Peggy Parish's much-loved Amelia Bedelia books for beginning readers, about a hapless maid who takes everything too literally. Syd Hoff wrote dozens of easy readers, typically about clever children and charming animals, including *Danny and the Dinosaur*, which some credit with starting the dinosaur craze among children.

Easy readers contain words that children can readily recognize or sound out. And words and phrases are frequently repeated for pedagogical purposes. Given these restrictions, the author has to devise an interesting story with engaging characters; it is quite a challenge. Today's children are lucky to have literate and enjoyable stories to learn to read by; easy readers far surpass the dull fare of the basal readers widely used in the last century.

Summary

It is never too early to begin sharing books with children. Even tiny infants can learn the enjoyment of holding a cardboard or cloth book. By the time they are age 2, they will be asking to have their favorite stories read to them. The time we have to share books with children is short indeed, for they grow up all too quickly. So it is very important that we don't waste that time on lackluster and mediocre books. Books for the very young are wonderfully varied. Alphabet and counting books can go far beyond instruction and can provide magical journeys into the imagination. Many books for the very young are designed to introduce such perceptual concepts as discerning shapes, colors, sizes, and opposites. Even though many of these books deal with concepts that young children may not be intellectually ready to grasp, books that are well executed, interesting to look at, and stimulating to the imagination can still fascinate them.

For the very young audience—infants and toddlers—board books, cloth books, and tactile books are durable and can be very entertaining. Books with moving parts go beyond being books; they are visually stimulating artworks and are not for children only. And when children have mastered the alphabet and move on to word recognition and reading, they will find waiting for them a wide selection of easy readers, books combining interesting stories with controlled vocabularies that they can enjoy on their own. These first experiences with books should be happy ones for children. Children's encounters with books should be frequent and varied, for a good book is food for both a child's mind and spirit.

For Reflection and Discussion

1. Locate and compare several alphabet or concept books. Identify the purpose of each book and its intended audience. Then evaluate it according to the criteria described in this chapter. Be sure to consider the illustrations, the specific content, any thematic thread running through the book, its appropriateness to the intended audience, and so on.

2. Plan an alphabet or concept book of your own. Identify the specific audience and choose a theme or design format. (It is not necessary to actually draw the pictures.) Make sure you can justify your choices.

3. Compare a pop-up version of a folktale with a standard version. Describe and evaluate the alterations that were made to accommodate the pop-up format.

4. Locate and read three or four easy readers, but choose each one from a different level (the levels are always numbered—0, 1, 2, 3, and so on—on the front cover). Describe the differences between the various levels in vocabulary and subject matter and treatment.

Works Cited

Baring-Gould, William S., and Ceil Baring-Gould. *The Annotated Mother Goose*. New York: Potter, 1962.

Butler, Francelia. *Skipping around the World: The Ritual Nature of Folk Rhymes*. New York: Ballantine, 1989.

Cianciolo, Patricia. "Visual Literacy and to Study Literature." *Jump Over the Moon*. Eds Pamela Barron and Jennifer Q. Burley. New York: Holt, 1984, 139–144.

Groff, Patrick. "Children's Literature Versus Wordless Books?" *Jump Over the Moon*. Ed. Pamela Barron and Jennifer Q. Burley. New York: Holt, 1984, 145–154.

Recommended Resources

Haining, Peter. *Movable Books: An Illustrated History*. London: New English Library, 1979.

Hopkins, Lee Bennett. "Pop Go the Books." *CLA Bulletin* 16 (Fall 1990): 10–12.

Kiefer, Barbara. "Critically Speaking: Literature for Children." *The Reading Teacher* (January 1985): 458–463.

Lindauer, Shelley L. Knudson. "Wordless Books: An Approach to Visual Literacy." *Children's Literature in Education* 19, 3 (1988): 136–142.

MacCann, Donnarae, and Olga Richard. *The Child's First Books*. New York: Wilson, 1973.

Pritchard, David. "'Daddy, Talk!' Thoughts on Reading Early Picture Books." *The Lion and the Unicorn* 7/8 (1983/84): 64–69.

Schoenfield, Madalynne. "Alphabet and Counting Books." *Day Care and Early Education* 10 (Winter 1982): 44.

Stewig, John Warren. "Alphabet Books: A Neglected Genre." In *Jump Over the Moon*. Ed. Pamela

Barron and Jennifer Q. Burley. New York: Holt, 1984, 115–120.

Thomas, Della. "Count Down on the 1–2–3's." *School Library Journal* 15 (March 1971): 95–102.

Books for Beginners: A Selected and Annotated Booklist

(Wordless picture storybooks are found in the booklist in Chapter 6.)

Mother Goose Books

Alderson, Brian, comp. *The Helen Oxenbury Nursery Rhyme Book.* Illus. Helen Oxenbury. New York: Morrow, 1986.
- A collection for very young readers with warm illustrations.

Briggs, Raymond, illus. *The Mother Goose Treasury.* New York: Coward, McCann & Geoghegan, 1966.
- A large collection with comic illustrations.

de Angeli, Marguerite, illus. *Book of Nursery and Mother Goose Rhymes.* Garden City, NY: Doubleday, 1953.
- A large collection fully illustrated in both black and white and color.

dePaola, Tomie, illus. *Tomie dePaola's Mother Goose.* New York: Putnam, 1985.
- For beginners as well as older readers, a large collection playfully illustrated.

Greenaway, Kate, illus. *Kate Greenaway's Mother Goose.* 1881. Several modern reprints.
- One of the earliest and still a favorite. A small book with delicate illustrations.

Grover, Eulalie Osgood, ed. *Mother Goose: The Original Volland Edition.* Illus. Frederick Richardson. (1915). New York: Derrydale, 1988.
- One of the earliest classic collections, A stunning book, now reprinted. Each of the more than 100 rhymes is accompanied by a full-page color illustration.

Gustafson, Scott. *Favorite Nursery Rhymes from Mother Goose.* New York: Greenwich Workshop, 2007.
- A book for beginners, with illustrations inspired by the great classic illustrators of the nineteenth and early twentieth centuries.

Hague, Michael, illus. *Mother Goose: A Collection of Classic Nursery Rhymes.* New York: Holt, 1984.
- A short collection for the very young, with striking illustrations.

Lobel, Arnold, illus. *The Random House Book of Mother Goose.* New York: Random House, 1986.
- A large, well-illustrated collection that has been recently reissued.

Long, Sylvia, illus. *Silvia Long's Mother Goose.* San Francisco: Chronicle, 1999.
- About 75 rhymes with very inventive illustrations, sometimes as much for the adult as for the child.

Marshall, James. *James Marshall's Mother Goose.* 1986. New York: Square Fish (Macmillan), 2009.
- Large colorful and comical illustrations.

Opie, Iona. *My Very First Mother Goose.* Illus. Rosemary Wells. New York: Candlewick, 1996.
- For beginners. Playful and colorful pictures accompany this collection of familiar rhymes.

Petersham, Maud, and Miska Petersham, illus. *The Rooster Crows: A Book of American Rhymes and Jingles.* New York: Macmillan, 1945.
- A collection of traditional American folk rhymes rather than Mother Goose rhymes.

Rackham, Arthur, illus. *Mother Goose.* 1913. New York: Marathon, 1978.
- A collection with Rackham's striking and gently humorous illustrations.

Sanderson, Ruth, illus. *Mother Goose and Friends.* Boston: Little-Brown, 2008.
- A book in which some of the traditional rhymes have been "sweetened" up.

Scarry, Richard, illus. *Richard Scarry's Best Mother Goose Ever.* New York: Golden Books, 1999.
- For beginners, with Scarry's characteristic cartoon animals.

Smith, Jessie Willcox, illus. *The Jessie Willcox Smith Mother Goose.* 1914. Several modern versions.
- The original version contains hundreds of rhymes and is the one you should look for to get the most for your money. The board book version is drastically stripped down.

Tripp, Wallace, illus. *Granfa' Grig Had a Pig and Other Rhymes Without Reason from Mother Goose.* Boston: Little, Brown, 1976.
- Contains both familiar and lesser-known rhymes.

Withers, Carl, collector. *A Rocket in My Pocket: The Rhymes and Chants of Young America.* Illus. Susanne Suba. New York: Holt, 1946.
- American folk rhymes, as told by children.

Wright, Blanche Fisher, illus. *The Real Mother Goose.* New York: Rand McNally, 1916.
- An old classic with many rhymes. Often reprinted in abridged versions, so look for the complete collection, which is a better deal.

Alphabet Books

Anno, Mitsumasa. *Anno's Alphabet.* New York: Harper, 1975.
- Clever illustrations of the letters that play tricks with the eye, in the vein of M. C. Escher.

Base, Graeme. *Animalia.* New York: Abrams, 1987.
- An animal alphabet with dramatic illustrations; a feast for the eye.

Bingman, Kelly. *Z Is for Moose.* Illus. Paul O. Zelinsky. New York: Greenwillow, 2012.
- An irrepressible moose cannot wait his turn in this very funny animal alphabet.

Burningham, John. *John Burningham's ABC's.* New York: Crown, 1985.
- A charming first alphabet book with simple cartoon pictures.

Elting, Mary, and Michael Folsom. *Q Is for Duck: An Alphabet Guessing Game.* 1980. Illus. Jack Kent. Logan, IA: Perfection Learning, 2005.
- For slightly older children, the alphabet in riddles and comical illustrations. A modern classic.

Gaiman, Neil. *The Dangerous Alphabet.* New York: HarperCollins, 2008.
- A story in which two children escape a succession of dangers as a boat takes them through haunted reaches.

Gerstein, Mordecai. *The Absolutely Awful Alphabet.* New York: Harcourt, 1999.
- A book where the letters of the alphabet are ghoulish, nasty, ugly, and weird—just the sort of things some young children love.

Gorey, Edward. *The Gashlycrumb Tinies.* New York: Houghton Mifflin, 1997.
- Catastrophes visit 26 hapless children in this alphabet book for teens and older. Showcases Gorey's characteristic dark humor—ghoulishly funny.

Green, Dan. *Wild Alphabet: An A to Zoo Pop-up Book.* London: Kingfisher, 2010.
- Inventive pop-up alphabet book, including animals both familiar and unusual.

Hudes, Quiara Alegria. *Bienvenidos a Mi Bario! (Welcomes to My Neighborhood!): A Barrio ABC.* New York: Scholastic, 2010.
- A multicultural alphabet book in which a young girl gives her friend an alphabetic tour of her neighborhood.

Isadora, Rachel. *City Seen from A to Z.* New York: Greenwillow, 1983.
- Stunning paintings (you will think they are photographs) in which letters are discovered in everyday objects.

Johnson, Stephen T. *Alphabet City*. New York: Viking Penguin, 1995.
- Letters of the alphabet are discovered in a cityscape. Remarkable illustrations and very original.

Kitchen, Bert. *Animal Alphabet*. New York: Dial, 1984.
- A wordless book with dramatic illustrations of animals, including some quite unusual ones.

Kontis, Alethea. *AlphaOops! The Day Z Went First*. Illus. Bob Kolar. New York: Candlewick, 2006.
- A book in which unruly letters bicker as they introduce themselves. Digital art captures the chaos.

MacDonald, Suse. *Alphabatics*. New York: Bradbury, 1986.
- A book in which animals morph into letters.

Martin, Bill, Jr., and John Archambault. *Chicka Chicka Boom Boom*. Illus. Lois Ehlert. New York: Simon & Schuster, 1989.
- A childhood classic for the very young with rollicking rhymes and comical illustrations. Don't miss this one.

McGuirk, Leslie. *If Rocks Could Sing: A Discovered Alphabet*. New York: Tricycle Press, 2011.
- Rocks in the shapes of objects are used to illustrate this imaginative alphabet book.

McLimans, David. *Gone Wild: An Endangered Animal Alphabet*. New York: Walker, 2006.
- Beautiful and clever illustrations in black and white dramatize the plight of rare animals.

Musgrove, Margaret. *Ashanti to Zulu: African Traditions*. Illus. Leo and Diane Dillon. New York: Dial, 1976.
- For older readers, an introduction to African culture in alphabet format.

Oxenbury, Helen. *Helen Oxenbury's ABC*. New York: Delacorte, 1983.
- A book with warm illustrations for very young children.

Pelletier, David. *The Graphic Alphabet*. New York: Scholastic, 1996.
- A book for older readers, in which the letters are drawn to depict the representative words. Very similar to Van Allsburg's *Z Was Zapped*.

Pinto, Sara. *The Alphabet Room*. New York: Bloomsbury, 2003.
- A book for very young children, with beautiful illustrations and a hide-and-seek alphabet game.

Rankin, Laura. *The Handmade Alphabet*. New York: Dial, 1991.
- A striking book that depicts the American Sign Language signs for each letter.

Seuss, Dr. *Dr. Seuss's ABC*. New York: Random, 1988.
- For beginners, the perfect book for learning letter shapes and sounds.

Sierra, Judy. *The Sleepy Little Alphabet: A Bedtime Story from Alphabet Town*. Illus. Melissa Sweet. New York: Knopf, 2009.
- A very funny rhyming story about the letters of the alphabet trying to go to sleep, but each one needing something first.

Spieker, Diana. *Alphabetica: Odes to the Alphabets*. Illus. Krista Skehan. San Francisco, CA: Personify Press, 2009.
- A book that presents the letters through a collection of concrete poetry, beautifully illustrated.

Thurlby, Paul. *Paul Thurlby's Alphabet*. Dorking, Surrey: Templar, 2011.
- A cleverly composed and refreshing alphabet book by a graphic artist who creates retro illustrations.

Van Allsburg, Chris. *Z Was Zapped*. Boston: Houghton Mifflin, 1987.
- A book for older readers, with stunning illustrations that depict disasters befalling the letters.

Wildsmith, Brian. *Brian Wildsmith's ABC*. New York: Watts, 1962.
- A book for beginners, with striking art in bold colors.

Counting, Concept, Tactile, and Movable Books

Anno, Mitsumasa. *Anno's Counting Book*. New York: Crowell, 1977.
- Clever illustrations play tricks on our eyes.

Bang, Molly. *Ten, Nine, Eight*. New York: Greenwillow, 1983.
- A counting book that goes in reverse.

Browne, Anthony. *One Gorilla: A Counting Book.* New York: Candlewick, 2013.
- An assortment of primates, evocatively drawn, to illustrate the concept of counting.

Burningham, John. *John Burningham's 123.* New York: Crown, 1985.
- A very good beginning book.

Carle, Eric. *Eric Carle's Opposites.* New York: Grosset and Dunlap, 2007.
- A beginner's book with full-page flaps the reader pulls to reveal opposites.

Cumpiano, Ina. *Quinito, Day and Night/Quinito, día y noche.* Illus. José Ramirez. San Francisco: Children's Book Press, 2008.
- A bilingual book about opposites found in our daily lives.

Falconer, Ian. *Olivia Counts.* New York: Atheneum, 2002.
- A book in which Olivia, the inimitable pig, learns to count.

Feelings, Muriel. *Moja Means One: A Swahili Counting Book.* Illus. Tom Feelings. New York: Dutton, 1971.
- A counting book with an introduction to a new culture.

Garne, S. T. *One White Sail.* San Marcos, CA: Green Tiger, 1992.
- A counting book with beautiful illustrations and a simple lyrical text.

Hoban, Tana. *Shapes, Shapes, Shapes.* New York: Greenwillow, 1986.
- A book of photographs that capture shapes in the real world.

Jay, Alison. *1, 2, 3: A Child's First Counting Book.* New York: Dutton, 2007.
- A book in which simple but striking illustrations make overtures to famous folktales.

Kunhardt, Dorothy. *Pat the Bunny.* New York: Golden Books, 1940.
- An early, and still favorite, tactile book for the very, very young.

Lionni, Leo. *A Color of His Own.* New York: Knopf, 1975.
- A book of simple collage illustrations that depict animals of different colors—except for the chameleon. A long-time favorite.

MacDonald, Suse. *Shape by Shape.* New York: Little, Simon, 2009.
- A book depicting basic shapes that morph into a prehistoric animal. Imaginative collage illustrations.

Marino, Gianna. *One Too Many: A Seek and Find Counting Book.* San Francisco, CA: Chronicle, 2010.
- A wordless counting book filled with a host of animals and some challenges for young children.

Murphy, Chuck. *Opposites (Slide 'n' Seek).* New York: Little Simon, 2001.
- An interactive book of opposites, one of a series by this illustrator.

Reinhart, Matthew. *Animal Popposites: A Pop-up Book of Opposites.* New York: Little Simon, 2002.
- A clever book about animals by one of the masters of the modern pop-up book.

Sabuda, Robert. *Winter's Tale: An Original Pop-Up Journey.* New York: Little, Simon, 2005.
- A stunning pop-up book about the magic of winter; this master of pop-up books has also created *Alice's Adventures in Wonderland, The Wonderful Wizard of Oz, The Night Before Christmas,* and many others.

Seder, Rufus Butler. *Gallop!* New York: Workman, 2007.
- Using a technique called scanimation, a board book that produces pictures in motion.

Seeger, Laura Vacaro. *Black? White! Day? Night! A Book of Opposites.* New York: Roaring Brook, 2006.
- With brightly colored cutouts and lift-up flaps, an interactive concept book in which things turn out to be the opposite of what they seem.

——. *Green.* New York: Roaring Brook Press, 2012.
- This book explores the many shades of green with striking die cut illustrations.

Shannon, George. *White Is for Blueberry.* Illus. Laura Dronzek. New York: Greenwillow, 2005.
- A book of colors with stunning illustrations and surprising subjects.

Sidman, Joyce. *Red Sings from the Tree Tops: A Year in Colors.* Illus. Pamela Zagarenski. New York: Houghton Mifflin, 2009.

- Colors combined with sounds and smells of the seasons in a richly imagined book.

Tafuri, Nancy. *The Big Storm: A Very Soggy Counting Book*. New York: Simon & Schuster, 2009.
  - A book in which attractive illustrations depict animals seeking shelter in a storm, increasing in number as they do.

Van Fleet, Matthew. *Monday the Bullfrog*. New York: Simon & Schuster, 2006.
  - A delightful tactile book in the shape of a frog; for the very young.

Wildsmith, Brian. *Brian Wildsmith's 1,2,3's*. New York: Watts, 1965.
  - A very good beginning counting book.

Wood, Audrey. *The Deep Blue Sea: A Book of Colors*. Illus. Bruce Wood. New York: Blue Sky Press, 2005.
  - A cumulative rhyme and distinctly colorful pictures introduce young children to colors.

6 Picture Storybooks

The Collaboration of Story and Art

Introduction

In *Alice's Adventures in Wonderland*, Alice asks, "What is the use of a book . . . without pictures or conversations in it?" Most young children express similar sentiments. Some of our most lasting memories are of the picture books we read as children—Ludwig Bemelmans's *Madeline*, Maurice Sendak's *Where the Wild Things Are*, and Chris Van Allsburg's *The Polar Express* are just a few of the perennially popular ones. These are the works that combine the art of storytelling with the art of illustration. The picture storybook is, in fact, a complex work of art requiring thoughtful conception and skillful execution.

We should point out that *Alice's Adventures in Wonderland* and this textbook are illustrated books; they are not picture books. In an illustrated book, the pictures supplement the text. In a true picture storybook, the pictures and the text work hand-in-hand: we can't have one without the other. The pictures not only tell the story, they add layers of meaning, frequently telling us much more than the words do.

This chapter will focus on how text and illustrations work together to form a satisfying picture book. Specifically, we will consider the key elements of the picture book, including storytelling techniques, artistic styles and media, and the overall book design.

Picture-Book Characteristics

The Tiger Who Came to Tea, written and illustrated by Judith Kerr, is a delightfully simple storybook. Sophie and her mother are having tea when a tiger unexpectedly knocks at the door and asks to join them. They graciously invite him in. Then the tiger proceeds to drink all their tea and to eat all the food on the table. Next he cleans out the cupboards and refrigerator, eating and drinking everything in sight. Then, as suddenly as he arrived, he thanks them and leaves. When Sophie's father arrives home, they tell him about the tiger who ate and drank them out of house and home, leaving them with nothing for dinner.

FIGURE 6.1 ■ In this illustration from Judith Kerr's *The Tiger Who Came to Tea*, the text merely tells us of the tiger's outrageous behavior, devouring all the food and drink in the house. The illustration, however, depicts Sophie's clear affection for the mysterious stranger who arrived unexpectedly for tea, removing any cause for the reader's concern.

Unabashed, Father suggests they put on their coats and go out to a café to eat. They enjoy a lovely dinner out, and the next day Sophie and her mother go shopping for more food. And they buy a huge tin of tiger food in case the tiger should return—"but he never did."

The illustrations are simple pencil and crayon drawings that capture life in postwar England, when many people had limited means, and going out to eat was a rare treat. The story's magical quality, a voracious talking tiger stopping by for tea, is treated as an ordinary event. The text sticks to the bare facts, but the illustrations reveal the characters' reactions—Sophie affectionately caressing the Tiger, for example (see Figure 6.1). What might have been a frightening experience is portrayed as inconvenient disruption of the daily routine—an exciting interlude and a wonderful mystery. And as readers, we want to believe in the story.

For nearly 50 years this has been one of the most popular picture books in England. It has been made into a play and even enjoys a Facebook page. Perhaps the book's popularity derives from its juxtaposition of mystery and familiarity, of the extraordinary and the everyday, of excitement and contentment. In short, *The Tiger Who Came to Tea* has what we look for in a good picture storybook, including

- an engaging and well-told story,
- illustrations that not only depict the narrative but enrich and extend the text,
- illustrations that capture the mood of the text, and,
- a pleasing balance between the illustrations and the text, with each complementing the other.

Picture-Book Stories

The term *picture book* describes a format—a book design—not a genre, which refers to a book's subject matter. In fact, picture books may deal with almost any subject. The picture-book text may be a folktale ("The Twelve Dancing Princesses" or "Rapunzel"—Color Plates C and E), a talking animal story (Beatrix Potter's *The Tale of Peter Rabbit*—Color Plate A), a realistic story (Robert McCloskey's *One Morning in Maine*), magical realism (David Wiesner's *Tuesday*—Color Plate D), a dream fantasy (Maurice Sendak's *Where the Wild Things Are*), nursery rhymes and concept books (see Chapter 5), or poetry (see Chapter 7). By the third grade most children have moved into chapter books and are beginning to see picture books as "babyish." However, in recent years we have seen the rising popularity of graphic novels, complex illustrated stories for older readers, which seem extensions and transformations of the picture book fitted to the tastes of our increasingly visual world. So it is helpful to understand how a picture book works, including both illustrations and text. Let's begin by examining the picture book stories—their plots, characters, and language.

Plot

The typical picture book contains 32 pages and fewer than 2,000 words (many have far fewer), which means that the author and illustrator must use the space wisely. When a storyline is involved, the text has to be simple and straightforward. If there is a plot (see Chapter 9), it may be dramatic, as in *The Tiger Who Came to Tea* or Beatrix Potter's *The Tale of Peter* Rabbit, which focuses on a single issue that must be resolved. Or, the plot may be episodic as in Ezra Jack Keats's *The Snowy* Day, which depicts a series of loosely related events usually united by a theme (what can a little boy do in the snow?).

We even find parallel plots in picture books. Robert McCloskey's *Blueberries for Sal* describes a girl (Sal) and her mother picking blueberries on a hill. Unbeknownst to them, on the other side of the hill, a mother bear and her cub are eating blueberries. Two sets of characters are engaged in their separate (or parallel) activities. In an unexpected mix-up, Sal ends up with the mother bear, and the cub ends up with Sal's mother—to the surprise of the mothers. Everything, happily, is straightened out in the end, and the proper families are reunited. The point is that a good picture-book story is engaging but not necessarily simplistic. It makes the child reader want to keep reading. The older the intended audience, the more sophisticated the story needs to be, or the more complicated the characters, which brings us to the next story element.

Character

The characters in a picture book tend to be identified by one or two dominant traits—for example, Peter Rabbit is curious and impishly rebellious. Ezra Jack Keats's Peter in *The Snowy Day* is a typically curious little boy delighting in the new snow. Children tend to identify with characters like themselves, and protagonists in picture books are most often young children or animals (who exhibit childlike qualities). In fact, we can usually determine the age of the intended reader by establishing the age of the protagonist. Keats's Peter appears to be about 5 years old—hence the intended reader can be assumed to be around age 4 or 5. (This is admittedly a little harder when the protagonist is a talking animal or a machine, like Mary Ann, the steam shovel in Virginia Lee Burton's *Mike Mulligan's Steam Shovel*, in which case we have to rely on the treatment of the subject and the language.)

Sometimes we learn about the characters through the text—what the author says about them—and sometimes through the pictures (and often through both at once). If we look at Figure 6.1, we find an example of the illustration adding an entirely new dimension, for the text never mentions the relationship between the tiger and Sophie. A tiger in the house could be a scary thing, but the illustration shows us there is nothing for Sophie to fear.

Language

Most children have a love for language and are fascinated with words and repetitive patterns. Notice how many stories include refrains, such as the classic "hundreds of cats, thousands of cats, millions and billions and trillions of cats" in Wanda Gág's *Millions of Cats.* Children even like made-up words, such as in the jolly tale *Master of All Masters*, retold by Joseph Jacobs, where the maid must learn odd new names for everyday items (a bed becomes a "barnacle," a cat a "white-faced simminy," and a fire a "hot cockalorum"—it is hilarious wordplay). Picture books can nicely play into a child's fascination with the miracle of language. And it is also good to remember that picture books are an important way to expand young children's vocabularies. So we should not be put off when an occasional big word (even one we don't know) pops up in a picture book. Beatrix Potter uses words like "implored," "exert," "disagreeable," "fortnight," and "camomile" in *The Tale of Peter Rabbit*—and children have been enjoying that book for over a century.

The picture-book format also requires that the language be carefully chosen to accompany the pictures. It can be very disconcerting when the words on a page do not actually refer to the illustrations we're looking at—and this does happen. A skillful picture-book designer will ensure that the words we are hearing and the pictures we are seeing actually correspond with each other.

Elements of Picture-Book Art

Picture-book art is narrative art; that is, it tells a story. But it often goes far beyond just telling a story. An artist—by applying lines, shapes, textures, and colors to a flat surface, and effectively using space and arrangement—can create the illusion of three dimensions or evoke specific emotional responses in us, such as joy or sadness, serenity or agitation. Let's examine the principal elements of graphic art to see how they are used in children's picture books.

Line

Lines convey meaning; they indicate the shapes of objects—for example, an artist uses a line to draw the shape of a dog—but lines can also suggest texture, depth, and motion. Horizontal lines suggest calm and stability (recalling firm, solid ground), whereas vertical lines suggest height and distance. Sharp and zigzagging lines suggest excitement and rapid movement (think of a lightning bolt). In Ludwig Bemelmans's illustration for *Madeline* (Figure 6.2) the lines direct our eyes from the bottom of the page to the top; because the walkway narrows at the top, we understand that the girls "in two straight lines" are moving away from us. The lines also suggest the orderliness of the convent school, overseen by the dominating figure of Miss Clavel at the bottom. In Nielsen's portrayal of the ball from "The Twelve Dancing Princesses" (Color Plate C) the sweeping curve of the lines suggests grace and elegance at once beautiful and otherworldly.

Shape

Like lines, shapes such as circles, ovals, squares, rectangles and triangles can define objects, and they can also elicit emotional reactions. Rounded shapes tend to suggest comfort, security, and stability, as seen in Zelinsky's portrait of Rapunzel's family (Color Plate E). They can also suggest spontaneity and a natural quality (as in Lawson's comical illustration for *The Story of Ferdinand*, Figure 6.3). Solid and geometric shapes—squares, rectangles, triangles, perfect circles, ovals—often appear more static even if the subject matter is unsettling (see *Jumanji*, Figure 6.4).

Space

We often do not think of space—literally the empty parts of the page—as an artistic element, but it is, in fact, very powerful. There is an old story about a Japanese artist who, when asked what was the most important part of a painting, replied, "The part that is left out." Space is actually what draws our attention to objects on the page. If a page contains very little empty space but is instead crowded with images, our attention is necessarily divided; we do not know exactly where to look. The lack of open space on a page may contribute to a claustrophobic or uneasy feeling (see *The Story of Ferdinand*, Figure 6.3) or

FIGURE 6.2 ■ *Madeline*, by Ludwig Bemelmans, is the first of several books about an irrepressible little girl in a Parisian convent school. The illustrations are interesting examples of expressionistic art. Notice the angularity of the figures and the exaggerated height of the nun, Miss Clavel, accompanying the 12 little girls who walk, as we are told, in "two straight lines" (surely a commentary on convent school discipline). The trees are more like ideas of trees; there is no attempt at realistic depiction. There is a carefree jocularity in these pictures that aptly characterizes the mood of the story.

He didn't look where he was sitting and instead of sitting on the nice cool grass in the shade he sat on a bumble bee.

FIGURE 6.3 ■ This illustration by Robert Lawson for *The Story of Ferdinand* by Munro Leaf is a good example of the correlation of picture and text. (Without the text, we might not understand what is about to happen to the bee.) Notice also how the various textures are depicted—the bull's hair, the bee's body, the clover. We should not overlook the comically expressive eye of the bee as it realizes it is about to be sat upon.

perhaps confusion or chaos (see *Jumanji*, Figure 6.4). However, a lot of empty space on a page can suggest loneliness, emptiness, or isolation, or it can direct our attention to certain objects. The illustration from Rohmann's *My Friend Rabbit* (Chapter 5, Figure 5.7) uses empty space in the bottom half of the illustration to force our eyes upward (so we feel we are looking to the treetops, where Mouse and Rabbit are stranded).

Texture

One of the illusions an artist creates is to give a flat surface (the paper) the characteristics of three dimensions and texture—the suggestion of fur, wood grain, smooth silk, and so on. Texture is achieved through the skillful use of the medium—paint layers, brush strokes, pencil marks, and so on. Texture generally evokes a realistic quality in an illustration. Notice the illusion of animal fur Van Allsburg creates in *Jumanji* (Figure 6.4) and *The Story of Ferdinand* (Figure 6.3).

FIGURE 6.4 ■ We, the viewers, are at a child's eye level, looking over the table and up at the menacing monkeys (made even more disturbing from this point of view) in this surrealistic pencil drawing from Chris Van Allsburg's *Jumanji*. The figures seem to crowd us, adding an almost claustrophobic feeling, and the whole scene appears to be a moment uncomfortably frozen in time—an appropriate mood for this story of a mysterious board game that comes to life.

Composition

The composition refers to the arrangement of the objects in a picture. Composition is important both to the narrative quality of an illustration and its emotional impact. For example, grouping many large shapes together may suggest stability (see *Rapunzel*, Color Plate E) or discomfort or uneasiness (see *Jumanji*, Figure 6.4), depending on how the shapes are organized on the page. John Burningham's illustration from *Mr. Gumpy's Outing* in Color Plate B is carefully divided into two parts—the upper half yellow, the lower half green. The cat is placed directly in the center, its bright orange face to the left, and a host of white daisies around its (hidden) legs and feet. The composition is balanced by the cat's tail jutting up boldly on the right side, reaching the very top edge of the illustration (and beyond).

COLOR PLATE A ● This watercolor from Beatrix Potter's *The Tale of Peter Rabbit* shows Peter brazenly eating radishes from Mr. McGregor's garden—defying his mother's warning. The style is quite realistic (aside from the fact that the animals are treated as people, but if rabbits could walk upright and wore clothes, they would look like this). Potter's light hand and delicate watercolors give her illustrations a warmth and charm that are uniquely hers.

COLOR PLATE B ● John Burningham is noted for his striking use of color, as seen in this portrait of a cat from *Mr. Gumpy's Outing*, a comical tale for very young readers. The style of the illustration is akin to naïve art, but there is an expressionistic quality in the unusual coloring and the cat that is entirely made of circles and rectangles, with two triangles for ears.

COLOR PLATE C • Kay Nielsen, a Danish artist of the early twentieth century, was strongly influenced by the Art Nouveau movement, characterized by stylized figures, graceful curving lines, and decorative organic motifs (usually floral). This illustration from "The Twelve Dancing Princesses" does not attempt a realist portrayal. Instead, the figures and the setting are very theatrical, proportions are exaggerated, and we are drawn to the exquisite detail. These elegant and ethereal creatures indeed belong to an enchanted world.

COLOR PLATE D ● David Wiesner's *Tuesday*, a delightfully surreal story about frogs taking flight on the lily pads one evening, is superbly illustrated by these surrealistic images. Surrealism is all about startling juxtapositions—very realistic frogs engaged in very unreal behavior. Wiesner uses a color palate of blues and lavenders, appropriate to the evening, and his details are exquisitely realistic—notice the patterns on the rotting log and delicate waterlily in bloom. But he does not take himself too seriously and thoroughly enjoys giving human expressions to the fishes gaping up from the pond and the dumbfounded turtle as they watch the smug frogs lift off on their fanciful night journey.

COLOR PLATE E ● Paul O. Zelinsky's dramatic illustration for *Rapunzel* is a deliberate attempt to evoke the feeling of Renaissance Italy. Everything from the evocative landscape to the carefully detailed architecture to the glorious clothing suggests the Italian fifteenth century. Renaissance art was strongly influenced by the realism of the art of classical Greece and Rome. Here the figure of Rapunzel, with the prince and their twins at the story's happy ending, is reminiscent of a Madonna by Raphael. There is an almost religious aura about the subject, and Zelinsky uses the rich colors of Raphael as well.

Perspective

Perspective, or point of view, refers to the artist's attempt to portray the world as we would see it through our eyes. So, for example, the farther away an object is, the smaller it appears, as in David Wiesner's illustration from *Tuesday* (Color Plate D), in which the distant moon appears smaller than the frogs being lifted into air on lily pads. Indeed, the viewer is seeing the frogs from the same point of view of the awestruck fish in the pond. Wiesner's use of perspective helps to make a fantastic event seem almost real—a style we call surrealism. Van Allsburg uses perspective to heighten the disturbing qualities of his surrealistic tale *Jumanji* (Figure 6.4). It is the story of a board game that comes to life, with frightening consequences. By using unusual perspectives the artist creates a sense of discomfort. We are viewing the scene from an unsettling angle, as if we were hiding behind the table. Films use the same technique to suggest that an unseen person (such as an intruder) is watching a character.

This is not to suggest that all use of perspective results in surrealistic art. Any artist wishing to achieve a sense of realism, works from a perspective. An artist may wish to change points of view from illustration to illustration—perhaps to avoid monotony, but more probably to make us see and think about things in specific ways. Perry Nodelman points out that most picture books give us the "middle shot." Close-ups and panoramic views are reserved for specific purposes—to emphasize character or to give us an overview, for example. Bemelmans gives us a bird's-eye view in Figure 6.2, and this contrasts interestingly with the viewpoint provided by Wiesner (Color Plate D), where the viewer is looking upward. Even in a brief picture book, an artist is able to provide a variety of perspectives to add depth and interest to the story.

Color/Black and White

Children are especially responsive to color, and very early on they choose "favorite" colors, which we like to imagine reflect their personalities. Color is one of the most emotionally evocative of artistic elements. Psychologists tell us that reds and yellows are warm or hot colors and suggest excitement, whereas blues and greens are cool or cold colors and suggest calm or quiet. These reactions may be embedded in our responses to the natural world— red and yellow are suggestive of warmth and happiness, and they are also the colors of sunlight and fire; blue we find to be soothing and melancholy perhaps because we associate it with calm waters or the broad expanse of the sky and the lonely universe beyond. Colors take on associative values—purple signifies royalty; green denotes envy or illness, but also life and renewal; red indicates danger, but also boldness; blue signals depression, but also loyalty and serenity; yellow suggests cowardice, but also cheerfulness; and so on. However, these responses are often cultural. In imperial China, for example, the color yellow was reserved for the emperor, and throughout Asia white is a traditional color of mourning, and brides often wear red.

Artists use color to establish the tone of a work. Beatrix Potter uses soft earthy colors in her pastoral story *The Tale of Peter Rabbit* (Color Plate A), whereas John Burningham, in his light-hearted story *Mr. Gumpy's Outing* (Color Plate B) experiments with a wilder, less conventional, palette. Kay Nielsen uses sharp contrasts that focus our attention on the dancing couple in "The Twelve Dancing Princesses" (Color Plate C), and the colors inside the palace suggest an artificial, almost otherworldly, elegance. David Wiesner turns to the deep blues and greens of the nighttime in *Tuesday* (Color Plate D). And Paul Zelinsky uses rich primary colors in his pleasant family portrait for *Rapunzel* (Color Plate E), in which he deliberately imitates the art of the Renaissance; the illustration is reminiscent of a portrait of the Holy Family by the great sixteenth-century Italian painter Raphael.

Some of the most-loved picture books, however, have no color at all. Wanda Gág uses simple black and white in *Millions of Cats*, as does Robert Lawson in *The Story of Ferdinand* (Figure 6.3). Chris Van Allsburg shows a strong preference for black and white (and many shades of gray) in his books, including *Jumanji* (Figure 6.4). Robert McCloskey likes to use monochrome—that is, just a single color. His *Make Way for Ducklings* is illustrated in sepia (a brown tone), and *Blueberries for Sal* is appropriately illustrated in blue. Professional photographers have long preferred black and white or monochrome for its evocative subtleties. Without color as a distraction, the viewers pay closer attention to the lines, shapes, composition, perspective, and texture. It is certainly a mistake to think that children require garish colors in their books or that they will reject books with black and white illustrations. Children's artistic intuition is often more subtle than we realize. And they are often far more open-minded than adults.

Artistic Media

The artistic medium is simply the material (or materials—*media*) an artist chooses to produce an illustration—pencil, ink, oils, watercolors, acrylics, woodblocks, and so on. Media are generally grouped into four broad categories: painterly techniques, graphic techniques, photography, and collage.

Painterly Techniques

Painterly techniques are those by which an artist creates an image by applying a medium (paint, chalk, ink, and so on) to a surface (usually paper) with an instrument (such as a brush, pen, or pencil). Paint itself consists of pigment (usually powdered) mixed with some liquid or paste to make it spreadable. Many variations are possible, depending on the medium used to mix with the pigment. Among the most common are the following:

- *Watercolors*, as their name implies, use water as the medium, resulting in transparent, typically soft, delicate pictures, as in Potter's *The Tale of Peter Rabbit* (Color Plate A).

- *Tempera* is made by mixing pigments with egg yolk or some other albuminous substance. Tempera is not as transparent as watercolor and can produce some brilliant hues. (See Maurice Sendak's *Where the Wild Things Are.*)

- *Gouache* (pronounced "gwash") is a powdered paint similar to tempera but mixed with a white base, resulting in a delicate hue. (See Margot Zemach's *Duffy and the Devil.*)

- *Oil paint* typically uses linseed oil as a base and is among the most opaque of media. One of the best examples is found in Paul O. Zelinsky's illustrations for *Rapunzel* (Color Plate E).

- *Acrylics* use a plastic base, a product of twentieth-century technology, and they produce very brilliant colors. (See Barbara Cooney's illustrations for Donald Hall's *The Ox-Cart Man.*)

- *Pastels* differ from the rest in that they are typically applied in powdered form (often with the fingers). (See Chris Van Allsburg's *The Wreck of the Zephyr.*)

- *Chalk*, *pencil*, *ink*, and *crayon* drawings, although technically not painting, follow the same general principles as painterly techniques. Chris Van Allsburg's *Jumanji* (Figure 6.4) is illustrated with pencil drawings, and Judith Kerr's drawings for *The Tiger Who Came to Tea* (Figure 6.1) were done in pencil and crayon.

Each of these media produces differing effects, and two or more may be used in combination as well.

Graphic Techniques

Graphic techniques refer to those methods by which the artist creates an image by cutting blocks or etching plates, inking them, and impressing them on a surface such as paper. As with painterly techniques, there are several varieties:

- *Woodblocks* were the very earliest form of reproducible art—dating from the late Middle Ages. The artist draws an image in reverse on a block of wood, then carves away all the areas that are not to be printed. Ink is then spread over the block and paper pressed onto it, resulting in the transfer of the image from block to paper (see Chapter 1, Figures 1.2 and 1.3).

- *Linocuts* are similar to woodblocks, but the artist uses blocks of linoleum rather than wood. (See Marcia Brown's *Dick Whittington's Cat.*)

- *Stone lithography* is a complex process that involves first drawing a design on a smooth, flat stone with a waxy mixture similar to a crayon. As in woodblocks, the image must be done in reverse. The stone is then treated with a chemical fixative, wetted with water, and finally inked. The ink sticks only to the waxed areas, and when paper is pressed onto the stone, an impression is made. (See Robert McCloskey's *Make Way for Ducklings*.)

Photography and Digital Art

Photography may be considered an artistic style as much as a technique. A good photograph requires a sense of composition—or the meaningful arrangement of objects to achieve a desired effect. In picture books, we normally expect something more creative than cell phone snapshots, and when photographs are used to tell stories, it is principally for realistic stories. Photographs are especially effective in informational books. When imaginatively used in black and white or in color, photography can be dramatic, beautiful, and highly expressive.

Since the 1990s, digital art—that is, art generated by a computer—has become more prevalent in children's picture books. One of the first artists to make a name in this field was J. Otto Seibold, beginning with *Mr. Lunch Takes a Plane Ride* (1993) written by Vivian Walsh and, most recently, Seibold's own *Lost Sloth*, a charming work for very young readers, are good examples of his work, which bears a resemblance to cubist abstraction, with its emphasis on geometric shapes. Yet it is not without detail, and the illustrations fit beautifully with the convoluted and comical storyline.

Collage

Collage consists of a combination of materials that are cut, torn, pasted, or otherwise assembled to create an artistic whole. "Collage" comes from the French word *coller*, meaning "to glue." The technique dates back to ancient China, but its modern use is traced to Pablo Picasso and George Braque. Artists may use paper, cloth, wood, plastic—the possibilities are limited only by the imagination. The trick is to combine the various parts into a harmonious whole. In children's books, collage has been successfully used by Ezra Jack Keats (*The Snowy Day*), Leo Lionni (*Frederick*), and Eric Carle (*The Very Hungry Caterpillar*).

Artistic Styles

An artist not only chooses a medium but a style as well. Artistic style refers to the visual characteristics of an illustration. We find a wide variety of sophisticated artistic styles represented in children's picture books. In the best examples, the artistic style fits the mood established by the text. Few illustrators fit neatly into a single artistic style. The best artists develop their own personal styles, drawn from their life experiences, education, individual tastes, and their specific talents. However, recognizing the wide-ranging talents of illustrators of children's books does increase our appreciation and respect for the art of picture-book illustration.

Realism

Realistic or representational art portrays the world with faithful attention to detail. Zelinsky's exquisite illustrations for *Rapunzel* (Color Plate E) are inspired by the realistic art of the Italian Renaissance, which was, in turn, influenced by the realistic art of classical Greece and Rome. The rich colors, the architectural and landscape detail, the elaborate clothing—all attest to the care with which Zelinsky is attempting to re-create the world of fifteenth- and sixteenth-century Italy. And Robert Lawson aims at realism in his depiction of the bee and Ferdinand—or what we can see of him (Figure 6.3).

Cartoon Art

Cartoons consist of exaggerated caricatures, never realistic, that are used for comic or satiric effect—there are no serious cartoons. They possess no subtlety and always exaggerate certain features—such as Mickey Mouse's ears, for example. Cartoon art is very popular in children's books, probably because of its playfulness. Cartoons, by their very nature, lack subtlety. They are simple, straightforward, and often outrageous, making them a frequent choice for illustrating nonsense, comical satire, and political points of view. Dr. Seuss's drawings are cartoons at their most delightful and outrageous: The colors are bold and the lines are distinct, but the features are distorted and any resemblance to reality is avoided. Eric Rohmann's illustrations for *My Friend Rabbit* (see Chapter 5, Figure 5.7) is an example of cartoon art, illustrating the nonsensical adventures of a mouse and rabbit. Always look for the exaggerated figures, the broad humor, and the simplistic color palette in cartoons—don't be too quick to identify any amusing illustration in a children's book as a cartoon. (Do not, for example, confuse Color Plates A and B as cartoons—Potter's illustration is far too realistic and Burningham's colors far too subtle for cartoon art.)

Folk Art

Folk art reflects a specific cultural or social group. It is often decorative, providing ornamentation for everyday utilitarian objects, such as dishes, pottery, furniture, jewelry, fabric, and so on. Because of its cultural associations, it is favored for illustrating folktales. Gerald McDermott's *Anansi the Spider* (see Chapter 8, Figure 8.7), with its geometric designs and bold colors, suggests western African influences. When Barbara Cooney illustrated Donald Hall's *The Ox-Cart Man*, a story set in New England in the early nineteenth century, she imitated the primitive folk art paintings of the period.

Naïve Art

Naïve art is made deliberately to resemble a child's drawings. The figures appear two-dimensional and usually disproportionate (for example, the head might be too big, the arms and legs do not bend, and so on). Judith Kerr's charming illustrations for *The Tiger Who Came to Tea* (Figure 6.1) contain many features of naïve art, which is perfectly suited to this both simple and wildly fanciful tale.

Art Nouveau

Although now rare in children's books, this style was a late-nineteenth-century reaction to the more formal academic art. It is characterized by organic motifs (especially floral designs), fluid lines, and highly stylized forms. Art Nouveau's most famous representative in the book world was Aubrey Beardsley, who was heavily influenced by oriental art, particularly Japanese watercolors. The result is a decorative and sophisticated style, exquisitely realized in the work of the Danish illustrator Kay Nielsen. Contrast Nielsen's stylized work (Color Plate C) with the more realistic art of Paul Zelinsky (Color Plate E).

Expressionism

Expressionism is another product of the twentieth century, with Marc Chagall, Wassily Kandinsky, and Paul Klee being among the most famous expressionists. These artists are not interested in realistic accuracy. They use distorted, misshapen figures, unusual perspectives, and colors that establish mood rather than depict reality. Again, true expressionism is rare in children's picture books, but in Bemelmans's illustrations for *Madeline* (Figure 6.2) we can see that the trees are playfully exaggerated shapes that only suggest trees. John Steptoe in *Daddy Is a Monster . . . Sometimes* exhibits expressionistic qualities, using a special style called *Les Fauves* ("the beasts").

Surrealism

Surrealism is another early-twentieth-century phenomenon—although some examples can be found as far back as the Renaissance in Hieronymus Bosch's disturbing paintings. A surrealist draws with realistic details—sometimes almost photographically realistic—but the subject matter is entirely unrealistic, using jarring juxtapositions that often result in an unsettling, sometimes nightmarish, quality. This style is used frequently by Chris Van Allsburg (see *Jumanji*, Figure 6.4).

Design and Meaning in Picture Books

Anyone who has read to a child from a picture book in which the pictures did not match up with the words on the page will understand how important picture-book design is. This matching up—which is called *juxtaposition*—is just one of many aspects of a successful picture book. Among the features important to the design and meaning of picture books are rhythm and movement, tension, and page layout.

Rhythm and Movement

John Warren Stewig defines *rhythm* as "controlled repetition in art" (76). Good picture-book design creates a sense of rhythm as we move from page to page—a rhythm that is suited to the nature of the narrative. In English and Western culture in general, we read our books, and therefore our pictures, from left to right. Some argue, therefore, that we identify most closely with objects on the left; protagonists often appear on the left and antagonists on the right. For example, Nielsen's illustration from "The Twelve Dancing Princesses" depicts the princess on the left (Color Plate C). In McDermott's illustration from *Anansi the Spider* (Chapter 8, Figure 8.7), the protagonist, the spider Anansi, appears on the left (as he is being devoured by a fish). And Peter Rabbit in Potter's illustration (Color Plate A) is on the left but looking toward the right (and therefore to the next page).

A quick perusal of Paul Zelinsky's illustrations in his *Rumpelstiltskin* reveals that the fiendish title character appears on the right side in 9 of the 11 illustrations in which he appears. But in Van Allsburg's illustration from *Jumanji* (Figure 6.4), the presumed protagonist, the girl in the doorway, is on the right, with the unsettling figures of the monkeys on the left. This reversal of the normal order of things may contribute to the apprehensive, eerie feeling that this illustration evokes—quite suited to the surrealistic story of an innocent game board mysteriously coming to life. Burningham's cat stares out at us from the left (Color Plate B), causing us to look first at its face and then to the rest of its body. Zelinsky's children (Color Plate E) have a similar orientation; they are turned with their backs to the left, and they are looking up to the right. Of course, these are not hard-and-fast rules, but, in general, story movement is from left to right. (We should note that the left-to-right orientation is purely conventional. Israeli picture books are designed to be read from right to left, since Hebrew texts are written in reverse of Western texts—right to left, back to front—and as a result the movement in the pictures is also from right to left.)

This movement also suggests another anomaly in the picture book: the interrupted rhythm that occurs when we read it. The movement is not continually forward; rather, we look at the pictures, then we read, then we look at the pictures again. The pictures create a starting and stopping pattern that the text must accommodate. This is why some picture book texts sound fairly inane when read without the pictures. Effective picture books are usually designed so that a natural pause occurs at the page turns. At the same time, the book should make us want to turn the page (either to be surprised or to have our expectations confirmed).

Tension

Good picture books create what Nodelman refers to as "directed tension"—in which the pictures are often at odds with or reach beyond the words, resulting in our heightened interest and excitement. One excellent example is Kerr's *The Tiger Who Came to Tea* (Figure 6.1), mentioned above.

Another fine example is Pat Hutchins's *Rosie's Walk*. The text of this book contains but one sentence—a string of prepositional phrases—describing Rosie's afternoon excursion "across the yard," "over the haystack," "around the pond," and so on, until she gets back "in time for dinner." But the illustrations show us that, unbeknownst to Rosie, a fox is stalking her, but his attempts to capture her meet with one comical disaster after another, until he is finally besieged by a hoard of bees and hightails it out of the story. The blissfully ignorant Rosie arrives back home in time for dinner. The effect of the book is entirely dependent on the tension between the text and the illustrations. It is this tension that makes us want to turn the page to see how Rosie will escape this time or to see how the fox is thwarted again. Books without such tension, where, for example, the pictures do no more than mimic the words or vice versa, can quickly become boring.

Page Layout

Another element of book design is the placement of the pictures and the text on the page. Here are some things to consider.

PAGE SIZE AND SHAPE ■ Many picture books are wider than they are high, and this makes them especially suited to narrative illustration (see *Tuesday*, Color Plate D). This shape allows for the depiction of landscapes, which are often crucial to storytelling. On the other hand, tall and narrow books tend to focus on character and diminish the setting (see *Madeline*, Figure 6.2 and *Rapunzel*, Color Plate E); a portrait in art is typically taller than it is wide (unless it is a portrait of an elephant). The size of a book also affects us. We often associate very small books and very large books with the youngest readers—small books are easy for little hands to handle and large books are eye catching. Medium sized books, however, are often more complex. The point is, that a book's size and shape are not randomly selected. In the best books, size and shape are appropriate to the subject and theme.

PAGE LAYOUT ■ We have already noted that pictures and text should be properly juxtaposed—that is, the text should correspond with the pictures. This is just common sense. But other considerations include the use of borders, vignettes, and panels. Borders frame the page and can enclose either text or illustrations. Contrast the irregular, almost informal, border Potter uses in Color Plate A with the very formal, clean-edged border used by Neilsen in Color Plate C and Zelinsky in Color Plate E. And notice how Bemelmans's trees in Figure 6.2 actually reach outside the border. In the discussion of *Where the Wild Things Are* below, we will see where borders can actually contribute to the meaning of a book.

A panel refers to the framing of two or more illustrations on the same page, allowing us to see several perspectives all at once. Mo Willems uses this to great effect in *Don't Let the Pigeon Drive the Bus* and others, in which he depicts the pigeon going through a series of moods as argues his case.

A vignette is a small, incidental picture that is integrated into the principal illustration or perhaps placed around the borders. It is often used to supply additional information and sometimes for humor. David Macaulay uses vignettes in his *The New Way Things Work*. This large, nonfiction picture book visually describes how hundreds of machines and devices work—from toasters to computers. On each page, Macaulay places tiny figures of wooly mammoths who wisecrack their way through the book. They add comic relief to a book that might overwhelm some readers.

One important feature in the layout of a picture book is the handling of the gutter, which is simply the crease made by the binding. A good book designer accommodates for this space and does not allow illustrations to get lost in the gutter between the pages. This is especially important when the illustrations are double-page spreads. Ideally the two pages perfectly come together at the gutter.

TYPOGRAPHY ■ Typography refers to the style and size of the lettering and the placement of the words on the page. The typeface can make a statement:

> *Some are elegant.*
>
> Some are casual.
>
> SOME ARE STYLIZED.
>
> Some are funky.

Some books use more than one typeface, often to identify varying speakers, as in Carolivia Herron's *Nappy Hair*. Sometimes we find hand lettering (used by Wanda Gág in *Millions of Cats* and Jean de Brunhoff in *The Story of Babar*). The placement of the text can range from the very formal—the text appearing in the same place on every page—to the very informal—the text moving about from page to page. In some books, the text forms patterns on the page, as in Lloyd Moss's *Zin! Zin! Zin! A Violin*, illustrated by Marjorie Priceman, where the words undulate in waves suggesting the musical sounds produced by various instruments. So the choice of typeface and placement of the text can have an important effect on our response to a picture book.

Picture-Book Layout: Three Examples

A brilliant text or an exquisite artwork will not guarantee a successful picture book, for the text and illustrations have to work together to form a pleasing and meaningful whole. Maurice Sendak's *Where the Wild Things Are* provides a good example of the way in which the layout of pictures and a well-worded text can enrich each other. As the story opens, Max, a rather naughty boy, is causing all manner of havoc about his house. The first pictures are small, with large white borders around them. Max is then sent to his room for his misbehavior. (We never see nor hear his mother, for this is Max's story.) Soon his room is transformed into a forest, and then an ocean tumbles by. Each succeeding picture grows larger and larger on the page, and the border recedes in size until it disappears altogether. Eventually the pictures overlap onto the facing page and finally become two-page spreads.

The accompanying text describes a magical event. Max steps into his private boat and sails to the land where the Wild Things are. There he becomes their king and presides over a "wild rumpus" during which the creatures, led by Max, do whatever they like (the dream of every child?). During the rumpus the pictures completely cover the pages, and there is no text whatsoever, which seems appropriate for this part of the story when Max is thoroughly absorbed in his dream fantasy and is most animal-like. Both language (a symbol of civilization) and the border enclosing the illustrations (perhaps signifying the necessary restraints imposed by civilized life) have vanished. Finally, Max tires of being king of the Wild Things and longs to be "where someone loved him best of all"—children really do want to have rules and order in their lives. So he sails back to the comfort of his bedroom, where he finds his supper waiting for him.

The pictures that depict Max's return (or, more accurately, his waking from a dream) gradually shrink, and the border returns—all suggesting a return to order in Max's life. At the end of the story, Max appears very much like a vulnerable little boy, no longer the wild thing who terrorized the household at the story's beginning. The final words describing his supper—"and it was still hot"—appear on a page without illustration, causing us to focus entirely on their meaning alone. These simple words bring us back to reality and, more importantly, imply unconditional parental love.

Perry Nodelman suggests that words in picture books accomplish three things, and we can find examples of all three in *Where the Wild Things Are*:

● Words express the emotional and narrative content of the pictures. ("The night Max wore his wolf suit and made mischief of one kind and another, his mother called him 'wild thing' . . . and he was sent to bed without eating anything.")

- Words express cause-and-effect relationships, either within parts of a single picture or within a series of pictures—for example, the words can indicate the passage of time between two pictures. ("That very night in Max's room a forest grew and grew . . . .")

- Words express what is important and what is not. (". . . he found his supper waiting for him—and it was still hot.") (Nodelman 215)

So we see that a successful picture book is a true collaboration of words and pictures as reflected in the overall design of the book.

Another inventive use of picture-book layout is found in John Burningham's *Come Away from the Water, Shirley.* This book portrays a day at the beach for the imaginative Shirley and her humdrum parents (and don't most children think their parents are humdrum?). The layout comprises a series of facing pages, with the left side depicting the dull routine of the parents and the right side depicting the imaginative world of Shirley at play. (Again, notice the left-to-right orientation; reversing this pattern would destroy the emphasis on Shirley's imaginative and completely subvert the story's purpose.) The parents' world is drawn in sparse colors on a large white background; the naïve style seems deliberately uninteresting. In contrast, Shirley's world is portrayed in rich colors suited to her lively imagination as she creates adventures on the beach (being captured by pirates, walking the plank, heroically escaping, and finding a buried treasure). Here the style is a form of expressionism—lively, vivid, with dramatic distortions. Our eyes, moving left to right, first see the dull adult world and then behold the wondrous world of childhood. The illustrations, then, create an irony in that the parents are illustrated with childlike drawings, and the child is illustrated with a sophisticated artistic style. (See Chapter 9 for a discussion of irony.) The text consists entirely of the mother's words, which are either admonitions to Shirley (which Shirley ignores) or empty promises. The contrasting illustrations and the incongruous text make for subtle ironies that will not be lost on many children.

David Wiesner's *The Three Pigs* is an inventive takeoff on the traditional folktale. The story opens very much like the familiar tale, until the pigs are unexpectedly blown out of their own story (by the wolf's huffing and puffing) and they find themselves as characters in search of a story, wandering in and out of other storybooks. Wiesner uses a variety of artistic styles throughout the book, indicating the various kinds of stories the pigs find—a cartoonish nursery rhyme, a romantic tale of a knight and a dragon, and so on. Not only do the artistic styles change between the various stories, so do the typefaces, each chosen to suit the specific tale. The wildly imaginative and comical story is a refreshing twist on a familiar folktale, and at the same time Wiesner invites us to explore the meaning of fiction and reality.

Of course, we do not always find such powerful symbolism in a book's layout. But books like these demonstrate the possibilities that lie in the picture book format, and they remind us of the importance of elements such as the style, size, and placement of illustrations. Words and pictures work together in a good picture book, and the resulting sum is something far greater and more rewarding than the individual parts.

Graphic Novels

Comic books have been around for decades, but in the past 20 years a new phenomenon has arisen—the graphic novel, which is a novel in comic-book format. The graphic novel is aimed at a somewhat older audience than most picture books, for these are books children read themselves. The texts are often lengthy and the stories complex. However, as in the picture book, the illustrations and the text of a graphic novel are equally important. In Japan, people of all ages read comics called manga, and although manga technically refers to comics of Japanese origin, the term is being rapidly adapted to any book-length work in graphic or comic book format. (The term *comic* is highly problematic since many of these works are not at all humorous, but at least it is a term everyone understands.) The comic-book format places illustrations in frames, with captions or dialogue bubbles, and in sequence. The sequencing conveys a specific meaning—it can suggest the passage of time or a shift of scenes, it can create suspense or shift the reader's attention, and so on.

Proponents of the graphic novel argue that it creates a bridge between the visual media (the media in which most young people are immersed) and the written media. The graphic novel can work very well with struggling readers—in much the same way that texts with pictures help students of a foreign language. Consequently, it can be argued that the graphic novel, rather than a distraction, is actually an enticement to reading. It is also argued that these works, in addition to developing visual literacy and getting young people to read, introduce such serious issues as philosophy, history, science, and ethics.

Certainly reading graphic novels is more intellectually demanding than watching television or texting messages to one's friends and relatives. And young people engrossed in graphic novels may be preferable to young people mesmerized by computer games or whiling away the hours on cell phones. Entire books have been written on the art of the graphic novel (see McCloud's *Understanding Comics* and *Reinventing Comics*). There is even an argument for the use of graphic novels in the classroom (see Yang, "Graphic Novels in the Classroom"). And in 2007, a graphic novel, Gene Luen Yang's *American Born Chinese*, was awarded the prestigious Michael Printz Award for distinguished young adult literature. And in 2008, Brian Selznick won the Caldecott Medal for *The Invention of Hugo Cabret*, which, at over 500 pages, contains many characteristics of the graphic novel.

Summary

Picture books, once thought of as objects of innocent amusement for toddlers, have metamorphosed into complex and sophisticated works of art that can be enjoyed by people of any age. The modern-day picture book represents a collaboration of both storytelling and visual art. It is a work in which the text and the illustrations share equally in the reading experience. This makes the picture book different from the illustrated book, in which the pictures merely decorate or elaborate on the text.

The text of the picture storybook is generally simple—but not simplistic. A good picture book contains an engaging plot and characters, it uses language that is both clear and evocative, and it is entertaining and, perhaps, thought provoking. Accompanying the text are illustrations, which are examples of narrative art. That is, the illustrations must tell a story—usually, but not always, the same story revealed by the text. And the illustrations contain the same elements we expect to find in any pictorial art—effective use of line, shape, space, texture, composition, and perspective.

The artistic medium—that is, oil, watercolor, pencil, woodblock prints, collage, photography, or digital graphics—is a choice the artist needs to make, as is the artistic style. The styles include everything from realism to expressionism, from naïve art to surrealism. Today's children can learn much about art simply by reading the many exquisite picture books available to them.

Picture books, to be successful, depend on careful design, and that design must somehow reflect the story's meaning. We look for rhythm and movement in the pictures, as well as tension in the book's layout, to add interest. Page layout is also important, for it determines such things as the size and shape of pages, the placement of text and pictures, the typography, and so on. Borders, panels, and vignettes are also at the artist's disposal when designing pages.

In recent years, the graphic novel has emerged as a popular form of children's and young adult literature. This hybrid of the comic book bridges the two worlds of visual media and literature. As such, many believe it can be an effective means of encouraging reading in a society that at times seems besotted by electronic imagery. The field of picture-book art is dynamic and invigorating. As adults, one of our most enjoyable obligations is to make sure children are acquainted with the rich spectrum of the modern picture book.

For Reflection and Discussion

1. Read a number of children's picture books on a specific topic or theme—friendship, siblings, grandparents, first day of school, pets, and so on. Determine which are the most effective and why.

2. Read at least five or six books illustrated by the same artist. Find some biographical information on the artist (try *Something About the Author* or *The Dictionary of Literary Biography* or *The Oxford Encyclopedia of Children's Literature* or other similar resources). What were the artist's specific artistic influences? What artistic features seem to set this artist apart from others? What particularly about this artist's work appeals to you?

3. Choose any good picture book (you might start with the lists below) and carefully examine the book's layout and design. Try to explain the decisions made by the illustrator and how they affect your response to the book. What especially makes this an effective picture book? Support your argument with specific examples.

4. Choose any good picture book (again, look at the lists below for starters) and consider how the illustrations add to and enrich the story. Do the illustrations affect our interpretation of the story? How?

5. Choose any graphic novel and read it. If you are already a fan of the graphic novel, explain what you look for in a good one. If this is your first experience, what is your response to the format? Try to find specific examples to support your responses.

Works Cited

Nodelman, Perry. *Words about Pictures: The Narrative Art of Children's Picture Books*. Athens: University of Georgia Press, 1988.

Stewig, John Warren. *Looking at Picture Books*. Fort Atkinson, WI: Highsmith Press, 1995.

Recommended Resources

Alderson, Brian. *Looking at Picture Books,* 1973. New York: Children's Book Council, 1974.

Bader, Barbara. *American Picturebooks from Noah's Ark to the Beast Within*. New York: Macmillan, 1976.

Barrett, Terry, and Kenneth Marantz. "Photographs as Illustrations." *The New Advocate* 17 (Fall 1989): 103–153.

Benedict, Susan, and Leonore Carlisle, eds. *Beyond Words: Picture Books for Older Readers and Writers*. Portsmouth, NH: Heinemann, 1992.

Cianciolo, Patricia. *Picture Books for Children*, 4th ed. Chicago: American Library Association, 1997.

Cummins, Julie, ed. *Children's Book Illustration and Design*. Glen Cove, NY: PBC International, 1992.

Dooley, Patricia. "The Window in the Book: Conventions in the Illustrations of Children's Books." *Wilson Library Bulletin* (October 1980): 108–112.

Gombrich, E. H. *The Image and the Eye: Further Studies in the Psychology of Pictorial Representation*. Ithaca, NY: Cornell University Press, 1982.

Kiefer, Barbara Z. *The Potential of Picturebooks: From Visual Literacy to Aesthetic Understanding*. Englewood Cliffs, NJ: Prentice Hall, 1995.

Lacy, L. E. *Art and Design in Children's Books: An Analysis of Caldecott Award Winning Illustrations*. Chicago: American Library Association, 1986.

Matulka, Denise I. *A Picture Book Primer*. Santa Barbara, CA: Libraries Unlimited, 2008.

McCloud, Scott. *Reinventing Comics: How Imagination and Technology Are Revolutionizing an Art Form*. New York: Harper, 2000.

——. *Understanding Comics: The Invisible Art*. New York: Harper, 1994.

Nikolajeva, Maria, and Carol Scott. *How Picture Books Work*. New York: Garland, 2000.

op de Beeck, Nathalie. *Suspended Animation: Children's Picture Books and the Fairy Tale of Modernity*. Minneapolis: University of Minnesota Press, 2010.

Roxburgh, Stephen. "A Picture Equals How Many Words? Narrative Theory and Picture Books for Children." *The Lion and the Unicorn* 7/8 (1983/84): 20–33.

Salisbury, Martin, and Morag Styles. *Children's Picture Books: The Art of Visual Storytelling*. London: Laurence King, 2012.

Shulevitz, Uri. *Writing with Pictures: How to Write and Illustrate Children's Books*. New York: Watson-Guptin, 1985.

Spitz, Ellen Handler. *Inside Picture Books*. New Haven, CT: Yale University Press, 1999.

Yang, Gene. "Graphic Novels in the Classroom." *Language Arts* 85, 3 (January 2008): 185–192.

Picture Storybooks: A Selected and Annotated Booklist

This is a list of some of the best children's picture storybooks, including timeless classics and more recent publications. The books are for a variety of age ranges, from toddler through about second grade. Also, look for other books by these illustrators and supplement this list with those at the end of Chapters 5, 8, and 12 and with the Caldecott and Greenaway Award books, listed in the Appendix.

*Denotes a book with a multicultural emphasis.

#Denotes a book dealing with sociological and/or psychological themes.

Allard, Harry, and James Marshall. *Miss Nelson Is Missing*. Illus. James Marshall. Boston: Houghton Mifflin, 1977.
- A comical tale of a clever, crafty schoolteacher and her students, with wild cartoon illustrations.

Allen, Jeffrey. *Mary Alice, Operator Number 9*. Illus. James Marshall. Boston: Little, Brown, 1975.
- A story of a community of talking animals that has trouble replacing a telephone operator. A great read-aloud.

Ardizzone, Edward. *Little Tim and the Brave Sea Captain*. 1936. New York: Penguin, 1983.
- A long-time favorite for older readers, featuring Ardizzone's lively sketches.

Bang, Molly. *When Sophie Gets Angry—Really, Really Angry . . .* New York: Greenwillow, 2004.
- A story of a young girl who experiences the emotional roller coaster of anger and eventually comes to terms with her feelings.

Bemelmans, Ludwig. *Madeline*. New York: Viking, 1937.
- A classic about an irrepressible girl in a Paris convent school, the first of a popular series.

Brett, Jan. *The Mitten*. New York: Putnam, 1989.
- A retelling of a familiar cumulative tale in which a succession of animals seek shelter in a lost mitten.

Brooke, L. Leslie. *Johnny Crow's Garden*. 1903. London: Warne, 1978.
- A longtime-favorite rhyming book in which talking animals frolic in Johnny Crow's garden.

#Brown, Margaret Wise. *The Dead Bird*. Illus. Remy Charlip. New York: HarperCollins, 2005.
- A touching story of children who find a dead bird and what they do.

——. *Goodnight Moon*. Illus. Clement Hurd. New York: Harper, 1947.
- A classic bedtime story about a bunny who doesn't want to go to sleep.

——. *The Runaway Bunny*. Illus. Clement Hurd. New York: Harper, 1942.
- A story of a bunny who comes up with inventive ideas to run away from home.

Browne, Anthony. *Voices in the Park*. New York: DK Ink, 1998.
- An outing in the park depicted from varying points of view. An unusual and complex picture book.

Bruel, Nick. *Bad Kitty*. New York: Roaring Brook Press, 2003.
- The first of several books featuring an irascible cat entangled in many misadventures. These books are hilarious.

#Bryan, Jennifer. *The Different Dragon*. Illus. Danamarie Hosler. Ridley Park, PA: Two Lives, 2006.
- A touching story about a boy living with his lesbian mothers.

Burningham, John. *Come Away from the Water, Shirley*. New York: Harper, 1977.
- A clever story about a day at the beach that juxtaposes the child's imagination and her parents' dull reality.

Burton, Virginia L. *The Little House*. Boston: Houghton Mifflin, 1942.
- A classic tale portraying the effects of the passage of time on a quaint house, which is the main character.

Carle, Eric. *The Very Hungry Caterpillar.* New York: Philomel, 1986.
- A perennial favorite among very young children as they watch a caterpillar turn into a butterfly.

*Clifton, Lucille. *Some of the Days of Everett Anderson.* Illus. Evaline Ness. New York: Holt, 1970.
- A small African American boy celebrates his life in the city; the first of a series about Everett Anderson.

#Cochran, Bill. *The Forever Dog.* Illus. Dan Andreasen. New York: HarperCollins, 2007.
- A sensitive and realistic treatment of the loss of a pet and, by extension, of death in general.

Cooney, Barbara. *Miss Rumphius.* New York: Viking, 1982.
- A beautifully illustrated book about the productive life of a New England woman.

Cronin, Doreen. *Click, Clack, Moo: Cows That Type.* Illus. Betsey Lewin. New York: Spotlight, 2006.
- A very funny story about some clever cows and a farmer.

——. *Diary of a Spider.* Illus. Harry Bliss. New York: HarperCollins, 2003.
- The title says it all—except that it is a very funny diary.

deBrunhoff, Jean. *The Story of Babar, the Little Elephant.* 1933. Several modern editions.
- A long-time-favorite tale about the adventures of an elephant.

#Demas, Corinne. *Saying Goodbye to Lulu.* Illus. Ard Hoyt. New York: Little, Brown, 2009.
- A first-person narrative of a young girl who must accept the death of her beloved dog.

#dePaolo, Tomie. *Nana Upstairs, Nana Downstairs.* New York: Putnam, 1973.
- A story featuring a boy's relationship with his grandmother and great-grandmother, and how he deals with their eventual deaths.

deRegniers, Beatrice Schenk. *May I Bring a Friend?* Illus. Beni Montressor. New York: Atheneum, 1964.
- A story of a young boy befriended by a king and queen. A wonderful rhyming tale with striking illustrations.

Duvoisin, Roger. *Petunia.* New York: Knopf, 1950.
- A modern fable about a silly goose who misunderstands the importance of books.

Emberley, Barbara. *Drummer Hoff.* Illus. Ed Emberley. New York: Prentice Hall, 1967.
- A cumulative tale with a Revolutionary War setting and striking woodcuts.

#Erlbruch, Wolf. *Duck, Death and the Tulip.* Minneapolis, MN: Lerner Publishing for Gecko Press, 2011. (First published in Germany, 2007.)
- A starkly simply but profoundly moving allegory about death.

Ets, Marie Hall. *Play with Me.* New York: Penguin, 1955.
- For very young children, a quiet tale of a little girl's wondrous adventure in nature.

#Falconer, Ian. *Olivia.* New York: Simon & Schuster, 2000.
- The first of many books about the irrepressible little pig Olivia, a modern-day feminist heroine.

*Feelings, Tom. *The Middle Passage: White Ships/Black Cargo.* New York: Dial, 1995.
- Powerful illustrations depict the horrific journey of the slaves from Africa to America.

Freeman, Don. *Corduroy.* New York: Viking, 1968.
- A long-time favorite about a teddy bear who wants a home.

Gág, Wanda. *Millions of Cats.* New York: Coward-McCann, 1928.
- Usually considered the first true American picture book, with charming black-and-white illustrations and a memorable refrain.

#Gallaz, Christophe. *Rose Blanche.* Illus. Roberto Innocenti. Mankato, MN: Creative Education, 1985.
- A picture book of the Holocaust, as seen through the eyes of a young German girl.

Geisert, Arthur. *Hogwash.* Boston: Houghton Mifflin, 2008.
- An intricately detailed wordless picture book about the pigs needing a bath.

Gerstein, Mordecai. *The Man Who Walked between the Towers.* New York: Roaring Brook, 2003.
- An account of an actual daredevil feat by an aerial artist in New York City in 1974.

Gramatky, Hardie. *Little Toot*. New York: Putnam, 1939.
- A classic story of an animated tugboat who comes to the rescue.

Gravett, Emily. *Dogs*. New York: Simon & Schuster, 2010.
- A book filled with enticing pictures of dogs of every shape and size.

——. *The Rabbit Problem*. New York: Simon & Schuster, 2010.
- A clever and lively book about a growing family of rabbits engaging in math.

Hall, Donald. *The Ox-Cart Man*. Illus. Barbara Cooney. New York: Penguin, 1983.
- Sensitive folk-art illustrations and a soothing poetic text relate this simple tale of New England in early nineteenth century.

Henkes, Kevin. *Kitten's First Full Moon*. New York: Scholastic, 2004.
- A story of a kitten who thinks the moon is a bowl of milk.

*Herron, Carolivia. *Nappy Hair*. Illus. Joe Cepeda. New York: Knopf, 1997.
- The joyful celebration of a young African American girl's hair.

Hutchins, Pat. *Rosie's Walk*. New York: Simon & Schuster, 1968,
- In this book of colorful, stylized illustrations, Rosie the hen takes a walk through the barnyard and never realizes the imminent danger lurking there.

Johnson, Crockett. *Harold and the Purple Crayon*. 1962. New York: Harper, 2012.
- A classic tribute to a child's imagination where Harold creates his own world with his purple crayon.

Joyce, William. *Rolie Polie Olie*. New York: Scholastic, 2001.
- Adventures on a planet inhabited by friendly robots.

Juster, Norton. *The Hello, Goodbye Window*. Illus. Chris Raschka. New York: Hyperion, 2005.
- A story in which a little girl describes her magical relationship with her grandparents.

*Keats, Ezra Jack. *The Snowy Day*. New York: Viking, 1962.
- A landmark book by a talented author/ illustrator in which a little African American boy has adventures in the snow.

Kerr, Judith. *The Tiger Who Came to Tea*. 1968. Somerville, MA: Candlewick, 2009.
- A simple tale about an unexpected guest; a favorite for nearly 50 years.

Kitamura, Satoshi. *Lily Takes a Walk*. New York: Dutton, 1987.
- A story of a little girl taking a walk with her dog, who has an overactive imagination.

Klassen, Jon. *This Is Not My Hat*. New York: Candlewick, 2012.
- A story of a brazen fish stealing a hat, but not without dire consequences.

Kraus, Robert. *Leo the Late Bloomer*. Illus. Jose and Ariane Aruego. New York: Simon & Schuster, 1987.
- The popular story of a young tiger who can't seem to do anything.

Krauss, Ruth. *The Backward Day*. Illus. Marc Simont. New York: Harper, 1950.
- The story of a boy who decides to do everything backward.

——. *The Carrot Seed*. Illus. Crockett Johnson. New York: Harper, 1945.
- A beautifully simple tale of a boy who plants and nurtures a seed with ultimate success; still popular after 60 years.

Langstaff, John M. *A Frog Went A-Courtin'*. Illus. Feodor Rojankovsky. New York: Harcourt, 1955.
- Award-winning illustrations and a favorite folk rhyme.

Leaf, Munro. *The Story of Ferdinand*. Illus. Robert Lawson. New York: Viking, 1936.
- Lovely black-and-white illustrations in the story of a gentle bull in Spain.

Lionni, Leo. *Frederick*. New York: Knopf, 1967.
- A story of a mouse who spends his days in contemplation while the others work—and then he repays them; one of many books by a popular author/illustrator.

——. *Inch by Inch*. New York: Knopf, 1967.
- The story of an inchworm who enjoys measuring everything, until he is asked to measure a song.

Liwska, Renata. *Little Panda*. New York: Houghton, 2008.
- A reassuring story told by a grandfather panda to his grandson.

Lobel, Arnold. *Fables*. New York: HarperCollins, 1980.
- Original fables in the spirit of Aesop.

Marshall, James. *George and Martha*. New York: Scholastic, 1972.
- A story of lovable anthropomorphic hippos with Marshall's characteristic cartoon illustrations.

Martin, Bill. *Brown Bear, Brown Bear, What Do You See?* Illus. Eric Carle. New York: Holt, 1967.
- Perfect for the very young in its combination of rhyme, rhythm, and repetition and the introduction to colors and animals.

McCloskey, Robert. *Blueberries for Sal*. New York: Viking, 1948.
- The story of a mix-up that occurs when a mother and her daughter and a bear and her cub go blueberry picking.

——. *Make Way for Ducklings*. New York: Viking, 1944.
- A classic tale of a family of mallard ducks in Boston.

*Muth, Jon. *Zen Shorts*. New York: Scholastic, 2005.
- A beautiful and thought-provoking book in which a magical panda shares Buddhist stories with three children.

Peet, Bill. *Encore for Eleanor*. Boston: Houghton Mifflin, 1985.
- One of many books by a great illustrator/storyteller—this one about an elephant who doesn't want to retire.

Pinkney, Jerry. *The Lion & the Mouse*. New York: Little, 2009.
- A familiar fable dramatically illustrated.

*Politi, Leo. *Pedro, the Angel of Olivera Street*. New York: Scribner, 1947.
- One of the earliest picture books featuring Latinos.

Portis, Antoinette. *Not a Box*. New York: HarperCollins, 2006.
- A charmingly simple book that explores the imaginative possibilities of a cardboard box.

Potter, Beatrix. *The Tale of Peter Rabbit*. London: Warne, 1901.
- The first of several talking animal tales by a celebrated illustrator.

Provensen, Alice, and Martin Provensen. *The Glorious Flight: Across the Channel with Louis Bleriot*. New York: Viking, 1983.
- A story based on a historical event, with striking full-color illustrations.

Raffi. *Baby Beluga*. New York: Crown, 1992.
- The story of a baby beluga whale discovering his independence.

Raschka, Chris. *A Ball for Daisy*. New York: Schwartz & Wade, 2011.
- A charming wordless picture book with lively drawings about a dog losing her favorite toy.

Rey, A. H. *Curious George*. Boston: Houghton Mifflin, 1973.
- The first of a popular series about an inquisitive monkey.

Rohmann, Eric. *My Friend Rabbit*. New York: Roaring Brook, 2002.
- An almost wordless picture book about a well-meaning, but hapless, rabbit.

Rosenthal, Amy Krouse. *Spoon*. Illus. Scott Magoon. New York: Hyperion, 2009.
- A clever and warmly humorous story about a little spoon examining his existence; see also Krouse and Magoon's *Chopsticks*.

#Rylant, Cynthia. *Dog Heaven*. New York: Blue Sky Press, 1995.
- Speculation on a dog's afterlife that is intended for grieving pet owners.

——. *When I Was Young in the Mountains*. Illus. Diane Goode. New York: Dutton, 1982.
- A book of recollections of childhood with sensitive illustrations.

*Say, Allen. *Grandfather's Journey.* New York: Houghton Mifflin, 1993.
- The story of a Japanese immigrant to America pulled between two cultures.

Seibold, J. Otto, and Vivian Walsh. *Mr. Lunch Takes a Plane Ride.* Illus. J. Otto Seibold, New York: Viking, 1993.
- A book in a series of favorites about a talking dog who engages in zany adventures.

Selznick, Brian. *The Invention of Hugo Cabret.* New York: Scholastic, 2007.
- More graphic novel than picture book, a fascinating quasi-mystery set in 1930s Paris.

Sendak, Maurice. *Where the Wild Things Are.* New York: Harper, 1963.
- An irascible boy's dream adventure—a modern classic. Not to be missed are the companion books, *In the Night Kitchen* and *Outside over There.*

Seuss, Dr. *And to Think That I Saw It on Mulberry Street.* New York: Vanguard, 1973.
- The first of many books by the wildly popular children's author/illustrator.

Simont, Marc. *The Stray Dog.* New York: HarperCollins, 2003.
- The story of a stray dog finding a home, charmingly illustrated.

Smith, Lane. *Grandpa Green.* New York: Roaring Brook, 2011.
- A boy's memories of his great-grandfather, told in a walk through his garden.

Steig, William. *Sylvester and the Magic Pebble.* New York: Windmill, 1969.
- The story of a little donkey who finds a magic pebble—and the trouble that ensues.

#Steptoe, John. *My Daddy Is a Monster . . . Sometimes.* New York: Viking, 1980.
- Unusual illustrations capture a father's changing moods.

Stewart, Sarah. *The Gardener.* Illus. David Small. New York: Farrar, Straus & Giroux, 1997.
- The story of a girl during the Depression creating a rooftop garden to cheer up her cantankerous uncle.

Swanson, Susan. *The House in the Night.* Illus. Beth Krommes. New York: Houghton Mifflin, 2009.
- A bedtime story in the form of a cumulative tale with stunning scratchboard illustrations.

Van Allsburg, Chris. *The Polar Express.* Boston: Houghton Mifflin, 1985.
- A classic Christmas story by a talented author/illustrator.

#Viorst, Judith. *The Tenth Good Thing about Barney.* Illus. Erik Blegvad. New York: Aladdin, 1987.
- A story in which children deal with the loss of a pet.

Waber, Bernard. *The House on East 88th Street.* Boston: Houghton Mifflin, 1962.
- An old favorite about a crocodile who makes his home with a human family. Its equally popular sequel is *Lyle, Lyle Crocodile.*

Wells, Rosemary. *Noisy Nora.* New York: Dial, 1973.
- A charming story about a disgruntled and neglected middle child in a mouse family.

Wiesner, David. *Flotsam.* New York: Clarion, 2006.
- The story of a boy fascinated with science who makes an unexpected discovery while exploring the beach.

——. *Tuesday.* New York: Clarion, 1991.
- A magical tale of a night when frogs float through the air on lily pads.

Willard, Nancy. *A Visit to William Blake's Inn.* Illus. Alice and Martin Provensen. New York: Perfection Learning, 1982.
- A collection of poems describing the guests coming to an inn, inspired by the work of the eighteenth-century poet William Blake. A Newbery Medal winner and a Caldecott Honor book, the first book to be honored in both categories.

Willems, Mo. *Don't Let the Pigeon Drive the Bus!* New York: Hyperion, 2003.
- The first of a series of books about the adventures of an irrepressible pigeon, including *The Pigeon Finds a Hot Dog* and *The Pigeon Wants a Puppy.*

——. *Knuffle Bunny: A Cautionary Tale*. New York: Hyperion, 2004.
- The first of a very funny series about a young girl's attachment to her stuffed bunny.

#Willhoite, Michael. *Daddy's Roommate*. Boston: Alyson, 1990.
- A young boy's description of the time spent with his gay father.

Williams, Vera B. *A Chair for My Mother*. New York: Greenwillow, 1982.
- A touching story for very young readers about a family that works together through hard times.

Yolen, Jane. *Owl Moon*. Illus. John Schoenherr. New York: Philomel, 1987.
- The story of a little girl and her father spending a magical winter evening looking for owls.

Yorinks, Arthur. *Hey, Al*. New York: Farrar, Straus & Giroux, 1986.
- A no-place-like-home tale of a poor janitor and his dog magically transported to a paradise.

Young, Ed. *Hook*. New York: Roaring Brook Press, 2009.
- A story of chickens hatching an eagle egg and then helping the eaglet to find his true home.

Zelinsky, Paul O. *Rapunzel*. New York: Dutton, 1997.
- A traditional retelling with stunning illustrations. One of several folktales Zelinsky has illustrated.

Zion, Gene. *Harry, the Dirty Dog*. Illus. Margaret Bloy Graham. New York: Harper, 1956.
- The hilarious tale of a dog who will do anything to avoid taking a bath—with very funny cartoon illustrations; the first of several books about Harry.

Zolotow, Charlotte. *Mr. Rabbit and the Lovely Present*. Illus. Maurice Sendak. New York: Harper, 1962.
- A quiet book about a little girl seeking a rabbit's advice on gifts.

7 Poetry

For the Love of Language

Introduction

From the soothing sounds of "Rock-a-bye baby" to the playful tunes of "Here we go 'round the mulberry bush" to the delightful nonsense of "Peter Piper picked a peck of pickled peppers," most young children have an instinct for poetry. It appeals to their fascination with language—its sound, its rhythm, its patterns, and ultimately its meaning.

In Chapter 5 we looked at Mother Goose rhymes, which are usually a child's first introduction to poetry. Sadly, we don't always nurture this early fascination with language as we should. Words become simply a means of communicating facts and ideas, and many young people forget the pleasure they had in the sheer sound and magic of language. In fact, rather too often the mention of poetry among teenagers evokes rolling eyes, groans, or worse. This is unfortunate, for poetry remains one of the most beautiful, powerful, and memorable ways to communicate human feelings. In this chapter we will look at the inner workings of poetry, the various kinds of poetry, and ways of bringing poetry alive for children.

Definition of Poetry

The poet Samuel Taylor Coleridge defined poetry as "the best words in their best order"; his good friend, the poet William Wordsworth, called it "the spontaneous overflow of powerful feelings." And Robert Frost described a poem as "where an emotion has found its thought and the thought has found the words." These definitions suggest poetry's elusive quality, but most agree that it has to do with the sound of language and the way language is used to express thought and feeling.

We discovered when we looked at Mother Goose rhymes that some poetry really doesn't make sense—but the rhymes, rhythm, and sounds make it fun. The same goes for much of nonsense verse, which we will discuss below. But if poetry consisted of nothing more than rhyme, rhythm, and clever sounds, we would tire of it quickly. The beauty of the best poetry is that it not only sounds good but its words move us and show us fresh ways of expressing ideas and of thinking about things. They create word pictures or images that make us feel joyful or sad or contemplative or inspired.

What follows is a brief discussion of the principal features of poetry—its sounds and the word pictures it creates—and how these all contribute to a poem's meaning and audience appeal.

Sounds in Poetry

As we have seen, a child's first introduction to poetry is through the sound of its language—specifically its rhyme and its rhythm.

Rhyme

Rhyme is, simply put, the repetition of similar sounds in a word, line, or stanza. End-rhyme is perhaps the most widely recognized rhyme in poetry; it occurs when the last words of two or more lines repeat the same sounds. Too often, end-rhyme devolves into trite and unimaginative rhymes, as in that old jingle,

> Roses are red, violets are blue,
> Sugar is sweet, and so are you.

And these quickly devolve into parodies:

> Roses are red, violets are blue,
> Your feet stink, and so do you.

But end-rhyme is often most enjoyable when it is unexpected, as in this example from Henry Wadsworth Longfellow:

> There was a little girl
> Who had a little curl
> Right in the middle of her forehead.
> When she was good
> She was very, very good,
> But when she was bad she was horrid.

In fact, English is not the easiest language in which to make end-rhymes. The popular rapper Eminem, setting out to disprove experts who claim that English has no rhyme for "orange," came up with this: "I put my or-ange four-inch door hinge in stor-age and ate por-ridge with Ge-orge" ("Eminem Finds Five Words"). Of course, he could have included "Blorenge," the name of a hill in Wales. And what about "purple"? Well, it rhymes with "curple" (a donkey's hind legs) and "hirple" (which means to limp)—at least according to one source (see Held). The problem is obvious: English end-rhymes can sometimes be hard to come by.

But repeated sounds don't always occur at the end of a line—or even at the end of a word. For example, we can repeat the initial sound of a word. We call this *alliteration*—as in "Billy Button bought a buttered biscuit" or "The thistle sifter sifted seven thick thistles."(Say that 10 times fast.) But as with most other things, alliteration is best in moderation, as in these lines from Alfred, Lord Tennyson's "The Eagle":

> He clasps the crag with crooked hands;
> Close to the sea in lonely lands,
> Ring'd with the azure world, he stands.
> The wrinkled sea beneath him crawls;
> He watches from his mountain walls,
> And like a thunderbolt he falls.

Notice how Tennyson sprinkles the consonant sounds *l*, and *w*, and hard *c* throughout the poem—at the beginning, the end, and in the middle of words. (This repetition of consonant sounds is called *consonance*.) Also, in the first stanza, Tennyson repeats certain vowel sounds as well, such as the short *a* in *clasps, crag, hands, azure,* and *stands*. (The repetition of vowel sounds is called *assonance*.) Notice, too, that all these repeated sounds are close enough to make the repetition effective but not so close as to make it annoying. Tennyson's use of sound is not accidental. The poet chose these words deliberately for their musical effect.

And listen to these lines from Robert Louis Stevenson's "The Moon." The poet makes use of alliteration, consonance, and assonance throughout the poem:

> The moon has a face like the clock in the hall;
> She shines on thieves on the garden wall,
> On streets and fields and harbor quays,
> And birdies asleep in the forks of the trees.

See how many examples of sound repetition you can find. (Remember that *quays* is pronounced as if it were spelled *keys*.) As adults, we sometimes overlook the sounds of language and concentrate only on the meaning. Fortunately, children are not so narrow, and they love to play with the sounds of language, and poetry lets them enjoy those sounds.

Rhythm

Just as important as rhyme is rhythm, the pattern created by the beats we find in spoken English. In English, we stress some syllables more than others. When these beats are placed into a regular pattern, we have rhythm. Read these lines of Shakespeare's:

> **Mer**rily, **mer**rily, **shall** I live **now**
> **Un**der the **blos**som that **hangs** on the **bough**

Do you hear the beat on the boldfaced syllables? We would mark it this way:

$$/ \sim \sim / \sim \sim / \sim \sim /$$

Each hash mark (/) indicates a strong beat. The rhythm results when we have a regular repetition of strong beats (or stressed syllables) accompanied by unstressed syllables. These combinations form patterns called meters. Very simply, there are four common meters, each having either two or three syllables. Listen for the patterns in the way we pronounce the following feminine names, each one representing a different meter:

> **Már**-y (a stressed syllable followed by an unstressed syllable—called a *trochee*)
>
> Ma-**ríe** (an unstressed syllable followed by a stressed syllable—called an *iamb*)
>
> **Már**-i-an (a stressed syllable followed by two unstressed syllables—called a *dactyl*)
>
> Mar-y-**ánne** (two unstressed syllables followed by a stressed one—called an *anapest*)

Experiment with your own name—can you determine which syllables should be stressed? Sometimes this takes practice. The trick is to speak the words naturally and not put an emphasis where there isn't one.

Few poems maintain a consistent rhythm throughout—for that would be terrifically monotonous, as in this:

> Máry hád a líttle lámb
> Its fléece was whíte as snów,
> And év'rywhére that Máry wént
> The lámb was súre to gó.

Every other syllable is stressed without fail, which contributes to the rather tedious sing-song quality of the verse. Most readers prefer poetry with a less insistent rhythm, as in these closing lines of Edward Lear's "The Owl and the Pussy Cat," describing the pair's wedding feast:

> They dined on mince and slices of quince,
> Which they ate with a runcible spoon;
> And hand in hand, on the edge of the sand,
> They danced by the light of the moon,
> The moon.
> The moon,
> They danced by the light of the moon.

Try marking the stressed syllables and notice the changes in rhythm from line to line. One reason certain poems are more enjoyable to read than others is that the rhythm is more pleasing.

Pictures in Poetry

A good poem creates pictures (or images) in our minds and makes us see something in a new way. If the images are not new and fresh, then the poem seems trite and dull (like "Roses are red, violets are blue"). Good poets try to awaken our senses—all of our senses—by describing things we can see, hear, taste, feel, or smell. The poet does this in one of two ways.

First, the poet can simply describe something in sensory terms—sight, sound, smell, touch, and taste. A rose, for example, may look red, feel smooth, smell sweet—I don't think we want to taste it. Second, the poet can compare one thing to something else using similes, metaphors, or personification ("it was light as a feather," "raining cats and dogs," "the angry sea"). We will look a little closer at each of these.

Sensory Description

SIGHT ▪ Poets use specific visual details to give us a picture and a feeling, as in John Clare's "Autumn":

> I love to see the cottage smoke
> Curl upward through the naked trees;
> The pigeons nestled round the cote
> On dull November days like these.

SOUND ▪ In these lines from "To Autumn," John Keats is describing the musical sounds of nature:

> Hedge-crickets sing; and now with treble soft
> The redbreast whistles from a garden-croft;
> And gathering swallows twitter in the skies.

Perhaps one of the most famous allusions to sound is found in Edgar Allan Poe's "The Raven," which opens with a raven rapping and tapping at the door:

> Once upon a midnight dreary, while I pondered, weak and weary,
> Over many a quaint and curious volume of forgotten lore—
> While I nodded, nearly napping, suddenly there came a tapping,
> As of some one gently rapping, rapping at my chamber door.
> "'Tis some visitor," I muttered, "tapping at my chamber door—Only this and
>   nothing more."

SMELL ▪ The sense of smell can be very evocative and call up past memories for us. Walt Whitman, a lover of nature, frequently uses the imagery of smell. In these lines he turns to warm and earthy smells of the out-of-doors: "The smell of apples, aromas from crush'd sage-plant, mint, birch-bark" and ". . . in the fragrant pines and the cedars dusk and dim."

TASTE ■ References to tastes can also be very suggestive, as in Mary O'Neill's description of the color brown: "Brown is cinnamon / and morning toast." And notice the combination of sensory images in these lines from Eliza Cook's poem "The Mouse and the Cake":

> A mouse found a beautiful piece of plum cake,
> The richest and sweetest that mortal could make;
> 'Twas heavy with citron and fragrant with spice,
> And covered with sugar all sparkling as ice.
>
> (Iona and Peter Opie. *The Oxford Book of Children's Verse.* Oxford: Oxford University Press, 1973.)

TOUCH ■ Walter de laMare calls on the sense of touch when he describes the experience of cool leaves brushing against skin: "Through the green twilight of a hedge / I peered with cheek on the cool leaves pressed." Here John Keats describes a cold St. Agnes's Eve (January 20)—and almost makes us shiver:

> St. Agnes' Eve—Ah, bitter chill it was!
> The owl, for all his feathers, was a-cold;
> The hare limp'd trembling through the frozen grass. . . .

Comparative Description

In addition to describing the world through sight, sound, taste, touch, and smell, poets help us better understand their messages by making comparisons. All of us make comparisons every day in our speaking—it's just that poets are a bit more imaginative. The three most common types of comparison are similes, metaphors, and personification.

SIMILE ■ A simile is a comparison between two things that uses *like* or *as*. We use similes all the time—"Busy as a bee," "Light as a feather," "Eat like bird," "Swim like a fish." We use similes to make our points clearer and, perhaps, to make our speech more colorful. Poets use similes for very much the same reasons. Notice all the similes in the following poem, "Kob Antelope," a poem from an anonymous poet from Yoruba in Africa:

> A creature to pet and spoil like a child.
> Smooth skinned
> stepping cautiously in the lemon grass.
> Round and plump

like a newly married wife.
The neck
heavy with brass rings.
The eyes
gentle like a bird's.
The head
beautiful like carved wood.
When you suddenly escape
You spread fine dust
like a butterfly shaking its wings.
Your neck seems long,
so very long
to the greedy hunter.

(Ulli Beier, trans., from *Yoruba Poetry:
An Anthology of Traditional Poems*, 1970.
Reprinted by permission of Bayreuth
African Studies.)

METAPHOR ▪ A metaphor is a little trickier than a simile because the comparison is not stated directly—it's done without *like* or *as*. A metaphor is an implied comparison. We also use metaphors every day—but often we don't recognize them because they have become so familiar. Sometimes our hearts are broken or we get cold feet; we use a computer mouse or visit a chat room—all these are metaphors. Some poems are made up entirely of metaphors. Read the following poem by Valerie Bloom:

Time's a bird, which leaves its footprints
At the corner of your eyes.
Time's a jockey, racing horses,
The sun and moon across the skies.
Time's a thief, stealing your beauty,
Leaving you with tears and sighs.
But you waste time trying to catch him,
Time's a bird and Time just flies.

("Time's a Bird" copyright © Valerie
Bloom 2000, from *Hot Like Fire* published
by Bloomsbury, reprinted by permission
of Valerie Bloom.)

Notice how Bloom applies each metaphor to a different aspect of time and notice how she weaves in other metaphors as well—such as comparing the sun and moon to racing horses. This is a good example of how metaphor enriches poetry.

PERSONIFICATION ▪ Personification is really a variation of simile or metaphor, in which the poet gives human qualities to an inanimate object, an abstract idea, or a force of nature. We speak of an "angry sea" or a "calm lake," a "cheerful room" or time "marching on." Notice how Robert Louis Stevenson describes the winter sun as a drowsy child in his poem "Winter-Time":

> Late lies the wintry sun a-bed,
> A frosty, fiery sleepy-head;
> Blinks but an hour or two, and then,
> A blood-red orange, sets again.

All these techniques help make us see things in ways we may not have thought of. And they help us to get in closer touch with the poet's feelings.

Kinds of Poetry

Poetry is a richly diverse genre that wears many clothes (to use a rather tired metaphor!). Two broad categories exist—narrative poetry, which tells a story, and lyric poetry, which describes a poet's feelings or emotions. And there are many variations.

Narrative Poetry and Ballads

A narrative poem includes characters, action, and plot. Robert Browning's "The Pied Piper of Hamelin" and Henry Wadsworth Longfellow's "The Song of Hiawatha" are two nineteenth-century verse narratives still in print today. The early twentieth-century poet Alfred Noyes wrote "The Highwayman," a tragic story of love and betrayal, ending with the violent death of the highwayman and his beloved. This narrative poem remains popular in England after more than a century.

For younger children ballads are probably more accessible than the longer narrative poems. A ballad is a short narrative poem, typically describing a single event or telling the exploits of a hero or heroine. Traditional ballads use the so-called ballad stanza, which contains four lines, each with eight syllables and with the second and fourth lines rhyming (that is, *a-b-c-b*), although many variations are found. One of the most famous ballads, "Barbara Allen," concerns tragic lovers and dates from the Middle Ages. The opening stanza sets the scene and introduces the main character:

> In Scarlet town, where I was born,
> There was a fair maid dwellin',
> Made every youth cry Well-a-way!
> Her name was Barbara Allen.

We learn that a young lad, Sweet William, is on his deathbed and begs to see Barbara Allen, but the hard-hearted maiden ignores him, and he dies. Then she is overcome by remorse and she, too, dies. They are buried near each other, and a red rose grows from his grave and a green briar grows from hers, and

> They grew and grew to the steeple top
> Till they could grow no higher,
> And there they twined in a true love's knot,
> Red rose around green briar.

It should not be surprising that both folk and country-and-western songs have been greatly influenced by the traditional ballad.

Lyric Poetry

In ancient Greece, poems were typically sung to music played on a stringed instrument called a lyre—thus, these poems were called lyrics. Today, we use the term *lyric poem* to refer to any shorter poem that expresses the poet's personal feelings or emotions. Lyric poems themselves come in an endless variety of forms—including cinquains, elegies, haiku, pastorals, odes, rondeaux, rondels, sestinas, sonnets, triolets, villanelles, and many more, with new ones still being created. Each form has its own rules for stanza length, line length, rhyme scheme, and so on. And there is also free verse, which ignores all the established rules.

What we look for in a lyric poem are fresh and thoughtful imagery, new ways of looking at things, and inventive use of rhyme and rhythm or language patterns. What follows are but a few examples of lyric forms that children enjoy—and this only scratches the surface. You should feel free to invent your own lyric form.

HAIKU ■ Japanese in origin, haiku typically consists of 17 syllables (the number of words doesn't matter) divided into three lines and is usually on the subject of nature and our relationship to nature, such as this example by Ruby Lytle:

> The moon is a week old—
> A dandelion to blow
> Scattering star seed.
> (From *What Is the Moon?* By Ruby Lytle. Reprinted
> with the permission of Tuttle Publishing.)

In this haiku, the metaphor of the stars as tiny seeds blown from the moon, like a whispery soft dandelion puff gone to seed, gives us a new way of thinking about the night sky and suggests a comforting pattern in creation. Haiku in English may have rhythm but usually does not rhyme. Its strength lies in its evocative imagery. Successful haiku uses metaphor to give us a fresh and imaginative look at something we may view as quite ordinary.

CINQUAINS ■ The cinquain is another old form, this time going back to medieval Europe. The term once seems to have included any five-line poem (*cinq* is French for "five"), but Adelaide Crapsey, in her volume titled *Verse*, created more precise rules stipulating that the five lines should contain two, four, six, eight, and two syllables, respectively. No rhyming is necessary, but quite often the first and last lines contain related ideas, are synonymous, or mirror each other. So this type of cinquain presents an interesting puzzle for the poet—and can be great fun for children to attempt.

Crapsey's cinquain titled "November Night" plays on the double meaning of the last word (and, incidentally, notice the simile in the third and fourth lines):

> Listen . . .
> With faint dry sound,
> Like steps of passing ghosts,
> The leaves, frost-crisp'd, break from the trees
> And fall.

FREE VERSE ■ Free verse, which became popular in the twentieth century, refers to poems that follow no established rules of form. Free verse comes closer to natural speech than most other poetry.

Now, of course, it goes without saying that very young children—through the early elementary and even middle elementary grades—prefer the sounds of rhythm and rhyme. For them, poetry is still closely allied with song. But by middle school, many students are ready to experiment with something more daring—poetry that seems to break the rules. So free verse has a definite place in the curriculum of the upper grades, and many fine works of free verse are available to them. The Yoruba poem quoted above, "Kob Antelope," makes up for its lack of rhyme and regular rhythm with its memorable concrete imagery and is a very good example of free verse.

We should never think that free verse means "free-for-all." Like all other poetry, it succeeds with crisp and imaginative images, thoughtful word choice, and carefully arranged sentences. The best writers of free verse know all about the conventions of poetry.

VISUAL POETRY ■ Also called concrete poetry or shape poetry, visual poetry consists of words arranged to take the shape of the poem's subject. Although visual poems go back at least to the seventeenth century, Lewis Carroll is credited with the first visual poem for children—"The Mouse's Tale" from *Alice's Adventures in Wonderland*. Characteristic of Carroll's love for puns, the poem is shaped, of course, like a mouse's tail. (See Figure 7.1.)

Today, visual poetry has become virtually a hybrid of literature and visual art. In fact, some visual poems almost defy reading aloud. One of the most famous examples of modern visual poetry is Reinhard Döhl's poem "Pattern Poem with an Elusive Intruder." It consists of multiple repetitions of the word *apple* making up the shape of an apple. The intruder is the slyly placed word *worm*, almost hidden in a lower corner of the apple. The poem was originally written in German, using the terms *apfel* and *wurm*—an example of a foreign-language poem that needs no translation.

Fury said to
a mouse, That
he met
in the
house,
'Let us
both go
to law:
I will
prosecute
you.—
Come, I'll
take no
denial;
We must
have a
trial:
For
really
this
morning
I've
nothing
to do.'
Said the
mouse to
the cur,
'Such a
trial,
dear sir,
With no
jury or
judge,
would be
wasting
our breath.'
' I'll be
judge,
I'll be
jury,'
Said
cunning
old Fury;
' I'll try
the whole
cause,
and
condemn
you
to
death.'"

FIGURE 7.2 ■ Robert Froman's "A Seeing Poem"

Source: Reprinted by permission of Mrs. Katherine Froman.

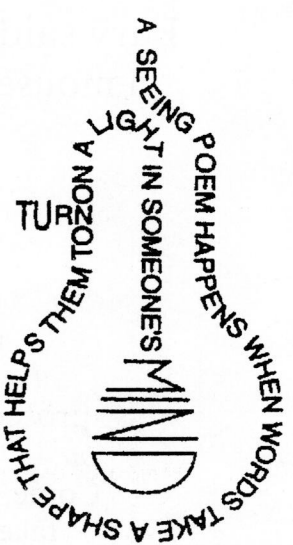

Visual poetry is often playful poetry—but it can be thoughtful as well. Visual poems present interesting challenges to readers in very much the same way that poetic imagery does in a conventional poem. A visual poem's impact relies heavily on its clever use of both language and design. Robert Froman's "A Seeing Poem" (see Figure 7.2) cleverly uses the form to define visual poetry itself.

LIMERICKS ■ The limerick is a five-line humorous poem in which the first, second, and fifth lines rhyme and the third and fourth lines rhyme. The fun of the limerick lies in its rollicking rhythm and its broad humor—a limerick is always comical. The following limerick has been attributed to President Woodrow Wilson:

> I sat next to the Duchess at tea;
> It was just as I thought it would be;
> Her rumblings abdominal
> Were simply phenomenal,
> And everyone thought it was me.

The limerick's form is easily imitated (often in subversive and off-color ways), and young children can have a great deal of fun creating their own.

Found Poetry

Poetry is all around us, just waiting for us to find it. So-called "found poetry" is created by taking words from other sources—books, newspapers, news releases, memos, signs, notices, advertisements of all sorts, restaurant menus, any place language can be found—and arranging the words into a poetic form. The purest found poem does not alter the words or word order. Dorothy Wordsworth, sister of the poet William Wordsworth, loved to walk in the countryside and then write down her feelings in a private journal. One of her prose sentences has been made into a poem merely by breaking it into lines:

> The lake was covered all over
> With bright silverwaves
> That were each
> The twinkling of an eye.

Without rhyme or regular rhythm, these lines sound poetic, giving us a lovely image of the lake.

Most found poems do not rhyme, but here is an unusual example taken from *An Elementary Treatise on Mechanics* (1819) by the philosopher William Whewell: "Hence no force, however great, can stretch a cord, however fine, into a horizontal line which is accurately straight." See what happens when the words are arranged this way:

> Hence no force, however great,
> can stretch a cord, however fine,
> into a horizontal line
> which is accurately straight.

Sometimes we might wish to tweak a passage the poetic effect. Take this sentence from Jeremy Bentham, the eighteenth-century English philosopher: "Stretching his hand up to reach the stars, too often man forgets the flowers at his feet," which we might adjust to read:

> Stretching our hands up
> To reach the stars,
> Too often we forget
> The flowers at our feet.

In 2011, a new journal was launched, *Found Poetry Review*, dedicated exclusively to publishing found poems, and the entries come from people of all ages. Found poetry can help children in several ways: It makes poetry a part of their everyday lives, removes the academic stigma often associated with poetry, encourages them to seek out their own found poems, and makes them more aware of the power and possibility of language.

NONSENSE VERSE ■ Nonsense verse, which defies all logic as we know it, is one of the most popular kinds of poetry among young children. It usually depicts ridiculous characters in outrageous situations. Take, for example, this limerick by Edward Lear:

> There was an Old Man with a beard
> Who said, "It is just as I feared!

> Two Owls and a Hen,
> Four Larks and a Wren,
> Have built a nest in my beard!"

However, nonsense verse may include made-up words, as in these lines from one of the most famous poems in the English language, Lewis Carroll's "The Jabberwocky," from *Through the Looking-Glass and What Alice Found There*:

> Twas brillig, and the slithy toves
> Did gyre and gimble in the wabe;
> All mimsy were the borogoves,
> And the mome raths outgrabe.

Our enjoyment comes from the playful language, the comic predicaments, the joy of the unexpected. Nonsense verse can also be subversive, going against society's conventions. And that may be its chief appeal for children, for after all, childhood is about testing the waters, discovering what works, finding out how far one can go, and what the grown-ups are hiding. Writing nonsense verse can be great fun for children—it is playful and encourages the creative use of rhythm, rhyme, and the sound of language in general, as in this popular example by Laura Richards:

> Once there was an elephant,
> Who tried to use the telephant—
> No! No! I mean an elephone
> Who tried to use the telephone—
> (Dear me! I am not certain quite
> That even now I've got it right.)
> Howe'er it was, he got his trunk
> Entangled in the telephunk;
> The more he tried to get it free,
> The louder buzzed the telephee—
> (I fear I'd better drop the song
> Of elephop and telephong!)

URCHIN POETRY ■ Joseph T. Thomas, Jr., uses the tantalizing term *urchin poetry* to describe the work of poets who are attempting to appeal to the earthier instincts in children that draw them to forbidden topics of childhood, especially sex, bodily functions, and excretions. Urchin poetry is identified by its subject matter and treatment and not by any prescribed poetic pattern. It almost always rhymes and has a rhythmic beat and is, in those respects, quite conventional. However, it is characterized by its fixation on bodily excretions, the outrageous, and the grotesque. Naturally, all these are fascinating to youth, perhaps largely because of the taboos associated with them.

The most famous poet in this vein is probably Shel Silverstein, whose *Where the Sidewalk Ends* and *A Light in the Attic* are filled with rollicking verses exploiting this material. With lines such as this from "Messy Room"—"And his smelly old sock has been stuck to the wall"—or his descriptions in "Sarah Cynthia Sylvia Stout"—"Gloppy glumps of cold oatmeal" and "Moldy melons, dried-up mustard"—Silverstein recognizes the value of a good "gross-out." Silverstein, in fact, is almost mainstream compared to the so-called "potty poets" whose obsessions with bodily excretions—always played for a laugh—have resulted in publications of many books of poetry (we will say nothing about the quality). And the justification for all this? It may be just one more way to entice those reluctant readers into the rich (if sometimes wacky) world of books.

PLAYGROUND POETRY ■ As we have seen, free verse, nonsense verse, and urchin poetry all seem to relish flaunting the rules, which at times seems to be a preoccupation of children in general. So it is not surprising that when children themselves experiment with poetry, they often challenge the status quo and break down social decorum. And where does this normally occur? On the playground—either literally or figuratively. Playground poetry (see Thomas) is the original urchin poetry, for it comes from the children themselves.

We have already suggested that children seem to have a natural affinity for poetry. Perhaps it is because poetry is one of the first literary forms introduced to them—in nursery rhymes, songs, and games. And it may have something to do with the fact that our bodies are tuned to natural rhythms—our heartbeats, for instance—and nature itself is filled with myriad patterns and rhythms. All this is speculative, but it is undeniable that children, left to their own devices, are constantly reciting and creating poetry—and it is usually a communal experience. This jump-rope rhyme was a favorite playground verse of my own daughters when they were in early elementary school:

Cinderella dressed in yella'
Went to town to see her fella'
On her way her girdle busted,
How many people were disgusted?
1, 2, 3, . . . [etc. until the jumper misses]

For another example, see Chapter 5, "Fudge, fudge, tell the judge." Playground poetry is very much like the traditional folktale in that it is passed along orally—often from child to child.

Playground poetry is also true living poetry—always spoken, rarely written down, and forever changing, adapting to new times, places, and circumstances. Consequently, the children themselves become poets (of sorts) as they add their individual touches to the verses. The example of "Cinderella" is popular because it mentions an "unmentionable"—a girdle. References to undergarments invariably get a rise from first and secondgraders. And the example "Fudge, fudge, tell the judge" is popular because of its fiendish violence.

But even these two poems are mild compared with what quite often is heard on the playground. I recall, for instance, this popular verse from my own childhood—and it is still in circulation—which is also urchin poetry at its most outrageous:

Great big gobs of greasy, grimy gopher guts,
Mutilated monkey feet,
Dirty little birdy feet,
Great big gobs of greasy, grimy gopher guts,
And me without a spoon!

Playground poetry is recited out of earshot of adults and is therefore the product of childhood unleashed. Here children can throw off the yoke of adult domination and safely release the anxiety, hostility, and pent-up frustrations that are perfectly normal aspects of growing up (although many adults like to pretend otherwise). This poetry contains all the language and imagery that are normally taboo for children. Profanity, sex, violence, and bodily functions are all typical features of this poetry. I offer neither a defense nor castigation of these poetic offerings—only a description.

Subversive poetry, including chants, parody, and the harmless cheers recited at sporting events, has always been, and always will be, an important part of childhood. Again, it serves as a much-needed outlet for pent-up childhood anxieties, doubt, fears, and frustrations. It is also an example of the creative process at work. Taste, refinement, and judgment will come with maturity, but art itself must begin with freedom of expression.

Sharing Poetry with Children

Studies of children's poetry preferences suggest, among other things, that (1) children prefer poetry that they can understand, (2) they prefer humorous poetry, (3) they prefer new poems to older ones, and (4) they do not like serious and contemplative poems (see Terry). However, such studies can be dangerous if we rely on them entirely to determine what poetry to share with children. Doing so would result in a further narrowing of taste among children and deprive them of many fresh and imaginative poems that they just might enjoy. For most elementary school children—and perhaps even older children—an oral approach to poetry makes the most sense. Because of its rhythmical and rhyming qualities, much of poetry begs to be read aloud. Figure 7.3 lists just a few ideas for using poetry in the classroom. The suggestions move generally from simplest to most complex. Many of these exercises can be done either individually or in groups. However, before beginning any of these projects, try sharing with the students several poems by a variety of poets. This should, in fact, become a regular part of the routine in a language arts classroom. Poetry inspires poetry.

FIGURE 7.3 ■ 25 Things to Do with Poetry

1. Read one new poem every day.
2. Memorize a favorite poem (that has at least six to eight lines).
3. Write a poem with lots of alliteration—for instance, a poem about Luis who is "lanky," "likeable," "lively," and "lucky."
4. Write a five-line poem in which every line rhymes at the end.
5. Make a list of your favorite sights, sounds, smells, tastes, and textures.
6. Drawing on the list you made in #5, write a poem of at least five lines about happiness.
7. Using as many sensory words as you can, write a poem about your most or least favorite food.
8. Compare two poems from different poets about your favorite season.
9. Using as many sensory words as you can, write a poem about your favorite season.
10. Make a list of *similes* that describe you, such as "happy as a clam," or "fast as lightning."
11. Make up a simile you have never heard before—and be sure you can explain it.
12. Make a list of *metaphors* that we often use, such as "a computer mouse," "putting your foot in your mouth," and "a skeleton in the closet."
13. Make up a metaphor you have never heard before—and be sure you can explain it.
14. Write a poem about your favorite color, using sights, sounds, smells, tastes, textures, and emotions you associate with the color. (See Mary O'Neill's *Hailstones and Halibut Bones*.)
15. Write a poem about yourself, using the letters of your name to begin each line.
16. Write a poem describing today's weather, using at least one simile or metaphor.
17. Write a parody of a nursery rhyme, using its rhyme scheme and rhythm, but give it a contemporary setting, something like this:

    Mayor Flubbins sat on a wall;
    Mayor Flubbins had a great fall.
    All the townspeople—women and men—
    Refused to return him to office again.

18. Write a limerick about a fictitious person, following this pattern:

    There was an old man from Peru
    Who dreamt he was eating his shoe.
    He awoke in the night?
    With a terrible fright
    And found it was perfectly true.

19. Write a haiku about your favorite season—just 17 syllables in 3 lines.
20. Write a poem using only *one-syllable* words, but with rhyme and rhythm.

(continued)

FIGURE 7.3 ■ 25 Things to Do with Poetry (*continued*)

21. Write a nonsense poem about an outrageous person or animal. Try using unusual rhyme and rhythm.
22. Write a poem that uses word sounds and rhythm in an unusual way—such as a galloping rhythm in a poem about horses or soothing sounds in a poem about sleep.
23. Write a visual poem about an object, with the lines making the shape of the object.
24. Create a found poem from a newspaper item, an advertisement, a menu, a sign, or anyplace there is written language.
25. Read a collection of poems by a favorite poet.

Summary

From the rhymes of Mother Goose to the jump-rope verse and limericks on the playground, poetry is a happy part of young children's lives. Perhaps, even in those formative years, children know instinctively what the eighteenth-century German philosopher Novalis said: "Poetry heals the wounds inflicted by reason." It is important that we nurture this initial love so that, as they grow older, children can appreciate the many facets of poetry—both the sound (the patterns of rhyme and rhythm) and the sense (including the exciting stories of narrative verse and the deep human emotion expressed in lyrics).

A poet is a visionary, one who sees the world in fresh and unusual ways and is capable of sharing that vision with the rest of us. It is important that we, as adults and teachers, overcome our own fears and apprehensions about poetry so that we can share its bounty. And the better we come to know poetry, the richer our experience will be. Although it is helpful to have some knowledge of poetic techniques and devices—rhythm, rhyme, metaphor, simile, personification—we should not get bogged down by terminology. The best way to learn to enjoy poetry is to read and hear lots of it, in all its rich variety. Poetry presents many opportunities for creative activities through which we can explore and appreciate the richness of the art form—oral recitation, illustration, and writing, to name a few. Few literary forms offer so much in pleasure and knowledge as poetry. Lovers of poetry are not born but made through patient and careful nurturing.

For Reflection and Discussion

1. Locate a collection of poems by a single poet. If possible, locate several collections by that poet. How would you describe this poetry to a friend? What are the poet's specific strengths? What are the poet's specific weaknesses? If you have found

several collections by the same poet, compare them. Has the poet exhibited any growth as a poet over the years?

2. Locate an anthology of poetry by several different poets and read through it. Which poems speak to you most clearly? What is it about those poems that seems to attract you? Is it form? The sound of the language? The meaning? Originality? A combination? From this experience, try to articulate your own feelings about poetry.

3. Compare two or more poems on the same subject written by different poets—for example, love poems, poems about the seasons, poems about childhood, poems about death. How do the poems differ in form? How do the poems differ in content? How do the poems differ in the way they make you feel? Can you explain these differences?

4. Find examples of what you would consider subversive poems—poems that test the boundaries of decorum or challenge the status quo. What is your response to them?

5. Add some of your own ideas to the list of suggestions in Figure 7.3.

Works Cited

Held, Carl. "Orange, Silver, Now Purple (More Lexical Lunacy)." *Games, Issue 207*, 29.1 (February 2005): 4–9, 16.

Terry, Ann. *Children's Poetry Preferences: A National Survey of the Upper Elementary Grades.* Urbana, IL: National Council of Teachers of English, 1984.

Thomas, Joseph T., Jr. *Poetry's Playground: The Culture of Contemporary American Children's Poetry.* Detroit, MI: Wayne State University Press, 2007.

Recommended Resources

Ciardi, John, and Miller Williams. *How Does a Poem Mean?* 2nd ed. Boston: Houghton Mifflin, 1975.

Higginson, William J., with Penny Harter. *The Haiku Handbook: How to Write, Share and Teach Haiku.* New York: McGraw-Hill, 1985.

Hopkins, Lee Bennet. *Pass the Poetry Please.* New York: Citation Press, 1972.

Hurst, Carol. "What to Do with a Poem." *Early Years* 11 (February 1980): 28–29, 68.

Kennedy, X. J. " 'Go and Get Your Candle Lit!' An Approach to Poetry." *Horn Book Magazine* 57, 3 (June 1981): 273–279.

Livingston, Myra. *Climb into the Bell Tower: Essays on Poetry.* New York: HarperCollins, 1990.

——. *Poem-Making: Ways to Begin Writing Poetry.* New York: HarperCollins, 1991.

Oliver, Mary. *A Poetry Handbook: A Prose Guide to Understanding and Writing Poetry.* San Diego, CA: Harcourt, 1994.

Vardell, Sylvia M. *Poetry Aloud Here! Sharing Poetry with Children in the Library.* Chicago: ALA, 2006.

Poetry For Children: A Selected Booklist

The first list includes anthologies—collections that include poems by many different poets. The second list includes books by individual poets.

Poetry Anthologies for All Ages

Adoff, Arnold, ed. *I Am the Darker Brother: An Anthology of Modern Poems by African Americans*, rev. ed. New York: Simon & Schuster, 1996.

Blishen, Edward, comp. *Oxford Book of Poetry for Children*. Illus. Brian Wildsmith. New York: Watts, 1963.

Carlson, Lori M., ed. *Cool Salsa: Bilingual Poems on Growing Up Latino in the United States*. New York: Holt, 1994.

De La Mare, Walter, ed. *Come Hither*, 3rd ed. Illus. Warren Chappell. New York: Knopf, 1957.

Demi, selector and illus. *In the Eyes of the Cat: Japanese Poetry for All Seasons*. Trans. Tze-si Huang. New York: Holt, 1992.

Dunning, Stephen, Edward Lueders, and Hugh Smith, comps. *Reflections on a Gift of Watermelon Pickle*. Glenview, IL: Scott, Foresman, 1967.

Elledge, Scott, ed. *Wider Than the Sky: Poems to Grow Up With*. New York: Harper, 1990.

Esbensen, Barbara Juster, comp. *Swing around the Sun*. Illus. Khee Chee Cheng, Stephen Gammell, and Janice Lee Porter. Minneapolis, MN: Carolrhoda, 2003.

Feelings, Tom, comp. and illus. *Soul Looks Back in Wonder*. New York: Dial, 1993.

Giovanni, Nikki, ed. *Hip Hop Speaks to Children*. Naperville, IL: Sourcebooks, 2008.

Harrison, Michael, and Christopher Stuart-Clark. *One Hundred Years of Poetry: For Children*. New York: Oxford University Press, 1999.

Hopkins, Lee Bennett, ed. *Sharing the Season: A Book of Poems*. New York: McElderry, 2010.

——. *Sky Magic*. Illus. Mariusz Stawarski. New York: Dutton, 2009.

Houston, James, ed. *Songs of the Dream People*. New York: Atheneum, 1972.

Eskimo and other Native American poems.

Janeczko, Paul B., ed. *A Kick in the Head: An Everyday Guide to Poetic Forms*. Illus. Chris Raschka. New York: Candlewick, 2005.

——. *A Poke in the I: A Collection of Concrete Poems*. Illus. Chris Raschka. Cambridge, MA: Candlewick, 2001.

Jones, Hettie, selector. *The Trees Stand Shining: Poetry of the North American Indians*. Illus. Robert Andrew Parker. New York: Dial, 1971.

Kennedy, X. J., and Dorothy Kennedy, eds. *Knock at a Star: A Child's Introduction to Poetry*, rev. ed. Illus. Karen Lee Baker. Boston: Little Brown, 1999.

Larrick, Nancy, ed. *Piping Down the Valleys Wild*. Illus. Ellen Raskin. 1968. New York: Dell, 1982.

Lewis, J. Patrick, comp. *National Geographic Book of Animal Poetry: 200 Poems with Photographs that Squeak, Soar, and Roar!* Washington, DC: National Geographic Children's Books, 2012.

Livingston, Myra Cohn, comp. *Dilly Dilly Piccalilli: Poems for the Very Young*. New York: McElderry, 1989.

——. *Lots of Limericks*. New York: Simon & Schuster, 1991.

Michael, Pamela, ed. *River of Words: Young Poets and Artists on the Nature of Things*. Minneapolis, MN Milkweed, 2008.

Moore, Lilian, ed. *Sunflakes: Poems for Children*. Illus. Jan Ormerod. New York: Clarion, 1992.

Nye, Naomi Shihab, selector. *This Same Sky: A Collection of Poems from Around the World*. New York: Macmillan, 1992.

Opie, Iona, and Peter Opie, eds. *The Oxford Book of Children's Verse*. New York: Oxford, 1973.

Orozco, José-Luis, selector-arranger. *De Colores and Other Latin-American Folk Songs for Children*. New York: Dutton, 1994.

Prelutsky, Jack, selector. *Read-Aloud Rhymes for the Very Young.* Illus. Marc Brown. New York: Knopf, 1987.

——. *The 20th Century Children's Poetry Treasury.* Illus. Meilo So. New York: Knopf, 1999.

Rampersad, Arnold, Marcellus Blount, and Karen Barbour, eds. *Poetry for Young People: African American Poetry.* New York: Sterling, 2013.

Schwartz, Alvin, selector. *And the Green Grass Grew All Around: Folk Poetry from Everyone.* Illus. Sue Truesdell. New York: Harper, 1992.

Vardell, Sylvia, and Janet Wong, comps. *The Poetry Friday Anthology: Poems for the School Year with Connections to the Common Core.* Princeton, NJ: Pomelo, 2012.

- Primarily for teachers, includes 36 poems for each grade from K to 5—one for every week of the school year. It needs to be supplemented by many other books.

Collections by Individual Poets

Many of these poets have published several books, so look for others as well. These books are suitable for elementary and middle school readers, and some collections, of course, are more sophisticated than others.

Adoff, Arnold. *Roots and Blues: A Celebration.* Illus. Gregory Christie. New York: Clarion Books, 2011.

Agard, John. *Half-caste and Other Poems.* North Pomfret, VT: Hodder/Trafalgar Square, 2005.

Agee, Jon. *Orangutan Tongs: Poems to Tangle Your Tongue.* New York: Hyperion, 2009.

Argueta, Jorge. *Talking with Mother Earth/Hablando con Madre Tierra.* Illus. Lucía Angela Pérez. Toronto: Groundwood/House of Anansi, 2006.

Blackaby, Susan. *Nest, Nook & Cranny.* Illus. Jamie Hogan. Watertown, MA: Charlesbridge, 2010.

Bloom, Valerie. *Hot Like Fire and Other Poems.* London: Bloomsbury, 2009.

Brooks, Gwendolyn. *Bronzeville Boys and Girls.* Illus. Faith Ringgold. New York: Amistad/HarperCollins, 2007.

Chandra, Deborah. *Balloons and Other Poems.* Illus. Leslie Bowman. New York: Farrar, Straus & Giroux, 1990.

Ciardi, John. *You Read to Me, I'll Read to You.* Illus. Edward Gorey. New York: HarperCollins, 1987.

Coatsworth, Elizabeth. *Under the Green Willow.* Illus. Janina Domanska. New York: Macmillan, 1971.

Cummings, E. E. *Hist Whist.* Illus. Deborah Kogan Ray. New York: Crown, 1989.

De La Mare, Walter. *Peacock Pie.* Illus. Barbara Cooney. New York: Knopf, 1961.

Dickinson, Emily. *My Letter to the World and Other Poems.* Toronto: Kids Can Press, 2008.

Dillard, Annie. *Mornings Like This: Found Poems.* New York: Harper, 1995.

Ehlert, Lois. *Oodles of Animals.* New York: Harcourt, 2008.

Elliot, David *In the Wild.* Illus. Holly Meade. New York: Candlewick, 2010.

Eliot, T. S. *Old Possum's Book of Practical Cats.* Illus. Edward Gorey. New York: Harcourt, Brace, Jovanovich, 1982.

Fleischman, Paul. *Big Talk: Poems for Four Voices.* Illus. Beppe Giacobbe. New York: Candlewick, 2008.

——. *A Joyful Noise: Poems for Two Voices.* New York: Harper, 1987.

A collection of poems meant for choral reading.

Florian, Douglas. *Lizards, Frogs, and Polliwogs.* New York: Harcourt, 2001.

Franco, Betsy. *Curious Collection of Cats.* Illus. Michael Wertz. San Francisco: Tricycle Press, 2009.

Froman, Robert. *Seeing Things: A Book of Poems.* New York: Crowell, 1974.

Frost, Helen. *Diamond Willow.* New York: Farrar, Straus & Giroux, 2008.

Frost, Robert. *Birches.* Illus. Ed Young. New York: Holt, 1988.

Giovanni, Nikki. *Spin a Soft Black Song.* Illus. George Martins. New York: Hill & Wang, 1985.

Greenberg, David T. *Bugs*. Illus. Lyn Munsinger. Boston: Little, Brown, 1997.

Greenfield, Eloise. *The Friendly Four*. Illus. Jan Spivey Gilchrist. New York: HarperColllins, 2006.

Hoberman, Mary Ann, and Linda Winston. *The Tree That Time Built: A Celebration of Nature, Science, and Imagination*. Illus. Barbara Fortin. Naperville, IL: Sourcebooks, 2009.

Holbrook, Sara. *Wham! It's a Poetry Jam: Discovering Performance Poetry*. Honesdale, PA: Boyds Mills, 2002.

Hopkins, Lee Bennett. *City I Love*. Illus. Marcus Hall. New York: Abrams, 2009.

Hughes, Langston. *The Dream Keeper and Other Poems*. New York: Knopf, 1994.

Jackson, Rob. *Weekend Mischief*. Illus. Mark Beech. Honesdale, PA: Wordsong, 2010.

Janeczko, Paul B. *Brickyard Summer*. New York: Orchard, 1989.

——. *Requiem: Poems of the Terezín Ghetto*. Cambridge, MA: Candlewick, 2011.

Jarrell, Randall. *The Bat Poet*. Illus. Maurice Sendak. New York: Macmillan, 1964.

Kennedy, X. J. *City Kids: Street & Skyscraper Rhymes*. Illus. Philippe Béha. Vancouver: Tradewind, 2010.

Kuskin, Karla. *Moon, Have You Met My Mother?* Illus. Sergio Ruzzier. New York: HarperCollins, 2003.

Lawson, JonArno. *Black Stars in a White Night Sky*. Illus. Sherwin Tjia. Toronto: Pedlar Press, 2006.

——. *Down in the Bottom of the Bottom of the Box*. Illus. Alec Dempster. Erin, Ontario: Porcupine's Quill, 2012.

Lear, Edward. *The Complete Verse and Other Nonsense*. Ed. Vivian Noakes. New York: Penguin, 2006.

Lewis, J. Patrick. *The House*. Illus. Roberto Innocenti. Minneapolis, MN: Creative Editions, 2009.

Livingston, Myra Cohn. *Calendar*. Illus. Will Hillebrand. New York: Holiday House, 2007.

Mado, Michio. *The Magic Pocket*. Trans. Empress Michiko of Japan. Illus. Mitsumasa Anno. New York: McElderry, 1998.

Mahy, Margaret. *Nonstop Nonsense*. Illus. Quentin Blake. New York: McElderry, 1989.

Marsalis, Wynton. *Jazz A·B·Z: An A to Z Collection of Jazz Portraits*. Illus. Paul Rogers. Cambridge, MA: Candlewick, 2005.

McCord, David. *One at a Time: His Collected Poems for the Young*. Illus. Henry Kane. Boston: Little, Brown, 1977.

Moore, Lilian. *Mural on Second Avenue and Other City Poems*. Illus. Roma Karas. New York: Candlewick, 2005.

Mordhorst, Heidi. *Pumpkin Butterfly: Poems from the Other Side of Nature*. Honesdale, PA: Wordsong/Boyds Mill Press, 2009.

Myers, Walter Dean. *Blues Journey*. Illus. Christopher Myers. New York: Holiday, 2003.

——. *Street Love*. New York: Amistad/HarperTempest, 2006.

Nash, Ogden. *The Best of Ogden Nash*. Chicago: Ivan R. Dee, 2007.

Nelson, Marilyn. *Fortune's Bones: The Manumission Requiem*. Asheville, NC: Front Street Books, 2004.

——. *A Wreath for Emmett Till*. Illus. Philippe Lardy. Boston: Houghton Mifflin, 2005.

Nye, Naomi Shihab. *A Maze Me: Poems for Girls*. Illus. Terre Maher. New York: Greenwillow, 2005.

——. *19 Varieties of Gazelle: Poems of the Middle East*. New York: Greenwillow, 2002.

O'Neill, Mary. *Hailstones and Halibut Bones*. Illus. John Wallner. New York: Doubleday, 1989.

Park, Linda Sue, *Tap Dancing on the Roof: Sijo (Poems)*. Pictures by Istvan Banyai. New York: Clarion, 2007.

Prelutsky, Jack. *The Frog Wore Red Suspenders*. Illus. Petra Mathers. New York: Greenwillow, 2002.

——. *Ride a Purple Pelican*. New York: Greenwillow, 1986.

——. *What a Day It Was at School!* Illus. Doug Cushman. New York: Greenwillow, 2006.

Richards, Laura. *Tirra Lirra: Rhymes Old and New*. 1932. Illus. Marguerite Davis. Boston: Little, Brown, 1955.

Roethke, Theodore. *Dirty Dinky and Other Creatures*. Selectors Beatrice Roethke and Stephen Lushington. New York: Doubleday, 1973.

Rosen, Michael J. *The Cuckoo's Haiku and Other Birding Poems*. Illus. Stan Fellows. Cambridge, MA: Candlewick, 2009.

Ruddell, Deborah. *A Whiff of Pine, a Hint of Skunk*. New York: Simon & Schuster, 2009.

Schertie, Alice. *Button Up! Wrinkled Rhymes*. Illus. Petra Mathers. New York: Houghton Mifflin Harcourt, 2009.

Shannon, George. *Busy in the Garden*. Illus. Sam Williams. New York: Greenwillow, 2006.

Sidman, Joyce. *Meow Ruff*. Illus. Michelle Berg. Boston: Houghton Mifflin, 2006.

Silverstein, Shel. *A Light in the Attic*. New York: Harper, 1981.

——. *Where the Sidewalk Ends*. New York: Harper, 1974.

Singer, Marilyn. *Mirror, Mirror: A Book of Reversible Verse*. Illus. José Masse. New York: Dutton, 2010.

Soto, Gary. *New and Selected Poems*. San Francisco: Chronicle Books, 1995.

Starbird, Kaye. *The Covered Bridge House*. Illus. Jim Arnosky. New York: Four Winds, 1979.

Stevenson, James. *Sweet Corn: Poems*. New York: Greenwillow, 1995.

Stevenson, Robert Louis. *A Child's Garden of Verses*. Illus. Jessie Willcox Smith. 1905. New York: Scribner's, 1969.

Swenson, May. *The Complete Poems to Solve*. New York: Macmillan, 1993.

Viorst, Judith. *If I Were in Charge of the World and Other Worries*. Illus. Lyn Cherry. New York: Atheneum, 1969.

Watson, Clyde. *Father Fox's Pennyrhymes*. Illus. Wendy Watson. New York: Crowell, 1971.

Whitman, Walt. *Voyages: Poems by Walt Whitman*. Selector, Lee Bennett Hopkins. Illus. Charles Mikolaycak. New York: Harcourt, 1988.

Wilbur, Richard. *Opposites*. New York: Harcourt, 1973.

Willard, Nancy. *Household Tales of Moon and Water*. New York: Harcourt, 1982.

——. *A Visit to William Blake's Inn*. Illus. Alice and Martin Provensen. New York: Harcourt, 1981.

Williams, Vera B. *Amber Was Brave, Essie Was Smart*. New York: Greenwillow, 2001.

Wong, Janet S. *A Suitcase of Seaweed and Other Poems*. New York: Simon & Schuster, 1996.

Worth, Valerie. *All the Small Poems and Fourteen More*. Illus. Natalie Babbitt. New York: Farrar, Straus & Giroux, 1994.

8 Folk Narratives

The Oldest Stories

Introduction

Folktales, legends, and myths are our oldest stories—and still some of the best. They contain gripping plots, exotic settings, magic, and wonder. They are at the core of all literature. In "Cinderella" we find the kernel of every romance. In "Hansel and Gretel" we find the essence of the coming-of-age story. In "Jack and the Beanstalk" we find the quintessential adventure story. In "Rumpelstiltskin" we find the mystery. And in "Little Red Riding Hood" we find the crucible of trickery and deceit (see Figure 8.1). In the folktale, human emotions, desires, fears, and hopes are stripped to their bare bones. They bring us to the very heart of humanity. The "folk" in folk narratives refers to the common people of a society—as opposed to professional writers, for example. Folk narratives, tradition tells us, are the stories the common people passed along by word of mouth, from generation to generation.

The folk narratives were the products of societies in which most people could not read—societies without books, televisions, computers, and film. These are also societies whose wells of knowledge depended on the spoken word. Consequently, we can never know who created the first versions of "The Frog King" or "Rapunzel" or "The Three Billy Goats Gruff." And we can never speak of the author of a folktale—only the reteller. And, by the same token, the tales come in many different versions—called "variants"—and no one can claim to know the original.

Although the myths and sacred tales about the origins of the world, the gods and goddesses, and the cultural heroes began as oral narratives centuries ago, most have long since been written down and become part of our literary culture (Homer's *Iliad*, the Old Testament, India's *Ramayana*, and so on). But most folk narratives (folktales, legends, tall tales, riddles, and so on) remained in the oral culture until fairly recently. It was only in the nineteenth century that collectors like Jacob and Wilhelm Grimm, Joseph Jacobs, Andrew Lang, Peter Asbjørnsen, Jørgen Moe, and others began to record the oral tales. And when they began looking at the tales from Africa, India, China, and the Americas, the collectors discovered striking similarities. African, Asian, and American Indian cultures all had their

FIGURE 8.1 ■ Gustave Doré's celebrated engraving for "Little Red Riding Hood" is typical of the drama—sometimes startling drama—with which he imbued all of his work.

own versions of "Cinderella" and "Little Red Riding Hood," for example. Whether the tales all sprang from a single source (as some argue) or whether they simply reflect the common thread of humanity's needs, hopes, fears, and desires (as most now believe), the truth may never be known. But their power and their influence on world culture cannot be denied.

The Elements of the Folk Narrative

Setting and Plot

"Once upon a time, in a kingdom far, far away"—so goes the traditional opening of the folk narrative. We rarely get anything more specific than this. It is true that folktale settings often suggest the place of origin—so Scandinavian folktales are set in cold, icy, and mountainous lands; German folktales are set in forested lands; Navajo folktales are set in the Southwestern desert; and so on. But we rarely find specific countries, cities, towns, or other places named. The setting remains distant in both time and place, and this allows it to be an enchanted place. We know from the beginning of the tale that this is a time and place where animals may talk, strange creatures may be found, and magic may occur. Folktale plots are generally of two types—dramatic or cumulative (see Chapter 9). A dramatic plot, composed of interdependent events reaching a climax and followed by a swift conclusion, is the familiar pattern of some of the most popular stories—"Cinderella," "Sleeping Beauty," and "Beauty and the Beast." The cumulative plot is one in which the same plot element is repeated, with slight variations, leading up to the climax; this plot device is usually found in tales for very young children, who find pleasure in the repetition. "The Gingerbread Man" and "The Turnip" are two popular examples.

Character

Much like the plots, folktale characters are simple and uncomplicated. Indeed, the characters often don't even have names, just stereotypical labels (the miller, the king, the wicked witch), or their names merely describe their character traits or appearance— "Beauty," "Prince Charming," "Snow White," or "Bluebeard." The characters are all one-dimensional. None ever displays any depth. None ever faces difficult psychological choices or torments. None ever ponders a problem very long. None ever undergoes any deep soul searching. A character's appearance betrays his or her personality. The lovely princess will always be beautiful and good and generous. Prince Charming will always be handsome and brave and faithful. The witch or ogre will always be ugly and selfish and cruel.

But, you may argue, what about the Beast in "Beauty and the Beast"? When we first see him, he is ugly and terrifying, but in the end, he is transformed into a handsome prince. But remember, he was always, deep inside, a handsome prince, for his ugly appearance is the result of an evil spell, which only a beautiful woman can break. A good and noble character's inner beauty cannot long be hidden, nor can a villain's ugliness.

So, if we have met Cinderella, then we recognize Sleeping Beauty, Snow White, Rapunzel, and dozens of other fair maidens from the folktales because they are, fundamentally, all alike; and Rumpelstiltskin is just a shorter, male version of the wicked witch who imprisoned Rapunzel, or the one who nearly ate Hansel and Gretel. Instead of being individuals, the folktale characters are types, some symbolizing goodness, humility, and generosity, others symbolizing greed, arrogance, and selfishness. We need no physical description. And perhaps it is better that way. Some critics even object to illustrating these tales because it deprives children of using their imaginations to create their own characters.

Here are some of the common character types found in folktales:

- *The beautiful maiden*—Usually helpless and at the mercy of some wicked guardian, she awaits the arrival of Prince Charming.
- *Prince Charming*—The hero is handsome and bold and deferential to beautiful maidens.

- *The wicked witch or ogre*—This villain is deformed and horrid looking, delighting in evil for evil's sake. We never learn, for example, that the witch might have been abused as a child or was the victim of a tragic love affair.

- *The faithful servant (or faithful companion)*—This character, whether servant or companion, serves as confidant to the hero or heroine.

- *The wise elder*—This character is generally a mysterious figure who sometimes speaks in riddles that the hero or heroine must unravel.

- *The helpful guide*—The hero or heroine is likely to encounter a guide, perhaps on a journey, and possibly a talking animal who is returning a favor performed by the hero or heroine.

- *The innocent babes*—Children, when they are heroes in the tales, tend to be much more clever than their adult counterparts; lacking the physical strength to overcome the villains, children must use their brains. Hansel and Gretel are good examples, outwitting the wicked witch, finding her treasure, and making their way back home.

- *The simpleton*—A usually lovable character whose foolishness may sometimes result in amazing good fortune. Who doesn't cheer on the underdog?

- *The ineffectual father*—The weak father figure's prominence in European folktales may suggest the prevalence of the mother in the raising of children—or it may suggest that women frequently told the stories.

- *The wicked stepmother*—This villain is an embodiment of evil and a figure found in folktales around the world. Some believe this character embodies the complex relationship between mother and child: We love the care she gives us but don't like the control she has over us; in folktales, we can love the deceased mother and hate the cruel stepmother, thus having it both ways. The witch in *Hansel and Gretel* is another version of this character.

- *The trickster*—Whether an animal or a human, we can't help liking this irascible, devilish, and endlessly fascinating character, who delights in wreaking havoc.

Language and Style

Since folktales were originally told orally, most of them still bear the traits we expect from oral literature. Folktales are characterized by an economy of language. Words are not wasted. The tales are brief and, sometimes, astonishingly to the point. In one version of "Hansel and Gretel," the fate of the poor woodcutter's selfish spouse is described in four words: "His wife had died." And that is that!

Like everything else about the folktale, the language is formulaic. Notice how many of the old European tales begin with the familiar formula "Once upon a time." In Africa, we often find tales that open with announcements such as "A story. A story. How does it go?" And we hardly have to mention the familiar ending "And they lived happily ever after." Then there are the magic words, such as "Mirror, mirror, on the wall" or "Open Sesame."

And we can't forget the repetitive language, such as that found in "The Three Pigs" ("Little pig, little pig, let me come in") or in "The Gingerbread Man," whose annoying title character taunts everyone with "Run, run, as fast as you can; You can't catch me, I'm the Gingerbread Man."

These patterns are integral to the folktale, reminding us that this is a story of the imagination, transporting us to another time and place. To eliminate the repetition or to change the pattern would destroy the magic.

Images and Symbols

Images are the pictures a storyteller (or poet) creates for us. They are the sights, sounds, tastes, textures, and smells that make a story memorable (see also the discussion, "Pictures in Poetry," in Chapter 7). Because folktales are so sparsely told and because they were originally oral tales, the images tend to be striking and bold—easy to visualize in the mind's eye and easy to remember. When we recall the popular tales from childhood, we find that we often associate many of them with specific, concrete objects: glass slippers, magic mirrors, poisoned apples, magic lamps, red riding hoods, and so on.

Sometimes an image becomes a symbol; that is, it stands for something greater than itself. Forests, for example, frequently represent the wild unknown—the opposite of civilization (just ask Little Red Riding Hood). Food often represents temptation or the object of desire. Think of Snow White and the apple (see Figure 8.2) or Hansel and Gretel and the gingerbread house. Rapunzel's long hair might be interpreted as a symbol of her womanhood, allowing her to escape her captor and find her future husband (see Figure 8.4). Also, the colors we associate with folktales are the strong colors—black, red, white—and the metallic—gold, silver, bronze. There are no subtle shades of gray, no pastels—these are stories without nuances, without subtleties. Of course, there is always the danger of over-reading when we begin to look for symbols. And often the child's reading is best: Sometimes a frog is just a frog.

Motifs

A motif is a recurring thematic element, a repeated pattern—such as color or shape in painting or a melody in music. In literature, a motif is an identifiable narrative element that recurs in a tale. Folktales, in part because of their oral origins, are rich in motifs. Motifs make it easy for storytellers to enhance and alter plots, adding features from other stories they know—sometimes for convenience, sometimes to stretch out the telling, sometimes to add a new message.

Some of the most commonly found folktale motifs include the following, many of which you will recognize immediately:

- Transforming humans being into beasts
- Imposing and breaking taboos (see the discussion below)

FIGURE 8.2 ■ Walter Crane's illustration for "Snow White," in which she is offered the temptation, the poisoned apple.

FIGURE 8.3 ■ Walter Crane's illustration for "The Sleeping Beauty."

- Using magical objects (sometimes working for the hero, sometimes against)
- Casting magical spells (again, working either for or against the hero)
- Going on a journey or quest
- Meeting a magical helper
- Enduring tests or trials
- Making, breaking, or keeping bargains
- Using deception (sometimes for the good)

These are only a few motifs and in their most generalized forms. Each motif may appear in hundreds of variations. As we read more and more tales, we begin to recognize these motifs and to see the common traits in tales from culture to culture. In "Rumpelstiltskin," for example, we see the motifs of bargains made and broken, the intervention of an enchanted being, the use of magic, and the imposing of tests. In "Little Red Riding Hood" we find the journey, the breaking of a taboo, and the use of deception.

Taboos

A taboo, which is a type of motif, is a very common element found in folktales. It is simply a prohibition against doing, touching, or even saying something because it might result in some supernatural retaliation. Taboos are commonly found in pre-industrial societies, where they serve as means of placating the gods or preserving the social order. (A taboo may consist of a dietary restriction—not eating certain foods, for example; or a sexual restriction—against incest or marrying within one's clan, for example; or it could consist of forbidden words—secret names that must not be spoken aloud; and so on.) Taboos serve many purposes, but one of the most important is establishing limits and setting boundaries. Rules and taboos help make up the moral world of the folktale, just as they do in our own lives. Without rules, all would be chaos. Even little children, when they make up games at play, are insistent on having rules. And once children begin to disregard the rules, the game falls apart, and someone calls "foul." (We will explore this further when we discuss fantasy in Chapter 10.)

Just as in life, when characters in a story break the rules, they must pay. Red Riding Hood is warned not to speak to strangers in the wood, Sleeping Beauty is cautioned to stay away from spinning wheels, and Cinderella is told she must leave the ball by midnight. And what happens when taboos are, inevitably, broken? Characters get eaten up or fall into a perpetual sleep or magic spells are broken. As in life, most of the important lessons have to be learned the hard way. Sometimes the punishment is mitigated—perhaps a hunter will come by and rescue Red Riding Hood; a prince will come by to awaken the Sleeping Beauty (see Figure 8.3); Cinderella will be given another chance to win her prince. And that, too, is what life sometimes brings us.

Types of Folk Narratives

Folk narratives come in many forms, and few generalities will encompass all of them. A few of the most common folk narrative types are described here, but categories often overlap, and these are only suggested as general guidelines.

Talking Animal Tales

Talking animals occur in many, many tales. But in some tales, animals are the main characters—anthropomorphized, of course. Many kinds of tales (we might indeed say most) contain talking animals—fables, merry tales, trickster tales and *pourquoi* tales. Then there are tales in which the characters are simply behaving like ordinary beings, living their everyday lives. These tales include some of the best-known stories—"The Three Pigs," "The Three Billy Goats Gruff," "Henny Penny". In most cases, humans do not appear or, if they do, they play decidedly minor roles. The characters move easily between the animal and human domains. Henny Penny is clearly a fowl of modest intelligence—but she's not the only one; the billy goats graze in the field but cleverly trick the troll; and the three pigs scarcely behave like pigs at all (except that they are attractive food items for wolves). And take the example of "The Musicians of Bremen-Town." An assortment of farm animals (a dog, a rooster, a donkey, they vary with the telling) run away from their masters, who plan to kill them because they are no longer useful—the dog can no longer hunt, the donkey can't pull the cart, and so on. The animals decide to go to Bremen-Town to become musicians (no, they have no musical talents we are aware of). On the way, they discover some robbers holed up in a cottage and counting their loot. The animals devise a plot to scare off the robbers, whereupon they settle down in the cottage with the treasure and live happily ever after, in comfortable retirement.

Fables

Another popular form of talking animal tale is the fable, a tale that uses animal characters allegorically to teach a specific lesson. In an allegory, the characters represent specific human types, such as greed, gullibility, selfishness, and so on. And the fable typically concludes with a clearly stated moral lesson. The following fable is taken from those attributed to the Greek teacher Aesop:

> *A very hungry fox came upon a vineyard where hung many bunches of the most delicious, the most luscious grapes you could ever wish to see. However, the grapes were staked to a high trellis, and the fox could not reach them, no matter how hard he tried. After many vain leaps, the exhausted fox gave up, exclaiming, "Oh, those grapes look green and sour. I didn't want them anyway." And off he went.*
>
> *The moral of the story is:* It is easy to find an excuse for not wanting what we cannot have.

This, of course, is the origin of the old expression "sour grapes." A fable, which does not always include talking animals, is always brief, features sharply defined characters, and a moral lesson is usually announced at the end, just in case we miss it.

Wonder Tales

Also referred to by the German term *Märchen* (roughly pronounced "mér-ken"), wonder tales are some of the most famous tales. Most people call these "fairy tales," even though few contain "fairies," but all include some form of magic. A wonder tale is a serious tale about characters who must overcome evil, usually with the aid of some magical power. These tales are often, but not necessarily, about aristocratic or royal people—they were the movie stars of their day. The heroes and heroines in wonder tales are typically young and beautiful and good. (Sometimes they are clever, but that is not a requirement, particularly if they have magical helpers on their side.) The stories are all formulaic, and they often contain the highly ritualized language and patterns we discussed above.

Wonder tales, especially those from Europe—"Cinderella," "Sleeping Beauty," "Rapunzel" (see Figure 8.4), and so on—are remarkable for their emphasis on worldliness. The heroes and heroines acquire wealth and power; gold, silver, and precious jewels occur frequently as rewards or objects of desire. In those tales that conclude with the hero and heroine marrying at the end and living happily ever after, we usually find that the happy couple are now a king and queen and live in a castle with servants at their beck and call. Poverty is seen as abhorrent, and wealth is an honorable goal. (Of course, we should remember that many of these tales are products of an earlier time, when most people lived in dire poverty and on the brink of starvation. The tales may be part of a wish-fulfilling fantasy.)

Merry Tales

Also called droll, noodlehead, or simpleton tales, these blatantly silly stories usually draw on animal or peasant characters who are portrayed as foolish or gullible,

FIGURE 8.4 ■ H. J. Ford's illustration for "Rapunzel."

presumably because of their lack of education or proper upbringing. A merry tale may include magical elements—talking animals, magic spells, enchanted creatures—but its chief trait is the foolishness of its main characters. The characters in myths, heroic legends, and wonder tales—who are often divine, royal, or aristocratic—take themselves quite seriously; there is nothing funny about "Cinderella" or "Beauty and the Beast." But the characters in merry tales are always ridiculous.

A merry tale allows us to let down our hair. Life requires comic relief, and merry tales provide that. They contain no lessons to be learned (except perhaps that the world has no shortage of fools). They turn the world upside down. After all, laughter is the result of an incongruous juxtaposition—the unexpected response, the out-of-place action.

Unlike in the wonder tale, where the hero usually ends up with a grand reward (the girl, the jewels, and the kingdom), the heroes of the merry tale do not always get what they want. But they seldom care. They accept life at face value and seem quite capable of making the best of a difficult situation—even when they themselves have caused the situation. Take this well-known example:

> A very poor couple were cutting wood for their fire one day when they heard a tiny voice cry, "Help me! Help me!" Lo and behold, it was a little imp caught beneath a great log. The couple lifted the log and released the poor imp.
>
> It turns out the imp had magical powers, and he said to them, "In gratitude for your kind assistance, I will grant you three wishes—but three only."
>
> The couple returned to their poor cottage and pondered their good fortune. The husband said, "We could wish for a great fortune or servants or a team of horses." The wife said, "Or we could wish for a fine house or new clothes or jewels."
>
> At last the husband said, "Right now I am exhausted and hungry. I just wish I had a pan full of sausages."
>
> Instantly, on the fire appeared a frying pan full of juicy sausages.
>
> The wife was furious. "You idiot! You have wasted one of our wishes on a pan of sausages! How I wish those sausages were on the end of your nose."
>
> Instantly, on the end of the husband's nose, appeared the string of sausages, straight from the frying pan.
>
> And try as they could, the couple were unable to pull the sausages from the man's nose.
>
> They now had one wish left. They could wish for money, servants, houses, jewels, but could they enjoy them if the man had to live the rest of his life with a string of sausages attached to the end of his nose? They had but one choice.
>
> They held each other's hand, closed their eyes, and together wished the sausages back in the frying pan. And so it happened.
>
> "At least," said the husband, "we got a fine supper of sausages out of it."

This tale, usually called "The Three Wishes," is a characteristic merry tale, and although we may lament the foolishness of the poor couple, something tells us that they are much happier now than if they had wished for riches and houses and clothes. The magic, unlike that in the wonder tale, does the characters more harm than good, and they decide they are better off without it. And, despite its obvious light-heartedness, the tale can cause us to think about what we might wish for had we the chance. Wishes reveal a great deal about human values and character.

Cumulative Tales

Cumulative tales use the cumulative plot device, in which a repetitive pattern—either repeated dialogue or repeated action or both—gradually builds up to a climax. A famous example is the story of "Henny Penny," which uses both repeated dialogue and action. Henny Penny is a foolish hen, who, when an acorn hits her on the head, thinks the sky is falling. So she runs off to tell the king. On her way, she tells her story to an equally foolish cock (Cocky Locky), a duck (Ducky Lucky), a goose (Goosey Loosey), and a turkey (Turkey Lurkey), each, in turn, joining her on her way to tell the king. At last they meet a clever fox (Foxy Loxy) who persuades them that a quicker way to the king is through his fox's den—and that is the last we ever see of the hen, the cock, the duck, the goose, and the turkey (although we are told that the fox and his family enjoyed a splendid repast that day).

Or consider the tale of "The Three Billy Goats Gruff," in which each succeeding goat is larger and fiercer than the last and has a deeper and gruffer voice. This pattern is known as *stylized intensification*, which is a fancy term for an element that becomes increasingly exaggerated with each repetition. We also find this in "The Three Pigs," with each pig building a house that is just a little sturdier than the last pig's. We see another variation in the Russian tale often referred to as "The Turnip," about an old man who grew a turnip that was so large he could not pull it out of the ground. His wife grabs onto him to help, then their granddaughter, their dog, their cat, all pulling together in a chain, but it not until a little mouse joins them that the turnip pops out of the ground. (The theme of this tale is expressed in that old saying about "the straw that broke the camel's back.")

Tall Tales and Local Legends

A tall tale describes exaggerated heroic feats by a fictional human character (such as Paul Bunyan, the legendary lumberjack, and Babe, his big blue ox, or Pecos Bill, the greatest cowboy). Such exaggerated tales are very popular in America, perhaps appealing to the American love affair with the "most extreme"—the biggest, tallest, richest, and so on.

A local legend describes similarly exaggerated feats but has its roots in historical fact. However, the lines between fact and fiction are blurred. A good example of a legend is the popular tale of William Tell that emerged from the Swiss movement for independence from Austria during the 1300s:

> *William Tell was a man of great physical strength and the most skilled marksman in Altdorf. One day, the wicked Austrian governor, named Gessler, caused a hat to be propped up on a stick*

in the town square and ordered the people to bow to it, signifying their submission to Austrian rule. The proud William Tell refused and was arrested. Gessler ordered Tell to shoot an apple off his son's head with a crossbow from a hundred paces—or else both would be executed. The brave Tell took the bow in his hand and aimed it at the apple balanced on his young son's head. He let the arrow fly, and it split the apple in two, sparing his son and freeing Tell, who eventually killed Gessler.

Although there is no concrete evidence that Tell ever existed, the story has been told for generations and has been the subject of a play and an opera—and his statue stands in Altdorf today. The specific local references and the mentioning of individuals' names make this a legend. Notice that, in this case, no magic is involved—only incredible skill. Legends have to have a touch of veracity.

Ghost Stories and Jump Tales

Young people revel in telling ghost stories at pajama parties and around campfires. We enjoy ghost stories because we enjoy the adrenaline rush when we are frightened—in a controlled environment. They appeal to our latent superstitious natures, our longing to believe in a world beyond the visible landscape. And there may also be a sense of emotional achievement we experience, much as when we accomplish a daring act—a sense of triumph at having heard a blood-curdling, horrifying story and coming away unscathed. Ghost stories are especially popular among adolescents, which suggests that these stories are, indeed, part of a rite of passage. The interactive ghost story—common around campfires and at pajama parties—involves the audience. These are often called "jump" tales—and you will see why from this example:

> *There was an old woman who lived all by herself, and she was very lonely. Sitting in the kitchen one night, she said, "Oh, I wish I had some company."*
>
> *No sooner had she spoken than down the chimney tumbled two feet from which the flesh had rotted. The old woman's eyes bulged with terror.*
>
> *Then two legs dropped to the hearth and attached themselves to the feet.*
>
> *Then a body tumbled down, then two arms and a man's head.*
>
> *As the old woman watched, the parts came together into a great, gangling man. The man danced around and around the room. Faster and faster he went. Then he stopped, and he looked into her eyes.*
>
> *"What do you come for?" she asked in a small voice that shivered and shook.*
>
> *"What do I come for?" he said. "I come—for YOU!"*
>
> *The storyteller shouts the last words, stamps his or her feet, and jumps at someone nearby.*

—(Schwartz, *Scary Stories*, 12)

Trickster Tales

The trickster is a mythological figure—sometimes a demi-god (half-god, half-human)—whose role is to challenge society's norms and rules. Many early societies celebrated their trickster figures because they were so entertaining. Among the American Indians we find Coyote and Raven and the little humpback figure of Kokopelli; in Europe, the fox was often a trickster. The trickster often sets out to break the rules—and when he does, sometimes good things happen and sometimes bad things happen. The Indians of the Pacific Northwest tell about the time when the world was in darkness. All the light was concealed in a box and jealously guarded by Old Man (a sort of ancestral god). But Raven came along and outwitted Old Man to get the light for himself. However, once light escaped from the box, there was no controlling it, and that is how we have light today (see Gerald McDermott's *Raven*).

A favorite African trickster is Anansi the Spider (see Figure 8.5). In one tale Anansi asks the Sky God for all the world's stories. The Sky God agrees, but only if Anansi can complete three tasks: Bring the Sky God a python, hornets, and a leopard. Through his cunning, he outwits the animals, and that is why Anansi today is the keeper of the world's stories. Everyone enjoys the trickster for his incorrigibility, his talent for survival, his unpredictability, his brazenness. Often the trickster does what we wish we could do if we had the courage. The trickster is a necessary part of society, always keeping the rest of us on our toes. It is easy to see why children love these figures.

Pourquoi Tales

Like trickster tales, *pourquoi* tales are partly mythological: They explain the origin of things (*pourquoi* is French for "why"). The story of Raven bringing light to the world, described above, is a very good example. A touching example comes from the Ojibwe and explains the origin of the Sleeping Bear Dune, a large sand dune on the northwestern shore of Michigan's Lower Peninsula:

> *A mother bear and her two cubs were swimming east across Lake Michigan when, in the midst of a great storm, the cubs tired and could go no longer. Their mother, who had reached the shore, watched helplessly as her cubs drowned in the lake. Unable to take her eyes from the water where her cubs perished, she died of grief. The mother bear's body was transformed by the Great Spirit Manitou into the mighty sand dune, and her cubs became the two islands known today as North and South Manitou Islands.*

Anansi, mentioned above as a trickster tale, is also a *pourquoi* tale, since it explains how humans (through Anansi) acquired the art of storytelling from the gods. As we mentioned above, all these categories are fluid and frequently overlapping. Folktales have always been organic creations, ever changing, crossing boundaries, and re-visioning the world.

FIGURE 8.5 ■ In this, one of hundreds of Anansi tales, the trickster spider is devoured by a fish, and his six sons, each with a distinctive talent, rescue him. But then Anansi must decide which one is to be rewarded. Gerald McDermott's illustrations were inspired by African folk art.

Myths and Traditional Epics

Myths are the sacred stories of a culture, and they form the basis of most religions. In fact, the term *myth* does not mean "falsehood," but rather refers to a sacred narrative usually explaining the origins of the world, of natural phenomena, of humankind, of sin, and of death. To people of Western cultures, the most familiar mythology outside the Judeo-Christian tradition is that of ancient Greece and Rome. Our daily lives are imbued with references to their gods and goddesses and their heroes. We have given their names to the planets, stars, and galaxies, and, on a more mundane level, months of the year (January, March, May, and June), body parts (Achilles tendon), cleaning agents (Ajax), synthetic fibers (Herculon), automobiles (Mercury), mapbooks (Atlas), athletic games (Olympics), and spacecraft (*Apollo* and *Gemini*), all of which derive from Greek or Roman mythology.

Another important influence on the Western tradition is Norse mythology, which reflects the harsh way of life engendered by the severe, yet dramatically beautiful, Scandinavian lands. In Norse mythology, the gods and goddesses were defenders of humanity against the mighty forces of evil. Like the Greek and Roman gods and goddesses, the Norse deities were anthropomorphic; that is, the gods and goddesses had human forms. But compared with the Greek deities, the Norse gods and goddesses were a much more serious lot, engaged in a perpetual struggle with the forces of evil—a struggle that they were destined eventually to lose. Individual codes of honor were highly esteemed in this war-conscious society. We remember the Norse gods in our days of the week: Tuesday is named for Tiw (the Norse god of war), Wednesday for Woden (the father of the gods), Thursday for Thor (the thunder god), and Friday for Fria (the goddess of fruits). This fascinating mythology still lingers with us.

The Greeks, Romans, and Norse, like the Hebrews, envisioned their deities in human form. Other cultures, however, have viewed their deities differently. For instance, the ancient Egyptian gods and goddesses were often depicted as part human and part animal. The Hindu deities took on many unusual forms, some possessing multiple heads and limbs, some blue in color, and so on. A culture's gods reveal much about its view of the universe and of humanity's role in that universe.

Throughout the world we find cultures with compelling myths to tell—from the wondrous stories of the American Indians, celebrating their belief in oneness with the natural world, to the deep well of tales from Africa and Asia, with their special brand of enchantment. Today these myths are becoming widely available in children's versions, and they are excellent methods of introducing world cultures. Many of the collections of folktales listed in the bibliography at the end of this chapter are retellings of mythological tales from around the world.

Related to the ancient myths are the heroic epics, which were originally part of the oral tradition and eventually written down. The popular heroes of ancient Greece and Rome include Achilles, Odysseus, Hector, Jason, and Perseus. In the Middle Ages we find the stories of the heroic Beowulf and of King Arthur and his knights. They were indeed the first superheroes, the prototypes of Superman, Batman, and Wonder Woman. Children's versions—such as Padraic Colum's *The Children's Homer* and *The Golden Fleece and the Heroes Who Lived before Achilles*, Rosemary Sutcliff's *The Light beyond the Forest* (about the medieval quest for the Holy Grail), and Michael Morpurgo's *Beowulf*—are all very popular.

The lasting influence of the great epics is evident in our modern-day fantasy fiction—which is the subject of the Chapter 10. Anyone who has seen such popular films as George Lucas's *Star Wars* series or Peter Jackson's *The Lord of the Rings* series or James Cameron's *Avatar* is well aware of this influence.

Folktales in the Classroom

Because of their brevity, straightforward narratives, sharply defined characters, and inventive qualities, folktales are a rich source of educational activities. For the youngest readers, these stories spark an interest in reading and storytelling. They help develop the imagination and can serve as a springboard to art projects (see Chapter 3). However, folktales offer a multitude of opportunities for older readers as well. (We never really outgrow them, as proven by their constant re-emergence in new dress on today's movie screens.) Figure 8.6 provides just a few suggestions. Only our imaginations limit the possibilities.

FIGURE 8.6 ■ A Dozen Things to Do with Folktales

1. Share a favorite folktale from memory—and make your retelling as dramatic as possible.
2. Join a group and prepare a story theater presentation of a favorite folktale.
3. Read a folktale (new or familiar) and make a list of the characters, along with the character traits each possesses.
4. Create a collage for your favorite folktale. Make sure it includes all the important elements of the story.
5. Compare two or more picture-book versions of the same tale and consider how the differences change the meaning. (Multiple versions are easy to find, especially of tales like "Little Red Riding Hood," "Hansel and Gretel," "Cinderella," and "The Three Pigs." Try to select vastly different versions.)
6. Make up a new ending for an old folktale—and explain how it changes the story's meaning.
7. Make up a folktale that includes each of the following objects in its plot—a rope, a bell, a mouse, an old oak tree, and a silk scarf (or any set of objects provided by your teacher).
8. Join a group and prepare a reader's theater performance of a folktale. (Excellent free reader's theater scripts from *Reader's Theater Editions*, at www.aaronshep.com, are designed to include a large number of readers and are perfect for class use.)
9. Read several parodies of folktales (David Wiesner's *The Three Pigs*, John Scieszka's *The True Story of the Three Little Pigs*, and Eugene Trivizas's *The Three Little Wolves and the Big Bad Pig*, for example). Join a group and prepare your own parody.
10. Use a folktale to demonstrate what a motif is (or a symbol or a protagonist or an antagonist or some other literary device).
11. Retell an old folktale in modern dress. It may or may not be a parody, for serious retellings occur all the time.
12. On your own or with a group, create an illustrated version of a favorite folktale. You are free to adapt it in any way you wish—but you will have to explain it.

Summary

Folktales and myths are our oldest stories, and they remain some of the best. Whether they are the high-minded tales of good triumphing over evil or the delightful absurdity of the merry tale or the inventiveness of the myths and legends, these tales have left an indelible mark on world culture. Folktales, legends, and myths continue to be popular because, as one scholar puts it, "they are survival tales with hope" (Zipes, *Why Fairy Tales Stick*, 27). And survival often means being opportunistic, exploitative, and selfish, which explains the harsh edge we find in many of the tales. These tales go right to the core of the eternal struggle of good and evil. They show us the dangers in greed, extravagance, and lack of self-control and the good in generosity, faithfulness, strength of character, and humility. Over and over again, we will find these messages woven into the fabric of these tales. In addition, the tales can be excellent introductions to the study of literature and of culture. And as we read tales from other lands and cultures, we come to realize that far more important than our differences are the ways we are all very much alike.

For Reflection and Discussion

1. Locate two different versions of the same folk narrative—two "Cinderella" stories or two "Three Little Pigs" stories, for example. Compare the presentation of the setting, the plot, the characters, the theme. What motifs do you find? Are there images or symbols? Compare the language used. Which do you think best captures the flavor of oral narrative? Explain.

2. Do you recall a favorite folktale from your childhood? Find a version of that tale and reread it. Why do you think it held such appeal for you? Was the story addressing some psychological need you may have felt? How do you respond to it today?

3. Locate a folktale from one of the older, traditional collections, such as the Grimm Brothers or Andrew Lang or Joseph Jacobs. Now find a modern version (picture book versions abound) and compare the two. What are the chief differences between them, and why do you think the modern version made the changes it did?

4. It is easy to find parodies of folktales (John Scieszka's *The True Story of the Three Little Pigs* is just one of the most famous ones). Locate one of these parodies and read it. Does the parody have a purpose? Does it succeed in that purpose? Does the parody work if we don't know the original tale? Explain.

Works Cited

Schwartz, Alvin, reteller. *Scary Stories to Tell in the Dark*. New York: HarperCollins, 1981.

Zipes, Jack. *Why Fairy Tales Stick: The Evolution and Relevance of a Genre*. New York: Routledge, 2006.

Recommended Resources

Armstrong, Karen. *A Short History of Myth*. Edinburgh: Cannongate, 2005.

Bernheimer, Kate, ed. *Mirror, Mirror on the Wall: Women Writers Explore Their Favorite Fairy Tales*. New York: Doubleday, 1998.

Bettelheim, Bruno. *The Uses of Enchantment: The Meaning and Importance of Fairy Tales*. New York: Knopf, 1976.

Bosma, Betty. *Fairy Tales, Fables, Legends, and Myths: Using Folk Literature in Your Classroom*, 2nd ed. New York: Teachers College Press, 1993.

Bottigheimer, Ruth, ed. *Fairy Tales and Society: Illusion, Allusion, and Paradigm*. Philadelphia: University of Pennsylvania Press, 1986.

——. *Grimms' Bad Girls and Bold Boys: The Moral and Social Vision of the Tales*. New Haven, CT: Yale University Press, 1987.

Campbell, Joseph. *The Hero with a Thousand Faces*, 2nd ed. Princeton, NJ: Princeton University Press, 1968.

Chase, Richard. *American Folk Tales and Songs*. New York: Dover, 1971.

Cook, Elizabeth. *The Ordinary and the Fabulous*. Cambridge, MA: Cambridge University Press, 1969.

Hettinga, Donald R. *The Brothers Grimm: Two Lives, One Legacy*. New York: Clarion, 2001.

Levorato, Alessandra. *Language and Gender in the Fairy Tale Tradition: A Linguistic Analysis of Old and New Story Telling*. Houndmills, UK: Palgrave Macmillan, 2003.

Lieberman, Marcia R. "'Some Day My Prince Will Come': Female Acculturation through the Fairy Tale." *College English* 34, 3 (1972): 383–395.

Lüthi, Max. *The European Folktale: Form and Nature*. Bloomington: Indiana University Press, 1982.

——. *Once Upon a Time: On the Nature of Fairy Tales*. 1970. Bloomington: Indiana University Press, 1976.

Petrone, Penny. *Native Literature in Canada: From the Oral Tradition to the Present*. Oxford: Oxford University Press, 1990.

Stone, Kay. "Fairy Tales for Adults: Walt Disney's Americanization of the Märchen." *Folklore on Two Continents*. Ed. N. Burlakoff and C. Lindahl. Bloomington: Indiana University Press, 1980.

——. "The Misuses of Enchantment: Controversies on the Significance of Fairy Tales." *Women's Folklore, Women's Culture*. Ed. Rosan A. Jordan and Susan J. Kalicik. Philadelphia: University of Pennsylvania Press, 1985.

Storr, Catherine. "Folk and Fairy Tales." *Children's Literature in Education* 17 (Spring 1986): 63–70.

SurLaLuneFairytales.com

- A useful and accessible website that provides information and discussion opportunities on the topic of folktales.

Tatar, Maria. *Off with Their Heads: Fairy Tales and the Culture of Childhood*. Princeton, NJ: Princeton University Press, 1992.

Thompson, Stith. *The Folktale*. New York: Holt, Rinehart and Winston, 1951.

Warner, Marina. *From the Beast to the Blonde: On Fairy Tales and Their Tellers*. New York: Farrar, Straus & Giroux, 1995.

Yolen, Jane. *Touch Magic*. New York: Philomel, 1981.

Zipes, Jack. *Breaking the Magic Spell: Radical Theories of Folk and Fairy Tales*. Austin: University of Texas Press, 1979.

——. *Don't Bet on the Prince: Contemporary Feminist Fairy Tales in North America and England*. London: Methuen, 1986.

——. *Fairy Tales and the Art of Subversion: The Classical Genre for Children and the Process of Civilization*. London: Heinemann, 1983.

——. *When Dreams Came True: Classical Fairy Tales and Their Tradition*. New York: Routledge, 1999.

Folk Narratives: A Selected and Annotated Booklist

Picture-Book Versions

Annotations have been included only if the title does not provide an adequate description.
*Tales from outside the western European tradition.

*Aardema, Verna. *Bringing the Rain to Kapiti Plain*. Illus. Beatriz Vidal. New York: Dial, 1981.
• A cumulative tale from Africa.

*——. *Why Mosquitoes Buzz in People's Ears*. Illus. Leo and Diane Dillon. New York: Dial, 1975.
• A strikingly illustrated African *pourquoi* tale.

Brown, Marcia. *Cinderella*. New York: Scribner's, 1954.

*Cendrars, Blaise. *Shadows*. Illus. Marcia Brown. New York: Scribner's, 1982.
• An African story.

*Climo, Shirley. *The Egyptian Cinderella*. Illus. Ruth Heller. New York: Crowell, 1989.

Cooney, Barbara. *Chanticleer and the Fox*. New York: Crowell, 1958.
• A European trickster tale.

*Demi. *The Firebird*. New York: Holt, 1994.
• Based on a favorite Russian folktale.

dePaola, Tomie. *Strega Nona*. New York: Prentice Hall, 1975.
• A comic Italian folktale.

Domanska, Janina. *Little Red Hen*. New York: Macmillan, 1973.

Galdone, Paul. *Hansel and Gretel*. New York: McGraw-Hill, 1982.

——. *Henny Penny*. New York: Clarion, 1979.
• A cumulative tale about a gullible hen who thinks the sky is falling.

*Haley, Gale. *A Story, a Story*. New York: Atheneum, 1970.
• An African tale about the origin of all the stories.

Hyman, Trina Schart. *Little Red Riding Hood*. New York: Holiday House, 1983.

Jarrell, Randall, reteller. *Snow White and the Seven Dwarfs*. Illus. Nancy Ekholm Burkert. New York: Farrar, Straus & Giroux, 1972.

*Johari, Harish. *Little Krishna*. Illus. Pieter Weltevrede. New York: Bear Cub, 2002.
• A Hindu tale about a favorite Hindu god.

Johnston, Tony. *The Cowboy and the Black-eyed Pea*. Illus. Warren Ludwig. New York: Putnam, 1992.
• A parody of the Princess and the Pea.

Kellogg, Steven. *Paul Bunyan: A Tall Tale*. New York: Morrow, 1984.

Lester, Julius. *John Henry*. Illus. Jerry Pinkney. New York: Dial, 1994.
• An American tall tale about a man of great strength.

*Louie, Ai-Ling. *Yeh-Shen: A Cinderella Story from China*. Illus. Ed Young. New York: Philomel, 1982.

Marshall, James. *Red Riding Hood*. New York: Dial, 1987.

*McDermott, Gerald. *Anansi the Spider*. New York: Holt, 1972.
• An African tale about an irrepressible trickster.

*——. *Arrow to the Sun*. New York: Viking, 1974.
• A creation tale from the Pueblo of the Southwest.

*——. *Raven: A Trickster Tale from the Pacific Northwest*. New York: Harcourt, 1993.
• A trickster tale about the bringing of light to humankind.

Moser, Barry, reteller. *The Three Little Pigs*. Boston: Little, Brown, 2001.

*Novesky, Amy. *Elephant Prince: The Story of Ganesh*. Illus. Belgin K. Wedman. San Rafael, CA: Mandala, 2004.

• A Hindu tale about the origin of all the stories.

Orgel, Doris, reteller. *The Bremen Town Musicians: And Other Animal Tales from Grimm*. Illus. Bert Kitchen. New Milford, CT: Roaring Brook, 2004.

Pinkney, Jerry, reteller. *Aesop's Fables*. New York: SeaStar/North-South, 2000.

• The famous talking animal moral tales from ancient Greece.

——. *Little Red Riding Hood*. New York: Little, Brown, 2007.

*Polacco, Patricia. *Babushka Baba Yaga*. New York: Philomel, 1993.

• A Russian tale featuring the famous witch.

*San Souci, Robert D., adapter. *Cendrillon: A Caribbean Cinderella*. Illus. Brian Pinkney. New York: Simon & Schuster, 1998.

*——, reteller. *Little Gold Star: A Spanish-American Cinderella*. Illus. Sergio Martinez. New York: HarperCollins, 2000.

Scieszka, John. *The Stinky Cheese Man and Other Fairly Stupid Tales*. Illus. Lane Smith. New York: Viking, 1992.

——. *The True Story of the Three Little Pigs*. Illus. Lane Smith. New York: Viking, 1989.

• Both of these books by Scieszka are parodies of traditional tales.

*Steptoe, John. *Mufaro's Beautiful Daughters: An African Tale*. New York: Lothrop, 1987.

Trivizas, Eugene. *The Three Little Wolves and the Big Bad Pig*. (1993) Illus. Helen Oxenbury. New York: Margaret McElderry, 1997.

• A parody with role reversal.

Weisner, David. *The Three Pigs*. Boston: Houghton Mifflin, 2001.

• A postmodern parody.

*Young, Ed. *Lon Po Po: A Red Riding Hood Story from China*. New York: Philomel, 1989.

Zelinsky, Paul O. *Rumpelstiltskin*. New York: Dutton, 1986.

• One of several strikingly illustrated European folktales by a talented illustrator.

Zemach, Harve, reteller. *Duffy and the Devil*. Illus. Margot Zemach. New York: Farrar, Straus & Giroux, 1973.

Zemach, Margot, reteller. *The Little Red Hen*. New York: Farrar, Straus & Giroux, 1983.

——. *The Three Little Pigs*. New York: Farrar, Straus & Giroux, 1988.

Folktale Collections

Asbjørnsen, Peter, and Jørgen Moe. *East O' the Sun and West O' the Moon*. New York: Dover, 1970.

• Scandinavian folktales.

*Bierhorst, John, ed. *The Dancing Fox: Arctic Folktales*. New York: Morrow, 1997.

*——. *Lightning Inside You: And Other Native American Riddles*. New York: Morrow, 1992.

*Bloch, Marie Halun. *Ukrainian Folk Tales*. New York: Coward, McCann, 1964.

Briggs, Katharine. *British Folk Tales*. New York: Pantheon, 1977.

*Bushnaq, Inea, trans. *Arab Folktales*. New York: Pantheon, 1986.

Calvino, Italo, ed. *Italian Folktales*. New York: Pantheon, 1980.

*Chandler, Robert, trans. *Russian Folk Tales*. New York: Shambhala/Random House, 1980.

Chase, Richard. *The Jack Tales*. Boston: Houghton Mifflin, 1971.

• American tall tales.

*Demi, adapter. *A Chinese Zoo: Fables and Proverbs*. New York: Harcourt, 1987.

*de Wit, Dorothy. *The Talking Stone: An Anthology of Native American Tales and Legends*. New York: Greenwillow, 1979.

Dickinson, Peter, reteller. *City of Gold and Other Stories from the Old Testament*. Illus. Michael Foreman. London: Gollancz, 1992.

*Fang, Linda, reteller. *The Ch'i-lin Purse: A Collection of Ancient Chinese Stories*. New York: Farrar, Straus & Giroux, 1995.

Glassie, Henry. *Irish Folk Tales*. New York: Pantheon, 1985.

Grimm, Jacob, and Wilhelm Grimm. *Household Stories*. Trans. Lucy Crane. New York: Dover, 1963.
- One of many editions dating from 1812 and onward.

*Gross, Ila Land. *Cinderella around the World*. New York: L.E.A.P., 2001.

Haley, Gail E., reteller and illus. *Mountain Jack Tales*. New York: Penguin, 1992.

*Hausman, Gerald, collector and reteller. *How Chipmunk Got Tiny Feet: Native American Origin Stories*. New York: HarperCollins, 1995.

*Haviland, Virginia. *Favorite Tales Told in India*. Boston: Little, Brown, 1973.

*Hodges, Margaret, reteller. *Hauntings: Ghosts and Ghouls from around the World*. Boston: Little, Brown, 1991.

Hurston, Zora Neale, collector. *Lies and Other Tall Tales*. Adapted and illus. Christopher Myers. New York: HarperCollins, 2005.

Jacobs, Joseph. *Celtic Fairy Tales*. 1891. New York: Dover, 1968.

——. *English Fairy Tales*. 1890. New York: Dover, 1967.

*Jaffe, Nina, and Steve Zeitlin. *While Standing on One Foot: Puzzle Stories and Wisdom Tales from the Jewish Tradition*. Illus. John Segal. New York: Holt, 1993.

*Jaffrey, Madhur. *Seasons of Splendour: Tales, Myths & Legends of India*. Illus. Michael Foreman. Harmondsworth, UK: Puffin, 1987.

*James, Grace, reteller. *Green Willow and Other Japanese Fairy Tales*. New York: Avenel, 1987.

*Joseph, Lynn. *The Mermaid's Twin Sister: More Stories from Trinidad*. New York: Clarion, 1994.

*Kherdian, David, reteller. *Feathers and Tails: Animal Fables from Around the World*. New York: Putnam, 1992.

Lang, Andrew. *The Blue Fairy Book*. 1889. New York: Dover, 1965.
- The first of a famous series of folktales from around the world, collected in the nineteenth century.

*Lester, Julius. *Black Folktales*. New York: Richard W. Baron, 1969.

*Lyons, Mary E., selector. *Raw Head, Bloody Bones: African-American Tales of the Supernatural*. New York: Scribners, 1991.

*Manitonquat (Medicine Story), reteller. *The Children of the Morning Light: Wampanoag Tales*. Illus. Mary F. Arquette. New York: Macmillan, 1994.

*Minford, John, trans. *Favourite Folktales of China*. Beijing, China: New World Press, 1983.

*Neil, Philip, reteller. *Fairy Tales of Eastern Europe*. Boston: Houghton Mifflin, 1991.

Nic Leodhas, Sorche. *Thistle and Thyme: Tales and Legends from Scotland*. New York: Holt, Rinehart and Winston, 1962.

Opie, Iona, and Peter Opie. *The Classic Fairy Tales*. New York: Oxford University Press, 1974.

Perrault, Charles. *Perrault's Fairy Tales*. Illus. Gustave Doré. 1867. New York: Dover, 1969.

*Phelps, Ethel Johnson. *The Maid of the North: Feminist Folk Tales from Around the World*. New York: Holt, Rinehart and Winston, 1981.

*Ross, Gayle. *How Rabbit Tricked Otter and Other Cherokee Trickster Stories*. Illus. Murv Jacob. New York: HarperCollins, 1994.

Rounds, Glen. *Ol' Paul, the Mighty Logger*. New York: Holiday House, 1936.

Schwartz, Alvin, reteller. *Ghosts! Ghostly Tales from Folklore*. New York: HarperCollins, 1991.

*Schwarz, Howard, and Barbara Rush, retellers. *The Diamond Tree: Jewish Tales from Around the World*. New York: HarperCollins, 1991.

*Singer, Isaac Bashevis. *Zlateh the Goat and Other Stories*. New York: Harper, 1966.
- Yiddish folktales.

Tatar, Maria, trans. and ed. *The Grimm Reader: The Classic Tales of the Brothers Grimm*. New York: Norton, 2010.

*Tehranchian, Hassan, adapter. *Kalilah and Dimnah: Fables from the Middle East*. New York: Harmony, 1985.

*Thompson, Vivian L. *Hawaiian Tales of Heroes and Champions*. New York: Holiday House, 1971.

*Vuong, Lynette Dyer. *The Golden Carp and Other Tales from Vietnam*. Illus. Manabu Saito. New York: Lothrop, 1993.

Yeats, W. B., and Lady Gregory. *A Treasury of Irish Myth, Legend, and Folklore*. New York: Avenel, 1986.

*Yep, Laurence, reteller. *Tongues of Jade*. New York: HarperCollins, 1991.
- Chinese tales.

*Yolen, Jane, ed. *Favorite Folktales from Around the World*. New York: Pantheon, 1986.

Epics and Myths

Colum, Padraic. *The Children's Homer: The Adventures of Odysseus and the Tale of Troy.* 1919. New York: Macmillan, 1982.

——. *The Children of Odin: The Book of Northern Myths.* 1920. New York: Macmillan, 1984.

——. *The Golden Fleece and the Heroes Who Lived before Achilles.* 1921. New York: Macmillan, 1983.

Green, Roger Lancelyn. *Heroes of Greece and Troy: Retold from the Ancient Authors.* New York: Walck, 1961.

*Hamilton, Virginia. *In the Beginning: Creation Stories from around the World.* New York: Harcourt Brace Jovanovich, 1988.

Hastings, Selina, reteller. *Sir Gawain and the Loathly Lady.* Illus. Juan Wijngaard. London: Walker Books, 1985.
An Arthurian tale.

Heany, Seamus, trans. *Beowulf.* New York: Farrar, Straus & Giroux, 2000.

*Henderson, Kathy. *Lugalbanda: The Boy Who Got Caught Up in a War.* New York: Candlewick, 2006.
A tale from Ancient Sumeria.

Hieatt, Constance, reteller. *Sir Gawain and the Green Knight.* New York: Crowell, 1967.

*Jendresen, Erik, reteller. *Hanuman: Based on Valmiki's Ramayana.* Illus. Ming Li. Berkeley, CA: Tricycle Press, 1998.
Tales from a classic Hindu epic.

Kimmel, Eric A. *The Hero Beowulf.* New York: Farrar, Straus & Giroux, 2005.

*McCaughrean, Geraldine. *The Bronze Cauldron: Myths and Legends of the World.* New York: Margaret K. McElderry, 1998.

*——. *The Crystal Pool: Myths and Legends of the World.* New York: Margaret K. McElderry, 1999.

*——. *The Golden Hoard: Myths and Legends of the World.* New York: Margaret K. McElderry, 1996.

*——. *The Silver Treasure: Myths and Legends of the World.* New York: Margaret K. McElderry, 1997.

Morpurgo, Michael. *Beowulf.* Cambridge, MA: Candlewick, 2006.

Philip, Neil. *The Tale of Sir Gawain.* Illus. Charles Keeping. New York: Philomel, 1987.

Sherwood, Merriam, trans. *The Song of Roland.* New York: McKay, 1938.

Steig, Jeanne. *A Gift from Zeus: Sixteen Favorite Myths.* Illus. William Steig. New York: HarperCollins, 2001.
A modernized, occasionally racy, retelling.

Sutcliff, Rosemary. *Beowulf.* London: Bodley Head, 1961.
• (Published in the United States as *Dragon Slayer.*)

——. *Black Ships before Troy: The Story of the Iliad.* New York: Delacorte, 1993.

——. *The Light beyond the Forest: The Quest for the Holy Grail.* New York: Dutton, 1980.

——. *The Road to Camlann.* New York: Dutton, 1982.

——. *The Sword and the Circle: King Arthur and the Knights of the Round Table.* New York: Dutton, 1981.

——. *The Wanderings of Odysseus.* New York: Delacorte, 1995.

*Tchana, Katrin Hyman, reteller. *Changing Woman and Her Sisters: Stories of Goddesses from Around the World.* Illus. Trina Schart Hyman. New York: Holiday House, 2006.

*Westwood, Jennifer, reteller. *Gilgamesh and Other Babylonian Tales.* New York: Coward McCann, 1970.

Williams, Marcia. *Greek Myths.* New York: Walker, 2006.

*Zeitlin, Steve. *The Four Corners of the Sky: Creation Stories and Cosmologies from around the World.* New York: Holt, 2000.

9 The Elements of Story

Reading Fiction

Introduction

Whether we are sharing Margaret Wise Brown's *Goodnight Moon* with a toddler, E. B. White's *Charlotte's Web* with a second grader, or Christopher Paul Curtis's *Bud, Not Buddy* with fifth and sixth graders, fictional stories all share one thing in common: They all portray the actions of imaginary characters. Why is it that we can read some stories over and over, and they stick with us forever, whereas we forget other stories as soon as we put down the book? Part of the answer, of course, has to do with us as readers and our individual interests and experiences (see Chapter 3). However, another part of the answer lies in the writer's skill as a storyteller—how he or she draws characters, constructs plots, details settings, and reveals themes. These are at the core of all stories, and in this chapter, which is an introduction to Chapters 10 and 11 on fantasy and realistic fiction, we will examine these elements to see what makes them work—or not work.

Narrative Point of View

Every story has to have a storyteller, whom we call the narrator. Never think of the narrator as the author—rather, think of the narrator as a mask that the author is adopting. Three common narrative approaches are found in children's fiction: first-person narrator, limited narrator, and omniscient narrator.

First-Person Narrator

Sometimes the narrator is also a character in the story, and this is called a first-person narrator. This is easy to identify, since the narrator refers to him- or herself as "I." Richard Peck opens his Newbery Honor book *A Long Way from Chicago* this way: "It was always August when we spent a week with our grandma. I was Joey then, not Joe: Joey

Dowdel, and my sister was Mary Alice. In our first visits we were still just kids, so we could hardly see her town because of Grandma. She was so big, and the town was so small" (1). Naturally, a first-person narrator can only tell us what he or she knows, feels, or experiences, but this is also the most intimate narrator. In Alice Childress's *A Hero Ain't Nothin' but a Sandwich*, we see the plight of Benjie, a 13-year-old African American boy struggling with heroin. The story is told from multiple points of view, including that of Benjie, his mother, grandmother, mother's boyfriend, teachers, and others. It is reminiscent of a documentary, in which we have to piece together the truth from the observations of several witnesses.

Limited Narrator

The limited narrator is an outside storyteller (that is, not a character within the story) whose viewpoint is limited to that of a single character. In other words, the limited narrator tells us only what that one character knows and feels. In the first chapter of *Little House in the Big Woods*, Laura Ingalls Wilder introduces her characters like this:

> *So far as the little girl could see, there was only the one little house where she lived with her Father and Mother, her sister Mary and baby sister Carrie. A wagon track ran before the house, turning and twisting out of sight in the woods where the wild animals lived, but the little girl did not know where it went, nor what might be at the end of it.*
>
> *The little girl was named Laura and she called her father, Pa, and her mother, Ma. In those days and in that place, children did not say Father and Mother, nor Mamma and Papa, as they do now.* (2–3)

The narrator's viewpoint is limited to Laura's, and we will not learn where the wagon track goes until she does. Like the first-person narrator, the limited narrator provides intimacy, but it is not restricted by the vocabulary or grammar of 5-year-old Laura.

Omniscient Narrator

The omniscient narrator is also an outside narrator, but one who knows the thoughts and feelings of all the characters in a story. *Omniscient*, in fact, means "all-knowing." Since both the omniscient narrator and the limited narrator are outside storytellers, it is not always obvious which is being used at first. E. B. White's *Charlotte's Web* opens with the exclamation of the young girl, Fern, "Where's Papa going with that axe?" We might suspect that this story is being told from Fern's point of view. But in the second chapter, the focus shifts to the little pig, Wilbur. Later on, we see things through the eyes of the farmer and hired hand and then through Fern's parents' eyes. This shifting viewpoint clearly identifies an omniscient narrator. The omniscient narrator is typically the most detached narrative viewpoint, but it also allows the reader to see the story from a variety of perspectives.

Setting

The setting includes the time, the geographical location, and the social circumstances in a story. A well-drawn setting helps establish the mood, the atmosphere. Wilder's *Little House on the Prairie*, for example, is set on the Great Plains in the latter half of the nineteenth century. So we read descriptions of the daily activities of the Ingalls family—poor settlers eking out a living in a place where wells are dug by hand, the nearest neighbor is miles away, and the family huddles in a log cabin behind a blanket for a door while wolves lurk perilously close outside.

Sometimes the setting almost becomes a character, challenging the protagonist to show his or her mettle. Setting is crucial in survival stories, such as Scott O'Dell's *Island of the Blue Dolphins* or Jean Craighead George's *Julie of the Wolves*, in which the protagonists are struggling to survive in hostile environments—inhospitable weather, dangerous wildlife, and tormenting isolation.

The setting can also be crucial when the story takes place in foreign lands (Lois Lowry's *Number the Stars* re-creates the atmosphere of Denmark during World War II), or in imaginary lands (remember Dorothy's remark in *The Wizard of Oz*, "Toto, I have a feeling we're not in Kansas anymore"), or in science fiction, where a future world must be envisioned. Indeed, one of the reasons these stories are so popular is because their settings permit readers to escape to imaginary places, where life is more exciting and where they may forget for a while the cares of their everyday lives.

Characters

A story is not likely to stick if it does not have believable and memorable characters. We often remember the characters long after we have forgotten a book's title or the specific details of its plot. Who can forget Pinocchio? Or Huck Finn? Or Wilbur and Charlotte? The creation of interesting characters is an essential part of any successful fictional story.

Character Types

The principal characters of a story include the protagonist (the main sympathetic character) and the antagonist (the chief opponent of the protagonist). We sometimes call these characters the hero and villain; however, protagonists are not always heroic, and antagonists are not always villainous. Protagonists might be strong, compassionate, and fearless, but they may also be bullheaded and rash. Antagonists might be dastardly, but they might also have an unexpected streak of generosity.

Usually a story includes several minor or supporting characters, who can be interesting in their own right—Long John Silver in *Treasure Island* or the Scarecrow in *The Wonderful*

Wizard of Oz, for example. Many times these minor characters are stock characters representing types rather than individuals—the flatterer, the show-off, the conceited, the tight-fisted, the addle-brained, the snob, and so on. When a character possesses the opposite traits of another character, we call him or her a foil character. "Foil" is a jeweler's term for a setting designed to making a jewel look bigger and brighter. So Templeton, the self-centered rat in *Charlotte's Web*, is a foil to Charlotte, and makes her kind and selfless nature seem all the more desirable.

Character Traits and Development

Each character may possess specific personality traits, but not all characters are as completely fleshed out as others. Some characters reveal fully developed personalities; these are the round characters. Charlotte, for example, is wise, compassionate, determined, and resourceful; Wilbur is at times happy, sad, frightened, loving, and so on. Other characters are only partially developed; these are the flat characters. We usually see just one side of them (the selfish rat Templeton, the stuttering goose, and the dim-witted farmhand are all examples of flat characters in *Charlotte's Web*).

In addition, some round characters may change through the course of the story; these are called dynamic characters. For example, at the beginning of *Charlotte's Web*, Wilbur is immature, self-absorbed, timid, and fearful, but by the end he becomes brave, selfless, and compassionate. Wilbur's transformation, his intellectual and psychological growth, is what makes him a dynamic character.

A single story will have very few dynamic characters—rarely more than one or two. Any more than that would take a very long book, indeed. Most characters are what we call static characters—that is, their personalities really do not change. The selfish rat, Templeton, is just the same rapscallion at the end of the story as at the beginning—he does a good deed only when there is something in it for him. Templeton is a flat and static character. Charlotte, on the other hand, is a well-rounded character, but she does not actually change. She is wise, kind, and compassionate from the very beginning—and she remains that way. In fact, we don't want her to change. This makes her a round but static character.

Character Revelation

And finally, we should consider how we learn about characters in a book. We gain our knowledge of characters in several ways:

- *What the narrator says about the character*—Although reliable, this usually is the least memorable way of getting to know a character (it's like learning about someone from a lecture).
- *What the other characters say about the character*—This evidence is only as reliable as the source; we must be wary of hidden motives or prejudices. Do we really trust what Templeton says about someone?

- *What the character says about him- or herself*—This information is usually quite reliable, but we should remember that people do not always mean what they say, nor do they always understand themselves. At the beginning of *Charlotte's Web*, for instance, can Wilbur really explain why he is so timid and so self-absorbed?
- *What the character actually does*—Actions, we all know, speak louder than words, and it is through actions that some of the most convincing evidence about character is revealed. The actions of Wilbur, Charlotte, and Templeton really tell us what the characters are like.

Plot

The novelist E. M. Forster once said, "The king died and then the queen died is a story. The king died, and then the queen died of grief is a plot" (86). The point is that the plot is not just a series of events; it is a series of *interrelated* events. In life, for example, you get someone else's mail by mistake, your phone rings and it's a wrong number, your neighbor cancels a luncheon engagement, and a friend asks you to take him to the dentist. This is not a plot—it's just a series of unfortunate events. In a plot, we expect every occurrence to have a purpose. The mail was deliberately switched so you wouldn't see the birthday cards that came. The so-called wrong number was a ruse to see if you were home. And your friend doesn't need a dentist appointment but just wants to get you out of the house so your neighbor can decorate for your surprise birthday party. The point is that a plot makes connections between the various incidents. Let's now look at three common plot patterns—dramatic, episodic, and parallel—and the journey device.

Dramatic Plot

A dramatic plot is a narrative based on a single major conflict that must be resolved. Typically, it begins by introducing the characters, setting, and conflict, which is followed by a rising action that intensifies gradually until reaching a peak or turning point. This is called the climax. The story then ends with a denouement or the conclusion that wraps up all the loose ends (see Figure 9.1). This structure, with its chronological arrangement, is probably the most familiar storyline; it is commonly found in mysteries, adventures, romances, folktales, and most picture-book stories. E. B. White's *Charlotte's Web* is a good example.

Episodic Plot

An episodic plot occurs when each chapter in a book is a self-contained dramatic story, with all the chapters tied together by characters and/or theme. Episodic plots are found in most weekly television sitcoms and dramas; each episode is complete in itself. Laura Ingalls

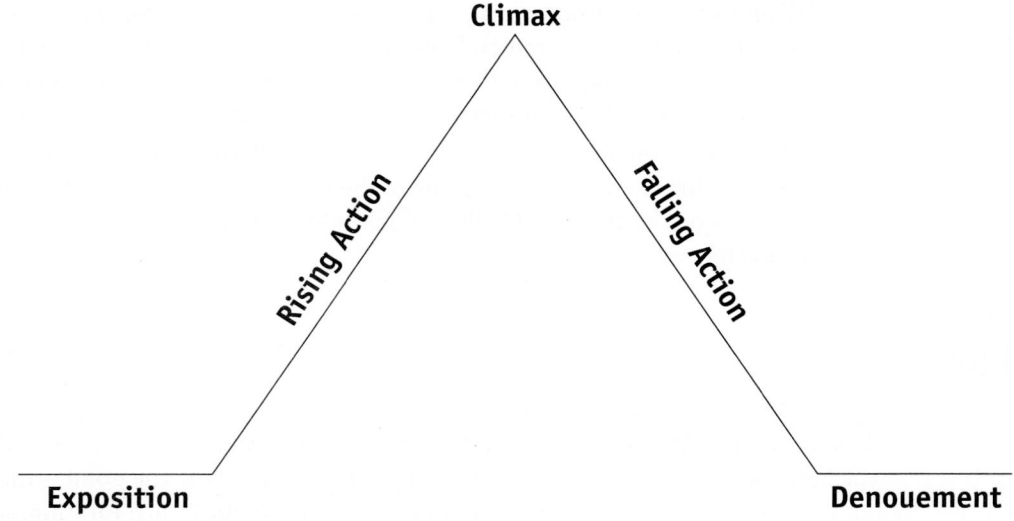

FIGURE 9.1 ■ Freytag's Pyramid, depicting the five major parts of most fictional stories.

Wilder's *The Little House in the Big Woods* uses an episodic plot, relating a series of adventures during a year in the life of a family in Wisconsin in the late nineteenth century: Each chapter focuses on a specific experience. C. S. Lewis uses an episodic plot in *The Voyage of the Dawn Treader*, one of the books of the Chronicles of Narnia, in which the characters encounter a series of exploits, most unrelated to the rest, while on a sea voyage to find the seven lost Lords of Narnia. If we were to diagram the episodic plot, it would look like a series of dramatic plots (see Figure 9.2).

Parallel Plot

When an author weaves two or more dramatic plots throughout a single book, we have a parallel plot structure. The plots are usually linked by a common character and/or a similar theme. Robert McCloskey's picture book *Blueberries for Sal* (see Chapter 6) is an unusual example of a parallel plot in a picture book.

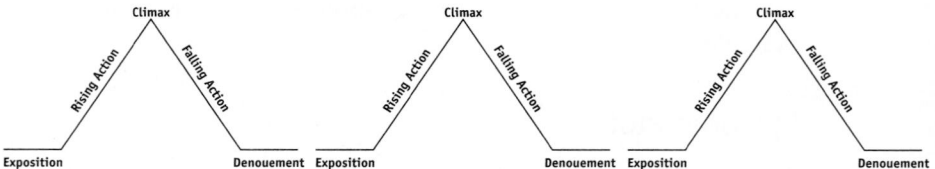

FIGURE 9.2 ■ An episodic plot usually functions like a series of dramatic plots, each part of the series being one episode or chapter.

One of the best examples of a parallel plot for older readers is Tove Jansson's *Moominsummer Madness*, in which we follow three sets of characters on a series of wacky adventures, all leading them to the same place at the end, where everything is happily resolved. The story is reminiscent of Shakespeare's *A Midsummer Night's Dream*, in which parallel stories of three sets of characters result in some bizarre mix-ups, to great comic effect.

The Journey

It has been said that in literature, there are really only two kinds of stories to tell: in one, a stranger comes to town; in the other, someone goes on a journey. Think of all the heroes and heroines you know who set off on journeys, from Peter Rabbit to Alice, Dorothy, the Pevensie children, and Harry Potter. Journeys make good plot devices because on a journey, the protagonist can meet new people, see new places, and experience new adventures.

Journeys are of two principal kinds—circular or linear. In a circular journey, the hero returns home in the end. On the simplest level, Peter Rabbit's journey into Mr. MacGregor's garden and back home is a circular journey (although it could have turned out much differently!). It is not surprising that most journeys in books for young readers are circular. In those early years, children still think returning home is best. Alice (*Alice's Adventures in Wonderland*) and Dorothy (*The Wonderful Wizard of Oz*) are among the best-known examples.

In a linear journey, the hero does not return home but makes a new one. As we might expect, this journey is more common in fiction for older readers. One unusual example involving a very young hero is Roald Dahl's *James and the Giant Peach*. James floats across the Atlantic Ocean (in a very large peach), accompanied by an assortment of very large insects and one worm, and he makes himself a new home in New York City. But whether the journey is circular or linear, the protagonist is always transformed as a result of the journey—for having gained knowledge and experience—and this makes the journey an ideal metaphor for life. In fiction for older readers we can look to the journeys of Ged, the hero of Ursula Le Guin's *A Wizard of Earthsea*, who traverses virtually his entire world—in search of himself.

Conflict

What makes a plot gripping is the conflict. Conflicts are sometimes depicted in terms of good versus evil or right versus wrong. For a story to hold our interest, something must be at stake. In most cases, a goal is to be accomplished and something achieved. A single story may contain more than one conflict, although one usually predominates. To see how a conflict is resolved is one reason we want to keep reading. But conflict has another important role, for it is the means by which the protagonist is allowed to transform, to grow, to mature. Conflicts come in several forms, and the four most prevalent in children's fiction are these: protagonist against another, protagonist against society, protagonist against nature, and protagonist against self. (A fifth, protagonist against fate, is rarely found in children's books.)

Protagonist against Another

The protagonist against another conflict occurs when two characters—namely the protagonist and the antagonist—are pitted against each other (see Figure 9.3). They may want the same thing (Cinderella and her wicked stepsisters all want to marry Prince Charming). Or perhaps they have conflicting desires (in *Charlotte's Web*, Wilbur wants to live, and the humans want to eat him). Or perhaps one character is determined to prevent another from achieving a goal (in Natalie Babbitt's *Tuck Everlasting*, the heroine, Winnie, must stop the villain from finding the spring of immortality and selling its water for profit).

Protagonist against Society

The protagonist against society conflict occurs when the protagonist is pitted against mainstream society and its values and mores (see Figure 9.4). We find this struggle in many stories of racial prejudice, such as Mildred Taylor's *Roll of Thunder, Hear My Cry*, depicting the struggle of an African American family against a community of white racists. But society can offer other challenges as well. Robert Cormier's *I Am the Cheese* depicts an innocent family in a hopeless struggle against government corruption. And Alice

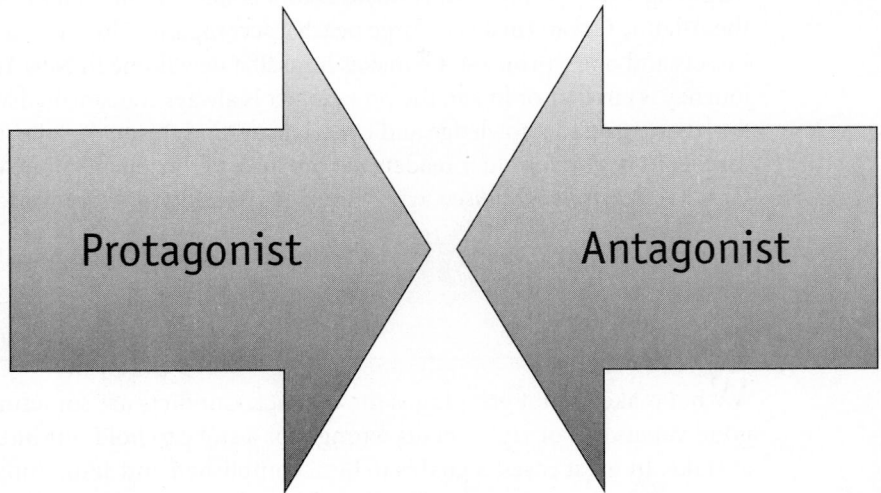

FIGURE 9.3 ■ The simplest conflict is that between good (the protagonist) and evil (the antagonist). The antagonist may be another person, or it may be nature itself.

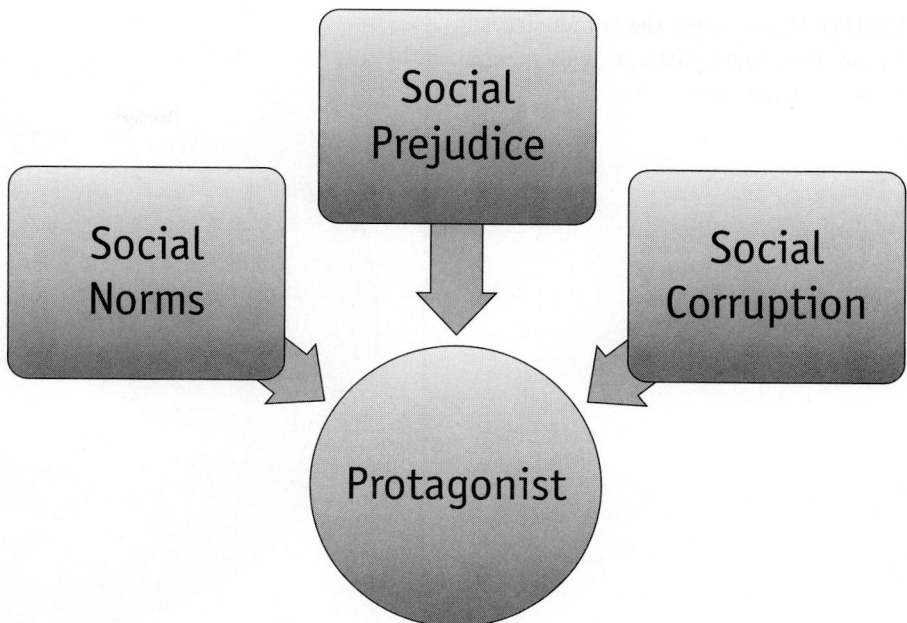

FIGURE 9.4 ■ Sometimes the protagonist is up against society as a whole, and society becomes the antagonist. The protagonist cannot defeat society, so he or she must try to change it.

Childress's *A Hero Ain't Nothin' but a Sandwich* portrays a teenage character, Benjie, plagued by drug addiction and at odds with his family, the school, and even his peers.

Protagonist against Nature

The protagonist against nature conflict occurs when the protagonist is engaged in a struggle for survival, usually alone in some natural wilderness or forbidding landscape (see Figure 9.5). For example, Scott O'Dell's *Island of the Blue Dolphins* is the story of a young woman abandoned on a deserted island and how she manages to live for 18 years. In Jean Craighead George's *Julie of the Wolves*, a young girl must survive the harsh climate of the Alaskan wilderness. In most modern treatments of this conflict, the protagonists usually survive because they learn how to live with nature—not fight against it.

Protagonist against Self

Here, the conflict is an emotional or intellectual struggle within the protagonist himself or herself (see Figure 9.6). Max in Sendak's *Where the Wild Things Are* (see the discussion in Chapter 6) is torn between wanting to be a monster (doing exactly as he pleases) and

FIGURE 9.5 ■ When the antagonist is nature, the protagonist's struggle is providing for basic human needs.

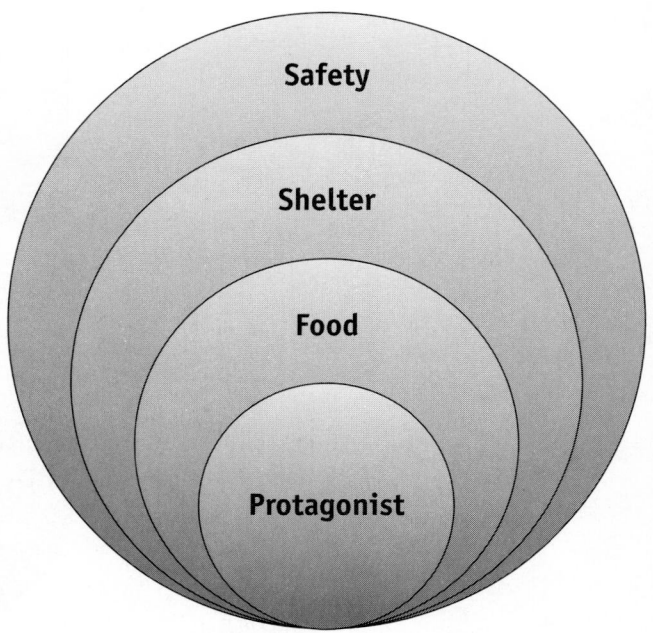

obeying his mother (doing what he probably knows is right). Max's real enemy is not his mother. It is himself. Judy Blume's *Are You There God? It's Me, Margaret* exposes the various emotional conflicts facing a girl in her early teens. And some would argue that Benjie (*A Hero Ain'tNothin' but a Sandwich*) is struggling against himself as much as he is with society. (A book can have more than one conflict.)

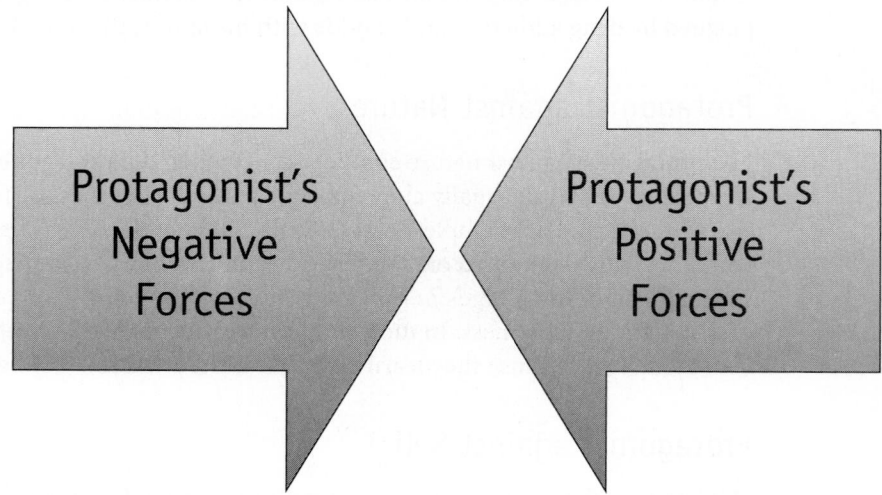

FIGURE 9.6 ■ Sometimes the protagonist is his or her own worst enemy. The struggle is then between the protagonist's strengths, hopes, and dreams and the protagonist's doubts, anxieties, and fears.

Style

A writer's style refers to the way language is used to tell stories in an engaging and effective way. What follows are some of the most frequently used storytelling techniques.

Exposition and Dialogue

Every story requires some background information—even if it is nothing more than a simple statement such as "Once upon a time." The narrator's explanations and descriptions are referred to as *exposition*. Exposition may be used to set the scene, introduce a character, and move the action along, as in this example from Laura Ingalls Wilder's *Little House in the Big Woods*:

> *When Laura and Mary had said their prayers and were tucked snugly under the trundle bed's covers, Pa was sitting in the firelight with the fiddle. Ma had blown out the lamp because she did not need its light. On the other side of the hearth she was swaying gently in her rocking chair and her knitting needles flashed in and out above the sock she was knitting.* (236)

Dialogue refers to the words spoken by the characters in the story to each other. (It is called monologue if only one character is involved.) Dialogue contributes a sense of drama to a story—we like to hear what the characters say to each other. Dialogue also allows the author to convey individual peculiarities, such as the goose's quirky speech in *Charlotte's Web* when she replies to Wilbur's inquiry about the time: "Probably-obably-obably about half-past eleven. . . . Why aren't you asleep, Wilbur?" (33). Charlotte's intellectual superiority over the other barnyard animals is clearly demonstrated by her greeting to Wilbur: "Salutations!" (35). In a play, the entire script is typically dialogue, in which case the necessary background or exposition has to be revealed through the characters' words.

Foreshadowing and Flashback

Foreshadowing refers to the dropping of hints about what is to come in the future, as when Little Red Riding Hood's mother warns her not to talk to strangers. Foreshadowing is used to create suspense (horror films are addicted to foreshadowing) and to prepare the reader for possibilities, which makes the plot more believable. Notice the sense of foreboding in the opening paragraph of Natalie Babbitt's *Tuck Everlasting*, the story of a lonely girl's encounter with a strange family who accidentally stumbled on a magical spring that bestows immortality on all who drink from it:

> *The first week of August hangs at the very top of summer, the top of the live-long year, like the highest seat of a Ferris wheel when it pauses in its turning. The weeks that come before are only a climb from a balmy spring, and those that follow a drop to the chill of autumn, but the first week of August is motionless, and hot. It is curiously silent, too, with blank white dawns and*

glaring noons, and sunsets smeared with too much color. Often at night there is lightning, but it quivers all alone. There is no thunder, no relieving rain. These are strange and breathless days, the dog days, when people are led to do things they are sure to be sorry for after. (3)

In this description of the novel's setting, the references to motionlessness, blank dawns, glaring noons, lightning quivering "all alone," and breathless days are all examples of foreshadowing, which prepares us for what is to come. Foreshadowing helps to unify a story, to make connections between the characters and their actions. In the well-constructed story, everything has a purpose; there are no loose ends, nothing is left undone.

The flashback is the device by which the narrator takes the reader back to a time and place before the story's present time. This is used in books for older readers but is unusual in stories for preschoolers, whose concept of time is not yet sophisticated enough to grasp the subtleties of the device. One very good example that children are familiar with is in Charles Dickens's *A Christmas Carol*, when the Ghost of Christmas Past takes Scrooge back to his youth. The flashback is usually used to reveal necessary background information, such as explaining why a character behaves in a certain way.

Tone

A story may be serious, humorous, satirical, passionate, sensitive, zealous, caustic, poignant, warm, and so on. This quality of fiction is referred to as tone. It is really the way an author treats the subject matter. Here are some of the most common tones found in children's books.

Didacticism

To be didactic simply means to teach, to be instructive. There is nothing wrong with didacticism. In fact, we expect didacticism in a textbook—like this one. But in literature didacticism can sound preachy and intrusive. Most fiction writers today generally try to avoid it. Beatrix Potter avoided a didactic tone in *The Tale of Peter Rabbit* by resisting the temptation to tell us how bad Peter has been (she doesn't have Peter confess his sins to his mother or promise to be a good bunny from now on, for example). Too often in didactic stories, the message overtakes the tale and we end up with stereotyped and underdeveloped characters, silly and contrived plots, and phony language.

In the eighteenth century (see Chapter 1), adults thought that all children's books should teach moral lessons. Consequently, these books all turned out to be didactic. Take one of the most famous examples, *The History of Little Goody Two-Shoes* (1765)—published by Newbery and written by an unknown author. This is the story of an orphan girl who has but one shoe. When a sympathetic rich man gives her a new pair, she goes about rejoicing that she now has "two shoes." As it turns out, the girl's name is Margery Meanwell, whose father had been ruined by two wicked men, Timothy Gripe and Farmer Graspall—well, you get the picture. Margery eventually becomes a popular teacher "who had the Art of moralizing and drawing Instructions from every Accident," and when her students lose a favorite pet, she reads "them a Lecture on the Uncertainty of Life, and the Necessity of being always prepared for Death." Eventually, her goodness brings her to the attention of a widowed lord who marries her, proving that virtue does, indeed, pay off. Not only is the tale didactic, instructing us that we should all be more like Goody Two-Shoes, but it is sentimental as well, which brings us to another subject.

Sentimentalism

Sentimentalism is the outward show of excessive emotion—or of emotion that is inappropriate to the circumstances. In other words, it is the expression of feeling without substance. Many tears are shed in *The History of Little Goody Two-Shoes*, and we are told that her death was "the greatest Calamity that ever was felt in the Neighbourhood" and that a monument "was erected to her Memory in the Church-yard, over which the Poor as they pass weep continually, so that the Stone is ever bathed in Tears." A later example of sentimentalism in children's books is found in the "Elsie Dinsmore" series, written by Martha Finley, beginning in 1867. Throughout the series, sweet Elsie Dinsmore bravely overcomes many heartbreaks and tribulations. But one critic complained, as far back as 1896, that "nothing can be more dreary than the recital of Elsie's sorrows and persecutions. Every page is drenched with tears." "Even," the critic continues, "on comparatively cheerful nights [Elsie] is content to shed 'a few quiet tears upon her pillow'" (Repplier, n.p.). This is a sure sign of a sentimental work.

Eleanor Porter's *Pollyanna*, made famous by a 1950s Disney film, is another good example of sentimentalism. The young heroine, through her incessant cheerfulness, transforms a perennially gloomy town into a place of "gladness." The problem with sentimentalism, as with most other excesses, is that it smacks of phoniness or insincerity, and is often simply silly.

Humor

Unlike didacticism and sentimentalism, humor is a welcome feature in all literature. Rare is the child who does not like a funny story. Most scholars agree that incongruity is the foundation of humor: We laugh at the tension resulting from something out of the ordinary. But humor is also elusive; whether we laugh at a joke depends on the teller (wording and timing are important) and on us (what we find hilarious others may find offensive or silly). Humor is age specific; what we find funny when we are 3 years old is seldom funny when we are 21. Katharine Kappas identifies various types of humor most commonly found in books for children up through early adolescence. They include exaggeration, incongruity, surprise, slapstick, absurdity, uncomfortable situations, ridicule, defiance, violence, and verbal humor. Some of these will seem surprising (or disturbing). But it is the child's penchant for physical humor that makes Roald Dahl's controversial works popular. In Dahl's *Charlie and the Chocolate Factory*, for example, several disagreeable children meet their ends in bizarre ways while touring a candy factory. Books such as these do not invite children to find humor in cruelty or the misfortunes of others. Rather, they allow children to release social and psychological tensions and give them a way of coping with uncomfortable, out-of-the-ordinary situations.

Humor is how all human beings express latent hostility. Take, for example, a familiar comic situation: A man steps on a banana peel, his heels go straight up in the air, and he lands on his behind. People laugh at this for several reasons. The movement is incongruous and unexpected, and it contains a touch of slapstick. It also makes the observers feel superior (they weren't the ones who fell), and they are relieved the man was not hurt. One of the important prerequisites for laughter provoked by someone else's misfortune is that the victim must seem to deserve the fate or the harm must not be critical. (The banana peel mishap is funnier if the victim is a pompous bore, but it is not so funny if the victim is a sweet, old lady—or if the victim dies, which results in dark or gallows humor. For a good example of this, see Edward Gorey's *The Gashlycrumb Tinies,* the morbid alphabet book briefly discussed in Chapter 5.)

It is through laughter that we learn to survive. Because it puts everyone on the same human level, laughter becomes the salve of the oppressed and the balm of the weak and vulnerable. And who in our society feels weaker and more vulnerable than a child? It is little wonder children find humor so indispensable to their well-being.

Parody

Parody is a literary imitation of another piece of literature, usually for comic effect. Parody is to literature what cartoon caricature is to art: Both exaggerate in order to ridicule. For a good antidote to sentimentalism, we can turn to Mark Twain's *The Adventures of Huckleberry Finn*, which contains a parody of nineteenth-century sentimentalism described above. Huck describes the character of Emmeline Grangerford, a young girl obsessed with death, who "kept a scrap-book . . . and used to paste obituaries and accidents and cases of patient suffering in it . . . and write poetry after them out of her own head" (Twain 144). Commenting on Emmeline's early death, Huck utters the classically unsentimental remark: "I reckoned that with her disposition she was having a better time in the graveyard." Twain's comic satire foreshadows the decline of sentimentalism in modern children's stories.

Parody implies a degree of sophistication; after all, if we are not familiar with the original work, we will not get the joke. Mark Twain's parody in his description of Emmeline Grangerford is funnier if we know about Elsie Dinsmore, for example. Once rare in children's fiction, parodies are becoming especially popular in children's picture books. Jon Scieszka's *The True Story of the Three Little Pigs* is a popular retelling of the familiar tale from the wolf's point of view (he was framed!). Another reversal is found in Eugene Trivizas's *The Three Little Wolves and the Big Bad Pig*, which has a heavy-handed but very funny message of nonviolence. And David Wiesner's *The Three Pigs* is a sophisticated tale that cleverly deconstructs the story and depicts the characters forming alliances with characters from other nursery stories. And in recent years political parodies of children's picture books have appeared, such as *Pat the Politician* by Julie Marcus and Susan Carp, a spoof on Dorothy Kunhardt's popular tactile book, *Pat the Bunny*. Of course, parodies like these are intended for adult readers. Parodies demonstrate the vitality of literature and can suggest to children new ways of interpreting old tales.

Irony

You may recall in *The Wonderful Wizard of Oz* that Dorothy undertakes a journey to seek the help of a wizard so she can get back home. On the way, she meets three new friends—a Scarecrow who wishes for brains, a Tin Woodsman who wishes for a heart, and a Cowardly Lion who wishes for courage. On the journey, each friend learns that he already possesses what he longed for—the Scarecrow is wise, the Tin Woodsman is kind and tender, and the Cowardly Lion is bold and fearless. On the other hand, the "all-powerful" Wizard of Oz is revealed to be a phony, an eccentric humbug. In the end, Dorothy finds that she had the ability to get home on her own all along (through the magic of her slippers, which are actually silver shoes in the book).

These are all examples of irony. Irony occurs when reality turns out to be different from what it first appeared. It can be intentional (as with the wizard, who knows he's a fraud) or circumstantial (as with Dorothy and her friends, who really are unaware of their own strengths). Irony adds layers to a story's meaning. It can be humorous. It can be tragic. It reminds us that the world is not always what it seems.

Sometimes irony can devolve into cynicism, which is the opposite of sentimentalism. The cynic believes that human nature is fundamentally corrupt and the world is a rotten place to be. Obviously, this is not a tone that is normally found in children's fiction. However, it is a feature of many of the works for adolescents written by Robert Cormier—*The Chocolate War*, *I Am the Cheese*, and others. Cormier deals with dark topics: a religious boy's school in which the priests are all corrupt, a government that betrays its own citizens. The characters in Cormier's books are thoroughly depraved, and society itself is utterly debased. Frankly realistic, Cormier offers no happy endings or even hopefulness, which, as you might imagine, has led to considerable controversy over his writings.

Theme

The plot is what happens in a story; the theme is what the story is really about. But the theme should not be regarded as a lesson to be learned. Recall the eighteenth-century moral writers (see Chapter 1), who insisted on hammering home their lessons and remember our discussion about didacticism above. We should see the theme as a fundamental principal or idea that the author is trying to convey. And to convey an idea, we need a complete thought. "Friendship" is a topic—it is not a theme. The idea that friendship requires us to make sacrifices—that is a theme. Today's readers prefer the theme to be woven into the fabric of the text—to emerge organically from the events of the story and the actions of the characters.

It is also important to remember that a book may have more than one theme—although one may predominate. *Charlotte's Web*, for example, explores the importance of friendship, the survival instinct in nature, and the inevitability of the cycle of life. The accompanying chart (see Figure 9.7) lists some popular children's books along with some possible themes, expressed through quotations from books or well-known people. The important thing is to note that the theme is an idea and that it is universal—applying to all people everywhere.

Another thing to keep in mind is that all fiction, whether fantasy fiction or realistic fiction, deals with the same types of themes—that is, there is no "fantasy" theme or "realistic" theme. All novels address the human condition—even when the novels are set in a galaxy far, far away and are populated with the most fantastical of creatures. It is the theme that gives the story its ultimate meaning. A recent British novel for young readers demonstrates this superbly. *A Monster Calls* was written by Philip Ness, but the idea came

FIGURE 9.7 ■ Themes Found in Popular Children's Books

Pippi Longstocking by Astrid Lindgren	"To be yourself in a world that is constantly trying to make you something else is a great achievement."—Ralph Waldo Emerson
Charlotte's Web by E. B. White	"There is nothing on this earth to be prized more than true friendship."—Thomas Aquinas
The Moffats by Eleanor Estes	"You don't choose your family. They are God's gift to you, as you are to them."—Desmond Tutu
Are You There, God? It's Me, Margaret by Judy Blume	"It takes courage to grow up and become who you really are."—e. e. cummings
Island of the Blue Dolphins by Scott O'Dell	"It's not the strongest or the most intelligent who will survive, but those who can best manage change."—Charles Darwin
Number the Stars by Lois Lowry	"Courage is being scared to death . . . and saddling up anyway."—John Wayne
Bridge to Terabithia by Katherine Paterson	"Grief is the price we pay for love."—Queen Elizabeth II
A Monster Calls by Patrick Ness and Siobhan Dowd	"If you speak the truth . . . you will be able to face whatever comes."—Ness and Dowd, *A Monster Calls*

from Siobhan Dowd, who did not live to see it realized. Set in modern-day England, it is the story of a 10-year-old boy, Conor, whose refuses to the face the fact that his mother is dying. His divorced father now lives with his new family in America, and his only other relative is his maternal grandmother, who seems controlling and entirely unable to comprehend Conor's world. Then, in the middle of the night, a terrifying monster in the form of a giant and ancient yew tree, comes to Conor's room and announces that he has some stories to tell Conor. Logic tells the boy that this is a dream (or nightmare), but telltale signs keep appearing (his bedroom floor is inexplicably strewn with poisonous yew berries, for example). The story moves between Conor's mysterious encounter with the monster, Conor's increasing inability to cope in school, and the events surrounding his mother's rapidly deteriorating condition—all leading to the inevitable climax. The monster's stories all lead up to the book's ultimate message: *Accepting death means letting go.* In the course of the book we see Conor behave outrageously—in ways that even he cannot understand, until the end, when we all understand.

It is a powerful story of love, sacrifice, and redemption—and even when we've finished the book, we are at a loss to describe it as either fantasy or realistic fiction. And it does not matter—for the theme addresses the universal human condition. The novels we remember the longest are the ones in which we discover a reflection of ourselves and our experiences—including the demons that haunt us and the unexpected angels that rescue us. And sometimes the demons and angels are ambiguous figures—and perhaps one in the same. Finally, it is the monster who reveals the theme when he tells Conor, "If you speak the truth . . . you will be able to face whatever comes" (203).

Ways of Reading Literature

Literary criticism examines, evaluates, and interprets works of literature. From time to time, as an educator, you may turn to articles or books about children's or young adult literature as a way to explore a work with young readers. Criticism often helps us understand a story or a novel or to see it in a different way. Here we will look very briefly at six common ways of reading and thinking about literature and how they might affect our reading of a familiar folktale, "Hansel and Gretel."

Formal Approach

A formal critic is interested in the form of a literary work—its language, its composition, and how the various parts come together to make a harmonious whole. Formalism, which was popular in the mid-twentieth century, examines how a story or book is constructed. Consequently, it focuses heavily on the elements discussed in the first part of this chapter and is particularly interested in how the various elements contribute to the work's overall unity.

Consider, now, a formal approach to "Hansel and Gretel," the story of the brother and sister abandoned in the woods by their wicked stepmother and wimpy father, who could no longer feed them. We begin by looking at the plot structure—a circular journey beginning and ending at home. We might also note the dichotomy of the wicked stepmother and the witch, who represent the same perverted values and must be defeated in order to resolve the tension. And we note the sharp contrasts between the two houses—the woodcutter's barren cottage and the witch's delicious home, made of gingerbread. All these elements contribute to the unity of the plot.

The strength of formal criticism is that it causes us to read the literature carefully and thoughtfully, and it provides a common vocabulary for the discussion of literature. But formal criticism often ignores the interconnectedness of literature, the influence of society on literature, and the facts of the author's life and experiences. Nor does it allow for the impact of the reader's personal experiences. For those, we look to other critical approaches.

Archetypal Approach

The psychologist and physician Carl Gustav Jung (1875–1961) believed in a collective unconscious shared by all human beings, something deep within us that contains the "cumulative knowledge, experiences, and images of the entire human race" (Bressler 92). Jung argued that this explains why people the world over respond to the same myths and stories (why we find Cinderella stories in virtually every culture on earth, for example). Jung identified certain human character types called *archetypes*—like the hero, the warrior, the wise old man or woman, the damsel in distress, the temptress, the trickster, and so on. These archetypes appear over and over again in stories from around the world, and they engage in similar patterns of behavior.

The basis of archetypal criticism—whose great champion was Northrop Frye—is that literature consists of variations on a great mythic cycle that follows this pattern:

- The hero begins life in a paradise (such as a garden).
- The hero is displaced from paradise (alienation).
- The hero endures a time of trial and tribulation, usually a wandering (a journey).
- The hero achieves self-discovery as a result of the struggles on that journey.
- The hero returns to paradise (either the original or a new, improved one).

As we pointed out above, the journey motif—either circular or linear—is very common in children's stories. If we return to *Hansel and Gretel*, we can immediately see the archetypal circular journey, during which the young hero and heroine encounter horrifying experiences involving an archetypal figure in the witch. They destroy the evil powers through wit and cunning and receive a boon in the form of the witch's jewels. Then, with the help of yet another archetypal figure, the white duck, perhaps representing Nature at last coming to their rescue, they return home triumphantly, to the open arms of their penitent father.

Archetypal criticism allows us to see the larger patterns of literature, although it tends to ignore the individual contributions of the author and the specific cultural and societal influences.

Historical Approach

The historical critic examines the culture and the society from which a literary work came and how these influences affect the literature. Historical criticism asks such questions as these:

- Who is the author, where did he or she come from, and what was his or her object in writing the work?
- How did the political events of the time influence what the writer wrote?
- How did the predominant social attitudes of the time influence the writer's outlook?
- What is the predominant philosophy that influenced the work?
- Were there any special circumstances under which the work was written?

One of the troubling aspects of "Hansel and Gretel" is how parents can be so callous as to abandon their children. We may also want to know the significance of the gingerbread house or why the witch dies in the oven. Of course, we do not know who wrote "Hansel and Gretel" nor exactly when it was first written, but it is certainly European and from the pre-industrial era (that is, before the eighteenth century), so we will begin there. So perhaps some of our questions about the tale can be answered by examining the historical context of the period when it likely originated.

Pre-industrial Europe was a time of widespread famine, and peasants lived on the verge of starvation. The overwhelming emphasis on food in the tale—the children drop bread crumbs, they are enticed by a gingerbread house from which they eat delicious candies, the witch is killed in her own oven, where she had planned to bake Hansel—may be partly explained by difficult times out of which the story rose. The abandonment of children might not have been so unusual a thing in a society that still did not necessarily condemn infanticide (particularly if the infant was a female). And even worse things happened. The historian Barbara Tuchman writes that during the fourteenth century "reports spread of people eating their own children, of the poor in Poland feeding on hanged bodies taken down from the gibbet" (24).

Seen within this context, "Hansel and Gretel" seems almost tame. Knowledge about the historical times in which a work was written can enrich our understanding. However, the historical approach often overlooks the literary elements and structure as well as the author's individual contributions.

Psychoanalytical Approach

Based on the work of Sigmund Freud in the early twentieth century, psychoanalytical criticism attempts to explain the reasons for human actions. Freud believed that the motivations for much of our behavior—our fears, our desires, our ambitions—lay hidden in our unconscious. Freud explained in great detail how he believed certain personality types developed—almost always as a result of some childhood experience, good or bad. He further believed that many artists were neurotics who used their art to vent their unconscious anxieties.

The psychoanalytical critic sees a work of literature as the outward expression of an author's unconscious mind, and it becomes the reader's or critic's task to discover the author's hidden fears, desires, and motivations. This type of criticism can coexist comfortably with other types, since it does not bother with either formalist or historical elements. To examine a work psychoanalytically is to probe the unconscious of the characters, to determine what their actions really reveal about them.

The most famous modern example of psychoanalytical reading of children's literature is Bruno Bettelheim's study of folktales, *The Uses of Enchantment* (1976). Here is a brief summary of Bettelheim's psychoanalytical interpretation of "Hansel and Gretel." He interprets the story as a symbolic representation of the child emerging from the developmental stage of oral fixation—when children want to put everything in their mouths. The tale is rife with food references. The children must be abandoned because of lack of food, they find a gingerbread house that they begin to eat, the house is inhabited by a cannibal witch. The gingerbread house, Bettelheim contends, "stands for oral greediness and how attractive it is to give in to it" (161). He goes yet a step further with the Freudian suggestion that the house is also a symbol of the human body, and that the children's devouring of the house symbolically represents their nursing. The witch personifies "the destructive aspects of orality" and also represents the threatening mother. On the other hand, the witch has jewels that the children inherit, but only when they have reached a higher stage of development, represented by the wisdom they use in deceiving and killing the witch. Bettelheim concludes, "This suggests that as the children transcend their oral anxiety, and free themselves from relying on oral satisfaction for security, they can also free themselves of the image of the threatening mother—the witch—and rediscover the good parents, whose greater wisdom—the shared jewels—then benefit all" (162).

Bettelheim's analysis is a great deal more complex than this, but such a summary does reveal some of the basic tenets of psychoanalytical criticism. And, as you can probably guess, one danger in psychoanalytical criticism is the tendency to overanalyze, to see every object as a symbol and every word as an expression of an unconscious desire or fear.

Feminist Approach

An offspring of the feminist movement of the mid-twentieth century, feminist criticism actually combines other critical methods while placing its focus on the questions of how gender affects a literary work, writer, or reader. The feminist approach might ask such questions as these:

- How are women portrayed in the work? As stereotypes? As individuals?
- How is the woman's point of view considered?
- Is male superiority implied in the text?
- In what way is the work affected because it was written by a woman? Or a man?

A major concern of feminist criticism is the masculine bias in literature. Historically, most works (including those written by women) were written from a masculine point of view and for male audiences. Literature has traditionally celebrated the masculine traits and cast aspersion on the feminine. Among the first works to come under attack were the folktales, with their stereotypically beautiful, helpless princesses who needed only a good man to set their lives aright and enable them to live happily ever after. In "Hansel and Gretel," we can see that the feminist critic might object to the portrayal of a woman as either a selfish wife or a cannibalistic witch. The mother/wife is, on the other hand, simply taking a desperate situation in hand, assuming authority where her ineffectual husband will not. Hansel, the boy, also proves equally ineffectual, marking the path with breadcrumbs that are quickly eaten by the birds and then finding himself imprisoned by the witch. It is Gretel who must take the decisive action and rescue them by cleverly deceiving the witch and then killing her. Gretel is, of course, an exception to the rule and refuses to fit into the traditional feminine mold.

The point is that we need to challenge the way we have traditionally read literature— from the point of view of a male-dominated society. Looking at a literary text from a feminist point of view can enrich a reading, making us aware of the complexity of human interaction. To read a text as a woman, according to some theorists, is to read it with "the skeptical purity of an outcast from culture" (Auerbach 156). To read a text as a woman "means questioning its underlying assumptions about differences between men and women that usually posit women as inferior" (Waxman 150). Feminist criticism therefore ultimately becomes cultural criticism.

Ecocriticism

Among the newest of critical approaches, ecocriticism (ecology + criticism) is an interdisciplinary approach to thinking about literature. Ecocriticism is a product of the environmental movement, often traced to the 1962 publication of Rachel Carson's *Silent Spring*, which warned of the widespread hazardous effects of pesticides on our environment. After that book, we could no longer take the natural world for granted, and the terms *ecology*, *environmentalism*, *natural*, and *green* have taken on special meaning in our society. So it is not surprising that readers would begin looking at literature in a new way. Ecocriticism looks at the presentation of nature and the environment in a work of literature:

- Does a story or poem view nature in a romantic way, seeing it as a cure for all humankind's ills or as an escape from the rat race of urban living?
- Does it attack human exploitation of the environment?
- Does it speculate on future environmental disasters?
- Does it argue for humanity's responsibility to protect the environment?

Much like feminist criticism, ecocriticism often argues a social agenda. Although this may be a stretch, a possible ecocritical reading of "Hansel and Gretel" might examine the role of the forest—a place that humans have not yet exploited or destroyed (although, remember, Hansel and Gretel's father is a woodcutter). The forest, in traditional folktales, is always depicted as a place of mystery and of danger. Yet it would seem that Hansel and Gretel are in much greater danger at home, within the clutches of their wicked stepmother. And what about the tempting gingerbread house in the forest? The very materials of the house—cakes, cookies, and candies—are unnatural, aberrations of the natural world, and therefore should be suspect to the children. In fact, the world in its natural state has not harmed them a bit. And nature seems to come to their rescue in the form of the white duck, who carries them safely across the water to their home. The natural world, for all its unpredictability, is far more accommodating to Hansel and Gretel than the human beings in their lives. (Their joy over the reunion with their father is, in fact, a bit perplexing, for he was deeply complicit in the abandonment plot.)

Summary

Our understanding of literature is enriched when we are acquainted with the writer's tools. So it is helpful to know about the role of the narrator, the setting, the use and development of character and plot. Equally important are the conflict and the theme, as well as such storytelling techniques as exposition, dialogue, foreshadowing, and flashback. The universal motif of the journey is pervasive in children's books and serves as a metaphor for our life's journey. Children fairly early on become aware of a writer's tone—is the story sad, happy, funny? And although young children will care little about literary criticism, it is helpful for those teaching children of all ages to know as much about the books they are teaching as possible. And, for those working with older readers, the various critical approaches can provide starting points for discussion and alternative ways of thinking about a work of fiction. The more we know about how literature works—how it is put together—the better we will appreciate its accomplishment.

All these elements are key to children's stories, just as they are to adult literature. The best children's stories consist of an engaging plot and memorable characters, and they leave us with an indelible impression. There is no reason we should not judge a children's book with the same rigorous literary standards we would use for an adult's book. Children deserve no less.

For Reflection and Discussion

1. Select any children's picture storybook and try to analyze it in terms of its narrative point of view, setting, character types, plot, conflict, and theme. As you consider each element, determine how effectively you believe the writer has succeeded in producing a literary work. Do you have suggestions for improving it?

2. Repeat the exercise above but this time using a folktale. See how your responses differ from the picture-book analysis.

3. Locate some parodies of children's stories. Children's picture books include many examples of folktale parodies. There are even parodies of children's books written for adults. See the various parodies of Margaret Wise Brown's classic *Goodnight Moon* (such as *Goodnight Bush*, a political parody by Gan Golen and Erich Origen). Consider what makes an effective parody. Try writing some guidelines.

4. Try to recall books from your own childhood that you now recognize as moralizing or sentimental. If you can locate them, reread them to see if they leave the same effect on you as they did the first time you read them.

5. Using a favorite children's book (even a picture book will work), attempt to apply a specific type of critical reading to it, such as a feminist or ecocritical or psychoanalytical approach.

Works Cited

Auerbach, Nina. "Engorging the Patriarch." In *Feminist Issues in Literary Scholarship*. Ed. Shari Benstock. Bloomington: Indiana University Press, 1987: 150–160.

Babbitt, Natalie. *Tuck Everlasting*. New York: Farrar, Straus & Giroux, 1975.

Bettelheim, Bruno. *The Uses of Enchantment: The Meaning and Importance of Fairy Tales*. New York: Knopf, 1976.

Bressler, Charles E. *Literary Criticism: An Introduction to Theory and Practice*. Englewood Cliffs, NJ: Prentice Hall, 1994.

Forster, E. M. *Aspects of the Novel*. 1927. New York: Harcourt Brace, 1954.

History of Little Goody Two-Shoes, The, 5th ed. London: Newbery and Carnan, 1768.

Kappas, Katherine H. "A Developmental Analysis of Children's Response to Humor."

The Library Quarterly 37 (January 1967): 67–77.

MacLachlan, Patricia. *Sarah, Plain and Tall.* New York: Harper & Row, 1985.

Ness, Patrick, and Siobhan Dowd. *A Monster Calls.* Illus. by Jim Kay. Somerville, MA: Candlewick Press, 2011.

Peck, Richard. *A Long Way from Chicago.* New York: Dial, 1998.

Repplier, Agnes. "Little Pharisees in Fiction." *Scribner's Magazine* (December 1896). www.readseries.com.

Tuchman, Barbara. *A Distant Mirror: The Calamitous 14th Century.* New York: Knopf, 1978.

Twain, Mark. *The Adventures of Huckleberry Finn.* 1884. New York: Random House, 1996.

Waxman, Barbara Frey. "Feminist Theory, Literary Canons, and the Construction of Textual Meanings." In *Practicing Theory in Introductory College Literature Courses.* Ed. James M. Calahan and David B. Downing. Urbana, IL: National Council of Teachers of English, 1991.

White, E. B. *Charlotte's Web.* New York: Harper, 1952.

Wilder, Laura Ingalls. *Little House in the Big Woods.* Illus. Garth Williams. New York: Harper & Row, 1953.

Recommended Resources

Boyd, Brian. *On the Origin of Stories: Evolution, Cognition, and Fiction.* Cambridge, MA: Belknap, 2009.

Cameron, Eleanor. *The Green and Burning Tree.* Boston: Little, Brown, 1969.

Cart, Michael. *What's So Funny? Wit and Humor in American Children's Literature.* New York: HarperCollins, 1995.

Dobrin, Sidney I., and Kenneth B. Kidd, eds. *Children's Culture and Ecocriticism.* Detroit, MI: Wayne State University Press, 2004.

Hearne, Betsy, and Roger Sutton, eds. *Evaluating Children's Books: A Critical Look.* Urbana: University of Illinois Press, 1993.

Horning, Kathleen T. *From Cover to Cover: Evaluating and Reviewing Children's Books*, rev. ed. New York: Collins, 2010.

Hunt, Peter. *Understanding Children's Literature*, 2nd ed. New York: Routledge, 2005.

May, Jill P. *Children's Literature and Critical Theory.* New York: Oxford University Press, 1995.

McGillis, Roderick. *The Nimble Reader: Literary Theory and Children's Literature.* New York: Twayne, 1996.

Nodelman, Perry. *The Hidden Adult: Defining Children's Literature.* Baltimore: The Johns Hopkins University Press, 2008.

Rudd, David, ed. *The Routledge Companion to Children's Literature.* New York: Routledge, 2010.

Tatar, Maria. *Enchanted Hunters: The Power of Stories in Childhood.* New York: Norton, 2009.

10 Fantasy

The World of Make-Believe

Introduction

Traditionally, children's fiction has been divided into two broad categories: realistic fiction and fantasy fiction. Realistic fiction portrays events that are possible; fantasy portrays the impossible. The distinction is sometimes blurred; Scott O'Dell's survival tale *Island of the Blue Dolphins*, a work of historical realism, and Louis Sachar's curious story *Holes*, which is contemporary realism, are in some ways as hard to believe as Astrid Lindgren's *Pippi Longstocking*, a fantasy about a girl with superhuman strength. And, at the end of the day, fantasy and realism actually deal with the same issues. Realistic novels such as Robert Cormier's *I Am the Cheese* (a chilling tale of government corruption) and Mildred Taylor's *Roll of Thunder, Hear My Cry* (about racism in the 1930s) depict the same social, psychological, and philosophical issues as fantasies like C. S. Lewis's Chronicles of Narnia, Phillip Pullman's His Dark Materials trilogy, and Suzanne Collins's Hunger Games trilogy.

Nevertheless, there is justification for observing the distinction between fantasy and realism since they do observe a different set of rules, and they often appeal to very different readers. Some people are fanatical devotees of fantasy, often of specific kinds of fantasy—science fiction, horror, or epic fantasy, for example. And still other readers insist on only true-to-life stories.

The enduring figures of the great fantasies—Alice, Dorothy and her motley companions, the irrepressible Mr. Toad of Toad Hall, Peter Pan, Wilbur the pig, and Charlotte the spider—are fixed indelibly on the cultural consciousness of our society and have helped shape our imaginations. It is difficult to exaggerate the influence of fantasy in our lives.

Modern fantasy has its roots in traditional folk narratives. However, fantasy differs from folk literature in that fantasy is a literary, not an oral, form. Each fantasy is a new creation coming from the pen of an individual writer using his or her own imagination. The settings, characters, and plots of a fantasy tend to be much more complex than those of the folktales. Also, fantasies do not contain the oral conventions found in the folk narratives. Consequently, fantasy poses certain challenges to readers, often taking them outside their comfort zones, giving them something they did not expect. It is also this challenge that attracts devoted readers.

Fantasy Fiction Characteristics

Fantasies, as we have noted, are stories of the impossible. In every fantasy there is some violation of the world's natural order as we understand it. A fantasy may contain ghosts, monsters or talking animals; it may involve time travel or magic. A fantasy story may be set in the distant future, on a faraway planet, in some make-believe land, in our own world, or in an alternate version of our world. But wherever the setting and whatever the fantasy elements, we will still find familiar human emotions and values—sadness, joy, fear, love, hate.

Fantasy seems always to have been popular with children. One of the earliest classics of children's literature is Lewis Carroll's *Alice's Adventures in Wonderland* (1865; see Figure 10.1).

FIGURE 10.1 ■ Sir John Tenniel's illustration for Lewis Carroll's *Alice's Adventures in Wonderland*, showing Alice discovering a passage into Wonderland.

And, in the first decade of the twenty-first century, J. K. Rowling's Harry Potter series was nothing less than a publishing phenomenon. So we ask, why do we read fantasy? What is its appeal? Here are some possible reasons:

- *Escape*—Fantasy can take us far away from our everyday world, to times that never were, to places that never existed; it lets us forget our everyday routines, our frustrations, our anxieties.
- *Excitement*—Fantasy can create a heightened thrill that goes far beyond anything we could ever know in our everyday lives, employing magical powers, space travel, time travel, and marvelous creatures.
- *Imagination*—Because it defies the rules and limitations we know and creates its own, fantasy invites us to think about things in different ways; it stretches our minds by giving us worlds and beings we may never have dreamed of before.
- *Thought-provoking ideas*—Fantasy can make us examine our values and all things familiar in a new light; sometimes the most bizarre of fantasies provide us the deepest insight into our own world, our own lives.

Readers who claim not to like fantasy may just not have found the right kind of fantasy for them. For fantasy comes in many varieties, shapes, and forms—from the sober epic or high fantasies to absurd comic fantasies to creepy ghost stories to clever science fiction and futuristic fantasies to charming talking animal fantasies. There truly is something for everyone.

The Qualities of Fantasy

What are the qualities of fantasy fiction that make it work and make it enjoyable? Accepting the fantasy world requires what the poet Samuel Taylor Coleridge called our "willing suspension of disbelief"—that is, our accepting the premises of the fantasy world (magic spells, enchanted objects, time travel, talking animals, dragons, wizards and witches, and so on). Now this does not mean that the entire burden rests with the reader. The writer has to get us to believe in the magic. The writer does this in several ways:

- By constructing a memorable fantasy world, either within our primary world or in a distinct secondary world
- By providing a set of consistent fantasy rules that readers can and want to accept as part of the fantasy
- By creating believable characters that readers can and want to identify with

Let's take a closer look at each of these.

The Fantasy World

A writer constructs a fantasy world in several different ways. In some fantasies, the magic actually intrudes in the primary world, the everyday world we live in. In Natalie Babbitt's *Tuck Everlasting*, Winnie Foster, a young girl in nineteenth-century America, accidentally stumbles across a magical spring, which bestows immortality on those who drink from it. The story is about how Winnie handles her knowledge of this secret magic. Mary Norton's *The Borrowers*, about the little people who live in our walls and floorboards, is another example of fantasy entering into the world we inhabit.

In other fantasies, one or more characters are transported from our world, the primary world, into a secondary world, where the magical elements occur. For example, in L. Frank Baum's *The Wonderful Wizard of Oz*, Dorothy is carried from Kansas to Oz by a cyclone (and then she has to find out how to get back home). Or, in C. S. Lewis's *The Lion, the Witch, and the Wardrobe*, the Pevensie children find a magical passage through the wardrobe into Narnia. Or, in the Harry Potter books, Harry must go to Platform 9¾ at King's Cross Station to get to Hogwarts.

And still other fantasies take place entirely in a secondary world. Take a story such as J. R. R. Tolkien's *The Hobbit*, which is set entirely in Middle Earth, a self-contained secondary world. No part of this story is set in our world. Many epic fantasies (such as Lloyd Alexander's Chronicles of Prydain or Ursula Le Guin's Earthsea cycle) or fantasies about space travel (such as those of Sylvia Engdahl) are examples. In these stories readers are brought into the secondary world from the beginning. And for some, it may take a chapter or two before the readers really understand what is going on—since everything is likely to be new and strange. (But this is often true in realistic fiction as well.)

The Fantasy Rules

Fantasy author Zilpha Snyder suggests that, regardless of the type, children demand two things from fantasy—that it contain *no nonsense* and that it contain *no treachery* (230). These, at first, may appear to be curious requirements: After all, isn't much of fantasy "nonsense"? And what does "treachery" have to do with fantasy? But Snyder argues convincingly that they are quite important.

All the best fantasies have their own rules. Somewhere near the beginning of most fantasy stories, we learn what the rules are. For example, a rule might be that anyone who drinks water from a special spring will never die (Babbitt's *Tuck Everlasting*). Or if the hall clock strikes 13 times, the protagonist will be able to venture back in time by stepping into the backyard (Philippa Pearce's *Tom's Midnight Garden*). Or the fantasy world might be a place where animals can talk and behave just like humans (Kenneth Grahame's *Wind in the Willows*). Snyder argues that a fantasy writer should not violate the rules once they have been established. This is very much like a game invented by children on the playground: They first make up the rules, and as long as everyone follows the rules, the game is fun. But when the players begin to ignore the rules, the game soon falls apart.

When Snyder refers to "treachery," she is asking the fantasy writer to let us believe in the fantasy even when we've finished reading it. You will recall that, at the end of the MGM movie *The Wizard of Oz*, we discover that Dorothy's entire adventure was just a dream; the adult characters all smile patronizingly at her as she insists it was real. However in L. Frank Baum's original story, the fantasy is very real. Dorothy *really* does go to Oz and experience adventures. The Scarecrow, the Tin Woodman, and the Cowardly Lion are real characters, and I suspect that this is what most children want to believe. (It's a little like wanting to believe in Santa Claus.) Once having made the commitment to believe, most readers do not like to find out that they have been deceived, that everything has been an elaborate hoax. Or, as a child might rightly say, it's not fair.

The Fantasy Characters

Many fantasy writers give us very unusual characters—characters we will never meet in real life. When we recall the great fantasies, it is often the characters we think of—Alice and all the odd creatures in Wonderland; the irascible puppet Pinocchio; the irrepressible Peter Pan; the independent Pippi Longstocking; the humble hobbit Bilbo Baggins; the determined orphan Harry Potter; and so on.

However, despite their unusual appearance or extraordinary powers or bizarre behavior, we are able to connect with them. And why is that? All fantasy characters have to be grounded in the common humanity that we all know. So the Scarecrow, the Tin Woodsman, and the Cowardly Lion from *The Wonderful Wizard of Oz* all possess specific human qualities that we can understand and associate ourselves with (see Figure 10.2). One of the most appealing qualities about *Charlotte's Web* is how White turn a potentially frightening creepy-crawly spider into one of children's literature's most beloved characters. He portrays Charlotte as wise, compassionate, and determined. We like her because of her human qualities. And for similar reasons, we dislike the selfish and power-hungry Wicked Witch of the West. In other words, fantasies are, in the end, about real life. They are just clothed in outlandish garb.

Types of Fantasy Fiction

Like folk literature, modern fantasy comes in many varieties. It may be comical or tragic, it may be frivolous or serious, it may take place in our world or in some imaginary world, it may include talking animals, fire-breathing dragons, or friendly ghosts. Any effort to classify modern fantasy is thwarted by this rich variety; nevertheless, it is helpful to make some tentative generalizations about common fantasy types. Keep in mind that some fantasies simply refuse to fit tidily into categories.

FIGURE 10.2 ■ Dorothy scolds the Cowardly Lion as the Scarecrow, the Tin Woodman, and Toto look on.

Animal Fantasy

Animal fantasies, in which animals talk and behave like humans, became popular in the early twentieth century. Indeed, in the eighteenth and early nineteenth centuries, many people believed that the idea of a talking animal was sacrilegious. With a few exceptions (Dorothy Kilner's *The Life and Perambulations of a Mouse*, 1783, and Mrs. Trimmer's *The Story of the Robins*, 1786), talking animal stories for children do not appear until the later nineteenth century. In the 1860s, Lewis Carroll included several talking animals in the Alice books. And Anna Sewell's *Black Beauty: The Autobiography of a Horse* (1877), originally for adults, remains extraordinarily popular today.

Beatrix Potter's picture-book fantasies—*The Tale of Peter Rabbit*, *The Tale of Benjamin Bunny*, and many others—are early examples of animal fantasy for very young children. These are the precursors of the multitude of talking animal stories in today's children's picture books—see the works of Jean de Brunhoff (*The Story of Babar* and its sequels), William Steig (*Sylvester and the Magic Pebble*, *Abel's Island*, and others), Ian Falconer (*Olivia* and its sequels), and Mo Willems (*Don't Let the Pigeon Drive the Bus* and the sequels), to name just a few.

But talking animals are not just for younger readers. Kenneth Grahame's classic *The Wind in the Willows*, first published in 1908 (see Figure 10.3), is a charming episodic tale set in the peaceful countryside of Edwardian England. It features a water rat, a mole, a badger, and a toad, leading comfortable lives in well-furnished homes, with good food,

FIGURE 10.3 ■ Ernest H. Shepard's illustration for Kenneth Grahame's *The Wind in the Willows*, showing Mole and Water Rat boating on the river.

hearty male companionship (the story virtually excludes women), and a few wild adventures—the most famous involving Mr. Toad and his fascination with fast motor cars.

In the 1920s, Hugh Lofting wrote the *Doctor Dolittle* books, tales of a talented veterinarian who is able to speak the languages of animals. In the 1930s and 1940s, Walter R. Brooks wrote of the comical adventures of a pig named Freddy and his talking animal friends on a farm in upstate New York. Over the course of the series, beginning with *Freddy Goes to Florida* (1927), Freddy becomes a detective, a politician, a pilot, and magician, and the books reflect the changing times during the Depression and World War II and into the 1950s. (He lives quite a long and exciting life for a pig.)

One of the most famous of all animal fantasies is E. B. White's *Charlotte's Web*, about Wilbur the pig and his friend, a spider named Charlotte. The plot revolves around a clever scheme to save Wilbur from being served up for Christmas dinner. In a similar vein is Dick King-Smith's comical *Babe, the Gallant Pig*, in which Babe is spared from the roasting pan by developing his skills as a sheepherder.

Among animal fantasies intended for older readers is Brian Jacques's very popular Redwall series, an example of heroic animal fantasy that draws its inspiration from medieval legends and romance. Richard Adams's *Watership Down* describes the plight of a society of rabbits forced from their homes by human encroachment. Similarly, Robert O'Brien's *Mrs. Frisby and the Rats of NIMH* is about a rat whose home, also threatened by humans, is saved by other rats who acquired advanced intelligence when they were subjects of scientific experiments. (Note the negative commentary on human society in both of these books.)

In all animal fantasy, the animals are anthropomorphized—they are given human feelings and human speech. This allows us to empathize with them, and, from their experiences, we learn something about ourselves and about humanity in general. (Conversely, we learn very little about real animals.)

Toy Fantasy

In 1883, an Italian author named Carlo Collodi (a pen name for Carlo Lorenzini) wrote *The Adventures of Pinocchio*, the story of a wooden puppet's quest to become a real boy. This was one of the first examples of a toy fantasy—stories in which toys come to life—and in many of these tales, the animated toys wish to become human. Toy fantasies enjoyed popularity in the 1920s and 1930s, with such works as Margery Williams Bianco's *The Velveteen Rabbit*, which remains a perennial favorite. It is not true, however, that all toys in these fantasies aspire to be humans. Rachel Field's *Hitty, Her First Hundred Years* is the first-person narrative of a doll who is reminiscing about her experiences over an entire century. This story reveals the peculiar advantages of toy protagonists over humans—toys may wear out, but they never die.

A. A. Milne's *Winnie-the-Pooh* and *The House at Pooh Corner* (first published in the 1920s) are among the best known of toy fantasies—although many readers are apt to see these as animal fantasies (a perfect example of how shaky classification schemes can be). Winnie and his friends are technically toys, although they have many of the characteristics of animals: The owl lives in a tree, the bear lives in a den and loves honey (or "hunny," as he says). The characters behave like a large, dysfunctional family, each member with a different physical or psychological hang-up—a hyperactive tiger, a manic-depressive donkey, a paranoid pig, a dyslexic owl, a feeble-minded bear (see Manlove 62). The allure of the stories, aside from their cuddly characters, is seeing how the toys manage in their world through love and loyalty.

Modern toy fantasies are most frequently in picture-book format (for example, Leo Lionni's *Alexander and the Wind-up Mouse* and Don Freeman's *Corduroy*), but Russell Hoban's *The Mouse and His Child* is a serious work of toy fantasy for older readers and is filled with sharp social satire. And we should not forget Lynn Reid Banks' *The Indian in the Cupboard* series and Disney's popular films beginning with *Toy Story*.

Magical Fantasy

It can be said that all fantasies contain magic. We might logically regard talking animals or toys as magical. However, aside from the talking, neither Wilbur the pig nor Winnie-the-Pooh is extraordinary. There are those fantasies, however, in which the magical element is the crux of the story. Take, for example, Astrid Lindgren's *Pippi Longstocking*—a story set in Sweden, perhaps in the 1940s (when it was written), and peopled with very ordinary human beings, except for Pippi herself. Pippi is a young girl, apparently orphaned, who lives by herself and does as she pleases. Her behavior is quite outrageous—which is why children love her. We do not worry about her being alone because she possesses superhuman strength (for which no explanation is ever given). Her magical strength makes her impervious to any danger and puts her on a superior footing to the adults in the story.

Another example is P. L. Travers's *Mary Poppins*, the story of an unconventional nanny with magical powers. She moves in with the Banks family—a rather stiff bunch of Londoners—and brings wonder into their lives, enabling them to finally find happiness. In both *Pippi Longstocking* and *Mary Poppins*, the magic helps give readers a fresh view of the world. These fantasies typically have contemporary settings, and we are constantly aware of the incongruity of the magical element. (Often the "normal" characters have to be convinced that the magic is real.) This is quite different from the magic in folktales, which is always taken for granted (see Chapter 8).

In magical fantasy stories, the magic itself is often conditional. William Steig's picture-book animal fantasy, *Sylvester and the Magic Pebble*, is the story of Sylvester, a young donkey who finds a pebble that will grant his wishes so as long as he holds onto it. When he encounters a hungry lion, Sylvester without thinking wishes he were a rock. Sylvester's wish is granted, and he is saved from the lion, but the poor donkey has been transformed into a rock, and the only way he can be restored is if someone finds the magic pebble and wishes the rock were Sylvester again. This is a good example of an animal fantasy that also operates as a magical fantasy. (There is nothing wrong with crossing categories if it makes sense.)

Similar conditions on the magical element occur in E. Nesbit's *Five Children and It*, the children are granted a new wish every day, but the wish ends with each sunset. And, in

Pippi Longstocking, only Pippi possesses superhuman strength. These are all good examples of how the "rules" of fantasy operate. Without the rules, chaos threatens. A magical power that is unlimited quickly becomes silly, uninteresting, and, in the child's eye, unfair.

Tall Tales

Closely related to magical tales are tall tales. In fact, *Pippi Longstocking* is little different from the characters in American tall tales like Paul Bunyan, except that in a tall tale, the exaggeration is taken to absurdity. (Of course, some may think it is absurd in *Pippi Longstocking,* too.) Paul Bunyan and his blue ox, Babe, are of stupendous size, and their feats include creating new rivers and carving canyons and leveling mountains. Tall tales seem to be largely an American phenomenon, characteristic of the American love of overstatement. The characters are outlandish, their feats unbelievable. Sid Fleischman's McBroom series for younger readers appears to have been inspired by the Paul Bunyan tales, and his stories for older readers, such as *The Ghost in the Noonday Sun* and *Chancy and the Grand Rascal,* are comical yarns set in nineteenth-century America and filled with eccentric characters. In another form of the tall tale, Lucretia Hale's *The Peterkin Papers,* written in the nineteenth century, describes the misadventures of a completely inept family. In the twentieth century, Harry Allard's picture books, illustrated by James Marshall, about the Stupids (Stupid being their family name) follow this tradition (*The Stupids Have a Ball,* *The Stupids Die,* and others).

The Enchanted Journey

Journey fantasies are almost always alternate-world fantasies—that is, they take place not in our world but in a fantasy world with a completely different set of rules. In these tales, the protagonist sets out—sometimes intentionally, sometimes by accident—through unfamiliar territory to accomplish some purpose. Journeys, as we saw in Chapter 9, have always been popular subjects for literature because they provide many opportunities for the protagonist to meet new characters and to engage in a variety of adventures. Journeys are also metaphors for character growth and development: Life itself is often referred to as a journey. Among the most famous journey fantasies for children are Lewis Carroll's *Alice's Adventures in Wonderland* and *The Wonderful Wizard of Oz.* The Swedish author Selma Lagerlöf wrote *The Wonderful Adventures of Nils,* describing a young boy's exciting travels across Sweden on the back of a goose—during which he learns about his homeland and himself as well.

Epic Fantasy

We frequently find the journey motif in another type of fantasy, the epic fantasy. An epic fantasy is an elaborate adventure story in which a kingdom or society is threatened by some powerful evil force (a vile monster, a wicked sorcerer or witch, a bloodthirsty conqueror). Coming to the rescue is a brave and mighty hero or heroine, who, usually with a band of worthy and stalwart companions, vanquishes the evil forces and restores peace and contentment to the people. Unlike the journey fantasies discussed above, epic fantasies are usually quite serious, and the hero or heroine is fighting against enormous odds for lofty ideals—which is why the epic fantasy is often referred to as "high fantasy." The stories often involve large numbers of characters and intricately woven plots, and it is not unusual for an epic fantasy to be published in a series of several books—three each in J. R. R. Tolkien's Lord of the Rings and Philip Pullman's His Dark Materials, five in Lloyd Alexander's Chronicles of Prydain, and seven each in C. S. Lewis's Chronicles of Narnia and J. K. Rowling's Harry Potter.

Many of these stories have as their models the great epics of the classical world—Homer's *Iliad* and *Odyssey* and Virgil's *Aeneid*—and the medieval tales of King Arthur and his gallant knights. The settings tend to be vast—that is, they deal with realms and empires, not households or cities. The hero/ine is often called to the task—and typically, in the beginning, feels unequal to the challenge. Also the hero/ine is an outsider, an orphan, or someone who is dispossessed (Harry Potter, for example, or Lyra in His Dark Materials). The villain represents ultimate evil and possesses unimaginable (but not invincible) power and commands the loyalty of a great force. The odds seem overwhelming. A journey is frequently involved, in which the hero/ine encounters many dangerous adventures. Invariably, a mysterious helper shows up just at the right time. Or, perhaps, a gift has been given the hero/ine, a gift that will later prove invaluable (Lyra's golden compass in His Dark Materials is a perfect example). Almost always, near the conclusion, a great battle occurs—often a battle between the massed forces of good and evil. These fantasies take the reader into strange new worlds and operate on the outer fringes of the imagination. The best of them enjoy a legion of devoted followers.

Miniature Fantasy

At nearly the opposite end of the spectrum from the epic fantasy is the miniature fantasy, the tale of miniaturized characters living their lives in diminutive circumstances. Children are captivated by the concept of smallness—they play with dollhouses and miniature railroads, keep little treasures in tiny boxes, and hide in small places. (See Griswold, 51–73.) Their own world is in many ways a miniature world of small dishes, clothes, and furniture. It is also interesting how many children's stories include small creatures—Snow White's seven dwarfs, Dorothy's Munchkins, Tolkien's hobbits, Stuart Little, and virtually all of Beatrix Potter's characters.

Jonathan Swift's journey to Lilliput, a land of tiny people, in the first book of *Gulliver's Travels* (1726), was one of the first works to portray a miniature society. Gulliver finds himself shipwrecked and inadvertently embroiled in a war between two nations of tiny people. And in the second book, Gulliver finds himself in Brobdingnag, a land of giants where he is now the miniature figure. The book demonstrates how size affects our view of the world. Mary Norton's beloved series beginning with *The Borrowers* portrays tiny people who live in our walls and steal all those things that inexplicably go missing. In these books, the fantasy world and the primary world intersect. Carol Kendall's *The Gammage Cup*, about the struggles of the Minnipin society against their ancient enemies, the Mushroom People, contains many features of the heroic fantasy, but on a small scale. Perhaps the greatest appeal these stories have for children is that they depict the triumph of smaller, cleverer people over the larger, but duller, bullies of the world. They present, as Griswold suggests, "alternatives to consensual notions of dimension and, consequently, adult notions of importance" (73). In other words, smallness in children's books is not mere "cuteness." It provides young readers with a provocative way of looking at reality, and one that they may readily identify with.

Supernatural and Time-Shift Fantasy

Supernatural and time-shift fantasies have an enthusiastic following. These include ghost and witch stories, stories of mysterious and unexplained occurrences, and stories of time travel. Most open in the primary world, and the fantasy element appearing as an aberration that must be corrected before the story ends. Ghost stories are perennial favorites with many young people. Robert Bright's *Georgie and the Robbers* is a picture book about a shy ghost, and the cartoon figure Casper the Friendly Ghost (also a popular film) has a long history. But older children generally prefer more threatening ghosts; indeed, the more horrifying and gruesome the story, the better some children seem to like it. Many people have deep within them something of the ambulance chaser. Nevertheless, the most thrilling tales of the supernatural are not those that dramatize and glamorize the blood and horror but those that leave something for our imaginations. Penelope Lively's *The Ghost of Thomas Kempe* is a popular and well-told example of a modern ghost story. Devoid of any grisly horror, Lively's novel explores the potential problems that a ghost from an earlier time might have in the modern world.

Related to the supernatural tales are stories that involve tricks with time—a ghost, after all, is simply a human presence moving about in a time other than that in which it lived. Philippa Pearce's *Tom's Midnight Garden* explores movement in and out of time and deals sensitively and seriously with human relationships. In a similar vein are Lucy Boston's Green Knowe books and Alan Garner's *Owl Service*, the latter of which is a somewhat sophisticated tale of the occult, drawing on mysterious ancient powers. The second volume of Terry Pratchett's Johnny Maxwell trilogy, *Johnny and the Dead*, is about a boy who communicates with dead spirits in a cemetery. Neil Gaimon's popular *Coraline*, in which a young girl accidentally discovers an alternate universe where she has a creepy "other mother" and "other father," is both haunting and funny.

Of course, we would be remiss not to mention Stephanie Meyer's incredibly successful vampire series, beginning with *Twilight* in 2005. In 2009, Meyer broke J. K. Rowling's record on the bestseller list. As often happens with writers who achieve enormous popularity, she has also received much criticism. Among the most frequent complaints is that the books are badly written and that the author is anti-feminist. At the very least, however, these works confirm the great popularity of supernatural fiction among young readers.

Science Fiction and Speculative Fiction

Mary Shelley's *Frankenstein* (1818) is often credited with being the first true work of science fiction. This is not an alternate-world fantasy but is set in our own world. Jules Verne, famous for his *Twenty Thousand Leagues under the Sea* and *From the Earth to the Moon*, also chose to set his science fiction in the primary world. In the twentieth century, a host of science fiction writers speculated on what would happen if we were to be invaded by aliens from outer space. H. G. Wells's *The War of the Worlds* was perhaps the most famous. These stories generally revolve around the earthlings desperately defending themselves as experts attempt to discover a means of defeating the invaders. Other science fiction writers place their stories in an alternate world—the earth in the future or on distant planets in faraway galaxies. The *Star Wars* film epics come to mind. Science fiction is a product of the technological world, but it is really just fantasy that replaces magic with technology. As one critic notes: "How different, after all, is a wizard with magic wand from a scientist with a microminiaturized matter-transformer? The reader does not know how either gadget works" (Roberts 90).

One writer of science fiction for young people, Sylvia Engdahl, prefers to call her work space fantasy because she is little concerned with technology or science. Instead, she sets her stories (*Enchantress from the Stars*, *The Far Side of Evil*, and others) in the distant future and on distant planets. These settings become merely the backdrop for her tales about the development of human civilization and its sociological and psychological implications. Many science fiction works deal with ethical problems facing humanity as science and technology outpace our development as human beings. Whether technological discoveries will be used for humanity's benefit or its destruction frequently becomes a theme of science fiction. Madeleine L'Engle, best known for *A Wrinkle in Time*, addresses such issues in her science fiction.

Robert Heinlein, one of the most notable science fiction writers of the twentieth century, also wrote books for young readers. His *Have Space Suit—Will Travel* is about a teenager who embarks on a series of adventures in outer space. Terry Pratchett's *Only You Can Save Mankind*, the first in his Johnny Maxwell series, describes the adventures of a boy who suddenly finds himself inside the computer game he was playing. Orson Scott Card's *Ender's Game*, about an alien invasion of earth, is inordinately popular despite (or because of) its violence (it is on the U.S. Marine Corps Professional Reading List). Science fiction, whether it is set on distant planets in some unknown time or on our own earth today, presents us with new paradigms, and it forces us to adopt new ways of thinking. Because of this, science fiction is also termed, quite appropriately, speculative fiction.

Dystopias

Lois Lowry's *The Giver* offers a bleak picture of a future civilization that has attempted to curb all emotions—very much like Plato would have liked in his *Republic*. Lowry's story shows us this chilling society through the eyes of its inhabitants—and we, the readers, must become the judges. The result can be unsettling—but it is also intensely thought provoking. *The Giver* is an example of an increasingly popular trend in fantasy fiction—the dystopia. Whereas a utopia portrays an ideal world, a dystopia depicts the opposite—a world where evil, corruption, injustice, poverty, and inhumanity prevail. Lowry shows a world where feelings, emotions, and sentiments are suppressed, and human beings become little more than automatons, unable to feel love, hate, joy, or sorrow.

Many consider Swift's *Gulliver's Travels,* mentioned above, one of the first dystopias. Swift's fantastical tale taking the protagonist, Lemuel Gulliver, to a series of strange lands is a sharply critical attack on the world he lived in—its foolishness, pettiness, and hypocrisy. Perhaps all societies should have a Swift to remind us when we are being foolish, lazy, careless, or cruel. This seems to be the great purpose of dystopian literature.

Several popular modern writers have taken to dystopian fiction. Suzanne Collins (the Hunger Games trilogy) depicts a society dominated by crass commercialism, Meg Rosoff describes the horrors of a future world war (*How I Live Now*), and James Dashner presents an unsettling view of the near-distant future (*The Maze Runner*). All dystopias are thinly veiled versions of our own world—or dire predictions of our world's future if we don't change our ways. In other words, they are wake-up calls.

Summary

Fantasy, like all other literature, changes with the tastes of a culture. Victorian fantasy—Lewis Carroll aside—was heavy with pointed morals and usually with some magical element intruding on the real world. The early twentieth century was the heyday of escapist fantasy—animal fantasies, toy and doll fantasies, and magical stories for younger readers—all perhaps in reaction to the upheaval caused by two world wars and a great worldwide economic depression. The 1950s saw a marked increase in fantasies for older children. (Talking animal fantasies remained popular in children's picture books.) More and more fantasies today deal with horrifying menaces. The rational fantasy world—such as that created by C. S. Lewis—has given way to a world in which irrational evil presents a constant threat. Psychological thrillers—done so successfully by the adult fantasist Stephen King—are now common among fantasies for children. R. L. Stine has written dozens of these types of fantasies.

Through the medium of fantasy, writers are able to explore complex ideas on a symbolic level that would otherwise be difficult to convey to young readers. Fantasy is perfectly suited to the thoughtful exploration of philosophical issues at a level that can be understood and appreciated by the child reader. Fantasy deliberately challenges our perceptions of reality and forces us to explore new, uncharted realms of thought. Unburdened by the conventions and prejudices of our own world, fantasy is ideally suited to present difficult social, political, and philosophical issues in an entirely new light. Many fantasies require of readers the patience and concentration to enter and embrace the writer's world. It is, after all, easier to read about the familiar and the everyday. But the readers who accept the challenge find great riches awaiting them.

The great psychologist Carl Gustav Jung wrote this of the importance of fantasy and its impact on the imagination and our lives:

> *The dynamic principle of fantasy is play, which belongs also to the child, and as such it appears to be inconsistent with the principle of serious work. But without this playing with fantasy no creative work has ever yet come to birth. The debt we owe to the play of the imagination is incalculable.* (82)

One critic has noted that "reading fantasy is not so much an escape *from* something as a liberation *into* something, into openness and possibility and coherence" and that we as readers get perspective on our world "by exploring a strange fictional place and learning how its pieces fit together" (O'Keefe 11–12). It is this challenge in fantasy that attracts its devoted readers.

For Reflection and Discussion

1. Read a fantasy novel—use the booklist below as a guide—and as you read, keep a journal. Read a chapter or two at a time and then spend five or ten minutes writing down your thoughts, observations, predictions—whatever comes to mind. Continue this process throughout the reading of the book. When you are finished, reread your journal entries and assess them. How accurate were your predictions? How do you feel about that? How did your ideas change in the process of reading the book?

2. Here is a challenge. Choose a fantasy novel that you would ordinarily not read—for example, if you are not a fan of science fiction, choose a popular science fiction novel. Read the book and give it a frank appraisal. If you liked it, why? If not, why not? And, more importantly, can you explain what about it might appeal to some readers? In other words, can you put yourself in the shoes of another?

3. Read a popular children's fantasy then do some research on the writer and the book. (See *Something about the Author* or *The Dictionary of Literary Biography* or *The Oxford Encyclopedia of Children's Literature* and other similar reference works, as well as biographies of the writers, if they are available.) Explain how your research made you feel differently about the book. Try to be as specific as you can.

4. Read a fantasy—perhaps from the booklist below—and consider what this story might be like had the writer chosen to use realistic fiction rather than fantasy. Could it have been done? Explain how you think the story would be different—in setting, characters, plot devices, and so on.

5. Read a fantasy—any fantasy will do—and then carefully explain the fantasy rules that operate throughout the story. Has the author stuck to the rules? Exactly how do the rules affect the fantasy as a story? How do they affect your enjoyment of the story? Do you have suggestions for improvement?

6. If you have a favorite fantasy character, try to compose a description of his or her personality. What is it that makes this character so appealing to you? What makes this character believable—despite the fact that he or she is a fantasy figure?

Works Cited

Griswold, Jerry. *Feeling Like a Kid: Childhood and Children's Literature.* Baltimore: Johns Hopkins University Press, 2006.

Jung, Carl Gustav, *Psychological Types.* New York: Harcourt, Brace, 1923.

Manlove, Colin. *From Alice to Harry Potter: Children's Fantasy in England.* Christchurch, New Zealand: Cyber editions, 2003.

O'Keefe, Deborah. *Readers in Wonderland: The Liberating Worlds of Fantasy Fiction.* New York: Continuum, 2003.

Roberts, Thomas J. "Science Fiction and the Adolescent." *Children's Literature: The Great Excluded* 2 (1973): 87–91.

Snyder, Zilpha Keatley. "Afterword." *Tom's Midnight Garden* by Philippa Pearce. New York: Dell, 1986: 230–232.

Recommended Resources

Aiken, Joan. "On Imagination." *The Horn Book* (November/December 1984): 735–741.

Alexander, Lloyd. "High Fantasy and Heroic Romance." *Horn Book Magazine* 47, 6 (December 1971): 577–584.

Attebery, Brian. *The Fantasy Tradition in American Literature: From Irving to Le Guin.* Bloomington: Indiana University Press, 1980.

Babbitt, Natalie. "Fantasy and the Classic Hero." *School Library Journal* (October 1987): 25–29.

Brennan, Geráldine, Kevin McCarron, and Kimberly Reynolds. *Frightening Fiction.* New York: Continuum, 2001.

Cameron, Eleanor. *The Green and Burning Tree.* Boston: Little, Brown, 1969.

Cooper, Susan. *Dreams and Wishes: Essays on Writing for Children.* New York: McElderry, 1996.

Dickinson, Peter. "Fantasy: The Need for Realism." *Children's Literature in Education* 17, 1 (1986): 39–51.

Egoff, Sheila. *Worlds Within: Children's Fantasy from the Middle Ages to Today.* Chicago: American Library Association, 1988.

Engdahl, Sylvia. "The Changing Role of Science Fiction in Children's Literature." *Horn Book Magazine* 47, 5 (October 1971): 449–455.

Hume, Kathryn. *Fantasy and Mimesis.* New York and London: Methuen, 1984.

Kuznets, Lois. *When Toys Come Alive: Narratives of Animations, Metamorphosis and Development.* New Haven, CT: Yale University Press, 1994.

Le Guin, Ursula. *The Language of the Night.* Ed. Susan Wood. New York: G. P. Putnam's Sons, 1979.

Lewis, C. S. "Three Ways of Writing for Children." *Horn Book Magazine* 39, 5 (October 1963): 459–469.

Marcus, Leonard E., ed. *The Wand in the Word: Conversations with Writers of Fantasy.* New York: Candlewick, 2006.

Marcus, Leonard S. "Picture Book Animals: How Natural a History?" *The Lion and the Unicorn* 7/8 (1983/1984): 127–139.

Martin, Philip. *A Guide to Fantasy Literature: Thoughts on Stories of Wonder and Enchantment.* Milwaukee, WI: Crickhollow Books, 2009.

Mendlesohn, Farah. *Rhetorics of Fantasy.* Middletown, CT: Wesleyan University Press, 2008.

Raynor, Mary. "Some Thoughts on Animals in Children's Books." *Signal* 29 (May 1979): 81–87.

Sale, Roger. *Fairy Tales and After: From Snow White to E. B. White.* Cambridge, MA: Harvard University Press, 1978.

Singer, Jerome. "Fantasy: The Foundation of Serenity." *Psychology Today* (July 1976): 33–37.

Smith, Karen Patricia. *The Fabulous Realm.* Lanham, MD: Scarecrow, 1993.

Sullivan, C. W. *Science Fiction for Young Readers.* New York: Greenwood, 1993.

Tolkien, J. R. R. *Tree and Leaf.* Boston: Houghton Mifflin, 1965.

Waggoner, Diana. *The Hills of Faraway: A Guide to Fantasy.* New York: Atheneum, 1978.

Westfahl, Gary. *Science Fiction, Children's Literature, and Popular Culture: Coming of Age in Fantasyland.* New York: Greenwood, 2000.

Wood, Michael. "Coffee Break for Sisyphus: The Point of Science Fiction." *New York Review of Books* 2 (October 1975): 3–4, 6–7.

Wullschläger, Jackie. *Inventing Wonderland: The Lives and Fantasies of Lewis Carroll, Edward Lear, J. M. Barrie, Kenneth Grahame, and A. A. Milne.* New York: Free Press, 1996.

Fantasy Fiction: A Selected and Annotated Booklist

No attempt has been made to identify reading levels. An individual's interests and abilities are the best guides.

Adams, Richard. *Watership Down.* New York: Macmillan, 1974.
- A heroic fantasy about a community of rabbits forced through habitat destruction on a perilous venture to find a new home.

Aiken, Joan. *The Wolves of Willoughby Chase.* New York: Doubleday, 1963.
- A gothic adventure story set in a fantasy English past.

Alexander, Lloyd. *The Book of Three.* New York: Henry Holt, 1964.
- Heroic fantasies set in the mythical kingdom of Prydain. This is the first of the Chronicles of Prydain, along with *The Black Cauldron* (1965), *The Castle of Llyr* (1966), *Taran Wanderer* (1967), *The High King* (1968), and *The Foundling and Other Tales of Prydain* (1970).

Atwater, Richard, and Florence Atwater. *Mr. Popper's Penguins.* Illus. Robert Lawson. Boston: Little, Brown, 1938.
- A comic tale of the antics surrounding a man who has received a crate of penguins from Antarctica.

Babbitt, Natalie. *Tuck Everlasting.* New York: Farrar, Straus & Giroux, 1975.
- The story of a young girl who finds a family that unwittingly drank from a stream of immortality.

Bailey, Caroline Sherwin. *Miss Hickory.* New York: Viking, 1968.
- The story of a crudely handmade doll that is abandoned by her family and must learn to fend for herself through a rough winter.

Barrie, Sir James. *Peter Pan.* 1911 (as *Peter and Wendy*). Several modern editions.
- A classic story of a boy who would not grow up. Originally a play (1904).

Baum, L. Frank. *The Wonderful Wizard of Oz.* 1900. Several modern editions.
- One of the most famous of all fantasy journeys.

Bond, Michael. *A Bear Called Paddington*. Boston: Houghton Mifflin, 1960.
- The story of a well-meaning and cuddly bear from "darkest Peru" who must adjust to life in London with Mr. and Mrs. Brown.

Boston, Lucy. *The Children of Greene Knowe*. New York: Harcourt, 1964.
- Ghost story set in an old English manor house, followed by five sequels.

Brooks, Walter R. *Freddy the Detective*. New York: Knopf, 1932.
- The first of 26 books about Freddy, "the smallest and cleverest" pig on the Bean farm, who pursues a myriad of wild adventures.

Cameron, Eleanor. *Wonderful Flight to the Mushroom Planet*. Illus. Robert Henneberger. Boston: Little, Brown, 1954.
- The story of two boys who travel in a spaceship to a nearby but invisible planet populated by miniature people.

Carroll, Lewis. *Alice's Adventures in Wonderland*. Illus. John Tenniel. 1865. Several modern editions.
- One of the greatest works of nonsense ever written. Followed by a sequel, *Through the Looking-Glass* (1871).

Colfer, Eoin. *Artemis Fowl*. New York: Viking, 2001.
- Exciting adventures of an anti-hero who kidnaps evil fairies; eight sequels followed.

Collins, Suzanne. *Gregor the Overlander*. New York: Scholastic, 2003.
- A science fiction epic about a hidden world beneath New York City. The first of the Underland Chronicles, which also includes *Gregor and the Prophecy of Bane* (2004), *Gregor and the Curse of the Warmbloods* (2005), *Gregor and the Marks of Secret* (2006), and *Gregor and the Code of Claw* (2007).

——. *The Hunger Games*. New York: Scholastic, 2008.
- A dystopia set in a future version of the United States. The first of the Hunger Games trilogy, along with *Catching Fire* (2009) and *Mockingjay* (2010).

Collodi, Carlo. *The Adventures of Pinocchio*. 1883. Several modern editions.
- The story of a rascally puppet who encounters many harrowing adventures in his quest to become a real boy.

Cooper, Susan. *Over Sea, under Stone*. New York: Simon & Schuster, 1965.
- An introduction to the characters featured in the Dark Is Rising series, based on Arthurian legend and a struggle between good and evil, along with *The Dark Is Rising* (1973), *Greenwitch* (1974), *The Grey King* (1975), and *Silver on the Tree* (1977).

Crossley-Holland, Kevin. *The Seeing Stone*. New York: Scholastic, 2001.
- The first of the Arthur trilogy, a retelling of the Arthurian legend, including *At the Crossing Places* (2002) and *King of the Middle March* (2004).

Dahl, Roald. *Charlie and the Chocolate Factory*. New York: Knopf, 1964.
- An outrageous dark comedy by a master storyteller about a boy and his trip through a chocolate factory.

——. *James and the Giant Peach*. New York: Knopf, 1961.
- A story about bizarre creatures sharing a hazardous journey across the Atlantic in a—you guessed it—giant peach.

——. *Matilda*. New York: Viking, 1988.
- The story of a child genius, her beloved teacher, and her dreadful parents. Typical Dahl dark comedy.

Dashner, James. *The Maze Runner*. New York: Delacorte, 2009.
- An adventure tale set in a grim world of the near future. The first of a trilogy including *The Scorch Trials* (2010) and *The Death Cure* (2011).

DuBois, William Pene. *Twenty-One Balloons*. New York: Viking, 1947.
- An outlandish tale of a strange land and its untimely destruction by a volcanic explosion.

Ende, Michael. *The Neverending Story*. 1979. Trans. Ralph Mannheim. New York: Doubleday, 1983.
- A fantasy story within a story, originally in German, about saving the world and winning a princess.

Field, Rachel. *Hitty, Her First Hundred Years*. New York: Macmillan, 1929.
- A doll's account of her adventures through an existence spanning a century.

Fleischman, Sid. *The Whipping Boy*. New York: Morrow, 1986.
- The adventures of a prince and his "whipping boy," who decide to run off together and grow up along the way.

Gaiman, Neil. *Coraline*. London: Bloomsbury, 2002.
- A horror story about a girl who finds herself trapped in a sinister alternate world.

Garner, Alan. *The Weirdstone of Brisingham*. London: Collins, 1960.
- A heroic fantasy that draws on Norse and Celtic lore, complete with wizards, elves, goblins, and more.

Goldman, William. *The Princess Bride*. New York: Harcourt, 1973.
- A fairy tale spoof with all the usual suspects.

Grahame, Kenneth. *The Wind in the Willows*. 1908. Several modern editions.
- The leisurely story of several animals living the good life in the Edwardian English countryside.

Heinlein, Robert. *Have Space Suit—Will Travel*. New York: Scribner's, 1958.
- Adventures in outer space from a celebrated science fiction author.

Hoban, Russell. *The Mouse and His Child*. New York: Harper, 1967.
- The story of two toy mice, joined at the hands, who eventually are discarded, pursued by a villainous rat, and long to become self-winding.

Jacques, Brian. *Redwall*. New York: Philomel, 1987.
- The first of a popular series of heroic fantasies (22 in all) featuring animals in the world of Redwall, which resembles a mythical England.

Jansson, Tove. *Comet in Moominland*. 1946. Trans. Elizabeth Portch. New York: Farrar, Straus & Giroux, 1990.
- The first of a series of magical tales about the wondrous Moomins and their eccentric friends, along with *Finn Family Moomintroll* (1948), *The Exploits of Moominpappa* (1950), *Moominsummer Madness* (1954), *Moominland Midwinter* (1957), *Moominpappa at Sea* (1965), and *Moominvalley in November* (1970).

Jarrell, Randall. *The Bat-Poet*. New York: Macmillan, 1964.
- The fable of a bat who can't sleep during the day and struggles to come to terms with his own individuality with the help of poetry.

Jones, Diana Wynne. *Howl's Moving Castle*. London: Metheun, 1986.
- A spoof on fairy tales in which a young girl boards a strange moving castle to find a way to remove a curse from herself.

Juster, Norton. *The Phantom Tollbooth*. New York: Random, 1961.
- The story of a boy whose magic toll booth transports him to the Kingdom of Wisdom.

Kendall, Carol. *The Gammage Cup*. New York: Harcourt, 1959.
- The tale of a heroic battle waged in a land of miniature peoples.

King-Smith, Dick. *Babe, the Gallant Pig*. New York: Random House, 1983.
- The charming story of a pig who learns to herd sheep. Made into a popular film.

Kipling, Rudyard. *The Jungle Book*. 1894. Several modern editions.
- Talking animal fables set in India, followed by *The Second Jungle Book*.

——. *Just So Stories*. 1902. Illus. Barry Moser. New York: Morrow, 1996.
- Classic animal fables set in India.

Lagerlöf, Selma. *The Wonderful Adventures of Nils*. 1906/1907. Various modern editions.
- A classic Swedish story of a boy journeying across Sweden on the back of a goose.

Lawson, Robert. *Rabbit Hill*. New York: Viking, 1944.
- A fable about the necessity of humans and animals living together.

L'Engle, Madeleine. *A Wrinkle in Time*. New York: Farrar, Straus & Giroux, 1962.
- A science fiction tale of children traveling through time and space. The first of a series of

five books, including *A Wind in the Door* (1973), *A Swiftly Tilting Planet* (1978), *Many Waters* (1986), and *An Acceptable Time* (1989).

Le Guin, Ursula. *A Wizard of Earthsea*. Boston: Houghton Mifflin, 1968.
- Adventures in a far-off world governed by wizards. The first of the Earthsea series, including *The Tombs of Atuan* (1971), *The Farthest Shore* (1972), *Tehanu* (1990), and *Other Wind* (2001).

Lewis, C. S. *The Lion, the Witch, and the Wardrobe*. 1950. New York: HarperCollins.
- The adventures of English children who find themselves in the magical world of Narnia. The first of the Chronicles of Narnia series, including *Prince Caspian* (1951), *The Voyage of the Dawn Treader* (1952), *The Silver Chair* (1953), *The Horse and His Boy* (1954), *The Magician's Nephew* (1955), and *The Last Battle* (1956).

Lindgren, Astrid. *Pippi Longstocking*. New York: Viking, 1950.
- The story of an extraordinary girl living in a very ordinary town—which she soon changes.

Lin, Grace. *The Starry River of the Sky*. New York: Little, Brown, 2012.
- The equally enchanting companion to *Where the Mountain Meets the Moon*, but with an earlier setting. The protagonist is a young boy who longs to find a way to restore the missing moon to the sky.

——. *Where the Mountain Meets the Moon*. New York: Little, Brown, 2009.
- A magical tale set in China about a young girl who sets off on a journey to find happiness for her parents, beautifully interwoven with traditional Chinese folktales.

Lively, Penelope. *The Ghost of Thomas Kempe*. Illus. Antony Maitland. New York: Dutton, 1973.
- The story of an English house haunted by a seventeenth-century poltergeist.

Lobel, Arnold. *Frog and Toad Are Friends*. New York: Harper, 1970.
- A series of short stories about inseparable friends, followed by a sequel, *Frog and Toad Together* (1972). Great for early readers.

Lofting, Hugh. *The Story of Dr. Dolittle*. New York: Stokes, 1920.
- A popular magical story of a doctor who learns to speak the languages of the animals. The first of a series of 12 books.

Lowry, Lois. *The Giver*. Boston: Houghton Mifflin, 1993.
- A chilling tale of life in the future. The first in a series, including *Gathering Blue* (2000), *The Messenger* (2004), and *Son* (2012).

McCaffrey, Anne. *Dragonflight*. New York: Ballantyne, 1968.
- Adventures set in the mythical pre-industrial world. The first of the series The Dragonriders of Pern, continued by McCaffrey's son, Todd McCaffrey.

McKinley, Robin. *The Hero and the Crown*. New York: Greenwillow, 1985.
- A heroic fantasy, one of the earliest to feature a female protagonist.

Miéville, China. *Un Lun Dun*. New York: Macmillan, 2007.
- An unusual tale of heroines overcoming evil in a wacky alternate world.

Milne, A. A. *Winnie-the-Pooh*. 1926. Illus. Ernest Shepard. New York: Dutton, 1961.
- A story of several endearing toy animals encountering comical adventures.

Nesbit, E. *Five Children and It*. London: Unwin, 1902.
- The story of five children who discover an ancient fairy, the Psammead, who can grant wishes. The first of the Psammead trilogy, including *The Phoenix and the Carpet* (1904) and *The Story of the Amulet* (1906).

Ness, Patrick. *The Knife of Never Letting Go*. New York: Candlewick, 2009.
- The first of the Chaos Walking dystopian trilogy, including *The Ask and the Answer* (2010) and *Monsters of Men* (2011).

——. *A Monster Calls (Inspired by an Idea by Siobhan Dowd)*. Illus. Jim Kay. New York: Candlewick, 2011.
- A powerfully told and dramatically illustrated story of a boy dealing with his mother's terminal illness and a monster that comes at night to tell him stories.

Nicholson, William. *The Wind Singer*. New York: Hyperion, 2000.
- A heroic adventure set in an alternate world. The first of the Windon Fire trilogy, along with *Slaves of the Mastery* (2001) and *Firesong* (2002).

Nix, Garth. *Mister Monday*. New York: Scholastic, 2003.
- The story of a young boy who finds himself master of the universe in this first of seven books in the Keys to the Kingdom series, each of which focuses on one of the seven deadly sins.

Norton, Mary. *The Borrowers*. New York: Harcourt, 1953.
- The first book in a series about tiny people who live in the walls and floorboards of our houses.

O'Brien, Robert. *Mrs. Frisby and the Rats of NIMH*. New York: Atheneum, 1971.
- The story of escaped laboratory rats helping a widowed field mouse relocate her home, where we learn about the rats' lab experiences.

Parish, Peggy. *Amelia Bedelia*. New York: Harper, 1963.
- The first of a series about a hapless housemaid who takes everything too literally.

Pearce, Philippa. *Tom's Midnight Garden*. New York: Dell, 1986.
- The story of a boy who accidentally finds a way to travel back in time.

Pratchett, Terry. *Only You Can Save Mankind*. London: Doubleday, 1992.
- The story of a boy who finds himself inside a computer game and the adventures that ensue. The first of the Johnny Maxwell trilogy, along with *Johnny and the Dead* (1993) and *Johnny and the Bomb* (1996).

Pullman, Philip. *The Golden Compass*. New York: Knopf, 1996.
- Originally published as *Northern Lights* in the United Kingdom, the epic adventures of a young girl and boy ina parallel world. The first of the His Dark Materials trilogy, along with *The Subtle Knife* (1997) and *The Amber Spyglass* (2000).

Reid Banks, Lynn. *The Indian in the Cupboard*. New York: Doubleday, 1981.
- The story of a magic cupboard that brings to life tiny toy creatures who become involved in a variety of adventures.

Rosoff, Meg. *How I Live Now*. New York: Penguin, 2004.
- A book about a third world war and its aftermath in the near future.

Rowling, J. K. *Harry Potter and the Philosopher's Stone*. London: Bloomsbury, 1997.
- The wildly popular adventures of an English orphan studying to become a wizard. The first of a series, along with *Harry Potter and the Chamber of Secrets* (1998), *Harry Potter and the Prisoner of Azkaban* (1999), *Harry Potter and the Goblet of Fire* (2000), *Harry Potter and the Order of the Phoenix* (2003), *Harry Potter and the Half-Blood Prince* (2005), and *Harry Potter and the Deathly Hallows* (2007).

Selden, George. *The Cricket in Times Square*. Illus. Garth Williams. New York: Farrar, Straus & Giroux, 1960.
- The adventures of a cricket from Connecticut attempting to make a go of it in New York City.

Sharp, Margery. *The Rescuers*. Boston: Little, Brown, 1959.
- A book about a beautiful and pampered mouse, Miss Bianca, who leads a daring rescue of an imprisoned poet. Also an animated film.

Snow, Alan. *Here Be Monsters!* New York: Atheneum, 2006.
- A darkly humorous fantasy in the vein of Roald Dahl in which a young boy has run afoul of some dastardly characters who wish to destroy him and the entire town.

Steig, William. *Abel's Island*. New York: Farrar, Straus & Giroux, 1976.
- A story of a mouse stranded on a deserted island who must learn to survive.

——. *Dominic*. New York: Farrar, Straus & Giroux, 1972.
- A story about a canine free spirit who sets off for a life of adventure—and finds it.

Thomas, Shelley Moore. *Good Night, Good Knight*. Illus. Jennifer Plecar. New York: Dutton, 2000.
- The first of a series of enchanting tales about a knight and his dragon friends.

Tolkien, J. R. R. *The Hobbit*. 1937. New York: Houghton Mifflin, Various editions.
- The prequel to the Lord of the Rings series is accessible to younger readers, whereas the series itself, which includes *The Fellowship of the Ring* (1954), *The Two Towers* (1955), and *The Return of the King* (1955), is for older readers.

Travers, P. L. *Mary Poppins*. New York: Harcourt, 1934.
- The tale of an acerbic nanny who brings order and joy to a stuffy London family.

Verne, Jules. *Twenty Thousand Leagues under the Sea*. 1864. New York: Penguin, 1987.
- A classic story of undersea adventures from the father of science fiction.

Wells, H. G. *The Time Machine*. 1895. New York: Bantam, 1982.
- One of the earliest and best time travel stories.

——. *The War of the Worlds*. 1898. New York: Putnam, 1978.
- One of the first novels about an invasion of Earth from outer space.

White, E. B. *Charlotte's Web*. New York: Harper, 1952.
- A classic tale of the friendship between a pig and a spider. Everyone should read this.

Williams, Margery. *The Velveteen Rabbit*. 1922. Illus. Michael Hague. New York: Holt, Rinehart & Winston, 1983.
- The story of a stuffed rabbit who longs to become a real animal—and, of course, does.

Yolen, Jane. *Dragon's Blood*. New York: Delacorte, 1982.
- A futuristic story featuring a species of dragons. The first in the Pit Dragon Chronicles, along with *Heart's Blood* (1984), *A Sending of Dragons* (1987), and *Dragon's Heart* (2009).

11

Realistic Fiction

The Days of Our Lives

Introduction

Realistic fiction attempts to describe the world as it is (or as it was, in the case of historical realism). A realistic novelist tries to make the characters and situations true to life and introduces nothing beyond the realm of possibility. Some writers portray the world as a bit rosier than it probably is, whereas other writers portray it as far darker than we hope it is. Our interest in realistic fiction derives from an inherent interest in the human condition and in the ways people face life's challenges, defeats, joys, and sorrows. When a writer re-creates an earlier time period, we call it *historical realism*, and when a writer describes his or her own time period, we call it *contemporary realism*. Although historical and contemporary realistic novels share many of the same subjects, plots, character types, and themes, a writer approaches each one a little differently. We will first consider the differences between historical and contemporary realism and then examine some of the prominent issues in realistic fiction in general.

Historical Realism

Definition and Background

Sir Walter Scott (1771–1832) virtually invented historical fiction in the early nineteenth century, with such novels as *Ivanhoe*, a romantic tale of the Middle Ages, and *Waverley*, about a Scottish rebellion against the English in 1745. Scott's books are for adults, but very quickly historical realism became popular with young readers, who were drawn by the exotic settings, colorful adventures, and heroic figures of the past. Soon writers like Robert Louis Stevenson (*The Black Arrow*, 1888) and Howard Pyle (*Otto of the Silver Hand*, 1888, see Figure 11.1) began writing historical fiction for young readers, and it remains popular to this day.

FIGURE 11.1 ■ This illustration is by Howard Pyle for his historical novel *Otto of the Silver Hand,* an adventure romance set in the European Middle Ages.

In the mid-nineteenth century, Alessandro Manzoni pointed out that the difference between a historian and a historical novelist is that the historian must deal with the "bare bones of history," whereas a historical novelist's job is "to put the flesh back on the skeleton that is history" (67–68). The "flesh" he is referring to is the fictional story that provides the intimate focus framed by the wider historical events in the novel. Think of Margaret Mitchell's story of Scarlett O'Hara and Rhett Butler against the background of the Civil War in *Gone with the Wind.* The historical novel has two faces: It is part history and part fabrication. Most readers of historical fiction like to feel that the history they are reading about is accurate, even if the story is fiction. At the same time, the writer's imagination has to give us an interesting story with engaging characters we want to get to know.

But, you might ask, don't all realistic novels eventually become historical fiction as they age? What about Louisa May Alcott's *Little Women*, for example, which is set in the 1860s? Is it historical fiction now? Actually, no. Alcott published the book in two volumes in 1868 and 1869—so it was set in what were then contemporary times. Alcott has no need to explain the social customs and mores of nineteenth-century New England; her readers would already have known about them. Nor is her interest in historical personages or events. Here is where historical realism differs from contemporary realism. In historical realism, the writer has a true sense of the past and understands that recreating a bygone era is crucial to the overall impact of the story. A rule of thumb is that true historical realism is set at least one generation (or about 20–25 years) prior to its writing.

To achieve a sense of authenticity, historical fiction usually includes some historic event as a key element in the story, such as the bombing of the Sixteenth-Street Baptist Church in Christopher Paul Curtis's *The Watsons Go to Birmingham—1963*, or the Danish evacuation of the Jews during World War II in Lois Lowry's *Number the Stars*, or the devastation of the Dust Bowl in the American Great Plains in the 1930s in Karen Hesse's *Out of the Dust*. But it is important to remember that historical fiction is *not* history—it is a fictional story with fictional characters. But at the very least, readers like to experience the genuine feeling of the past when they read historical fiction.

Capturing the Period

How do writers capture the feeling of the past? In part, through the accumulation of specific details. Karen Hesse's *Out of the Dust* is written as the journal of a young girl struggling in the Oklahoma Dust Bowl during the worst of the Depression in the mid-1930s. In simple, yet eloquent, free verse, she tells us about the relentless sandstorms and hardships the people had to endure—wetting sheets and blankets to place over windows and doors to absorb the blowing sand or stringing up ropes so people could find their way from house to barn in the blinding storms. Both the courage and the desperation of the people struggling to survive are movingly portrayed through these vivid details.

Another way a writer can evoke the feeling of the past is through authentic dialogue. We know that nineteenth-century Americans did not speak the same way that Americans of today speak. (Indeed, teenagers of the 1980s did not speak like the teenagers of today—in the 1980s, no one "texted" anybody, and Twitter and Facebook were unheard of, nor did anyone get "unfriended.") The following brief passage from Irene Hunt's Civil War story *Across Five Aprils* shows how the author uses the language of the period to make the setting and characters more authentic:

> *The young man got to his feet grinning. "Sure, Red, glad to oblige. Hear you been blowin' off at the mouth at some of the cracker-barrel heroes agin."*
>
> *Milton shrugged. "Word gets around fast."*
>
> *"Ben Harris was in fer a minute." The young man shook his head. "You jest ain't goin' to be happy till you git dressed up in tar and feathers, are you, Red?"* (78)

The dialect is that of uneducated rural Americans in the 1860s. The passage refers, of course, to the nineteenth-century practice of literally covering victims with tar and feathers as a form of public chastisement. Some readers find dialect difficult to read, at least at first. But it is frequently necessary if we are to get the true flavor of a time and place.

Another thing to look for in historical fiction is the *anachronism*—that is, anything that is out of place in the time period—a silly example would be George Washington talking on a cell phone with his officers. A good historical novelist is also a good historical researcher. Along with items, attitudes can be anachronistic. An example is found in Avi's *True Confessions of Charlotte Doyle*, a Newbery Honor book. It is the story of a 13-year-old girl sailing to America in 1832. On the voyage, she outmaneuvers the ship's wicked captain and ultimately replaces him at the helm. Anne Scott MacLeod, although admitting the story is a "fine vicarious adventure story," calls it also "preposterous," objecting not only to the age of the protagonist but to her gender in the context of nineteenth-century attitudes (see MacLeod 29–31). Some readers are willing to accept anachronisms if the story is redeemed in other ways—excitement, rich characters, or purely for comic effect, for example.

Historical fiction can interest young readers in a historical period and encourage them to read nonfiction works about the history itself. It can also be a good supplement to a history class. Reading one of the many novels about the Holocaust and World War II (Lois Lowry's *Number the Stars*, Hans Richter's *Friedrich*, or John Boyne's *The Boy in the Striped Pajamas*, for example) can give young readers a compelling sense of what it was like to live through the period. On the other hand, historical fiction should never be allowed to substitute for genuine history.

Contemporary Realism

Definition and Background

Contemporary realism is set during or very near the time of its writing. Consequently, writers of contemporary fiction, unlike historical novelists, can take many things for granted. For instance, no writer of contemporary fiction today would have to define a mall, a cell phone, an iPad, or digital downloads. In other words, a contemporary novelist already shares a common body of knowledge with the readers. So we can expect less background information about the time and place in contemporary fiction than in historical fiction. An exception occurs when the story is set outside the culture of the general reader; in that case, the writer is obligated to provide background material about the culture, the climate, social customs, beliefs, and so on. (In fact, contemporary fiction set in a foreign culture is similar to historical fiction in that regard. For example, Margaret Craven's very beautiful short novel, *I Heard the Owl Call My Name,* has a setting contemporary with its publication date, 1973, but the story takes place in the remote Indian village of Kingcome on the coast of British Columbia. Many of the Indians still cling to their ancient customs, which are described in loving detail, as they struggle to remain untouched by the encroaching modern world. The setting gives a timeless quality to this moving story of personal courage and dignity in the face of life and death.)

Contemporary realism for children dates to the nineteenth century, with works such as Charlotte Yonge's *The Daisy Chain* (1856), the story of a large English family dealing with the death of the mother, and, as we have already mentioned, Alcott's *Little Women*. And there is that granddaddy of school stories, Thomas Hughes's *Tom Brown's School-Days* (1857). The school story (almost always about boys) is usually set in a boarding school, where the youthful characters enjoy a degree of freedom away from their parents' watchful eyes. It is common in children's and young adult stories to find children separated from their parents; some child protagonists are orphaned or from single-parent homes, away at boarding school or summer camp, or sometimes simply lost. The point is that characters who have some independence can be much more interesting to read about than those who are attached to their mother's apron strings. Also in the nineteenth century, adventure stories (like Mark Twain's *The Adventures of Tom Sawyer*) and survival stories (in the vein of Daniel Defoe's classic *Robinson Crusoe* [1719]) were popular with young readers. Defoe's book inspired R. M. Ballantyne's *The Coral Island* (1857), the story of three young boys stranded on a remote Pacific island who survive because of their perseverance and ingenuity.

New Realism and the Problem Novel

Up until the mid-twentieth century, most contemporary stories for young readers tended toward sentimentalism (see Chapter 9) or at least romanticism—painting life as generally rosy even if there were occasional rough patches. But this began to change in the mid-twentieth century, when romanticism and sentimentalism were replaced by honest, sometimes harsh, realism—at least this was true of many books for older readers. Beginning in the 1960s the so-called new realism surfaced; it introduced to children's and young adult literature raw emotions (lots of shouting and crying), franker language (gritty street talk), and bolder ideas (sex, drugs, and gangs). In fact, with the coming of new realism, little remained that was taboo for the young adult novel.

With the coming of new realism, books for young adult readers began to address a wide variety of issues that were formerly avoided: racial prejudice (works by Mildred Taylor and Virginia Hamilton), teenage gangs (Walter Dean Myers's *Scorpions*), drug abuse (Alice Childress's *A Hero Ain't Nothin' but a Sandwich*), homosexuality (M. E. Kerr's *"Hello," I Lied*), child abuse (Mirjam Pressler's *Halinka*), mental illness (James Bennett's *I Can Hear the Mourning Dove*), sexual abuse (Cynthia Voigt's *When She Hollers*), and many others.

Many of these books also fit into a subcategory often called the *problem novel*, which is really a variation on the so-called social novel for adults (which go back as far as Charles Dickens in the nineteenth century). The problem novel tends to be narrowly focused on a single hot-button issue—often controversial—and depicts the teenage protagonist's initiation into the adult world. As a consequence, they are also often coming-of-age stories (though generally not very deep), leaving the protagonist "sadder but wiser" at the end. S. E. Hinton's *The Outsiders,* published in 1967, is considered among the first of the modern problem novels for teenagers or young adults. Hinton's book is a starkly realistic portrayal of teenage street gangs (and Hinton herself was a teenager when she wrote the book).

Too often problem novels contain predictable plots, shallow characters, and trite dialogue. Sometimes they are sensationalized and devolve into melodrama—they are the soap operas of young adult literature. Perhaps most seriously, many of them imply that teenage problems have simplistic solutions. Of course, their predictability and easy answers make them very popular with young readers, as evidenced by the success of the Sweet Valley High series and the Baby-Sitters Club series. But at their best, problem novels explore significant psychological and sociological issues with sensitivity, and they give us vivid, complex characters.

Judy Blume's name has long been associated with the problem novel. Her *Forever* was one of the first books for young readers to deal frankly with sex (which also got it banned in many places), and her *Blubber* describes the cruelty inflicted by children on an overweight girl. Blume's *Tiger Eyes,* for young adult readers, is a good example of the finely crafted problem novel, examining a teenager's coping with her father's senseless murder and the changes it brought to her life.

Nor should we overlook another important trend in both contemporary and historical realism, and that is the increasing attention to cultural diversity. We can now find books about a wide variety of cultural groups—books that are sensitive to cultural practices and beliefs, as well as to the problems many cultures face in a rapidly changing, global, and technological world. The booklists at the end of this chapter and at the end of Chapter 4 include many of these titles.

Topics in Realistic Fiction—Historical and Contemporary

Perhaps the most common subject in books for readers in the middle grades and older is coming of age—moving from childhood into puberty and adolescence. Many books for younger readers, although not technically coming-of-age stories, are about children coping with life's inevitable changes. Good examples are Beverly Cleary's *Ramona* books, Patricia MacLachlan's *Arthur, for the Very First Time,* Katherine Paterson's *The Great Gilly Hopkins,* and Grace Lin's *The Year of the Dog.*

For older readers, the issues become more complicated. They face dramatic and often perplexing changes in their physical bodies, in their social encounters, and in their intellectual grasp of things. Most readers are drawn to stories about people like themselves facing extraordinary situations. If you want a fancy term for these coming-of-age books, it is the German word *Bildungsroman*, which means roughly "a formation or building story," a story of how characters come to be what they are. Many of the great classic novels of youth and adolescence are coming-of-age stories—from Charlotte Brontë's romantic love story *Jane Eyre* to Charles Dickens's *Great Expectations* to Mark Twain's *Huckleberry Finn*, all written in the nineteenth century. And in the twentieth century we have John Knowle's *A Separate Peace* (about a terrible secret among young schoolboys), J. D. Salinger's brutally frank (but very funny) *Catcher in the Rye* (about a troubled youth), Harper Lee's powerful *To Kill a Mockingbird* (about social injustice), and William Golding's chilling *Lord of the Flies* (about the dark side of human nature), all of which have acquired the status of classics.

Coming of age necessarily involves gaining wisdom—but it is always at the expense of innocence and involves loss of freedom from care. At the end of these stories, the protagonist has learned something about him- or herself, about people, and about the world. Invariably, the protagonist is a sensitive and curious individual who is looking for answers, trying to understand his or her own physical and emotional changes, and learning about the ways of the world. We should note that coming-of-age stories do not have to be realistic fiction. In fact, many of the greatest fantasies are also about growing up—from Ursula Le Guin's Earthsea cycle to Philip Pullman's His Dark Materials trilogy to Suzanne Collins's Hunger Games trilogy. These are all about characters who mature physically, psychologically, emotionally, and socially—sometimes against their will but always of necessity. This is the great theme of literature for children in the middle grades and older.

What follows is a brief discussion of some of the most popular topics we find in realistic fiction—in both historical realism and contemporary realism (for they both deal with the same subjects and themes). Many of these novels are coming-of-age stories, and many will fit into more than one of these categories. This is only intended as a general guide to suggest the breadth and richness of realistic fiction.

Family Relationships

The great Russian writer Tolstoy opened his novel *Anna Karenina* with the famous line "All happy families are all alike; each unhappy family is unhappy in its own way" (1). Certainly from a writer's point of view, a family without conflict would make a dull story indeed. But, in fact, most early family stories for young readers depict happy families—although they are not without their troubles. Louisa May Alcott's *Little Women* (see Figure 11.2) portrays the March family—four sisters and their mother (father is off fighting in the Civil War). There is sibling rivalry, the family lives on the edge of poverty, there are failed romances, and tragedy even strikes as one of the sisters falls ill and dies. But the Marches triumph with their general spirit of optimism and genuine love for each other. In the early twentieth century, Eleanor Estes wrote a series of books about the Moffat family (beginning with the *The Moffats*, first published in 1941), an impoverished family living in Connecticut just

FIGURE 11.2 ■ J. S. Eland's sentimental illustration for an early edition of Louisa May Alcott's popular domestic story *Little Women* depicts Amy playing dress-up, a typical pastime for middle-class, nineteenth-century girls.

after World War I. They, too, are a family of four siblings—this time two boys and two girls—and their widowed mother. The family's poverty is a constant source of conflict in their lives, but they always manage, everyone helps out, and no one grumbles. Their source of strength, as with the Marches, is the family unit.

These books are fairly typical of the family stories of the nineteenth and early twentieth centuries (and it is curious how many of these early "family" stories depict single-parent families). As the twentieth century progressed, the family story transformed. More and more, instead of happy families overcoming poverty and occasional hardship, we find families torn by internal dissension and fractured by tragic circumstances. Cynthia Voigt's *Homecoming* and its sequels are the stories of the four Tillerman children, two boys and two girls, who have been abandoned by their mother in a Connecticut parking lot. Under the leadership of Dicey, the elder sister, they set off to find their grandmother, a woman they've never met, in far-off Maryland. When they finally reach their grandmother, she turns out to be cold, distant, and cantankerous. This is hardly the happy family circle depicted by Alcott and Estes. However, in the end, through perseverance, sacrifice, and forgiveness, the family manages to pull together. The theme is essentially the same as it has always been in the family story (the need for mutual sacrifice, forgiveness, and unconditional love), but the romantic vision has been replaced by one more starkly realistic. There is, for instance, no happy reunion with their mother, who dies from a drug overdose. The current trend in family stories for children, unsurprisingly, is to focus on fractured, blended, and dysfunctional families or families in crisis. Single-parent homes are commonplace—although it is frequently due to divorce rather than widowhood, as in the past.

Beverly Cleary, famous for her humorous stories of Ramona Quimby and Henry Huggins, all depicting happy families, herself became part of the general trend in 1983 with *Dear Mr. Henshaw*. This Newbery Medal–winning novel is written as a series of letters and journal entries by a young boy coming to terms with his parents' divorce. But some families are in even more dire straits. Bill and Vera Cleaver's *Where the Lilies Bloom* portrays a family of orphaned siblings trying to make it on their own in their impoverished Appalachian home; the children even have to bury their father themselves. In still a different vein is Patricia MacLachlan's *Baby*, the story of a family, recently bereaved from the death of an infant, who find, on its doorstep, an abandoned baby. This poetic tale is one of healing and redemption.

If the message of the modern family story remains positive, it does suggest that the family is a diverse organism, intricately complicated, sometimes tragic, but ultimately worth fighting for.

Friendship

Very few books for young readers do not involve the forming of friendships. Indeed, as children grow older, friendships often become as important as family ties, and in many cases they're more important. Susan Patron's *The Higher Power of Lucky*, which won the 2007 Newbery Medal, bridges the narrow gap between stories of family and stories of friends. It actually treats the disintegration of one family—Lucky's mother is dead and her father has deserted her—and the creation of a new family that includes, of all people, her father's second wife (now divorced). Stories about friendships include the subjects of making new friends, keeping old ones, disagreements among friends, and discovering unusual or unlikely friends. In many modern novels, it is with the support of good friends that young people cope with difficult home lives. An early example is Frances Hodgson Burnett's much-loved *The Secret Garden*, which describes the forming of a friendship between two children, one orphaned and one neglected (see Figure 11.3). Lucy Maud Montgomery's equally popular *Anne of Green Gables* shows an orphan adapting to an unconventional family (an elderly brother and sister) and forming friendships in a new environment. In Eleanor Estes's *The Hundred Dresses*, a girl from an impoverished family and immigrant background is subjected to cruel taunts for being

FIGURE 11.3 ■ Charles Robinson's illustration from Frances Hodgson Burnett's popular classic, *The Secret Garden*, originally published in 1910, about the redemption of a sullen orphan girl living on the moors of northern England.

Source: "There were Trees . . . and a Large Pool with an Old Grey Fountain in its Midst", Charles Robinson (1870–1937). Colour lithograph. Private Collection/© Look and Learn/The Bridgeman Art Library.

different but is eventually embraced by new friends. One of the most popular modern children's stories on the subject of making new and unlikely friends is Kate DiCamillo's *Because of Winn-Dixie*, about a girl being raised by her father and adjusting to a new home in Florida, where she makes friends with an assortment of quirky characters and a dog.

But friendships have their rocky spots, and books dealing with friendship usually reveal relationships being put to the test and emerging stronger. Louise Fitzhugh's *Harriet the Spy* is a good example. It is the story of a fiercely independent only child who has to learn the value of friendship the hard way—after she has done her best to drive all her friends away. E. L. Konigsburg's *The View from Saturday* describes a motley crew of youthful intellectuals who come from a wide variety of religious and ethnic backgrounds (and supported, incidentally, by a wheelchair-bound teacher). In all these stories, the message is that friendships do not just happen, they are forged with considerable effort and sacrifice—and they come with inestimable rewards. In other words, friendships are an extension of (and sometimes a replacement for) family relationships.

Adventure and Survival

Modern realistic adventure and survival stories are the heirs of Daniel Defoe's *Robinson Crusoe*. An adventure tale depicts the realistic, often harrowing, adventures of a protagonist, who often must struggle against formidable, usually adult, antagonists. The setting is frequently in a faraway place, which requires a journey. The hero or heroine's life or wellbeing is threatened in a series of close scrapes. The protagonist escapes, usually through a combination of agility and cleverness. (Great strength is usually not a requirement.) Adventure stories, written largely for boys, first became popular in the nineteenth century. Robert Louis Stevenson was among the most famous authors of adventure stories, with such classics as *Kidnapped* and *Treasure Island*. Jack London's animal story *The Call of the Wild* is a long-time favorite realistic adventure story, in which the main character is a dog who is taken from his California home by a cruel man who forces him to pull dogsleds in Alaska. Eventually, the dog escapes and seeks his ancestral roots with the wolves.

A popular variation of the adventure story is the survival story—also descended from *Robinson Crusoe*—in which the protagonist is stranded (alone or with just a few friends or family members) in an unfamiliar and often dangerous place and must figure out how to remain alive and be rescued. However, few modern survival stories subscribe to Defoe's optimistic portrayal of a wild tropical paradise where the hero carves out a life of luxury (complete with a servant). Instead, modern survival stories portray the hardships and isolation that face most of the protagonists, who are usually humbled before the forces of nature. They adapt their lifestyles to their surroundings. Scott O'Dell's *Island of the Blue Dolphins*, which first appeared in 1960, is a work of historical fiction based on an actual incident from the early nineteenth century. This was one of the first modern survival stories to adopt this new and far more realistic approach to survival narratives. O'Dell conveys the message that, in real life, survival means sacrifice, suffering, adaptation, and often loneliness. Jean Craighead George (*Julie of the Wolves* and *My Side of the Mountain*) and Harry Mazer (*Snowbound* and *The Island Keeper*) have followed O'Dell's example, portraying heroes and heroines who learn to live in harmony with the natural world and who often come to respect nature above the civilizing forces of humanity. In other words, they become aware of the ecosystem (see the discussion of ecocriticism in Chapter 9).

Perhaps the most chilling, but among the most important, survival stories of modern times are those about children surviving the Holocaust. Some of these are actual memoirs and are therefore nonfiction—*The Diary of Anne Frank* being the most famous, although, in fact, Anne Frank herself did not survive. Judith Kerr's *When Hitler Stole Pink Rabbit* is a novel, which was inspired by the author's own harrowing experience escaping Hitler's Germany. And John Boyne's exceedingly popular *The Boy in the Striped Pajamas* is a purely fictional and powerful account of life in Auschwitz as seen through the eyes of a 9-year-old boy.

A key element in any survival story is its detailing of the means of survival. We see the protagonist gathering food, finding shelter from the elements, securing protection from threatening forces, and learning how to combat loneliness. Survival stories depict the individual overcoming adversity and, in the process, achieving self-awareness, which includes recognizing one's strengths and shortcomings and understanding one's innermost needs and desires.

Social Outcasts

Stories of social outcasts deal with individuals who must struggle to become part of society and who are, for one reason or another, regarded as outside the mainstream. Mark Twain's irrepressible hero Huckleberry Finn is perhaps the original outsider. Scorned by society and with only one true friend, Jim, an escaped slave, he faces a rough-and-tumble world with tenacity and bravery, ultimately achieving acceptance (although by that time he is not sure he wants it).

It would be easy to argue that most fictional stories today are, to one degree or another, about "outsiders," including books such as Fitzhugh's *Harriet the Spy*, Burnett's *The Secret Garden*, DiCamillo's *Because of Winn-Dixie*, and many others. That they are outsiders is what makes the characters compelling. In recent years, authors have become increasingly interested in those "outsiders" who have long been neglected in children's literature— people shunned by society because they are troubled emotionally, disadvantaged physically, or challenged mentally. Katherine Paterson, in *The Great Gilly Hopkins*, portrays an emotionally troubled child placed in a foster home. *The Language of Goldfish* by Zibby Oneal describes a young girl plagued with mental illness and suicidal tendencies. *The Pigman* by Paul Zindel is about a developing relationship between two teenagers and a lonely elderly man. Robert Cormier's *Tenderness* is a chilling portrait of a teenage serial killer; you can't get much further outside than that.

Sexuality

Once virtually ignored in children's books—indeed, many adults tried to pretend that it did not exist—sexuality in its many manifestations is now an important subject in children's and, especially, adolescent literature. Judy Blume's *Are You There, God? It's Me, Margaret* is, in part, about a young girl coping with the onset of menses. Frankly, one of the values in novels about sexuality is that they provide children with necessary information that might help them through the very difficult period of puberty. (Too often, parents neglect this responsibility.) And Paul Zindel helped to open up the discussion of premarital sex, rape, and teenage pregnancy in *My Darling, My Hamburger.*

Issues important to lesbian, gay, bisexual, transgendered, and questioning (LGBTQ) individuals were at one time virtually ignored in books for teen readers. Indeed, they were not only ignored but were taboo until the 1980s. Many writers are now recognizing sexual orientation as an important social issue about which children need sensitive education. A pioneering work in this field is John Donovan's *I'll Get There. It Better Be Worth the Trip*, which appeared in 1969, a groundbreaking work about a teenager's coming to terms with his homosexuality. Other significant contributions include Marion Dane Bauer's *Am I Blue?: Coming Out from the Silence* (a selection of short stories on gay and lesbian themes by various writers) and M. E. Kerr's *Deliver Us from Evie* (about a teenage lesbian). Alex Sanchez is best known for his Rainbow Boys trilogy, coming-of-age stories about three gay and bisexual friends.

As we might expect, all these books are frequently challenged and occasionally banned. But fortunately, with more enlightened attitudes, they are gradually becoming standard reading fare and are showing up on more and more reading lists. This is a testament to the tolerance and sensitivity of today's youth, which is a refreshing change from the stifling, judgmental, and hypocritical world of the past.

The true dark side of sexuality is sexual abuse. This issue is at the heart of Laurie Halse Anderson's *Speak*, the story of a young girl's difficult recovery from rape and how she once again finds her voice and her identity. Even more chilling is Elizabeth Scott's *Living Dead Girl*, about a pedophile abducting a 10-year-old girl and holding her for five years.

Of course, any book on sexuality for young people is going to face some controversy, but we need to recognize the distinction between serious books about sexuality and books that exploit sex (or pornography). The best books are honest and forthright while avoiding the lascivious. Without responsible writers creating sensitive and intelligent stories, many young people would learn about sexuality from ill-informed friends and neighbors—or worse. As with most other topics, knowledge always trumps ignorance.

Death and Dying

Death is actually one of the oldest subjects we find in children's literature. In eighteenth-century children's books, characters were always dying—the virtuous winging their way to heaven and the wicked consigned to the pits of hell. In the nineteenth century, the fire and brimstone were omitted, and death became an object of sentimentalism, cleverly parodied by Mark Twain in *Huckleberry Finn*. (See the discussion of parody in Chapter 9.)

It may be that earlier generations were better equipped emotionally to handle death than we are today—not because they had any answers but because they simply were not afraid to face death as a fact of life. They were surrounded by death; they lived with it. Today, we confine it to institutions—impersonal hospitals and nursing homes. In addition, modern science has led us to believe in miracles and has almost lulled us into a false sense of our own invulnerability. So when death does come, it seems an anomaly—an unwelcome stranger in our society. We deny it, bargain with it, rage against it—we can't even utter its name (people no longer "die"; instead, they "pass away" or, rather inaccurately, "pass"). It is the difficulty of acceptance that is the subject of most children's books on the subject.

We have seen in Chapter 2 that for the very youngest children, the subject of death is often broached by portraying the death of an animal. And many books for middle and upper elementary readers depict the deaths of beloved pets. Marjorie Kinnan Rawlings's *The Yearling* and Wilson Rawls's *Where the Red Fern Grows* are two celebrated examples. For older readers, the deaths of friends and family members are the more frequent subjects. Writing about death is often quite personal. Mollie Hunter's *A Sound of Chariots* reflects the author's own deep grief following the death of her father. Lois Lowry's *A Summer to Die* is based on the death of Lowry's sister. And Katherine Paterson wrote *Bridge to Terabithia* as an assuagement for her young son, who had lost his best friend in a tragic accident. These writers all present death without sentimentality but with great sensitivity. In *Bridge to Terabithia* we can observe the protagonist, Jesse, move through the stages of grief as he attempts to come to terms with loss—and, as always, there are no answers, only ultimate acceptance and memory.

The deaths that are often the most difficult to accept are the unexpected and premature ones. James Lincoln Collier and Christopher Collier's *My Brother Sam Is Dead*, a historical novel about two brothers fighting on opposites sides during the American Revolution, is among the earliest books for young people depicting a wartime casualty. And, the once-unspeakable subject of teen suicide is the subject of Richard Peck's *Remembering the Good Times* and John Green's *Looking for Alaska*. Once again we see the move in children's literature toward greater realism, more frankness and honesty, and greater intensity. Unlike the writers of the eighteenth century, who found their comfort in religious salvation, many writers today present death as the natural completion of the great circle of life or a tragic consequence over which we have little control and which we must learn to accept.

Mysteries and Puzzlers

Mysteries and puzzlers are often escapist fiction, creating a world somehow more exciting, more dangerous, and more interesting than we imagine our own to be. The mystery, first popularized in the early nineteenth century by Edgar Allan Poe and later refined by Arthur Conan Doyle, the creator of Sherlock Holmes, has long been a favorite of young readers.

Detective mysteries lend themselves to serialization, and we even find series for beginning readers. One of the most popular of these—Cynthia Rylant's High-Rise Private Eyes series—features a talking rabbit and raccoon (so it is technically a fantasy but that is immaterial—and unimportant to second graders). The hero of Donald Sobol's Encyclopedia Brown series, also for younger readers, is known for his intellect. And Betsy Byars's Herculeah Jones series relates the adventures of the young daughter of a police officer and a private detective. And we can't overlook Nancy Drew and the Hardy Boys, whose formulaic stories, written by various ghostwriters over many years, remain popular.

The mystery always involves the solving of a puzzle—often a crime. The success of a mystery depends on the writer's clever planting of clues and the ingenuity of the puzzle and its solution. The puzzle must not be too easily solved, or the reader will lose interest. And the solution to the mystery must seem logical once all the pieces are put together, or the reader will feel deceived. A mystery writer must keep a delicate balance, knowing just how much to reveal and when. For many readers, mysteries become addictive.

Sports

Very popular among an important group of readers is the sports story, which actually has its origin in the boys' magazines of the nineteenth century. As full-blown books, however, they are a twentieth-century phenomenon. One of the most popular of the early sports writers was Clair Bee, whose books, beginning with *Touchdown Pass* in 1948, are all about a high school athlete, Chip Hilton. The stories promote high moral character and good sportsmanship.

Sports tales are usually coming-of-age stories, particularly when the protagonist gains self-knowledge through participation in sports, as in the works of Matt Christopher (*The Fox Steals Home*) and Chris Crutcher (*Athletic Shorts*). In the hands of a talented writer, a sports story can be a compelling study of human nature—the importance of sportsmanship and fair play, the striving for individual excellence, the challenge of meeting goals.

Animals

Animal stories in realistic fiction usually describe relationships between humans and animals, although we can find a few in which the animals themselves become the central figures—Jack London's *The Call of the Wild*, mentioned above, is a good example. Realistic animal stories first appeared in the late nineteenth and early twentieth centuries, and they seem to have been most popular in North America. Canadians Ernest Thompson Seton (*Wild Animals I Have Known*) and Charles G. D. Roberts (*Red Fox*) wrote stories depicting animals realistically (that is, they don't talk or wear clothes) but giving them personalities (some human connection is necessary).

The most common realistic animal stories are actually about humans who have developed attachments to animals. Some of the best known include Mary O'Hara's *My Friend Flicka* (a horse), Eric Knight's *Lassie Come Home* (a heroic collie), and Marguerite

Henry's *Misty of Chincoteague* (about the famous wild horses of Assateague and Chincoteague islands, off the coast of Virginia). We have already mentioned above two of the most beloved animal stories—Rawlings's *The Yearling* and Rawls's *Where the Red Fern Grows*—both about humans coping with an animal's death. Recent developments can be seen in Phyllis Reynolds Naylor's Newbery Award–winning *Shiloh*, about animal abuse, and Carl Hiaasen's *Hoot*, a story of the effects of habitat destruction. So the animal story becomes an excellent vehicle for raising environmental awareness in young readers.

A Word about Verse Novels

In the nineteenth century it briefly became fashionable to write novels in poetry rather than prose—we call them verse novels. Robert Browning's *The Ring and the Book*, published in installments from 1868 to 1869, is one of the most famous verse novels. Then they fell out of fashion until rather recently. In the 1990s they began to appear in children's literature. Virginia Euwer Wolf's *Make Lemonade*, appearing in 1993, was one of the first young people's novels to use verse. And Karen Hesse's verse novel *Out of the Dust* won the Newbery Medal in 1998. Verse novels for young readers typically use free verse, in other words, without rhythm or regular rhyme. The writing also tends to be sparse, with just a few crisp lines to each page. Consequently, the effective verse novel must rely heavily on suggestive imagery to convey the setting, the character, and the plot details. In many instances, the story is told in the protagonist's words. An interesting variation on the verse novel is the verse biography (biography will be discussed in Chapter 12). Margarita Engle's *The Poet Slave of Cuba* is a biography of a nineteenth-century Cuban poet, Juan Francisco Manzano, an uneducated slave who had a talent for poetry in which he described his difficult life. Engle chose to use her own poems to tell his life story. Books written in verse for young readers reflect the constantly evolving nature of literature for children.

Summary

Realistic fiction, whether historical or contemporary, is enormously diverse. It is also difficult to pigeonhole. A single novel such as Hiaasen's *Hoot* contains numerous themes, including the importance of making new friends, the difficulty of adapting to a new environment, the need to protect the environment, and the value of learning to stand up for oneself and for important principles.

Historical fiction includes stories that authors set in the past and in which the historical setting is integral to the plot. This fiction can bring to life the world of the past and pique young readers' curiosity about historical times and places. Contemporary realism includes stories set in the author's present, which generally relieves the author from the responsibility of explaining many specific cultural and social details.

In both historical and contemporary fiction we find a wide variety of topics, including stories about family, friendship, outsiders, growing up, survival, mysteries, sports, and more. Most address the importance of human connections, assuming personal responsibility, perseverance, and realizing individual potential. Reading a good realistic novel is an excellent way to overcome our narrow prejudices, to get to know people different from us, and to understand human motivation and desire. Ironically, we invariably learn that people, wherever they are, whatever their history or heritage, are very much like us after all.

For Reflection and Discussion

1. Choose two works of historical fiction that deal with the same time period or same historical issue—for example, the American Civil War or the Holocaust. Read and compare the novels on the basis of their specific subject matter, themes, style, character development, and so on. What are the fundamental differences? Does one seem more effective than the other? Why?

2. Choose one work of historical fiction on a time period or subject that interests you. Read the novel and then do some research into the actual history. For example, you might look at a novel dealing with American Indians, such as Scott O'Dell's *Walk Two Moons*, and then read something about the actual "Long Walk." Determine whether the novelist has faithfully portrayed the spirit of the time. Be prepared to explain why or why not.

3. Choose a novel of contemporary realism and, as you read, keep an informal journal. Read a chapter or two at a time and then spend a few minutes writing down your thoughts, observations, or predictions—whatever comes to mind. Continue this process throughout the reading of the book. When you are finished, reread your journal entries and assess them. Were your predictions and assessments of the characters accurate? Did the author pull any surprises? If so, did this help the story?

4. Choose a problem novel—a book for middle and high school readers that focuses on one particular problem of growing up (physical, social, psychological, and so on)—and read it, paying attention to how the problem is portrayed and what resolution occurs. How would you assess the book on its depiction of the problem and the credibility of the resolution? (Is it oversimplified? Inaccurate? Didactic or preachy?)

5. Choose a work of children's realistic fiction that addresses your personal interests—history, sports, mystery, romance, animals, and so on. (Use the booklist below for ideas.) Read the book closely, taking notes as you do. When you are finished, assess the book using some of the information gathered from this chapter and from Chapter 9. Was the book successful? What were its particular strengths? Its weaknesses?

Works Cited

MacLeod, Anne Scott. "Writing Backward: Modern Models in Historical Fiction." *The Horn Book Magazine* (January/February 1998): 26–33.

Manzoni, Alessandro. *On the Historical Novel.* 1850. Trans. Sandra Bermann. Lincoln: University of Nebraska, 1984.

Tolstoy, Leo. *Anna Karenina.* Trans. Richard Pevear and Larissa Volokhonsky. London: Penguin, 2000.

Recommended Resources

Alston, Anne. *The Family in English Children's Literature.* New York: Routledge, 2008.

Connelly, Mark. *The Hardy Boys Mysteries, 1927–1979: A Cultural and Literary History.* Jefferson, NC: McFarland, 2008.

Cornelius, Michael G., and Melanie E. Gregg, eds. *Nancy Drew and Her Sister Sleuths: Essays on the Fiction of Girl Detectives.* Jefferson, NC: McFarland, 2008.

Crowe, Chris. *More Than a Game: Sports Literature for Young Adults.* Lanham, MD: Scarecrow, 2003.

Gavin, Adrienne, and Christopher Routledge, eds. *Mystery in Children's Literature: From the Rational to the Supernatural.* New York: Palgrave Macmillan, 2001.

Gillespie, John T. *Historical Fiction for Young Readers (Grades 4–8): An Introduction.* Santa Barbara, CA: Libraries Unlimited, 2008.

Hinton, S. E. "Teenagers Are for Real." *New York Times Book Review* 27 (August 1967): 26–29.

Nixon, Joan Lowry. "Clues to the Juvenile Mystery." *The Writer* 90 (February 1977): 23–26.

Nodelman, Perry. "How Typical Children Read Typical Books." *Children's Literature in Education* 12 (Winter 1981): 177–185.

Paterson, Katherine. *Gates of Excellence: On Reading and Writing Books for Children.* New York: Elsevier/Nelson, 1981.

Rees, David. *The Marble in the Water.* Boston: The Horn Book, 1980.

——. *Painted Desert, Green Shade: Essays on Contemporary Writers for Children and Young Adults.* Boston: The Horn Book, 1984.

Thiel, Elizabeth. *The Fantasy of Family: Nineteenth-Century Children's Literature and the Myth of the Domestic Ideal.* New York: Routledge, 2007.

Townsend, John Rowe. *Written for Children: An Outline of English-Language Children's Literature,* 6th ed. Lanham, MD: Scarecrow, 1996.

Wilkin, Binnie Tate. *Survival Themes in Fiction for Children and Young People,* 2nd ed. New York: Scarecrow, 1993.

Zornado, Joseph. "A Poetics of History: Karen Cushman's Medieval World." *The Lion and the Unicorn* 21, 2 (1997): 251–266.

Historical Realism: A Selected and Annotated Booklist

Very little historical realism is written for children in the lower elementary grades, but some of these titles may appeal to upper elementary readers. No attempt has been made to identify reading levels. An individual's interests and abilities are the best guides. Also, check the booklists at the end of Chapter 4 for historical novels on other cultures.

Denotes a book with a multicultural emphasis.

#*Denotes a book dealing with mature sociological and/or psychological themes.*

*Anderson, Laurie Halsie. *Chains.* New York: Atheneum, 2008.
- A young black girl's search for freedom during the American Revolution. An excellently researched and powerfully told story.

——. *Fever 1793.* New York: Simon & Schuster, 2000.
- The story of a young girl's survival during a fever outbreak in eighteenth-century America.

*——. *Forged.* New York: Atheneum, 2010.
- A sequel to *Chains,* about the plight of runaway slaves during the American Revolution. Equally powerful.

Avi. *Crispin: The Cross of Lead.* New York: Hyperion, 2002.
- The story of a fourteenth-century English peasant boy who encounters adventures as he flees punishment for a crime he did not commit.

——. *The True Confessions of Charlotte Doyle.* New York: Orchard, 1990.
- The account of a young girl's harrowing adventures on the high seas in the nineteenth century.

Brink, Carol Ryrie. *Caddie Woodlawn.* 1936. Various modern editions.
- The adventures of a girl on the frontier in nineteenth-century America. Based on the life of the author's grandmother.

*Bruchac, Joseph. *Code Talker: A Novel about the Navajo Marines of World War Two.* New York: Penguin, 2005.
- Based on the true story of the use of the Navajo language for secret messages during World War II.

Collier, James Lincoln, and Christopher Collier. *My Brother Sam Is Dead.* New York: Four Winds Press, 1974.
- The story of two brothers finding themselves on opposite sides during the American Revolution.

Conrad, Pam. *Pedro's Journal: A Voyage with Christopher Columbus, August 3, 1492–February 14, 1493.* New York: Scholastic, 1992.
- The experiences and observations of a young boy aboard Columbus's *Santa Maria* on the voyage to the Americas.

*Curtis, Christopher Paul. *The Watsons Go to Birmingham—1963.* New York: Delacorte, 1995.
- A story in which a 9-year-old African American boy and his family from Michigan witness racial violence in the Deep South.

Cushman, Karen. *Catherine, Called Birdy.* New York: Clarion, 1994.
- The diary of a thirteenth-century English girl who flouts social norms.

de Angeli, Marguerite. *The Door in the Wall.* New York: Doubleday, 1949.
- The story of a young boy in medieval England who overcomes physical hardships and performs acts of heroism.

*Dorris, Michael. *Morning Girl.* New York: Hyperion, 1992.
- A young native girl's account of the devastating effects of the European arrival in the Bahamas in 1492.

Estes, Eleanor. *The Moffats.* New York: Harcourt, 1941.
- Adventures of four siblings in Connecticut in the late 1910s.

Forbes, Esther. *Johnny Tremain.* Boston: Houghton Mifflin, 1946.
- A classic story of a patriot boy in Boston during the Revolutionary War.

Fritz, Jean. *The Cabin Faced West.* New York: Coward, 1958.
- A story about a young girl who must adjust to life in the frontier in late eighteenth-century Pennsylvania.

Frost, Helen. *Crossing Stones.* New York: Foster/Farrar, 2009.
- A verse novel about a girl wrapped up in American political and social affairs during World War I.

Gray, Elizabeth Janet. *Adam of the Road.* New York: Viking, 1942.

- The adventures of an 11-year-old boy traveling through thirteenth-century England.

*Greene, Bette. *Summer of My German Soldier*. New York: Dial, 1973.
- A tragic story of American anti-Semitism during World War II.

Hahn, Mary Downing. *Hear the Wind Blow: A Novel of the Civil War*. New York: Clarion, 2003.
- A story about a Confederate soldier setting off to find his brother during the final days of the Civil War.

Henry, Marguerite. *King of the Wind*. New York: Rand, 1948.
- A story loosely based on the life of Sham, a seventeenth-century Arabian horse who became the ancestor of all future thoroughbreds.

*Hesse, Karen. *Letters from Rifka*. New York: Holt, 1992.
- The story of a young Russian Jewish girl immigrating to America in the early twentieth century.

——. *Out of the Dust*. New York: Scholastic, 1997.
- A verse novel about a young girl living in the Dust Bowl during the 1930s.

*Ho, Minfong. *The Clay Marble*. New York: Farrar, Straus & Giroux, 1991.
- A story of a young girl separated from her family in war-torn Cambodia in 1980.

Hunt, Irene. *Across Five Aprils*. New York: Follett, 1964.
- The story of a northern family's experiences during the course of the American Civil War.

*Kadohata, Cynthia. *Kira-Kira*. New York: Atheneum, 2004.
- A story about a Japanese-American girl growing up in the 1950s who must face the death of her sister.

*Lowry, Lois. *Number the Stars*. Boston: Houghton Mifflin, 1989.
- A story about a Danish girl bravely facing the horrors of German occupation and anti-Semitism during World War II.

MacLachlan, Patricia. *Sarah, Plain and Tall*. New York: Harper, 1985.
- A look into the nineteenth-century West, where a brother and sister must adjust to their father's mail-order bride.

*Mead, Alice. *Dawn and Dusk*. New York: Farrar, Straus & Giroux, 2007.
- The story of a 13-year-old boy in the Iraq War of the 1980s.

*O'Dell, Scott. *Island of the Blue Dolphins*. Boston: Houghton Mifflin, 1960.
- A classic survival story about a young American Indian girl alone on a deserted island.

*Orlev, Uri. *The Island on Bird Street*. Trans. Hillel Halkin. Boston: Houghton Mifflin, 1984.
- The story of a young Jewish boy in Warsaw, who survives on his own during World War II.

*Park, Linda Sue. *A Single Shard*. New York: Dell, 2001.
- The story of a young, determined potter in twelfth- century Korea.

Peck, Richard. *Remembering the Good Times*. New York: Delacorte, 1985.
- A look at teenagers dealing with the suicide of a close friend.

#——. *A Year Down Yonder*. New York: Dial, 2000.
- Comical adventures of a young boy during the Great Depression.

Pyle, Howard. *Otto of the Silver Hand*. 1888. Various modern editions.
- A classic tale of courage and honor about a young boy in thirteenth-century Germany who earns his way to knighthood.

*Richter, Conrad. *Light in the Forest*. New York: Knopf, 1953.
- The story of a white boy kidnapped at age 4 and raised by American Indians who must deal with divided loyalties when, years later, he is returned to his birth parents.

*Richter, Hans Peter. *Friedrich*. New York: Holt, 1970.
- The shattering tale of two German boys—a Jew and a Gentile—growing up during Hitler's rise to power.

Sayres, Meghan Nuttall. *Anahita's Woven Riddle*. New York: Amulet, 2006.
- A story set in late nineteenth-century Persia, in which four men compete in a battle of wits for the hand of a clever young nomadic woman.

Schlitz, Laura Amy. *A Drowned Maiden's Hair: A Melodrama.* New York: Candlewick, 2006.
- A tale in the gothic vein of an orphaned girl in the early twentieth century unwittingly partaking in fraudulent séances to bilk wealthy clients.

——. *Good Masters! Sweet Ladies! Voices from a Medieval Village.* New York: Candlewick, 2007.
- Life in thirteenth-century England is described in a series of monologues and dialogues of young people. Ideal for classroom reading aloud and theater.

*Schmidt, Gary D. *Lizzie Bright and the Buckminster Boy.* New York: Clarion, 2004.
- The story of a young boy who faces the reality of racism when his family moves to the Maine coast in the early twentieth century.

Speare, Elizabeth George. *The Witch of Blackbird Pond.* Boston: Houghton Mifflin, 1958.
- A young woman's tale of heroism during the witch scares in colonial America.

Stead, Rebecca. *When You Reach Me.* New York: Wendy Lamb Books, 2009.
- A slice of life from New York in 1979 in which a sixth-grade girl discovers mysterious notes from an unknown person claiming to know the future.

Stevenson, Robert Louis. *Kidnapped.* 1886. Several modern editions.
- The adventures of a youth caught up in the Jacobite rebellion in eighteenth-century Scotland.

Sutcliff, Rosemary. *The Mark of the Horse Lord.* New York: Walck, 1965.
- An ex-gladiator's adventures in Roman Britain in the first century.

Vining, Elizabeth Gray. *Adam of the Road.* New York: Viking, 1942.
- The story of an 11-year-old boy in thirteenth-century England who sets out to find his father.

Walsh, Jill Paton. *The Emperor's Winding Sheet.* New York: Farrar, Straus & Giroux, 1974.
- An exciting tale set in 1453, during the fall of Constantinople.

Wilder, Laura Ingalls. *Little House in the Big Woods.* New York: Harper, 1932.
- The first book in a series about growing up in the nineteenth century, followed by *Little House on the Prairie* (1932), *Farmer Boy* (1933), *On the Banks of Plum Creek* (1937), *By the Shores of Silver Lake* (1939), *The Long Winter* (1940), *Little Town on the Prairie* (1941), *These Happy Golden Years* (1943), and *The First Four Years* (1971).

Wiles, Deborah. *Countdown.* New York: Scholastic, 2010.
- An 11-year-old girl's experiences during the Cuban missile crisis in 1962. A documentary novel that includes actual photos and news clippings from the period to re-create the atmosphere, it is the first in the projected Sixties Trilogy.

Williams, Susan. *Wind Rider.* New York: Laura Geringer/HarperCollins, 2006.
- The story of a talented young horsewoman who faces the challenges of living in prehistoric Asia.

Contemporary Realism: A Selected and Annotated Booklist

Most of these books are for readers in about third grade and older. An individual's interests and abilities are the best guides. Look for other titles by these authors and see the booklists at the end of Chapter 4 for contemporary novels on other cultures.

**Denotes a book with a multicultural emphasis.*

\#*Denotes a book dealing with mature sociological and/or psychological themes.*

#Acampora, Paul. *Defining Dulcie.* New York: Dial, 2006.
- The account of a 16-year old coping with the death of her father.

Alcott, Louisa May. *Little Women.* 1868–1869. Several modern editions.
- The story of the four sisters in the March family living in New England during the Civil War.

#Anderson, Laurie Halse. *Speak*. New York: Farrar, Straus & Giroux, 1999.
- A sensitive book that explores the effects of sexual abuse on a teenage girl.

#Bauer, Marion Dane, ed. *Am I Blue?: Coming Out of the Silence*. New York: HarperCollins, 1994.
- A collection of short stories by various authors on the subject of gay and lesbian teenagers.

#Bennett, James. *I Can Hear the Mourning Dove*. Boston: Houghton Mifflin, 1990.
- A book that explores the healing process in an emotionally disturbed teenage girl.

*#Block, Francesca Lia. *Weetzie Bat*. New York: HarperCollins, 1989.
- This surrealistic and sympathetic look at alternative lifestyles is the first of a popular series.

#Blume, Judy. *Are You There, God? It's Me, Margaret*. New York: Bradbury, 1970.
- A book about a young girl confronting a host of coming-of-age problems, from the onset of menses to seeking answers to religious faith.

——. *Tales of a Fourth Grade Nothing*. New York: Dutton, 1972.
- A long-time favorite about young Peter Hatcher's comic trials and tribulations.

#——. *Tiger Eyes*. Scarsdale, NY: Bradbury, 1981.
- A story about a teenage girl coping following a family tragedy and a move across the nation.

*#Boyne, John. *The Boy in the Striped Pajamas*. Oxford, UK: David Fickling Books, 2006.
- A book about the horrors of life in Auschwitz, as seen through the innocent eyes of a young boy.

Burnett, Frances Hodgson. *The Secret Garden*. 1909. Various modern editions.
- The classic tale of Mary Lennox and her discoveries while living with her mysterious uncle on the Yorkshire moors.

Burnford, Sheila. *The Incredible Journey*. Boston: Little, Brown, 1961.
- An animal survival story about two dogs and a cat journeying together across Canada.

*#Childress, Alice. *A Hero Ain't Nothin' but a Sandwich*. New York: Coward, 1973.
- The story of an African American teenager's struggle with drugs, told from multiple viewpoints.

#Cleary, Beverly. *Dear Mr. Henshaw*. New York: Morrow, 1983.
- The letters of a young boy coping with his parents' recent divorce.

——. *Henry Huggins*. New York: Morrow, 1950.
- The comic adventures of Henry during his third-grade year. A modern classic.

——. *Ramona the Pest*. New York: Morrow, 1968.
- One of eight books focusing on the adventures of Ramona, a friend of Henry Huggins. A perennial favorite among early elementary readers.

Cleaver, Bill, and Vera Cleaver. *Where the Lilies Bloom*. Philadelphia: Lippincott, 1969.
- A story about orphaned Appalachian children struggling to survive in dire circumstances.

#Cormier, Robert. *The Chocolate War*. New York: Pantheon, 1974.
- A dark tale about social corruption pervading a private religious school.

#——. *I Am the Cheese*. New York: Bell, 1987.
- The tragic story of an innocent family who become the victims of massive government abuse.

*Craven, Margaret. *I Heard the Owl Call My Name*. New York: Bantam, 1973.
- The story of a young priest who comes to a Kwakiutl Indian village in British Columbia, where he faces life's most difficult challenges.

*Creech, Sharon. *Walk Two Moons*. New York: Harper, 1994.
- A book narrated by a young girl of American Indian heritage, about the extraordinary events during a difficult year of adjustment.

#Crutcher, Chris. *Athletic Shorts*. New York: Greenwillow, 1991.
- A collection of short stories about teenage athletes, including two with gay themes.

Defoe, Daniel. *Robinson Crusoe*. Retold by Steven Zorn. Philadelphia: Running Press, 2002.
- A version of Defoe's classic survival story retold for younger readers.

#Donovan, John. *I'll Get There. It Better Be Worth the Trip*. New York: Harper & Row, 1969.
- One of the first young adult novels to deal with homosexuality.

Farley, Walter. *The Black Stallion*. New York: Random House, 1944.
- An adventure classic about a boy and a horse who survive a shipwreck and become inseparable. One of the best horse stories ever written, and the first of a series.

Fitzhugh, Louise. *Harriet the Spy*. New York: Harper, 1964.
- The story of a precocious young girl in New York City who proves too wise for her own good.

#Ford, Michael Thomas. *Suicide Notes*. New York: Harper, 2008.
- A 15-year-old gay teenager's examination of his life after a botched suicide attempt; at once irreverent, funny, and poignant.

#Fox, Paula. *Eagle Kite*. New York: Orchard, 1995.
- A somber story of a boy wrestling with family secrets as his father is dying of AIDS.

George, Jean Craighead. *Julie of the Wolves*. New York: Harper, 1972.
- A survival story of a Yupik girl stranded in the Arctic wilderness.

Gipson, Fred. *Old Yeller*. New York: Harper, 1956.
- The story of the friendship between a Texas boy and his dog.

#Green, John. *Looking for Alaska*. New York: Dutton, 2005.
- The story of a 16-year old who must come to terms with the suicide of her best friend.

Hest, Amy. *Remembering Mrs. Rossi*. New York: Candlewick, 2007.
- A story in which a third-grade girl and her father cope with the death of her mother.

Hiaasen, Carl. *Hoot*. New York: Bantam, 2005.
- A story with an environmental message that features eccentric characters, including an assortment of animals.

#Hinton, S. E. *The Outsiders*. New York: Viking, 1967.
- One of the first novels of new realism, the story of teenage gangs—actually written by a teenager.

Hunt, Irene. *Up a Road Slowly*. New York: Follett, 1967.
- A moving coming-of-age story about an orphaned girl who faces difficult adjustments when she goes to live with her spinster aunt, a teacher.

Kerr, Judith. *When Hitler Stole Pink Rabbit*. New York: Puffin, 1971.
- The semi-autobiographical story of a young girl's escape from Nazi Germany.

#Kerr, M. E. *Deliver Us from Evie*. New York: Harper, 1994.
- The story of Evie's family adjusting to her announced lesbianism.

Kerrin, Jessica Scott. *Martin Bridge, Ready for Takeoff!* Toronto: Kids Can, 2005.
- The first in a series of books containing short stories about an inventive third grader's adventures.

Kinney, Jeff. *Diary of a Wimpy Kid*. New York: Amulet, 2007.
- The trials and tribulations of a middle schooler. The first of an immensely popular series, including *Rodrick Rules* (2008) and *The Last Straw* (2009).

Kipling, Rudyard. *Kim*. 1901. Several modern editions.
- A classic tale of life in late-nineteenth-century India, through the eyes of a young boy. See also *Captain Courageous*, a coming-of-age story about a boy on the high seas.

Kjelgaard, Jim. *Big Red*. New York: Holiday, 1956.
- The story of the friendship between a boy and his Irish setter.

Knight, Eric. *Lassie Come Home*. Philadelphia: Winston, 1940.
- The classic tale of a boy and his dog, a prize collie. Set in Great Britain.

Knowles, John. *A Separate Peace*. London: Secker & Warburg, 1959.
- A modern classic about a tragedy at a New England boys' school.

Konigsburg, E. L. *From the Mixed-up Files of Mrs. Basil E. Frankweiler*. New York: Atheneum, 1967.
- A clever mystery story set in the Metropolitan Museum of Art in New York City.

——. *The View from Saturday*. New York: Atheneum, 1996.
- The story of several extraordinary children of varying backgrounds preparing for a quiz contest.

London, Jack. *The Call of the Wild*. 1903. Many modern editions.
- A classic realistic animal story of a family dog who is stolen from California and lives with a cruel master in Alaska before escaping and returning to the life of his ancestors.

Lowry, Lois. *A Summer to Die*. Boston: Houghton Mifflin, 1977.
- The story of a girl coping with the death of her sister.

MacLachlan, Patricia. *Arthur, for the Very First Time*. New York: HarperCollins, 1994.
- The story of 10-year-old Arthur's transformative summer on his great uncle's farm.

——. *Baby*. Logan, Iowa: Perfection Learning, 1995.
- A moving story of loss and redemption that begins with the discovery of an infant left in a basket in a driveway.

McCloskey, Robert. *Homer Price*. New York: Viking, 1943.
- The comic adventures of an imaginative boy living in small-town Ohio.

Montgomery, Lucy Maude. *Anne of Green Gables*. 1908. Several modern editions.
- The popular tale of a young girl adopted by an elderly brother and sister on Prince Edward Island, Canada.

*Morpurgo, Michael. *Kensuke's Kingdom*. New York: Scholastic, 2003.
- The story of an elderly Japanese man, stranded on an island for 40 years, who rescues an 11-year-old boy from the sea.

Mowat, Farley. *Owls in the Family*. Boston: Little, Brown, 1962.
- A comical tale of a boy and his two pet owls.

*Myers, Walter Dean. *Scorpions*. New York: Harper, 1988.
- The story of a young African American boy who is pressured to become a gang member.

*——. *Street Love*. New York: HarperCollins, 2006.
- A verse novel about a teenage romance in Harlem.

Naylor, Phyllis Reynolds. *Shiloh*. New York: Atheneum, 1991.
- A story about a young West Virginia boy who finds a mistreated beagle pup and faces ethical issues.

Nesbit, E. *The Story of the Treasure Seekers*. London: Unwin, 1899.
- A book about six children who try to recover their family's lost fortune. The first of the Bastable Children trilogy, along with *The Wouldbegoods* (1901) and *The New Treasure Seekers* (1904).

Palacio, R. J. *Wonder*. New York: Knopf, 2012.
- A story about a boy with a physical deformity entering a mainstream fifth-grade class.

Paterson, Katherine. *Bridge to Terabithia*. New York: Crowell, 1977.
- The story of a friendship between a young girl and boy that ends in tragedy.

——. *The Great Gilly Hopkins*. New York: Crowell, 1978.
- The story of a difficult but clever foster child and her efforts to reunite with her mother.

Paulsen, Gary. *Hatchet*. New York: Bradbury, 1987.
- The story of a young boy who must survive on his own after a plane crash, with only a hatchet.

Peck, Richard. *Secrets of the Shopping Mall*. New York: Delacorte, 1979.
- The story of a young boy and girl trying to escape the clutches of a gang by hiding out in a mall.

Peck, Robert. *A Day No Pigs Would Die.* New York: Knopf, 1972.
- The moving story of a 13-year-old boy who must grow up quickly. Set in rural Vermont.

Ransome, Arthur. *Swallows and Amazons.* 1930. Several modern editions.
- The first of a series of 12 outdoor adventure stories set in the British Isles.

Rawlings, Marjorie Kinnan. *The Yearling.* New York: Scribner's, 1938.
- A powerful tale set in central Florida of a boy who raises a fawn but must make a terrible choice. The only children's book that has ever won the Pulitzer Prize.

Rawls, Wilson. *Where the Red Fern Grows.* New York: Doubleday, 1961.
- A classic, heart-rending tale of a boy and his two dogs in the Ozarks.

Rylant, Cynthia. *Missing May.* New York: Scholastic, 1992.
- The story of a young girl coping with the death of her beloved foster mother.

Sachar, Louis. *Holes.* New York: Farrar, Straus & Giroux, 1998.
- A sort of tragicomedy—verging on fantasy—about a boy who must solve a mystery while he is incarcerated at a detention camp in Texas.

Salisbury, Graham. *Lord of the Deep.* New York: Delacorte, 2001.
- The story of a 13-year-old boy coming of age on a deep-sea fishing trip in the Pacific with his stepfather.

#Sanchez, Alex. *Rainbow Boys.* New York: Simon & Schuster, 2001.
- A portrayal of the experiences of gay teens. The first book in a trilogy that also includes *Rainbow High* (2003) and *Rainbow Road* (2005).

#———. *So Hard to Say.* New York: Simon & Schuster, 2004.
- A sensitive exploration of a young boy's grappling with his own sexuality. One of the few novels on sexual orientation aimed at early teens.

#Scott, Elizabeth. *Living Dead Girl.* New York: Simon Pulse, 2008.
- The chilling story of a young girl's five-year abduction by a sex abuser. For older readers.

Smith, Doris Buchanan. *A Taste of Blackberries.* New York: Crowell, 1973.
- A book about a young boy who must come to terms with the death of a friend.

Sobol, Donald. *Encyclopedia Brown, Boy Detective.* 1963. Several later editions.
- The first of a series of popular detective stories for elementary school readers.

*Spinelli, Jerry. *Maniac Magee.* Boston: Little, Brown, 1990.
- A tall tale about a boy bringing together a racially divided community.

Stevenson, Robert Louis. *Treasure Island.* 1883. Various modern editions.
- A classic pirate tale, complete with buried treasure and a villain with a wooden leg.

*Taylor, Theodore. *The Cay.* New York: Doubleday, 1969.
- The story of an 11-year-old white boy, blinded in a wartime accident, who survives with the help of an older black man on a deserted Caribbean island.

#Tolan, Stephanie S. *Listen!* New York: HarperCollins, 2006.
- The story of a 12-year-old girl who learns to accept the tragic death of a mother, with the magical help of a stray dog.

Twain, Mark. *The Adventures of Huckleberry Finn.* 1884. Several modern editions.
- A classic tale about an irascible boy on an adventure down the Mississippi.

———. *The Adventures of Tom Sawyer.* 1876. Several modern editions.
- The classic tale of a boy's life along the Mississippi in the mid-nineteenth century.

Voigt, Cynthia. *Homecoming.* New York: Atheneum, 1981.
- Four siblings abandoned by their mother make a difficult journey to their grandmother's. First of the seven books in the Tillerman cycle.

#Wolf, Virginia Euwer. *Make Lemonade.* New York: Holt, 1993.

- A verse novel about a young girl who babysits for the children of an unwed teenage mother and the relationship that develops. The first of a series of three, followed by *True Believer* (2001) and *This Full House* (2009).

*Woodson, Jacqueline. *Locomotion.* New York: Putnam, 2003.
- A story in which an 11-year-old orphaned African American boy reveals his hopes, fears, and frustrations through a series of poems.

Wynne-Jones, Tim. *Some of the Kinder Planets.* New York: Kroupa, 1995.

- A collection of short stories, both serious and amusing, often off-beat, involving a variety of young characters, male and female.

#Zindel, Paul. *My Darling, My Hamburger.* New York: Harper, 1969.
- A groundbreaking story in which teenagers confront the issues of premarital sex, rape, and pregnancy.

#———. *The Pigman.* New York: Harper, 1968.
- The story of two teenagers forming an unusual bond with a lonely old man.

CHAPTER

12 Nonfiction

Telling It Like It Is

Introduction

A famous television detective from the 1950s, Joe Friday of *Dragnet*, was fond of remarking, "All we want are the facts, ma'am." The purpose of nonfiction is, of course, to convey factual information; however, as Dr. Latham, a nineteenth-century English physician, said, a good book must contain "important facts, duly arranged, and reasoned upon with care" (43). Good nonfiction is not a mere catalogue of information or an almanac of data. It is a well-written book, designed to engage us, inform us, and entertain us.

The earliest nonfiction for children consisted of dreary tomes prepared for use in the schoolroom. They often contained rather dry catalogues of facts and figures for young readers to absorb, master, or memorize. Beginning in the mid-twentieth century, a new attitude toward nonfiction emerged. This was the notion that a work of nonfiction could be just as interesting, just as beautiful, just as inspiring as a good work of fiction. Among the earliest were histories for young readers. In fact, the very first winner of the Newbery Medal, in 1922, was Hendrik van Loon's *The Story of Mankind*, a history of the human race. Today, many talented writers are producing high-quality nonfiction for young readers, including books on history, science, nature, the arts, psychology, and sociology. In this chapter we will examine what to look for in a good work of nonfiction and what is currently available for young readers.

Characteristics of Nonfiction

The best nonfiction contains a clear purpose suited to the audience, factual information that is accurate and objectively balanced, a style that is clear and engaging, and a format or design that effectively conveys the material.

Purpose and Audience

Nonfiction is didactic; it has a specific instructional goal—from teaching the sounds of the alphabet to explaining the cycles of life or the movement of the stars to describing the life of a famous person. Each work also has a specific audience, ranging from preschoolers and toddlers to young adults and older adults. Naturally, the intended audience will determine the contents and the approach of the book. To determine this, we have to answer a few questions: How much do the intended readers know? How much can we expect them to grasp? What is going to keep them interested? What details can be included?

A Medieval Feast by Aliki is a picture book for early elementary readers that describes life in the European Middle Ages. To appeal to this young audience, the author combines a fictional framing story—the king is coming to dine—with colorful illustrations that provide a vivid portrait of medieval life. Ruth Heller's popular Chickens Aren't the Only Ones, about animals who lay eggs, and The Reason for a Flower, which introduces young readers to the world of plants, both include striking and colorful illustrations and clear and straightforward textual explanations (see Figure 12.1).

On the other hand, the works of Russell Freedman (Lincoln: A Photobiography and others) and Jim Murphy (An American Plague and others) are aimed at older readers. These books have full-length texts and are illustrated with photographs or drawings taken from the historical periods they describe. The authors also include reading lists, indexes, and other helpful aids for older readers. As always, we have to judge a book in terms of its intended audience.

Factual Information

In fiction, we don't have to worry about the accuracy of facts—most of them are made up anyway. In nonfiction, accuracy is crucial. But "facts" themselves can be tentative things. In The Reason for a Flower, mentioned above and first published in 1983, Ruth Heller refers to fungi as plants. But in 2007, fungi were reclassified and put into their own kingdom—neither plant nor animal. In other words, what we think are "facts" may change with new information. (See the discussion below about Pluto.) Moreover, science is not the only field where new discoveries are being made. Historians, for example, also keep uncovering new materials—forgotten letters, secret memos, newly discovered artifacts. So, a history of the Civil War written in 1950 may be less accurate than one written last year. Nothing is static.

As facts can change, so can attitudes. A good example is seen in a survey of children's biographies of Christopher Columbus. Early books (such as Ingri and Edgar Parin d'Aulaire's Columbus, 1955) depict Columbus as a heroic figure, braving the unknown and bringing sophisticated European culture to the benighted Indians. Recent books (notably David Adler's Christopher Columbus, Great Explorer (1991) and Milton Meltzer's Christopher Columbus and the World around Him (1990) depict Columbus in a less flattering light, emphasizing his mercenary nature as well as his heinous treatment of the

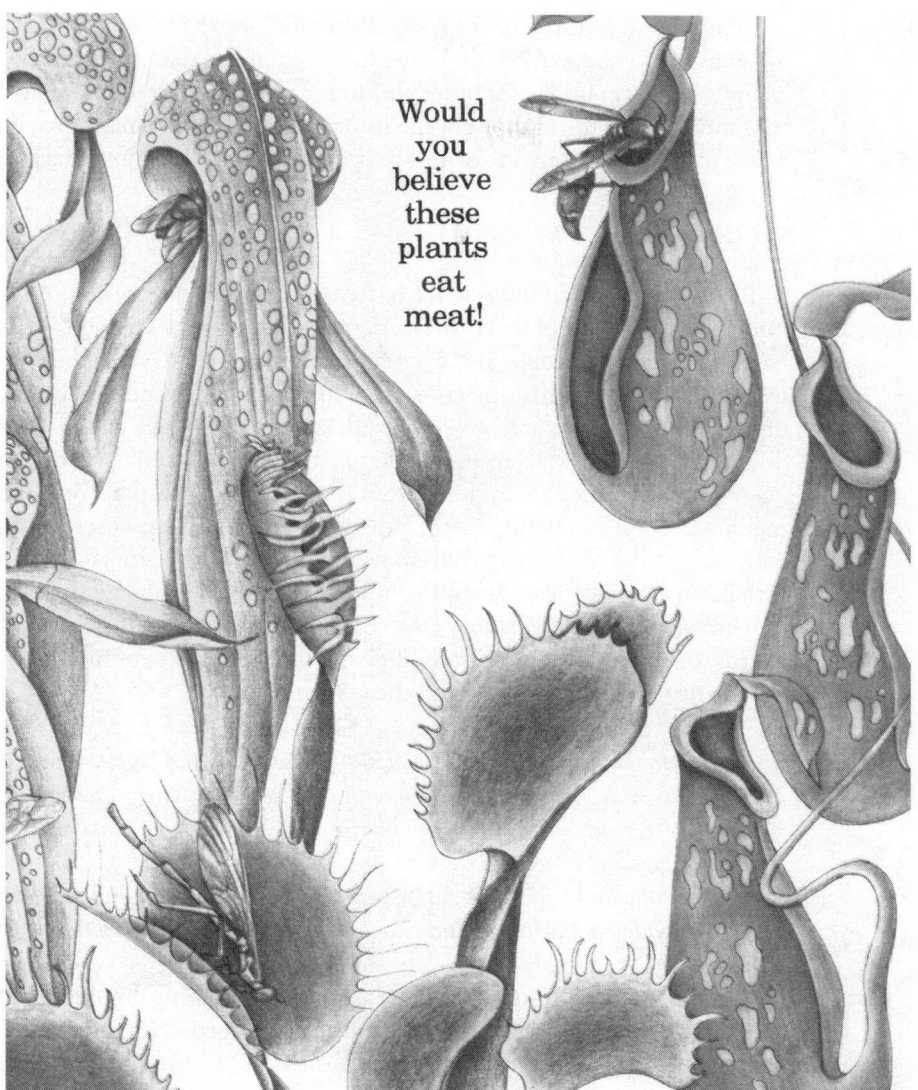

Would you believe these plants eat meat!

FIGURE 12.1 ■ Ruth Heller's elegant drawings for her picture-book introduction to botany, *The Reason for a Flower*, depicts meat-eating plants in action and is sure to captivate many young readers.

native population. And perhaps in some future time, his reputation will be once again re-evaluated. Consequently, we should always need to consider when a book was written (which may differ from its publication date). However, this doesn't mean that newer books are always better than the old ones; that is just not true.

Compared to those of the past, nonfiction books for today's young readers are more likely to offer solid evidence—in the form of figures, data, and charts—to support claims. Many nonfiction books for older children now include resource material and bibliographies that show where the author got the information, and this helps give integrity to the work. These features also provide evidence that the writer didn't just make up this stuff.

Style

Millicent Selsam, a noted science writer for children, once said, "A good science book is not just a collection of facts" (62). A good science book conveys, in Selsam's words, "something of the beauty and excitement of science" (65). She is referring to style—the writer's choice of words, the construction of sentences and paragraphs, and the organization of the material. Perhaps the first rule of style is that the writing be clear. It does not matter how accurate the text is if we cannot understand what it's saying. Terms need to be identified in language young readers can grasp. Here is where the language of metaphor comes in handy (see Chapter 7). When Selsam describes the white spots on a baby deer's coat as looking "like spots of sunlight on the forest floor" (*Hidden Animals*), she is making a comparison (a simile, in fact) to help us visualize the subject.

Jim Arnosky, in *Watching Desert Wildlife*, describes his observations on birds, snakes, lizards, deer, and other desert wildlife. At the conclusion of his work, he sums up his experience and its meaning with these words:

> *I went to the desert to feel the heat of the desert sun and breathe the dry air. I went to the desert to see its wide open places. I went with my eyes open wide, watchful for snakes and scorpions, and alert, ready to see all the wonderful wild animals who make their homes amid the thorns and spines.*
>
> *I came home from the desert with a fresh new outlook on nature and wildlife. I felt bigger and broader, happy in the knowledge that I had discovered another world.* (n.p.)

A good writer of nonfiction has a gift for describing complex information in language that is clear, precise, succinct, and beautiful—indeed, the language of science is often quite poetic.

Format

Format refers to the physical presentation of material, specifically how the pages and chapters are laid out. Readers in the upper elementary grades and beyond rarely expect to find illustrations in their novels. But a nonfiction book is another kettle of fish. A book filled with facts can be overwhelming. And some facts are easier to explain graphically than with words alone. A book's format also includes such matters as typeface, chapter and division headings, and various auxiliary features, such as a table of contents, bibliography, index, and so on. Let's take a brief look at some of these.

TABLE OF CONTENTS ■ A book for older readers is likely to contain a table of contents—an outline showing what the book covers. A helpful table of contents contains clear and accurate headings (rather than merely clever ones) and demonstrates the logic of the book's organization.

FOOTNOTES/ENDNOTES ■ Many nonfiction books include footnotes, which are placed at the bottom of the page, or endnotes, which are placed at the end of each chapter or at the back of the book. These notes provide additional information the author found interesting and useful but not necessarily crucial to the content of the book. Sometimes these notes contain suggestions for additional readings or fascinating tidbits of extraneous information. (Footnotes and endnotes are occasionally more interesting than the text!)

GLOSSARY ■ A nonfiction work may include a glossary, which is a specialized dictionary of important terms used throughout the book. A glossary defines terms as they are used specifically in the text. This is particularly helpful if the book uses a lot of technical terms or is about a topic unfamiliar to most people. See the glossary at the back of this book for an example.

BIBLIOGRAPHY ■ To help readers explore the subject further, many works of nonfiction contain a bibliography, or a list of resources, that identifies materials (books, articles, films, and so on) on a specific subject. Usually in nonfiction for children and adolescents, the bibliography consists of a reading list of relevant books young readers might find interesting.

INDEX ■ A nonfiction work for older readers (middle school and beyond) is likely to contain an index. Always at the very end of the book, an index is a list of the important subjects discussed in the book, along with the page numbers where readers can find specific information. The purpose of an index is to enable readers to use the book as a reference source—that is, if readers want to find out something specific, they can locate the topic in the index without having to read through the entire book. See the index to this book.

Illustrations

The illustrations in a nonfiction book may include drawings, photographs, diagrams, graphs, charts, or any other nontextual matter used to explain key ideas.

Photographs are very popular in nonfiction because of their accuracy and sense of authenticity. History books and biographies may use period photographs that were actually taken during the historical era covered in the book (Freedman's *Lincoln: A Photobiography*). Books about the sciences and arts make good use of photography as well when they want to convey accurate details (Celia Bland's *Bats*).

Sometimes, however, a photograph will just not work. Then the author turns to drawings. For example, in her book on human reproduction, *Mommy Laid an Egg; Or, Where Do Babies Come From?* Babette Cole uses comical cartoon drawings depicting aspects of human anatomy and sexuality. Tony De Saulles's cartoon drawings for Nick Arnold's *The Body Owner's Handbook* substitute for actual photographs of human internal organ, which could be unsettling. David Macaulay's *Cathedral* describes the process of building a medieval cathedral, and his exquisite pen-and-ink drawings more than make up for the absence of photographs, which, of course, do not exist. And then we find books in which the illustrations are beautiful works of art in themselves, such as Steve Jenkins's collage creations in his animal book *Biggest, Strongest, Fastest* (see Chapter 5, Figure 5.6).

The Eyewitness Juniors series seems inspired by television and electronic media, containing information in small doses on pages filled with an array of illustrations (see Figure 12.2). These books serve as stimulating introductions and springboards to more sophisticated treatments. Similarly, Seymour Simon's *Out of Sight: Pictures of Hidden Worlds* contains a series of stunning photographs, all produced through technologically sophisticated means, showing us such things as the interior of a living human heart or the head of a ladybug or the formation of new stars in a galaxy 7,000 light years away.

Maps are very helpful in both history and geography books. Janis Herbert's *The Civil War for Kids*, for example, includes several maps, including battlefield maps. Map reading is an important skill too easily overlooked in this day of global positioning systems, and young readers might need the help of such works as Scot Ritchie's picture storybook *Follow That Map! A First Book of Mapping Skills* and Sara Finelli's *My Map Book*.

Charts, diagrams, and tables are used in a wide variety of nonfiction books. A history book might include a timeline that places events in chronological order. A biography might include a genealogy chart—or family tree—illustrating family relationships. A science book might include a diagram, which is simply a labeled drawing. A book on dance might include a diagram of a dance movement—something that is very difficult to capture in a photograph. A table is a means of organizing information into rows and columns to make it more accessible or to help compare items; for example, a table might be used to show how various kinds of animals differ in their diet, habitat, life span, and so on. Tables can pack a lot of information into a small space.

The key to all these visual aids is that they be clear, unambiguous, and easy to follow, and they help us understand the subject. We want illustrations that are accurately labeled with helpful captions. Illustrations without captions leave us guessing about what we're looking at. That's not helpful. Finally, each illustration should have a very clear purpose. Illustrations should not be mere decoration.

Types of Nonfiction

For the sake of convenience, we will divide nonfiction into five types: science and nature; arts and leisure; human growth and development; history, society, and culture; and biography and autobiography. Each of these very broad categories requires a slightly different approach.

Hatching out

Most reptiles lay eggs. Some eggs have leathery shells, and others have hard shells, like hens' eggs. And some reptiles don't lay eggs at all. They give birth to live young, just like humans do.

1 When it's time to break out, the baby hog-nosed viper's egg shrivels, because the baby has used up all the yolk inside.

2 The baby snake makes the first cut in its shell with a special tiny egg tooth. Pushing with its snout, it pokes its head out.

3 The snake stays inside its safe shell for hours, or even days, before it finally crawls out.

4 The baby snake is a miniature version of its parents. Once it's hatched, it does not need to be looked after by Mom.

Empty shell

FIGURE 12.2 ■ In this illustration from Mary Ling's *Amazing Crocodiles & Reptiles* we see the hatching of a viper, with four stages of the process captured in photography by Jerry Young and carefully labeled.

Science and Nature

Books about science and nature include many topics: the life sciences (animals and plants), the earth sciences (rocks, minerals, the weather, the environment), astronomy, mathematics, and technology.

As might be expected, books about animals are among the most popular of the science books, particularly with younger readers. Even the youngest children find almost any book about animals appealing. In recent years a number of fine books have been written on unusual and threatened animal species, including the puffin, the panda, and the bald eagle. Series such as Save Earth's Animals and Eye to Eye with Endangered Species are raising young readers' awareness about the fragility of animal life on our planet. Typically these books describe the animals' life cycles, habits, and importance in the larger frame of the natural world and, often, what is being done to save them. Jim Brandenburg is a noted environmentalist and photographer who has written many books for children, including his *Face to Face with Wolves*, an intimate portrait of the threatened Arctic wolf.

Gail Gibbons's *From Seed to Plant* and Ruth Heller's *The Reason for a Flower* (mentioned earlier) illustrate one of nature's most elemental tales—the growth of a plant from a tiny seed—and they invite hands-on experiences. Plants, of course, are not naturally cuddly, nor do they have expressive personalities (except possibly for the Venus flytrap). So a writer must emphasize other qualities, such as a plant's beauty, its uniqueness, and its importance to us and our ecosystem. It is not only the animal world that is threatened with extinction, and we are beginning to see books alerting young children to the potential disappearance of our plant life as well. Richard C. Vogt's *Rain Forests*, one of the Insiders series from Simon & Schuster, provides plentiful information about rain forests worldwide, along with three-dimensional illustrations.

Astronomy is an exciting, if challenging, subject for children, and making it understandable for young readers requires a great deal of ingenuity. In *Exploring the Night Sky*, science writer Terence Dickinson describes the immense size of the solar system, using an extended metaphor:

> *A model of the solar system gives an idea of its size and the sizes of its various members. Let's use a major-league baseball stadium located in the centre of a large city for the model. The sun, the size of a baseball, rests on home plate. Mercury, Venus, Earth and Mars, each about the dimensions of the ball in a ballpoint pen, are, respectively, 1/8, 1/5, 1/3 and 1/2 of the way to the pitcher's mound. A pea near second base is Jupiter. In shallow centre field is a smaller pea, Saturn. Uranus, the size of this letter O, is at the fence off in deep centre field. Neptune and Pluto, a letter O and a grain of salt in our model, are just outside the park.* (26)

He continues with the baseball field metaphor, noting that the nearest star to our solar system "would be a baseball in another city more than 1,000 miles away" (26).

However, Dickinson's passage would soon become outdated. When first published in 1987, the details were deemed accurate; the solar system contained nine planets. Then,

FIGURE 12.3 ■ David Aguilar's stunning drawing suggesting what Uranus might look like from its moon, Miranda, captures both the majesty and the mystery of the solar system.

about 20 years later, the scientific community downgraded Pluto to the status of a dwarf planet. This downgrade occurred because recent data had revealed that Pluto did not possess all the properties to qualify it as a planet; for example, it was not big enough to clear other things out of its orbit. Then, just as we were getting accustomed to that view of the solar system, more knowledge was gathered, and new books, such as David Aguilar's *13 Planets: The Latest View of the Solar System*, published in 2011, have been based on that information, adding the planets Pluto, Haumea, Makemake and Eris (see Figure 12.3).

An unusual series of science books produced in Great Britain by Nick Arnold is fiendishly called Horrible Science. It is referred to in the cover material as "Science with the squishy bits left in!" This series now includes numerous titles on all aspects of science, and each book contains cartoonish and often outrageous drawings by Tony De Saulles. The titles themselves are tantalizing, including *Chemical Chaos*, *Fatal Forces*, and *Nasty Nature*. In *The Body Owner's Handbook* Arnold describes in detail the functions of our organs, what can go wrong, and how to best care for our bodies; it is billed as "the guide you simply can't live without." It reads like a manual for auto care, and the author delights in giving his teen audience the gruesome, the unsavory, and the indelicate details they love so much. Although the texts and illustrations are light-hearted in tone, the subjects and explanations are quite serious, and the books provide a great deal of interesting and useful information.

One book of scientific explanations that is not to be missed is David Macaulay's near monumental *The Way Things Work* (originally published in 1988 and expanded and updated in 1998 in *The New Way Things Work*). This hefty volume explores all the realms of the earth sciences—mechanics, physics (even nuclear physics), electronics, and chemistry. With amazing clarity and simplicity and with the help of hundreds of clever drawings, Macaulay explains a phenomenal number of complex ideas and processes. He ties the entire work together by using cartoon figures of woolly mammoths to demonstrate the various properties and scientific principles involved. For example, the mammoths are used to represent "force" or "effort." (The cartoon figures, incidentally, do not trivialize the subject matter in this case; instead, they clarify complex ideas—such as jet propulsion and the operation of computers.) In this way, Macaulay uses metaphor to illustrate an abstract concept and humor to make his explanations understandable and enjoyable. This book has enormous appeal for adults as well as young people.

Arts and Leisure

Unfortunately, modern American society has typically regarded the arts as luxuries or pastimes. When school budgets are cut, art programs are often the first to go. But art feeds the soul as well as the mind, and it is an indispensable part of a child's education. As with anything else, most people find art more meaningful when they can participate in it— perform the music or the dance, act in the play, paint the picture, or form the sculpture. Nevertheless, books can offer instructions, expand experiences, pique curiosity, and develop taste. Historical surveys of the various art forms provide useful perspectives; it is always important to know what has gone before us. Marc Aronson's *Art Attack: A Short Cultural History of the Avant-Garde*, for example, describes a specific movement in modern art.

William Latch's *Can You Hear It?* provides an excellent introduction to classical music for younger readers. Robert Levine's *Story of the Orchestra*, for somewhat older readers, includes material about classical music and orchestral instruments. Both of these books are accompanied by CDs.

David Macaulay (mentioned above for *The Way Things Work*) has created a series of picture books that bridge science, history, and art. Each book focuses on a specific type of building and explains how it is built. The buildings rage from an Egyptian pyramid (*Pyramid*) to a medieval castle (*Castle*) and cathedral (*Cathedral*) to a modern skyscraper

(*Unbuilding*). Macaulay pays close attention to technical detail and also includes information about the society of the builders. Obviously, Macaulay's books straddle our categories—and there is nothing wrong with that.

Books on sports, hobbies, film, theater, drawing, and painting are all available. Many of these tend to be how-to or instructional books, and often the most interesting books on sports or art or theater are the biographies of athletes, artists, actors, and writers. But more about biography below. There seems to be no end to the subjects covered in nonfiction— there are even very clever picture books on language (which may not seem much like leisure to you, but it's not quite science either!). Lynn Truss's *Eats, Shoots & Leaves: Why Commas Do Make a Difference* is a light-hearted way of approaching punctuation. (There actually is an adult version of this book as well.)

Human Growth and Development

Books about human growth and development are the most recent additions to nonfiction books for children. They include such psychological and sociological concerns as family relationships, friendship and other human interaction, sexual growth and development, physical and emotional challenges, and death and dying.

As you might imagine, books on sexuality are in high demand. Gail Saltz's *Changing You: A Guide to Body Changes and Sexuality* and Jacqui Bailey's *Sex, Puberty, and All That Stuff: A Guide to Growing Up* both include straightforward text with cartoon drawings. The casual approach and the comical illustrations remove the mystery of sex, as well as some of its allure.

As children reach puberty, they need certain books that are addressed specifically to males or females. Jeremy Daldry's *The Teenage Guy's Survival Guide: The Real Deal on Girls, Growing Up and Other Guy Stuff* sets out to assuage some of the teenage angst that plagues every boy. And for teenage girls there are books such as Debra Beck's *My Feet Aren't Ugly! A Girl's Guide to Loving Herself from the Inside Out*. An important part of growing up is learning that we are fundamentally like everybody else. Another area that is finally receiving the attention it deserves is the issue of sexual preference. Dan Savage's *It Gets Better: Coming Out, Overcoming Bullying, and Creating a Life Worth Living* is a collection of essays and testimonials from people famous and not-so-famous, including President Obama, Hillary Clinton, and British Prime Minister David Cameron, intended to provide words of encouragement to LGBTQ (lesbian, gay, bisexual, transgender, and questioning) teenagers who are victims of bullying.

In Chapter 5 we briefly discussed the treatment of death in books for children, pointing out that sometimes a well-written fictional work can provide comfort and understanding in experiencing loss. And sometimes young people simply need to hear the facts. Earl A. Grollman's *Straight Talk about Death for Teenagers: How to Cope with Losing Someone You Love* is an example of a thorough and straightforward discussion of the many facets of this very difficult topic. Regardless of the subject matter, young readers need honesty, sensitivity, and accuracy in their nonfiction.

History, Society, and Culture

Another very large category encompasses books on topics such as political and social history, geography, and religion. As we have seen in the preceding chapters, we can learn a great deal about people and places through well-written realistic fiction and even through the traditional folktales. However, along with these fictional works, we need to know certain facts to gain a fuller understanding of and appreciation for a culture. Even children in the early elementary years can be drawn into historical subjects. We have already mentioned Aliki, whose picture books on historical and cultural subjects are ideally suited to young readers. One favorite is *Mummies Made in Egypt*, which describes the complicated process by which the ancient Egyptians embalmed their dead. Also on an Egyptian subject is James Cross Giblin's *Secrets of the Sphinx*, which includes stunning artwork by Bagram Ibatoulline. It is filled with information about one of the most intriguing monuments of the ancient world, presented for readers in the middle grades.

Books for older readers generally have longer texts and fewer illustrations; most are illustrated books rather than picture books. The best writers of history try to depict the past faithfully, including the unpleasant, the controversial, and the vile along with the good, the glorious, and the inspirational. Of particular note are Milton Meltzer (*The Black Americans: A History in Their Own Word* and *Brother Can You Spare a Dime? The Great Depression: 1929–1933*), Russell Freedman (*Cowboys of the Wild West*), and Jim Murphy (*An American Plague: The True and Terrifying Story of the Yellow Fever Epidemic of 1793*). Each of these writers has a lively writing style and provides engaging details; period photographs, news clippings, and other archival materials; and reading lists, endnotes, indexes, and other helpful features for serious readers.

Good historical nonfiction for children about non-Western cultures—Asian, African, South American, even European—is a bit more difficult to find, but it is out there. Russell Freedman, in fact, has written a fine study of the great Chinese philosopher Confucius (*Confucius and the Golden Rule*). Adeline Yen Mah's *China: Land of Dragons and Emperors*, an acclaimed history of China for young readers, is an example that needs to be emulated.

Religion is a sensitive area for many people, and writers on religious subjects are wise to be mindful of the delicate nature of this topic. There is a difference between informing and preaching. If approached purely from an informational point of view, books on religion can help children learn about their own heritage as well as about religions and cultures around the world. Mary Pope Osborne's *One World, Many Religions: The Way We Worship* is one example of a book that tries to find the common thread of humanity in the world's many faiths.

Biography and Autobiography

Biographies and autobiographies are simply books about the lives of people—living or dead, famous or infamous or unknown. A biography is the story of a person's life written by someone else; if a person writes his or her own life story, it's called an autobiography.

Biographies for young readers began to appear as early as the 1920s and 1930s. These early ones tended to romanticize their subjects. Ingri and Parin d'Aulaire's biographies of Abraham Lincoln and Christopher Columbus, for example, place the subjects on a pedestal, where they appear a bit too perfect and too heroic, and they lack a flesh-and-blood quality. Today, most biographers prefer to portray their subjects as real-life characters—warts and all. But rather than debunk the heroes, this approach makes them easier to like; perhaps we just don't trust someone who seems too perfect.

Take, for example, Russell Freedman's *Lincoln: A Photobiography*, which opens with this anecdote:

> *At first glance, most people thought he was homely. Lincoln thought so too, referring once to his "poor, lean, lank face." As a young man he was sensitive about his gawky looks, but in time, he learned to laugh at himself. When a rival called him "two-faced" during a political debate, Lincoln replied, "I leave it to my audience. If I had another face, do you think I'd wear this one?"* (1)

What sets heroes apart from everyone else is not that they have no weaknesses but that they succeed despite their weaknesses. Doesn't that make their triumph more impressive?

COMPLETE, PARTIAL, AND COLLECTIVE BIOGRAPHIES ▇ Writers may take one of many possible approaches to biography. A complete biography covers a subject's entire life, from cradle to grave. These can range from simple picture-book biographies (Aliki's *The Story of Johnny Appleseed*, for example) to complex works (such as Freedman's *Lincoln: A Photobiography*).

Other biographies cover only one phase of the subject's life. These partial biographies tend to focus on specific themes or periods of the subject's life. One very popular biographical series, The Childhood of Famous Americans, includes fictionalized biographies that focus chiefly on the subject's childhood and teen years (Augusta Stevenson's *George Washington: Young Leader*, for example). Presumably these books will pique the young readers' curiosity so that, in time, they will want to read full-length biographies of their favorite people, but we should keep in mind that these are not authentic biographies (more on them below), and they take many liberties with the facts.

Sometimes we find collective biographies, which include brief sketches of the lives of several people who are linked by a common thread: scientists, first ladies, sports figures, musicians, and so on. One of the most famous of all collective biographies is President John F. Kennedy's best-selling *Profiles in Courage*, about the lives of some lesser-known American heroes. Originally for adults, it has been edited for younger audiences. Such books make good introductions to the lives of famous people and may encourage readers to find more thorough biographies.

AUTHENTIC AND FICTIONALIZED BIOGRAPHIES ▇ It is important to distinguish between an authentic biography, which deals exclusively in facts, and a fictionalized biography, which modifies some facts for the sake of story. We turn again to Freedman's *Lincoln: A*

Photobiography. This book contains nothing that cannot be verified by solid evidence. Lincoln's words quoted above are drawn from material of the period—they are not made up. If dialogue is used in an authentic biography (which is not common), it has to be supported by historical documents (such as letters or diaries) or verifiable personal recollections.

In fictionalized biography, a writer may invent scenes and/or dialogue—usually to make the story more dramatic, more interesting. Fictionalized biographies are often easily recognized by their use of dialogue. So, in Jean Lee Latham's Newbery Award–winning *Carry on, Mr. Bowditch*, the story of a real-life mathematician, we find a gripping adventure story. But the dialogue (which Latham could not possibly have had access to), the absence of an index, and the detailed descriptions of young Bowditch as an indentured servant all reveal this as fictionalized biography. It is not that fictionalized biographies are fundamentally unreliable; we should simply not use them as reference works. Their purpose is entertainment and, perhaps, to encourage us to read further about the subject.

Nor should we think that an authentic biography is just a series of boring facts. Listen to the folksy quality of this passage from Robert Quackenbush's authentic picture-book biography *Mark Twain? What Kind of Name Is That?*:

> *Samuel Langhorne Clemens—river pilot, gold miner, frontier reporter, humorist, and this nation's best-loved author—claimed that two important events took place on November 30, 1835. One was the appearance in the night sky of Halley's Comet—an event that comes only once every seventy-five years—and the other was his birth in Florida, Missouri. Sam loved telling jokes and playing tricks. He claimed that he couldn't remember what his first lie was, but he told his second lie when he was only nine days old. He had pretended that a diaper pin was sticking him, and he'd hollered as loud as he could. This brought him extra loving attention—until his trickery was found out, that is. Sam's mother thought he might get hit by a bolt of lightning one day, on account of all the mischief he caused as he was growing up in Hannibal, Missouri, with his older brother Orion, his older sister Pamela, his younger brother Henry, and nineteen cats.* (9)

Yes, much is omitted about young Sam Clemens's childhood, but in this short paragraph we learn several facts, we get a good idea of his character, and most readers will want to read on. It is just what we want from good biography.

We need to say a word about biographical fiction: It is fiction, not nonfiction. And in fact, biographical fiction can even be fantasy, such as in Robert Lawson's *Captain Kidd's Cat* (about the pirate Captain Kidd), *I Discover Columbus*, and *Ben and Me* (about Benjamin Franklin)—all told by animals who knew them. These books are purely delightful, which is just what they were intended to be. But we should *not* mistake them for history. And, perhaps like fictionalized biography, they may inspire a young reader to seek out authentic biographies of these people.

AUTOBIOGRAPHY ■ An autobiography is a book written about one's own life. Sometimes, an autobiographer will write about only one part of his or her life—childhood and adolescence, for example, or the early adult years, or specific career experiences. Autobiographies are usually more informal than biographies, often taking the form of memoirs or reminiscences. Many individuals believe they don't have to research their own lives (after all, who should know their lives better than they do?), and so they rely on their recollections of events. Consequently, specific dates are frequently missing from autobiographies, and seldom do we find any documentation. Not only are facts suspect in an autobiography, but so is the interpretation. What is more important to the writer of an autobiography—the truth or the subject's image?

Nevertheless, what famous people say about themselves can be both enlightening and entertaining. An autobiography can also be a great source for discovering an individual's character traits, likes and dislikes, innermost feelings—things that are not so easily hidden. Several children's authors have written their autobiographies for young readers, including Betsy Byars's *The Moon and I*, Phyllis Reynolds Naylor's *How I Came to Be a Writer*, Jean Fritz's *Homecoming: My Own Story*, and Roald Dahl's *Boy: Tales of Childhood*.

Nonfiction and the Common Core Curriculum

As was pointed out in Chapter 3, the new Common Core Curriculum recommends that at least 50 percent of an elementary school student's reading should be from nonfiction and that by high school it should increase to 70 percent. We also looked at the arguments for and against these recommendations, and there is no need to repeat them here. However, if nonfiction is to become a significant part of a student's required reading, then the least we can do is try to make sure that the nonfiction is of the best possible quality. The following guidelines provide some suggestions for things to look for when evaluating nonfiction.

- The book's overall appearance is appealing
- The format is suited to the content and the intended audience
- The language and content are appropriate for the intended audience
- The writing style is clear, accessible, and engaging
- The content is accurate, thorough, and objective
- The content reflects solid and up-to-date research
- The content is clearly and logically organized
- The illustrations are accurate, helpful, and well-placed
- The organizational apparatus (table of contents, notes, glossary, bibliography, index, etc.) is logical and helpful

Ideally, when we finish a work of nonfiction, we find ourselves wanting to read further—not because the book we just finished was inadequate but because it nurtured our curiosity and made us hungry for more.

Summary

Fiction and nonfiction often have similar ends—to help us understand the world we live in and to give us pleasure. The difference is that fiction does it through a made-up story, whereas nonfiction sticks to factual evidence. Nonfiction books, once thought of as chiefly dull, utilitarian works, have risen to a higher stature in recent years, some even having received children's literature's most prestigious awards.

Good nonfiction writers give us facts in a way that sparks our interest and stirs our imagination. They know that truth, as the old expression goes, is "stranger than fiction." Facts themselves are not dull, but how they are presented may be. Nonfiction writers have to combine the spellbinding skills of the storyteller with the knowledge of the scholar and researcher.

This is no easy task, for nonfiction, like fiction, is judged on its ability to keep our interest. But unlike fiction, nonfiction is also judged on the quality of its research, the accuracy of its facts, and the integrity of its explanations. Nonfiction also requires a clear purpose and audience, balance and an objective, and accuracy and sufficient detail—as well as being enjoyable to read. Most nonfiction for children includes illustrations that should extend our knowledge, explain the complicated, and unravel the mysterious. These illustrations should not be mere ornamentation. A nonfiction book may also include supplementary materials, such as a table of contents, a glossary, a list of references, and an index—all designed to help the reader use the book more effectively.

Topics in nonfiction include works about science and nature; arts and leisure; human growth and development; history, society, and culture; and biography and autobiography. Regardless of the topic, a well-constructed nonfiction work is not simply a loose collection of facts (something like a *Guinness Book of Records*—interesting to read in bits and pieces but hardly a gripping story). The best nonfiction is well crafted, carefully designed, and precisely written. It helps us understand our world and ourselves, and it urges us to read on, to learn more. In the end, like the best fiction, nonfiction speaks to the strength and resilience of the human spirit and to the unending wonder of the universe.

For Reflection and Discussion

1. Locate and read at least three or four information books on the same topic but for different age levels—a picture book for preschoolers, a picture book for early elementary, and a chapter book for children in the middle grades, for example. Determine the specific audience and purpose for each book. What are the chief differences in treatment among the books? Consider the factual differences, the differences in tone, and the differences in layout and presentation. How successful is each book, given its specific audience and purpose?

2. Choose any biography written for children (of any age). After reading the book, locate some factual information about the subject—from reliable online sources, biographical dictionaries or encyclopedias, adult biographies, and so on. Evaluate the children's biography for its accuracy, its thoroughness, and its effectiveness in capturing the personality of the subject. In light of your research, what are the book's strengths and weaknesses?

3. Try your hand at writing an explanation of a concept for young children. The following are some examples of possible topics:

   a. What makes night and day?

   b. What are the differences between a solid, a liquid, and a gas?

   c. What are the seasons? What makes them?

   d. Who was George Washington Carver, and why is he important?

   e. What happens when our heart beats?

   Be sure to determine your audience's age level: Are they preschoolers? Early elementary children? Middle schoolers? And be sure to write for your audience. You may want to include illustrations. (Don't worry; if you're not an artist, you can pull materials off the Web.) When you're finished, have a child from your target audience read your explanation. How successful was your explanation?

Works Cited

Arnosky, Jim. *Watching Desert Wildlife*. Washington, DC: National Geographic Society, 1998.

Dickinson, Terence. *Exploring the Night Sky*. Willowdale, Ontario: Firefly, 1987.

Freedman, Russell. *Lincoln: A Photobiography*. New York: Clarion, 1987.

Latham, P. M. *The Collected Works*. Vol. II. London: New Sydenham Society, 1877.

Selsam, Millicent E. "Writing about Science for Children." In *Beyond Fact: Nonfiction for Children and Young People*. Ed. Jo Carr. Chicago: American Library Association, 1982, 61–65.

Recommended Resources

Aiken, Joan. "Interpreting the Past." *Children's Literature in Education* 16 (Summer 1985): 67–83.

Baxter, Kathleen A., and Marcia Agness Kochel. *Gotcha Good! Nonfiction Books to Get Kids Excited about Reading*. Santa Barbara, CA: Libraries Unlimited, 2008.

Burton, Hester. "The Writing of Historical Novels." In *Children and Literature: Views and Reviews*. Ed. Virginia Haviland. Glenview, IL: Scott, Foresman, 1973, pp. 299–304.

Carr, Jo, ed. *Beyond Fact: Nonfiction for Children and Young People*. Chicago: American Library Association, 1982.

Carter, Betty, and Richard F. Abrahamson. *Nonfiction for Young Adults: From Delight to Wisdom*. Phoenix, AZ: Oryx Press, 1991.

Cianciolo, Patricia. *Informational Picture Books for Children*. Chicago: American Library Association, 2000.

Epstein, William H. "Introducing Biography." *Children's Literature Association Quarterly* 12 (Winter 1987): 177–179.

Fisher, Margery. *Matters of Fact: Aspects of Non-fiction for Children*. New York: Crowell, 1972.

Ford, Danielle. "More Than the Facts: Reviewing Science Books." *The Horn Book Magazine* 78, 3 (May/June 2002): 265–271.

Fraser, Elizabeth. *Reality Rules! A Guide to Teen Nonfiction Reading Interests*. Santa Barbara, CA: Libraries Unlimited, 2008.

Fritz, Jean. *And Then What Happened, Paul Revere?* New York: Coward, McCann & Geoghegan, 1973.

Garfield, Leon. "Historical Fiction for Our Global Times." *The Horn Book* (November/December 1988): 736–742.

Gottleib, Robin. "On Nonfiction Books for Children: Tradition & Dissent." *Wilson Library Journal* (October 1974): 174–177.

Kendall, Paul Murray. *The Art of Biography*. 1965. New York: Norton, 1985.

Mallet, Margaret. *Making Facts Matter: Reading Non-fiction 5–11*. London: Paul Chapman, 1992.

Marcus, Leonard. "Life Drawing: Some Notes on Children's Picture Book Biographies." *The Lion and the Unicorn* 4 (Summer 1980): 15–31.

Moore, Ann W. "A Question of Accuracy: Errors in Children's Biographies." *School Library Journal* 31 (February 1985): 34–35.

Segel, Elizabeth. "In Biographies for Young Readers, Nothing Is Impossible." *The Lion and the Unicorn* 4 (Summer 1980): 4–14.

Weinberg, Steve. "Biography: Telling the Untold Story." *The Writer* (February 1993): 23–25.

Wilms, Denise M. "An Evaluation of Biography." In *Jump Over the Moon*. Ed. Pamela Barron and Jennifer Burley. New York: Holt, Rinehart & Winston, 1984, pp. 220–225.

Nonfiction: A Selected and Annotated Booklist

The following list does not even scratch the surface of what is available in nonfiction for children and is only intended to suggest the wide variety of quality books available. Reading levels are only suggestions. An individual's interests and abilities are the best guides. The dates are generally for the most recent edition.

Science and Nature

Pre-K–Grade 4

Arnosky, Jim. *Thunder Birds: Nature's Flying Predators*. New York: Sterling, 2011.
- a picture book about the great birds of prey by a celebrated naturalist.

——. *Watching Desert Wildlife*. Washington, DC: National Geographic, 2002.
- Stunning illustrations and a text for beginning readers.

Bang, Molly. *Common Ground: The Water, Earth, and Air We Share*. New York: Scholastic, 1997.
- A picture book that argues for conservation of our natural resources.

Batten, Mary. *Hungry Plants*. Illus. Paul Mirocha. New York: Random House, 2004.
- A story of carnivorous plants, illustrated from the insect's viewpoint.

Bland, Celia. *Bats.* Chicago: Kidsbooks, 1997.
- Photographs capture the life of bats; a book in the Eyes on Nature series on various animals.

Brandenburg, Jim. *Face to Face with Wolves.* Washington, DC: National Geographic, 2010.
- Photographs accompany an intimate look at the Arctic wolf.

Branley, Franklyn. *The Air Is All Around You.* Illus. John O'Brien. New York: HarperCollins, 2006.
- One of many in a popular series of picture books on science (Let's-Read-and-Find-Out Science); for younger readers and with hands-on projects.

Brown, Laurie Krasny, and Marc Brown. *Dinosaurs to the Rescue! A Guide to Protecting Our Planet.* Boston: Little, Brown, 1992.
- An ecological guidebook for the very young.

Cobb, Vicki. *I Face the Wind.* Illus. Julia Gorton. New York: HarperCollins, 2003.
- One of a series of accessible science books by Cobb, this one on the science of wind.

Cole, Joanna. *The Magic School Bus and the Climate Challenge.* Illus. Bruce Degen. New York: Scholastic, 2010.
- One of the popular and long-running series of Magic School Bus adventures.

Floca, Brian. *Moonshot: The Flight of* Apollo 11. New York: Atheneum, 2009.
- A handsomely illustrated and well-told story of a historic space mission.

Gibbons, Gail. *From Seed to Plant.* New York: Holiday, 1993.
- One of Gibbons's many accessible nonfiction picture books about nature.

Heller, Ruth. *Chickens Aren't the Only Ones.* St. Louis, MO: Turtleback, 1999.
- A fascinating look at egg-laying animals, colorfully illustrated; from the World of Nature series.

——. *The Reason for a Flower.* New York: Puffin, 1999.
- A colorful introduction to the makeup of flowers.

Henderson, Douglas. *Asteroid Impact.* New York: Penguin, 2001.
- A dramatically illustrated story of the asteroid scientists believe may have destroyed the dinosaurs.

Hopkinson, Deborah. *Sky Boys: How They Built the Empire State Building.* Illus. James F. Ransome. New York: Schwartz & Wade, 2006.
- Part science, part history, describing the building of the world's tallest building in 1931.

Jenkins, Steve. *Biggest, Strongest, Fastest.* Boston: Houghton Mifflin, 1995.
- Extreme facts about animals, depicted in collage illustrations.

——. *Life on Earth: The Story of Evolution.* Boston: Houghton Mifflin, 2002.
- A good introduction to evolution, illustrated with Jenkins's characteristic collages.

Lyon, George Ella. *All the Water in the World.* Illus. Katherine Tillotson. New York: Atheneum, 2011.
- An explanation for young readers of the complexities of the water cycle with stunning art and beautiful language.

McCarthy, Meghan. *Astronaut Handbook.* New York: Knopf, 2008.
- An informative and funny book all about the science of space travel—for toddlers.

Miche, Mary. *Nature's Patchwork Quilt: Understanding Habitats.* Illus. Consie Powell. Nevada City, CO: Dawn Publications, 2012.
- A book of lively illustrations and good explanations of various animal habitats.

Schwartz, David M. *Millions to Measure.* Illus. Steven Kellogg. New York: HarperCollins, 2003.
- A book whose playful illustrations help explain the concept of measuring.

Selsam, Millicent. *Hidden Animals.* New York: Harper & Row, 1967.
- A book with fascinating nature photography that demonstrates the camouflage of animals. Unfortunately out of print.

Simon, Seymour. *Guts: Our Digestive System.* New York: HarperCollins, 2005.
- An excellent introduction for young readers.

——. *Our Solar System*, rev. ed. New York: HarperCollins, 2007.
- A tour of the solar system with full-color photographs. One of dozens of fine science books by Simon for younger children.

——. *Out of Sight: Pictures of Hidden Worlds*. New York: Chronicle Books, 2002.
- Imaginative photographs of nature.

Tara, Stephanie Lisa. *Snowy White World to Save*. Illus. Alex Walton. CreateSpace, 2013.
- Picture-book treatment of the effects of global warming on the polar ice caps.

Vogt, Richard C. *Rain Forests*. New York: Simon & Schuster, 2009.
- Packed with information and three-dimensional illustrations.

For Grades 4 and Above

Aguilar, David. *13 Planets: The Latest View of Our Solar System*. Washington, DC: National Geographic, 2011.
- A book illustrated with computer art that is based on the most recent scientific data.

Arnold, Nick. *The Body Owner's Handbook*. Illus. Tony De Saulles. New York: Scholastic, 2002.
- Hilarious explanations of how the body works. See the many other science titles by Arnold and De Saulles in the Horrible Science series.

Bryson, Bill. *A Really Short History of Nearly Everything*. New York: Delacorte, 2009.
- A book filled with amazing scientific facts and richly illustrated.

Dickinson, Terry. *NightWatch: A Practical Guide for Viewing the Universe*, 4th ed. Illus. Adolf Schaller. Richmond Hill, Ontario: Firefly, 2006.
- A very good introduction to astronomy.

Farrell, Jeanette. *Invisible Enemies: Stories of Infectious Disease*, rev. ed. New York: Farrar, Straus & Giroux, 2005.
- A book filled with interesting facts about seven major killers.

Hague, Bradley. *Alien Deep: Revealing the Mysterious Living World at the Bottom of the Ocean*. Washington, DC: National Geographic, 2012.
- A fascinating explanation of underwater exploration.

Kerrod, Robin, and David Hughes. *Visual Encyclopedia of Space*. New York: DK Children, 2006.
- A compact book filled with hundreds of illustrations covering all aspects of space.

Krautwurst, Terry. *Night Science for Kids: Exploring the World after Dark*. Asheville, NC: Lark Books, 2005.
- An interactive approach to discovering nature in the nighttime.

Kurlansky, Mark. *World without Fish*. Illus. Frank Stockton. New York: Workman, 2011.
- A book about the interconnections between biology, economics, politics, climate, and so on.

Macaulay, David. *The New Way Things Work*. Boston: Houghton Mifflin, 1998.
- Meticulously illustrated explanations of the workings of everything from pop-up toasters to computer chips.

Masoff, Joy. *Oh, Yuck! The Encyclopedia of Everything Nasty*. Illus. Terry Sirrell. New York: Workman, 2000.
- A well-researched book that appeals to young teenagers.

McCutcheon, Chuck. *What Are Global Warming and Climate Change? Answers for Young Readers*. Albuquerque: University of New Mexico Press, 2010.
- An objective approach to a still controversial subject.

Murray, Elizabeth A. *Death: Corpses, Cadavers, and Other Grave Matters*. Minneapolis, MN: Twenty-First Century Books, 2010.
- A book filled with fascinating details, written by a forensic scientist.

Pringle, Laurence. *Billions of Years, Amazing Changes: The Story of Evolution*. Illus. Steve Jenkins. Honesdale, PA: Boyds Mill Press, 2011.
- A lively explanation of evolution by a celebrated science writer. Look for the many other titles by Pringle.

Ride, Sally, and Susan Okie. *To Space and Back*. New York: Lothrop, 1986.
- The personal experiences of the first American woman in space.

Spangler, Steve. *Naked Eggs and Flying Potatoes: Unforgettable Experiments That Make Science Fun*. Austin, TX: Greenleaf, 2010.

- A lively collection of a wide variety of experiments suited to middle schoolers.

St. George, Judith. *The Brooklyn Bridge: They Said It Couldn't Be Built*. New York: Putnam, 1982.
- A book that's part history and part engineering, with period photographs.

Taylor-Butler, Christine. *The Digestive System*. New York: Children's Press, 2008.
- A very good introduction to this subject.

Turner, Pamela S. *The Frog Scientist*, reprint ed. New York: Sandpiper, 2011.
- A book about the scientist who discovered the ill effects of pesticides on frogs.

Walker, Sally M. *Fossil Fish Found Alive: Discovering the Coelacanth*. Minneapolis, MN: Carolrhoda, 2002.
- The story of finding a fish once thought to be extinct, illustrated with color photographs.

Arts and Leisure

For Pre-K to Grade 4

Aliki. *William Shakespeare and the Globe*. New York: HarperCollins, 1999.
- A picture-book introduction to the Elizabethan theater.

Banks, Kate. *Max's Words*. Illus. Boris Kulikov. New York: Farrar, Straus & Giroux, 2006.
- A book about a little boy who decides to collect words.

Brown, Marc. *Your First Garden Book*. New York: Trumpet, 2009.
- Gardening projects for beginner.

Herzog, Brad. *Little Baseball*. Illus. Doug Bowles. Ann Arbor, MI: Sleeping Bear, 2011.
- A board book that introduces baseball to the youngest readers. See also *Little Football*.

Latch, William. *Can You Hear It?* New York: Abrams, 2006.
- An introduction to classical music for children from about second grade and up, with an accompanying CD. Produced with the Metropolitan Museum of Art.

Lipsey, Jennifer. *My Very Favorite Art Book: I Love to Paint*. Asheville, NC: Lark, 2005.
- A practical approach to art for elementary school children. One of a series by Lipsey, including *I Love to Draw*, *I Love to Collage*, and others.

Pulver, Robin. *Punctuation Takes a Vacation*. Illus. Lynn Rowe Reed. New York: Holiday, 2003.
- A comical picture-book story that illustrates the use of punctuation.

Raimondo, Joyce. *Imagine That: Activities and Adventures in Surrealism*. New York: Watson-Guptill, 2008.
- A great introduction to surrealism for young children, including hands-on activities. The first in the Art Explorers series, including *Express Yourself* (expressionism), *What's the Big Idea?* (abstract art), *Make It Pop* (pop art), and *Picture This* (impressionism), all by the same author.

Truss, Lynn. *Eats, Shoots & Leaves: Why, Commas Do Make a Difference*. Illus. Bonnie Timmons. New York: Putnam, 2006.
- Picture-book fun with punctuation; great for early elementary language study. A popular adult version, with the same author and title, also exists.

For Grades 4 and Above

Ancona, George. *Cutters, Carvers, and the Cathedral*. New York: Lothrop, 1995.
- A book about the building of St. John the Divine, the largest cathedral in the United States.

Aronson, Marc. *Art Attack: A Short Cultural History of the Avant-Garde*. New York: Clarion, 1998.
- An introduction to twentieth-century art.

Berman, Len. *The Greatest Moments in Sports*. New York: Sourcebooks Jabberwocky, 2009.
- Twenty-five episodes in modern sports, selected by a sportscaster whose personal biases are reflected. One of a series of interesting sports books by this author.

Bierhorst, John. *A Cry from the Earth: Music of the North American Indians.* Santa Fe, NM: Ancient City Press, 1992.
  - An introduction to American Indian music, song, and dance.

Carter, David A., and James Diaz. *The Elements of Pop-Up.* New York: Simon & Schuster, 1999.
  - A practical book on how to make pop-up books.

Crisfield, Deborah W. *The Everything Kids' Soccer Book: Rules, Techniques, and More about Your Favorite Sport.* New York: Adams Media, 2009.
  - One of the Everything Kids series of informative books about children's sports, including Bob Schaller's book on baseball, Schaller and Dave Harnish's on basketball, and Greg Jacobs's on football.

DK Publishing. *Dance.* New York: DK, 2012.
  - A composite book covering all aspects of dance, from history to dance movements.

Evans, Dilys. *Show and Tell: Exploring the Fine Art of Children's Book Illustration.* San Francisco: Chronicle Books, 2008.
  - An excellent introduction for children and adults.

Helsby, Genevieve. *Those Amazing Musical Instruments! Your Guide to the Orchestra Through Sounds and Stories.* New York: Sourcebooks Jabberwocky, 2007.
  - An exploration of the various musical instruments in the orchestra; includes a CD.

Hughes, Langston. *The First Book of Jazz.* New York: Ecco, 1997.
  - Originally written in 1955, still a fine introduction by a great poet.

LeBoutillier, Nate. *The Best of Everything Baseball Book.* Mankato, MN: Capstone, 2011.
  - A compendium of facts about baseball. The same author has a companion book on basketball.

Levine, Robert. *The Story of the Orchestra: Listen while You Learn about the Instruments, the Music and the Composers Who Wrote the Music!* Illus. Meredith Hamilton. New York: Black Dog & Leventhal, 2000.
  - An introduction to both classical music and to musical instruments.

Macaulay, David. *Cathedral: The Story of Its Construction.* Boston: Houghton Mifflin, 1973.
  - Just one of many informative picture books, including *Castle*, *Mosque*, and *Pyramid*, on the art and science of architecture.

Metropolitan Museum of Art. *Monet's Impressions.* New York: Chronicle Books, 2009.
  - An introduction to Monet, using the artist's own words and paintings.

——. *Vincent's Colors.* New York: Chronicle Books, 2005.
  - An introduction to Van Gogh, using the artist's own words and paintings.

Roche, Art. *Art for Kids: Comic Strips: Create Your Own Comic Strips from Start to Finish.* New York: Sterling, 2011.
  - A superb introduction for children. See also the author's *Cartooning*.

Temple, Kathryn. *Art for Kids: Drawing: The Only Drawing Book You'll Ever Need to Be the Artist You've Always Wanted to Be.* Asheville, NC: Lark, 2005.
  - An excellent resource for young artists.

Human Growth and Development

For Pre-K to Grade 4

Bang, Molly. *When Sophie Gets Angry.* New York: Blue Sky Press, 1999.
  - A picture-book story of a child dealing with anger that is frank and realistic.

Brown, Laurie Krasny, and Marc Brown. *What's the Big Secret? Talking about Sex with Girls and Boys.* Illus. Marc Brown. Boston: Little, Brown, 1997.
  - A good introduction for very young children with cartoon illustrations and accurate information. One of many similar books by this husband-and-wife team; see also *Dinosaurs Divorce*, *How to Be a Friend: A Guide to Making Friends and Keeping Them*, and *When Dinosaurs Die: A Guide to Understanding Death*.

Carlson, Nancy. *How to Lose All Your Friends.* New York: Puffin, 1997.

- A humorous look at bratty behavior—and how to avoid it.

Cole, Babette. *Mommy Laid an Egg! Or Where Do Babies Come From?* New York: Chronicle, 1996.
- A light-hearted but factually accurate introduction to sex and reproduction.

Ekster, Carol Gordon. *Where Am I Sleeping Tonight?* Illus. Sue Rama. Weaverville, CA: Boulden, 2008.
- A picture book describing the initial struggles and confusion facing two children when their parents divorce.

Goodman, Susan E. *The Truth about Poop.* Illus. Elwood H. Smith. New York: Viking, 2004.
- Perhaps more than we wanted to know about bodily elimination, but young readers will be captivated.

Harris, Robie H. *It's Not the Stork! A Book about Girls, Boys, Babies, Bodies, Families and Friends.* Illus. Michael Emberley. New York: Candlewick, 2008.
- About those sensitive issues parents have so much trouble discussing.

——. *Who Has What? All about Girls' Bodies and Boys' Bodies.* Illus. Nadine Bernard Westcott. New York: Candlewick, 2011.
- Accurate yet accessible answers to all those questions young people ask that many grownups wish they didn't.

Jeffers, Oliver. *The Heart and the Bottle.* New York: Philomel, 2010.
- A powerful exploration of grief and overcoming it, told with moving symbolism.

Kaplow, Julie, and Donna Pincus. *Samantha Jane's Missing Smile: A Story about Coping with the Loss of a Parent.* Illus. Beth Spiegel. Washington, DC: Magination, 2007.
- A realistically presented story of a young girl's coping with the death of her father.

Levins, Sandra. *Was It the Chocolate Pudding? A Story for Little Kids about Divorce.* Illus. Bryan Langdo. Washington, DC: American Psychological Association, 2005.
- A discussion about divorce for young children.

Meiners, Cheri J. *Cool Down and Work through Anger.* Minneapolis, MN: Free Spirit, 2010.
- Practical ways for children to cope with anger. One of the Learning to Get Along series, by the same author, which also includes the books *Join In and Play* and *Talk and Work It Out.*

Mills, Joyce C. *Gentle Willow: A Story for Children about Dying.* Illus. Michael Chesworth. Washington, DC: Magination, 1993.
- A book about accepting death—one's own and that of a loved one.

Newman, Lesléa. *Daddy, Papa, and Me.* Illus. Carol Thompson. Berkeley, CA: Tricycle Press, 2009.
- A toddler spends a day with its two dads, a gay couple; a companion book, *Mommy, Mama, and Me*, describes similar experiences but with a lesbian couple.

Riggs, Shannon. *Not in Room 204: Breaking the Silence of Abuse.* Illus. Jaime Zollars. New York: Whitman, 2007.
- A well-told story that raises awareness of child abuse at home—a difficult subject but one not to be ignored.

Rosen, Michael. *Michael Rosen's Sad Book.* Illus. Quentin Blake. New York: Candlewick, 2005.
- A moving book about dealing with grief; it is sad but very insightful.

Saltz, Gail. *Changing You: A Guide to Body Changes and Sexuality.* Illus. Lynn Avril Cravath. New York: Puffin, 2009.
- A factual but informal approach for readers about 6 and older.

Spelman, Cornelia Maude. *When I Miss You.* Illus. Kathy Parkinson. New York: Whitman, 2000.
- An animal family is used to explore human emotions, one of the Way I Feel series by this author, including *When I Feel Scared, When I Feel Jealous,* and others.

Stickney, Doris. *Water Bugs & Dragonflies: Explaining Death to Children.* Cleveland, OH: Pilgrim Press, 2004.
- Death is explained through the allegory of metamorphosis.

For Grades 4 and Above

Bailey, Jacqui. *Sex, Puberty, and All That Stuff: A Guide to Growing Up.* Illus. Jan McCafferty. Hauppauge, NY: Barron's Educational, 2004.
- A humorous approach with cartoon illustrations.

Beck, Debra. *My Feet Aren't Ugly! A Girl's Guide to Loving Herself from the Inside Out*, rev. ed. New York: Beaufort Books, 2011.
  - An amusing book designed to build self-confidence.

Belge, Kathy, and Marke Bieschke. *Queer: The Ultimate LBGT Guide for Teens.* San Francisco: Zest Books, 2011.
  - A humorous, personal, and honest approach to the subject.

Bode, Janet. *Death Is Hard to Live with: Teenagers and How They Cope with Loss.* New York: Delacorte, 1993.
  - A collection of personal stories written by teenagers.

Daldry, Jeremy. *The Teenage Guy's Survival Guide: The Real Deal on Girls, Growing Up and Other Guy Stuff.* Boston: Little, Brown, 1997.
  - Frank and occasionally irreverent, the American version of a British book titled *Boys Behaving Badly.*

Dee, Catherine. *The Girls' Guide to Life: Take Charge of Your Personal Life, Your School Time, Your Social Scene, and Much More!* 2nd ed. Boston: Little, Brown, 2005.
  - Information and accompanying activities on a wide variety of subjects of interest to girls about 10 and older.

Grollman, Earl A. *Straight Talk about Death for Teenagers: How to Cope with Losing Someone You Love.* Boston: Beacon Press, 1993.
  - A book that deals with a wide variety of issues, such as accidental death, suicide, long-term illness, and the death of a parent or a friend.

Harris, Robie H. *It's Perfectly Normal: Changing Bodies, Growing Up, Sex, and Sexual Health.* Illus. Michael Emberley. New York: Candlewick, 2009.
  - An excellent introduction for upper elementary readers.

Huegel, Kelly. *GLBTQ: The Survival Guide for Gay, Lesbian, Bisexual, Transgender, and Questioning Teens*, rev. ed. Minneapolis, MN: Free Spirit, 2011.
  - A valuable resource for teenage readers.

Pardes, Bronwen. *Doing It Right: Making Smart, Safe, and Satisfying Choices about Sex.* New York: Simon Pulse, 2013.
  - Frank discussions from a sex educator.

Savage, Dan. *It Gets Better: Coming Out, Overcoming Bullying, and Creating a Life Worth Living.* New York: Plume, 2012.
  - A collection of essays directed toward teens.

Stout, Glen. *Able to Play: Overcoming Physical Challenges.* New York: Sandpiper, 2012.
  - Personal stories of four professional athletes who have physical disabilities.

History, Society, and Culture

For Pre-K to Grade 4

Alexander, Heather. *A Child's Introduction to the World: Geography, Cultures, and People.* Illus. Meredith Hamilton. New York: Black Dog and Leventhal, 2010.
  - A colorful introduction to world cultures.

Aliki. *A Medieval Feast.* New York: HarperCollins, 1986.
  - Lively illustrations and interesting facts about a great occasion during the Middle Ages.

——. *Mummies Made in Egypt.* New York: Crowell, 1979.
  - A factual account of mummification, complete with detailed drawings.

Amery, Heather. *Then and Now*, rev. ed. Illus. Peter Firmin. London: Usborne, 2008.
  - A picture-book explanation of how things change over time.

Coombs, Rachel. *A Year in a Castle.* Minneapolis, MN: First Avenue, 2009.
  - A book illustrated in great detail and filled with interesting facts about Medieval life; one book in the Time Goes By series, including Nicholas Harris's *A Day in the City* and *A Year at a Farm* and Elizabeth Havercroft's *A Year on a Pirate Ship*, among many others.

Fowler, Alan. *Africa*. New York: Children's Press, 2002.
- One of several by this author for the Rookie Read-About Geography Series for very young children, including *Antarctica, Asia, Australia, Europe, North America*, and *South America*.

Frank, John. *The Tomb of the Boy King*. Illus. Tom Pohrt. New York: Farrar, Straus & Giroux, 2001.
- A picture-book account of the discovery of King Tutankhamen's tomb.

Knowlton, Jack. *Geography from A to Z: A Picture Glossary*. Illus. Harriet Barton. New York: HarperCollins, 1997.
- Arranged like dictionary, but with geographical terms; useful for early elementary readers; see also Knowlton's *Maps and Globes*, an introductory geography for very young children.

Mara, Will. *The Seven Continents*. New York: Children's Press, 2005.
- Geography for the very young, part of the Rookie Read-About Geography series.

Millard, Anne. *A Street through Time*. New York: DK Children, 1998.
- Young children watch history unfold as the panorama of history is revealed at a single riverside site over 12,000 years.

Ritchie, Scot. *Follow That Map! A First Book of Mapping Skills*. Toronto: Kids Can Press, 2009.
- A good introduction to maps and how to use them.

Smith, David J. *If the World Were a Village: A Book about the World's People*. Illus. Shelagh Armstrong. Toronto: Kids Can, 2002.
- A fascinating book that imagines the world's population as a village of 100 people. A good introduction to thinking about ecology.

For Grades 4 and Above

Bartoletti, Susan Campbell. *Black Potatoes: The Story of the Great Irish Famine*. Boston: Houghton Mifflin, 2001.
- The story of a bleak episode in nineteenth-century history.

Bealer, Alex W. *Only the Names Remain: The Cherokees and the Trail of Tears*. Boston: Little, Brown, 1972.
- The tragic tale of the forced Cherokee relocation in the 1830s.

Bowker, John. *World Religions: The Great Faiths Explored and Explained*, rev. ed. New York: DK Publishing, 2006.
- A fully illustrated examination of many of the world's great religions.

Chang, Ina. *A Separate Battle: Women and the Civil War*. New York: Dutton, 1991.
- The seldom-told story of the contributions of women during this national tragedy.

Colman, Penny. *Corpses, Coffins, and Crypts: A History of Burial*. New York: Holt, 1997.
- The intriguing survey of an unusual, and often ignored, subject.

——. *Rosie the Riveter: Women Working on the Home Front in World War II*. New York: Crown, 1995.
- A book about the contributions of women during World War II.

Cooper, Ilene. *The Dead Sea Scrolls*. Illus. John Thompson. New York: Morrow, 1997.
- A good introduction to the discovery and meaning of these ancient Jewish documents.

Deary, Terry. *Horrible History of the World*. Illus. Martin Brown. New York: Scholastic, 2007.
- Especially appealing to middle-school readers, part of the popular Horrible Histories Handbooks series; great fun, if not always entirely accurate.

Freedman, Russell. *Cowboys of the Wild West*. New York: Tickner & Fields, 1985.
- One of many fine works of historical nonfiction by this writer.

Giblin, James Cross. *Secrets of the Sphinx*. Illus. Bagram Ibatoulline. New York: Scholastic, 2004.
- An award-winning exploration of the theories surrounding a mysterious Egyptian sculpture.

Gombrich, E. H. *A Little History of the World*. Illus. Clifford Harper. New Haven, CT: Yale University Press, 2008.
- First written in German in 1935, still a remarkable feat, a brief overview of all human history.

Greenfeld, Howard. *The Hidden Children*. New York: Clarion, 1993.
- A gripping account of children saved from the Holocaust of World War II.

Ippisch, Hanneke. *Sky: A True Story of Resistance During World War II*. New York: Simon & Schuster, 1996.
- A book about the heroic efforts to rescue the Jews from the Holocaust, written by a member of the Dutch resistance. A moving work despite some stylistic impediments.

Kantar, Andrew. *29 Missing: The True and Tragic Story of the Disappearance of the* S.S. Edmund Fitzgerald. East Lansing: Michigan State University Press, 1998.
- The story of one of the most famous shipwrecks on the Great Lakes.

Levine, Ellen. *Darkness over Denmark: The Danish Resistance and the Rescue of the Jews*. New York: Holiday House, 2000.
- A good nonfiction companion to Lois Lowry's award-winning *Number the Stars*.

Marrin, Albert. *Year of Dust: The Story of the Dust Bowl*. New York: Puffin, 2009.
- An excellent description of the 1930s, with both back-story and warnings for the future. Superbly illustrated with period photographs.

McWhorter, Diane. *A Dream of Freedom: The Civil Rights Movement from 1954 to 1968*. New York: Scholastic, 2004.
- A book movingly illustrated with period photographs.

Meltzer, Milton, ed. *The Black Americans: A History in Their Own Words, 1619–1983*. New York: Crowell, 1984.
- A book filled with moving personal accounts.

——. *Brother, Can You Spare a Dime? The Great Depression: 1929–1933*. New York: New American Library, 1977.
- Powerful personal stories that recount the period.

Morimoto, Junko. *My Hiroshima*. 1987. New York: Puffin, 1990.
- The author's personal experiences as a youth in Hiroshima when the atomic bomb was dropped.

Murphy, Jim. *An American Plague: The True and Terrifying Story of the Yellow Fever Epidemic of 1793*. New York: Clarion, 2003.
- The story of a tragic and little-known episode.

——. *The Great Fire*. New York: Scholastic, 1995. An account of the great Chicago fire of 1871.

Myers, Walter Dean. *Now Is Your Time! The African-American Struggle for Freedom*. New York: HarperCollins, 1991.
- A book that recounts the individual stories of people involved in the civil rights movement.

Osborne, Mary Pope. *One World, Many Religions: The Way We Worship*. New York: Knopf, 1996.
- An overview of the beliefs and practices of seven major world religions.

Stanley, Jerry. *I Am an American: A True Story of Japanese Internment*. New York: Crown, 1994.
- A book about racial prejudice that resulted in the abuse of Japanese Americans during World War II.

Yen Mah, Adeline. *China: Land of Dragons and Emperors*. 2004. New York: Delacorte, 2009.
- An overview of China's long and turbulent history.

Biographies and Autobiographies

For Pre-K to Grade 4

Adler, David A. *Lou Gehrig: The Luckiest Man Alive*. Illus. Terry Widener. New York: Harcourt, 1997.
- A picture-book biography of the great baseball player.

Aliki. *The Story of Johnny Appleseed*. New York: Perfection Learning, 1971.
- The life of the man who planted apple trees and good will all over the Midwest in the early nineteenth century.

Anderson, M. T. *Handel, Who Knew What He Liked.* Illus. Kevin Hawkes. Cambridge, MA: Candlewick, 2001.
- A picture-book biography of the great eighteenth-century composer.

Bauer, Marion Dane. *Martin Luther King, Jr.* Illus. Jamie Smith. New York: Scholastic, 2009.
- One of a series of picture-book biographies.

Borden, Louise. *A. Lincoln and Me.* Illus. Ted Lewin. New York: Scholastic, 2009.
- A clever introduction to Abraham Lincoln, through the eyes of a modern-day boy who shares his birthday.

Brown, Don. *Odd Boy Out: Young Albert Einstein.* Boston: Houghton Mifflin, 2004.
- A picture-book story of the famous scientist's early years.

Bryant, Jen. *River of Words: The Story of William Carlos Williams.* Illus. Melissa Sweet. Grand Rapids, MI: Eerdmans, 2008.
- A picture-book story about the life of a famous American poet.

Fritz, Jean. *Bully for You, Teddy Roosevelt!* New York: Putnam, 1991.
- The life of the president told for younger readers; one of many picture-book biographies of American figures by Fritz.

Giovanni, Nikki. *Rosa.* Illus. Bryan Collier. New York: Holt, 2005.
- A brief, richly illustrated biography of Rosa Parks.

Greenfield, Eloise. *Mary McLeod Bethune.* 1977. Illus. Jerry Pinckney. New York: Crowell, 1994.
- A picture-book biography of a great African American educator.

Hill, Laban Carrick. *Dave the Potter.* Illus. Bryan Collier. New York: Little, Brown, 2010.
- A beautifully told story of the life of a slave in nineteenth-century South Carolina who became a celebrated potter.

Lawrence, Jacob. *Harriet and the Promised Land.* New York: Windmill, 1968.
- A picture-book biography of one-time slave and heroine of the Underground Railroad Harriet Tubman.

McCarthy, Meghan. *The Incredible Life of Balto.* New York: Knopf, 2011.
- A lively biography of the great Alaskan sled dog.

McDonnell, Patrick. *Me . . . Jane.* New York: Little, Brown, 2011.
- A brief picture-book biography of Jane Goodall, the celebrated primate expert.

Quackenbush, Robert. *Mark Twain? What Kind of a Name Is That?* New York: Aladdin, 1990.
- A picture-book biography of the famous writer, appropriately light-hearted.

Raboff, Ernest. *Pablo Picasso.* New York: Doubleday, 1968.
- A picture-book biography of the celebrated artist; one of a series.

Sis, Peter. *Starry Messenger: Galileo Galilei.* New York: Farrar, Straus & Giroux, 1996.
- A picture book about the life of the great astronomer.

——. *The Tree of Life: Charles Darwin.* New York: Farrar, Straus & Giroux, 2003.
- A picture book about the life of the scientist who articulated the theory of evolution.

Stanley, Diane, and Peter Vennema. *Good Queen Bess: The Story of Elizabeth I of England.* Illus. Diane Stanley. New York: Four Winds, 1990.
- A picture-book biography of the great English queen; one of many biographies from this husband-and-wife team.

——. *Shaka: King of the Zulus.* Illus. Diane Stanley. New York: Morrow, 1988.
- A picture-book biography of a famous African warrior-king.

Steig, William. *When Everybody Wore a Hat.* New York: HarperCollins, 2003.
- A picture-book autobiography of a popular children's author and illustrator.

Venezia, Mike. *The Beatles.* New York: Scholastic, 1997.
- A picture-book biography of the famed band.

For Grades 4 and Above

Allen, Thomas B. *Harriet Tubman, Secret Agent: How Daring Slaves and Free Blacks Spied for the Union During the Civil War.* Washington, DC: National Geographic, 2006.
- A book filled with fascinating information about the Underground Railroad.

Andronik, Catherine M. *Wildly Romantic: The English Romantic Poets: The Mad, the Bad and the Dangerous.* New York: Henry Holt, 2007.
- A lively collective biography of Wordsworth, Coleridge, Byron, Shelley, and Keats.

Bitton-Jackson, Livia. *I Have Lived a Thousand Years: Growing Up in the Holocaust.* New York: Simon & Schuster, 1997.
- The personal account of a Holocaust survivor.

Bruchac, Joseph. *A Boy Called Slow: The True Story of Sitting Bull.* New York: Philomel, 1995.
- An engaging account of the great Lakota chief.

——. *Pocahontas.* New York: Harcourt, 2003.
- The story of the Powhatan princess, told from two points of view—hers and John Smith's.

Byars, Betsy. *The Moon and I.* New York: Harper Collins, 1996.
- The autobiography of an award-winning children's author.

Dahl, Roald. *Boy: Tales of Childhood.* New York: Farrar, Straus & Giroux, 1984.
- Lively reminiscences of the author of *Charlie and the Chocolate Factory.*

Engle, Margarita. *The Poet Slave of Cuba: A Biography of Juan Francisco Manzano.* New York: Holt, 2006.
- A verse biography of a celebrated Cuban poet, who was also a slave.

Ferris, Jeri. *Native American Doctor: The Story of Susan La Flesche Picotte.* Minneapolis, MN: Carolrhoda, 1991.
- A book about the first American Indian woman to graduate from medical school.

Fleischman, Sid. *Escape! The Story of the Great Houdini.* New York: Greenwillow, 2006.
- A book about the life of the fascinating escape artist.

Frank, Anne. *The Diary of a Young Girl: The Definitive Edition.* Ed. Otto H. Frank and Mirjam Pressler. Trans. Susan Massotty. New York: Doubleday, 1995.
- A young girl's candid reflections on her life while hiding from the Nazis in Amsterdam during World War II; perhaps the most famous personal memoir to come out of the war.

Freedman, Russell. *Confucius and the Golden Rule.* New York: Clarion, 2002.
- Life and thought of the great Chinese philosopher.

——. *Eleanor Roosevelt: A Life of Discovery.* New York: Clarion, 1993.
- The life of the famed first lady; one of many illustrated biographies by Freedman.

——. *Lincoln: A Photobiography.* New York: Clarion, 1987.
- The life of the great Civil War president, illustrated with archival material.

Fritz, Jean. *The Double Life of Pocahontas.* New York: Puffin, 1983.
- The story of the life of the famous Powhatan princess who was torn between two worlds.

——. *Homesick: My Own Story.* New York: Putnam, 1982.
- A children's author recounting of her own childhood.

Gerstein, Mordicai. *What Charlie Heard.* New York: Farrar, Straus & Giroux, 2002.
- The story of the life of American classical composer Charles Ives.

Gibbin, James Cross. *Charles A. Lindbergh: A Human Hero.* New York: Clarion, 1998.
- The story of the life of the celebrated pilot who first flew solo over the Atlantic.

Heiligman, Deborah. *Charles and Emma: The Darwins' Leap of Faith.* New York: Holt, 2009.

- The story of the personal and professional life of Charles Darwin.

Kherdian, David. *The Road from Home: The Story of an Armenian Girl*. New York: Greenwillow, 1979. (Later re-issued with the subtitle *A True Story of Courage, Survival and Hope*.)
- A book about the childhood experiences of the author's mother, a survivor of the Armenian holocaust of 1915.

Krull, Kathleen. *Lives of the Artists: Masterpieces, Messes (and What the Neighbors Thought)*. Illus. Kathryn Hewitt. Orlando, FL: Harcourt, 1995.
- A lively collection of brief biographies.

——. *Lives of the Presidents: Fame, Shame (and What the Neighbors Thought)*. Illus. Kathryn Hewitt. Orlando, FL: Harcourt, 1998.
- Another lively collection of brief biographies.

Lanier, Shannon, and Jane Feldman. *Jefferson's Children: The Story of One American Family*. New York: Random House, 2000.
- A book about the multiracial family legacy of the third president.

Latham, Jean Lee. *Carry On, Mr. Bowditch*. New York: Houghton Mifflin, 1955.
- A fictionalized biography of an unlikely hero, an American colonial mathematician.

Matthews, Elizabeth. *Different Like Coco*. New York: Candlewick, 2007.
- The story of the life of the famed fashion designer Coco Chanel.

Mora, Pat. *A Library for Juana: The World of Sor Juana Inéz*. Illus. Beatriz Vidal. New York: Knopf, 2002.
- A biography of an unusual seventeenth-century female scholar in Mexico.

Myers, Walter Dean. *At Her Majesty's Request: An African Princess in Victorian England*. New York: Scholastic, 1999.
- The life of an orphaned African princess raised in England under the protection of Queen Victoria.

Naylor, Phyllis Reynolds. *How I Came to Be a Writer*. New York: Atheneum, 2001.

- The memoir of the author of *Shiloh*, focusing on her writing.

Parks, Rosa, with Jim Haskins. *I Am Rosa Parks*. Illus. Will Clay. New York: Dial, 1997.
- An autobiographical account of the life of the famous civil rights leader.

Rappaport, Doreen. *John's Secret Dreams: The Life of John Lennon*. Illus. Bryan Collier. New York: Hyperion, 2004.
- A book about the life of the most controversial member of the Beatles.

Redsand, Anna. *Viktor Frankl: A Life Worth Living*. New York: Clarion, 2006.
- The biography of a Holocaust survivor and renowned psychiatrist.

Reich, Susanna. *Clara Schumann: Piano Virtuoso*. New York: Clarion, 1999.
- A book about one of the few celebrated female composers and musicians of the nineteenth century.

Reiss, Johanna. *The Upstairs Room*. New York: HarperCollins, 1972.
- A stark autobiographical account of a Dutch girl's survival during World War II.

Severance, John B. *Gandhi: Great Soul*. New York: Clarion, 1997.
- A book about the life of Mahatma Gandhi.

Siegal, Aranka. *Upon the Head of a Goat: A Childhood in Hungary, 1939–1944*. New York: Farrar, Straus & Giroux, 1985.
- An autobiographical account of a Jewish girl's life during World War II.

Singer, Isaac Bashevis. *A Day of Pleasures: Stories of a Boy Growing Up in Warsaw*. New York: Farrar, Straus & Giroux, 1969.
- Reminiscences of a Nobel Prize–winning author.

Stevenson, Augusta. *George Washington: Young Leader*. New York: Aladdin, 1971.
- A fictionalized biography focusing on the first president's youth; part of the Childhood of Famous Americans series.

Szabo, Corinne. *Sky Pioneer: A Photobiography of Amelia Earhart*. Washington, DC: National Geographic, 1997.
- The story of the adventurous life of the pioneering woman pilot.

Thomas, Jane Resh. *Behind the Mask: The Life of Queen Elizabeth I*. New York: Clarion, 1998.
- A handsome biography of the great English queen.

Tillage, Leon Walter. *Leon's Story*. Illus. Susan L. Roth. New York: Farrar, Straus & Giroux, 1997.
- An autobiographical account of an African American's struggle in the mid-twentieth century.

Van der Rol, Ruud, and Rian Verhoeven. *Anne Frank: Beyond the Diary*. New York: Viking, 1993.
- Richly illustrated with photographs, an excellent companion to the famous diary.

Yates, Elizabeth. *Amos Fortune, Free Man*. New York: Dutton, 1950.
- The story of a nineteenth-century American slave who managed to buy his freedom.

Appendix

Children's Book Awards

American Awards

The Newbery Medal

The Newbery Medal is named for John Newbery, a British entrepreneur who pioneered children's book publishing in the eighteenth century. The award is, however, an American award, presented annually by the American Library Association to the most distinguished contribution to children's literature published in the United States. Runners up are given Newbery Honor Awards, but in the interest of space, Honor books have been omitted from here, except for those from 2000 and beyond; the complete list is readily found at the Newbery Award online site. As with any other such award, there has not always been general agreement with the decisions. However, the list does include some of the finest writing for young people in the past century.

1922	*The Story of Mankind* by Hendrik Willem van Loon, Liveright
1923	*The Voyages of Doctor Dolittle* by Hugh Lofting, Lippincott
1924	*The Dark Frigate* by Charles Hawes, Little, Brown
1925	*Tales from Silver Lands* by Charles Finger, Doubleday
1926	*Shen of the Sea* by Arthur Bowie Chrisman, Dutton
1927	*Smoky, the Cowhorse* by Will James, Scribner's
1928	*Gay Neck, the Story of a Pigeon* by Dhan Gopal Mukerji, Dutton
1929	*The Trumpeter of Krakow* by Eric P. Kelly, Macmillan
1930	*Hitty, Her First Hundred Years* by Rachel Field, Macmillan
1931	*The Cat Who Went to Heaven* by Elizabeth Coatsworth, Macmillan
1932	*Waterless Mountain* by Laura Adams Armer, Longmans, Green (McKay)
1933	*Young Fu of the Upper Yangtze* by Elizabeth Foreman Lewis, Winston
1934	*Invincible Louisa: The Story of the Author of* Little Women by Cornelia Meigs, Little, Brown
1935	*Dobry* by Monica Shannon, Viking
1936	*Caddie Woodlawn* by Carol Ryrie Brink, Macmillan
1937	*Roller Skates* by Ruth Sawyer, Viking
1938	*The White Stag* by Kate Seredy, Viking
1939	*Thimble Summer* by Elizabeth Enright, Holt, Rinehart & Winston
1940	*Daniel Boone* by James Daugherty, Viking
1941	*Call It Courage* by Armstrong Sperry, Macmillan
1942	*The Matchlock Gun* by Walter D. Edmonds, Dodd, Mead
1943	*Adam of the Road* by Elizabeth Janet Gray, Viking
1944	*Johnny Tremain* by Esther Forbes, Houghton Mifflin
1945	*Rabbit Hill* by Robert Lawson, Viking

1946 *Strawberry Girl* by Lois Lenski, Lippincott

1947 *Miss Hickory* by Carolyn Sherwin Bailey, Viking

1948 *The Twenty-One Balloons* by William Pène du Bois, Viking

1949 *King of the Wind* by Marguerite Henry, Rand McNally

1950 *The Door in the Wall* by Marguerite de Angeli, Doubleday

1951 *Amos Fortune, Free Man* by Elizabeth Yates, Aladdin

1952 *Ginger Pye* by Eleanor Estes, Harcourt Brace Jovanovich

1953 *Secret of the Andes* by Ann Nolan Clark, Viking

1954 *… and Now Miguel* by Joseph Krumgold, Crowell

1955 *The Wheel on the School* by Meindert DeJong, Harper

1956 *Carry On, Mr. Bowditch* by Jean Lee Latham, Houghton Mifflin

1957 *Miracles on Maple Hill* by Virginia Sorensen, Harcourt Brace Jovanovich

1958 *Rifles for Watie* by Harold Keith, Crowell

1959 *The Witch of Blackbird Pond* by Elizabeth George Speare, Houghton Mifflin

1960 *Onion John* by Joseph Krumgold, Crowell

1961 *Island of the Blue Dolphins* by Scott O'Dell, Houghton Mifflin

1962 *The Bronze Bow* by Elizabeth George Speare, Houghton Mifflin

1963 *A Wrinkle in Time* by Madeline L'Engle, Farrar, Straus & Giroux

1964 *It's Like This, Cat* by Emily Cheney Neville, Harper

1965 *Shadow of a Bull* by Maia Wojciechowska, Atheneum

1966 *I, Juan de Pareja* by Elizabeth Borten de Trevino, Farrar, Straus & Giroux

1967 *Up a Road Slowly* by Irene Hunt, Follett

1968 *From the Mixed-up Files of Mrs. Basil E. Frankweiler* by E. L. Konigsburg, Atheneum

1969 *The High King* by Lloyd Alexander, Holt, Rinehart & Winston

1970 *Sounder* by William H. Armstrong, Harper

1971 *Summer of the Swans* by Betsy Byars, Viking

1972 *Mrs. Frisby and the Rats of NIMH* by Robert C. O'Brien, Atheneum

1973 *Julie of the Wolves* by Jean Craighead George, Harper

1974 *The Slave Dancer* by Paula Fox, Bradbury

1975 *M. C. Higgins, the Great* by Virginia Hamilton, Macmillan

1976 *The Grey King* by Susan Cooper, Atheneum

1977 *Roll of Thunder, Hear My Cry* by Mildred D. Taylor, Dial Press

1978 *Bridge to Terabithia* by Katherine Paterson, Crowell

1979 *The Westing Game* by Ellen Raskin, Dutton

1980 *A Gathering of Days: A New England Girl's Journal 1830–32* by Joan Blos, Scribner

1981 *Jacob Have I Loved* by Katherine Paterson, Cromwell

1982 *A Visit to William Blake's Inn: Poems for Innocent and Experienced* by Nancy Willard, Harcourt

1983 *Dicey's Song* by Cynthia Voigt, Atheneum

1984 *Dear Mr. Henshaw* by Beverly Cleary, Morrow

1985 *The Hero and the Crown* by Robin McKinley, Greenwillow (Morrow)

1986 *Sarah, Plain and Tall* by Patricia MacLachlan, Harper

1987 *The Whipping Boy* by Sid Fleischman, Greenwillow (Morrow)

1988   *Lincoln: A Photobiography* by Russell Freedman, Clarion/Houghton Mifflin

1989   *Joyful Noise: Poems for Two Voices* by Paul Fleischman, Harper

1990   *Number the Stars* by Lois Lowry, Houghton Mifflin

1991   *Maniac Magee* by Jerry Spinelli, Little, Brown

1992   *Shiloh* by Phillis Reynolds Naylor, Atheneum

1993   *Missing May* by Cynthia Ryland, Orchard

1994   *The Giver* by Lois Lowry, Houghton Mifflin

1995   *Walk Two Moons* by Sharon Creech, HarperCollins

1996   *The Midwife's Apprentice* by Karen Cushman, Houghton Mifflin

1997   *The View from Saturday* by E. L. Konigsburg, Atheneum

1998   *Out of the Dust* by Karen Hesse, Scholastic

1999   *Holes* by Louis Sachar, Farrar, Straus & Giroux

2000   *Bud, Not Buddy* by Christopher Paul Curtis, Delacorte
        Honor Books: *Getting Near to Baby* by Audrey Couloumbis, Putnam; *26 Fairmount Avenue* by Tomie de Paola, Putnam; *Our Only May Amelia* by Jennifer L. Holm, HarperCollins

2001   *A Year Down Yonder* by Richard Peck, Dial
        Honor Books: *Hope Was Here* by Joan Bauer, Putnam; *The Wanderer* by Sharon Creech, HarperCollins; *Because of Winn-Dixie* by Kate DiCamillo, Candlewick; *Joey Pigza Loses Control* by Jack Gantos, Farrar, Straus & Giroux

2002   *A Single Shard* by Linda Sue Park, Houghton Mifflin
        Honor Books: *Everything on a Waffle* by Polly Horvath, Farrar, Straus & Giroux; *Carver: A Life in Poems* by Marilyn Nelson, Front Street

2003   *Crispin: The Cross of Lead* by Avi, Hyperion
        Honor Books: *The House of the Scorpion* by Nancy Farmer, Atheneum; *Pictures of Hollis Woods* by Patricia Reilly Giff, Random House; *Hoot* by Carl Hiaasen, Knopf; *A Corner of the Universe* by Ann M. Martin, Scholastic; *Surviving the Applewhites* by Stephanie S. Tolan, HarperCollins

2004   *The Tale of Despereaux: Being the Story of a Mouse, a Princess, Some Soup, and a Spool of Thread* by Kate DiCamillo, Candlewick
        Honor Books: *Olive's Ocean* by Kevin Henkes, Greenwillow; *An American Plague: The True and Terrifying Story of the Yellow Fever Epidemic of 1793* by Jim Murphy, Clarion

2005   *Kira-Kira* by Cynthia Kadohata, Atheneum
        Honor Books: *Al Capone Does My Shirts* by Gennifer Choldenko, Putnam; *The Voice that Challenged a Nation: Marion Anderson and the Struggle for Equal Rights* by Russell Freedman, Clarion; *Lizzie Bright and the Buckminster Boy* by Gary D. Schmidt, Clarion

2006   *Criss Cross* by Lynne Rae Perkins, Greenwillow
        Honor Books: *Whittington* by Alan Armstrong, Random House; *Hitler Youth: Growing Up in Hitler's Shadow* by Susan Campbell Bartoletti, Scholastic; *Princess Academy* by Shannon Hale, Bloomsbury; *Show Way* by Jacqueline Woodson, Putnam

2007   *The Higher Power of Lucky* by Susan Patron, Simon & Schuster
        Honor Books: *Penny from Heaven* by Jennifer L. Holm, Random House; *Hattie Big Sky* by Kirby Larson, Delacorte; *Rules* by Cynthia Lord, Scholastic

2008   *Good Masters! Sweet Ladies! Voices from a Medieval Village* by Laura Amy Schlitz, Candlewick
        Honor Books: *Elijah of Buxton* by Christopher Paul Curtis, Scholastic; *The Wednesday Wars* by Gary D. Schmidt, Clarion; *Feathers* by Jacqueline Woodson, Putnam

2009   *The Graveyard Book* by Neil Gaiman, illustrated by Dave McKean, HarperCollins
        Honor Books: *The Underneath* by Kathi Appelt, illustrated by David Small, Atheneum; *The Surrender Tree: Poems of Cuba's Struggle for Freedom* by Margarita Engle, Henry Holt; *Savvy* by Ingrid Law, Dial/Walden Media; *After Tupac & D Foster* by Jacqueline Woodson, G.P. Putnam's Sons

2010   *When You Reach Me* by Rebecca Stead, Random House

Honor Books: *Claudette Colvin: Twice Toward Justice* by Phillip Hoose, Farrar, Straus & Giroux; *The Evolution of Calpurnia Tate* by Jacqueline Kelly, Henry Holt; *Where the Mountain Meets the Moon* by Grace Lin, Little, Brown; *The Mostly True Adventures of Homer P. Figg* by Rodman Philbrick, Scholastic, Inc.

2011   *Moon over Manifest* by Clare Vanderpool, Delacorte Press
Honor Books:*Turtle in Paradise* by Jennifer L. Holm, Random House; *Heart of a Samurai* by Margi Preus, Amulet Books; *Dark Emperor and Other Poems of the Night* by Joyce Sidman, Houghton Mifflin; *One Crazy Summer* by Rita Williams-Garcia, Amistad

2012   *Dead End in Norvelt* by Jack Gantos, Farrar, Straus & Giroux
Honor Books: *Inside Out & Back Again* by Thanhha Lai, HarperCollins; *Breaking Stalin's Nose* by Eugene Yelchin, Henry Holt

2013   *The One and Only Ivan* by Katherine Applegate, HarperCollins
Honor Books: *Splendors and Glooms* by Laura Amy Schlitz, Candlewick; *Bomb: The Race to Build—and Steal—the World's Most Dangerous Weapon* by Steve Sheinkin, Roaring Brook Press; *Three Times Lucky* by Sheila Turnage, Dial Books

The Caldecott Medal

Named for the British illustrator Randolph Caldecott, the Caldecott Medal has been awarded annually since 1938 by the American Library Association for the most distinguished picture book published in the United States. Runners up are given Caldecott Honor Awards, but in the interest of space, Honor books have been omitted here, except for those from 2000 and beyond; the complete list is readily found at the Caldecott Award online site. The Caldecott Award is given to the illustrator, not the writer. Unless indicated otherwise, the illustrator is the author.

1938   *Animals of the Bible* by Helen Dean Fish, illustrated by Dorothy P. Lathrop, Stokes

1939   *Mei Li* by Thomas Handforth, Doubleday

1940   *Abraham Lincoln* by Ingri and Edgar Parin d'Aulaire, Doubleday

1941   *They Were Strong and Good* by Robert Lawson, Viking

1942   *Make Way for Ducklings* by Robert McCloskey, Viking

1943   *The Little House* by Virginia Lee Burton, Houghton Mifflin

1944   *Many Moons* by James Thurber, illustrated by Louis Slobodkin, Harcourt Brace Jovanovich

1945   *Prayer for a Child* by Rachel Field, illustrated by Elizabeth Orton Jones, Macmillan

1946   *The Rooster Crows …*, illustrated by Maud and Miska Petersham, Macmillan

1947   *The Little Island* by Golden MacDonald, illustrated by Leonard Weisgard, Doubleday

1948   *White Snow, Bright Snow* by Alvin Tresselt, illustrated by Roger Duvoisin, Lothrop

1949   *The Big Snow* by Berta and Elmer Hader, Macmillan

1950   *Song of the Swallows* by Leo Politi, Scribner's

1951   *The Egg Tree* by Katherine Milhouse, Scribner's

1952   *Finders Keepers* by William Lipkind, illustrated by Nicholas Mordvinoff, Harcourt Brace Jovanovich

1953   *The Biggest Bear* by Lynd Ward, Houghton Mifflin

1954   *Madeline's Rescue* by Ludwig Bemelmans, Viking

1955   *Cinderella, or the Little Glass Slipper* by Charles Perrault, translated and illustrated by Marcia Brown, Scribner's

1956   *Frog Went A-Courtin'* edited by John Langstaff, illustrated by Feodor Rojankovsky, Harcourt Brace Jovanovich

1957   *A Tree Is Nice* by Janice May Udry, illustrated by Marc Simont, Harper

1958   *Time of Wonder* by Robert McCloskey, Viking

1959   *Chanticleer and the Fox,* adapted from Chaucer and illustrated by Barbara Cooney, Crowell

1960   *Nine Days to Christmas* by Marie Hall Ets and Aurora Labastida, illustrated by Marie Hall Ets, Viking

1961   *Baboushka and the Three Kings* by Ruth Robbins, illustrated by Nicolas Sidjakov, Parnassus

1962   *Once a Mouse …* by Marcia Brown, Scribner's

1963   *The Snowy Day* by Ezra Jack Keats, Viking

1964   *Where the Wild Things Are* by Maurice Sendak, Harper

1965   *May I Bring a Friend?* by Beatrice Schenk de Regniers, illustrated by Beni Montresor, Atheneum

1966   *Always Room for One More* by Sorche Nic Leodhas, illustrated by Nonny Hogrogian, Holt, Rinehart & Winston

1967   *Sam, Bangs & Moonshine* by Evaline Ness, Holt, Rinehart & Winston

1968   *Drummer Hoff* by Barbara Emberley, illustrated by Ed Emberley, PrenticeHall

1969   *The Fool of the World and the Flying Ship* by Arthur Ransome, illustrated by Uri Shulevitz, Farrar, Straus & Giroux

1970   *Sylvester and the Magic Pebble* by William Steig, Windmill (Simon & Schuster)

1971   *A Story A Story* by Gail E. Haley, Atheneum

1972   *One Fine Day* by Nonny Hogrogian, Macmillan

1973   *The Funny Little Woman* retold by Arlene Mosel, illustrated by Blair Lent, Dutton

1974   *Duffy and the Devil* by Harve Zemach, illustrated by Margot Zemach, Farrar, Straus & Giroux

1975   *Arrow to the Sun* adapted and illustrated by Gerald McDermott, Viking

1976   *Why Mosquitoes Buzz in People's Ears* retold by Verna Aardema, illustrated by Leo and Diane Dillon, Dial Press

1977   *Ashanti to Zulu: African Traditions* by Margaret Musgrove, illustrated by Leo and Diane Dillon, Dial Press

1978   *Noah's Ark* by Peter Spier, Doubleday

1979   *The Girl Who Loved Wild Horses* by Paul Goble, Bradbury

1980   *Ox-Cart Man* by Donald Hall, illustrated by Barbara Cooney, Viking

1981   *Fables* by Arnold Lobel, Harper

1982   *Jumanji* by Chris Van Allsburg, Houghton Mifflin

1983   *Shadow* by Blaise Cendrars, illustrated by Marcia Brown, Scribner's

1984   *The Glorious Flight: Across the Channel with Louis Blériot July 25, 1909* by Alice and Martin Provensen, Viking

1985   *Saint George and the Dragon* by Margaret Hodges, illustrated by Trina Schart Hyman, Little, Brown

1986   *The Polar Express* by Chris van Allsburg, Houghton Mifflin

1987   *Hey, Al* by Arthur Yorinks, illustrated by Richard Egielski, Farrar, Straus & Giroux

1988   *Owl Moon* by Jane Yolen, illustrated by John Schoenherr, Philomel (Putnam)

1989   *Song and Dance Man* by Karen Ackerman, illustrated by Stephen Gammell, Knopf

1990   *Lon Po Po: A Red-Riding Hood Story from China* by Ed Young, Philomel (Putnam)

1991   *Black and White* by David Macaulay, Houghton Mifflin

1992   *Tuesday* by David Wiesner, Clarion

1993   *Mirette on the High Wire* by Emily Arnold McCully, Putnam

1994   *Grandfather's Journey* by Allen Say, Houghton Mifflin

1995   *Smoky Night* by Eve Bunting, illustrated by David Diaz, Harcourt

1996   *Officer Buckle and Gloria* by Peggy Rathmann, Putnam

1997   *Golem* by David Wisniewski, Clarion

1998   *Rapunzel* by Paul O. Zelinsky, Dutton

1999   *Snowflake Bentley* by Jacqueline Briggs Martin, illustrated by Mary Azarian, Houghton Mifflin

2000   *Joseph Had a Little Overcoat* by Simms Taback, Viking
          Honor Books: *Sector 7* by David Wiesner, Clarion; *The Ugly Duckling* by Jerry Pinkney, Morrow; *When Sophie Gets Angry—Really, Really Angry …* by Molly Bang, Scholastic; *A Child's Calendar* by John Updike, illustrated by Trina Schart Hyman, Holiday

2001   *So You Want to Be President?* by Judith St. George, illustrated by David Small, Philomel
Honor Books: *Casey at the Bat* by Ernest Thayer, illustrated by Christopher Bing, Handprint; *Click, Clack, Moo: Cows That Type* by Doreen Cronin, illustrated by Betsy Lewin, Simon & Schuster; *Olivia* by Ian Falconer, Atheneum

2002   *The Three Pigs* by David Wiesner, Clarion/Houghton Mifflin
Honor Books: *The Dinosaurs of Waterhouse Hawkins* by Barbara Kerley, illustrated by Brian Selznick, Scholastic; *Martin's Big Words: The Life of Dr. Martin Luther King, Jr.* by Doreen Rappaport, illustrated by Bryan Collier, Hyperion; *The Stray Dog* by Marc Simont, HarperCollins

2003   *My Friend Rabbit* by Eric Rohmann, Roaring Brook
Honor Books: *The Spider and the Fly* by Mary Howitt, illustrated by Tony DiTerlizzi, Simon & Schuster; *Hondo and Fabian* by Peter McCarty, Holt; *Noah's Ark* by Jerry Pinkney, Seastar/North-South

2004   *The Man Who Walked between the Towers* by Mordicai Gerstein, Roaring Brook Press
Honor Books: *Ella Sarah Gets Dressed* by Margaret Chodos-Irvine, Harcourt; *What Do You Do with a Tail Like This?* by Steve Jenkins and Robin Page, Houghton Mifflin; *Don't Let the Pigeon Drive the Bus* by Mo Willems, Hyperion

2005   *Kitten's First Full Moon* by Kevin Henkes, Greenwillow
Honor Books: *The Red Book* by Barbara Lehman, Houghton Mifflin; *Coming on Home Soon* by Jacqueline Woodson, illustrated by E. B. Lewis, Putnam; *Knuffle Bunny: A Cautionary Tale* by Mo Willems, Hyperion

2006   *The Hello, Goodbye Window* by Norton Juster, illustrated by Chris Raschka, Hyperion
Honor Books: *Rosa* by Nikki Giovanni, illustrated by Bryan Collier, Henry Holt; *Zen Shorts* by Jon J. Muth, Scholastic; *Hot Air: The (Mostly) True Story of the First Hot-Air Balloon Ride* by Marjorie Priceman, Simon & Schuster; *Song of the Water Boatman and Other Pond Poems* by Joyce Sidman, illustrated by Beckie Prange, Houghton Mifflin

2007   *Flotsam* by David Wiesner, Clarion
Honor Books: *Gone Wild: An Endangered Animal Alphabet* by David McLimans, Walker; *Moses: When Harriet Tubman Led Her People to Freedom* by Carole Boston Weatherford, Hyperion

2008   *The Invention of Hugo Cabret* by Brian Selznick, Scholastic
Honor Books: *Henry's Freedom Box: A True Story from the Underground Railroad* by Ellen Levine, illustrated by Kadir Nelson, Scholastic; *First the Egg* by Laura Vaccaro Seeger, Roaring Brook/Neal Porter; *The Wall: Growing Up Behind the Iron Curtain* by Peter Sis, Farrar, Straus & Giroux/Frances Foster; *Knuffle Bunny Too: A Case of Mistaken Identity* by Mo Willems, Hyperion

2009   *The House in the Night* by Susan Marie Swanson, illustrated by Beth Krommes, Houghton Mifflin
Honor Books: *A Couple of Boys Have the Best Week Ever* by Marla Frazee, Harcourt; *How I Learned Geography* by Uri Shulevitz, Farrar, Straus & Giroux; *A River of Words: The Story of William Carlos Williams* by Jen Bryant, illustrated by Melissa Sweet, Eerdmans

2010   *The Lion & the Mouse* by Jerry Pinkney, Little, Brown
Honor Books: *All the World* by Liz Garton Scanlon, illustrated by Marla Frazee, Beach Lane Books; *Red Sings from Treetops: A Year in Colors* by Joyce Sidman, illustrated by Pamela Zagarenski, Houghton Mifflin Harcourt

2011   *A Sick Day for Amos McGee* by Philip C. Stead, illustrated by Erin E. Stead, Roaring Brook Press
Honor Books: *Dave the Potter: Artist, Poet, Slave* by Laban Carrick Hill, illustrated by Bryan Collier, Little, Brown; *Interrupting Chicken* by David Ezra Stein, Candlewick

2012   *A Ball for Daisy* by Chris Raschka, Random House
Honor Books: *Blackout* by John Rocco, Disney; *Grandpa Green* by Lane Smith, Roaring Brook Press; *Me ... Jane* by Patrick McDonnell, Little, Brown

2013   *This Is Not My Hat* by Jon Klassen, Candlewick
Honor Books: *Creepy Carrots!* by Aaron Reynolds, illustrated by Peter Brown, Simon & Schuster; *Extra Yarn* by Mac Barnett, illustrated by Jon Klassen, HarperCollins Publishers; *Green* by Laura Vaccaro Seeger, Roaring Brook Press; *One Cool Friend* by Toni Buzzeo, illustrated by David Small, Dial Books; *Sleep Like a Tiger* by Mary Logue, illustrated by Pamela Zagarenski, Houghton Mifflin

The Mildred L. Batchelder Award

Presented annually by the American Library Association, this award recognizes the most outstanding children's book originally translated from a language other than English.

1968   *The Little Man* by Erich Kastner, translated by James Kirkup, illustrated by Rich Schreiter, Knopf, 1966

1969   *Don't Take Teddy* by Babbis Friis-Baastad, translated by Lise Somme McKinnon, Scribner, 1967

1970   *Wildcat under Glass* by Alki Zei, translated by Edward Fenton, Holt, Rinehart & Winston, 1968

1971   *In the Land of Ur: The Discovery of Ancient Mesopotamia* by Hans Baumann, translated by Stella Humphries, illustrated by Hans Peter Renner, Pantheon Books, 1969

1972   *Friedrich* by Hans Peter Richter, translated by Edite Kroll, Holt, Rinehart & Winston, 1970

1973   *Pulga* by Siny Rose Van Iterson, translated by Alexander and Alison Gode, Morrow, 1971

1974   *Petros' War* by Alki Zei, translated by Edward Fenton, Dutton, 1972

1975   *An Old Tale Carved Out of Stone* by Aleksandr M. Linevski, translated by Maria Polushkin, Crown, 1973

1976   *The Cat and Mouse Who Shared a House* by Ruth Hurlimann, translated by Anthea Bell, Walck, 1974

1977   *The Leopard* by Cecil Bodker, translated by Gunnar Poulsen, Atheneum, 1975

1978   No award given

1979   *Konrad* by Christine Nostlinger, translated by Anthea Bell, illustrated by Carol Nicklaus, Watts, 1977, and *Rabbit Island* by Jorg Steiner, translated by Ann Conrad Lammers, illustrated by Jorg Muller, Harcourt Brace Jovanovich, 1978

1980   *The Sound of Dragon's Feet* by Alki Zei, translated by Edward Fenton, Dutton, 1979

1981   *The Winter When Time Was Frozen* by Els Pelgrom, translated by Raphael and Maryka Rudnik, Morrow, 1980

1982   *The Battle Horse* by Harry Kullman, translated by George Blecher and Lone Thygesen-Blecher, Bradbury, 1981

1983   *Hiroshima No Pika* by Toshi Maruki, translated by the author, Lothrop, 1982

1984   *Ronia, the Robber's Daughter* by Astrid Lindgren, translated by Patricia Crampton, Viking, 1983

1985   *The Island on Bird Street* by Uri Orlev, translated by Hillel Halkin, Houghton Mifflin, 1984

1986   *Rose Blanche* by Christophe Gallaz and Roberto Innocenti, translated by Martha Coventry and Richard Graglia, illustrated by Roberto Innocenti, Creative Education, 1985

1987   *No Hero for the Kaiser* by Rudolf Frank, translated by Patricia Crampton, illustrated by Klaus Steffans, Lothrop, 1986

1988   *If You Didn't Have Me* by Ulf Nilsson, illustrated by Eva Ericksson, translated by Lone Thygesen-Blecher and George Blecher, McElderry, 1987

1989   *Crutches* by Peter Hartling, Lothrop, 1988

1990   *Buster's World* by Bjarne Reuter, translated by Anthea Bell, Dutton, 1989

1991   *A Handful of Stars* by Rafik Schami, translated by Rika Lesser, Dutton, 1990

1992   *The Man from the Other Side* by Uri Orlev, translated by Hillel Halkin, Houghton Mifflin, 1991

1993   No award given

1994   *The Apprentice* by Pilar Molina Llorente, translated by Robin Longshaw, illustrated by Juan Ramón Alonso, Farrar, Straus & Giroux, 1993

1995   *The Boys from St. Petri* by Bjarne Reuter, translated by Anthea Bell, Dutton, 1994

1996   *The Lady with the Hat* by Uri Orlev, translated by Hillel Halkin, Houghton Mifflin, 1995

1997   *The Friends* by Kazumi Yumoto, translated by Cathy Hirano, Farrar, Straus & Giroux, 1996

1998   *The Robber and Me* by Josef Holub, edited by Marc Aronson, translated by Elizabeth D. Crawford, Holt, 1997

1999   *Thanks to My Mother* by Schoschana Rabinovici, edited by Cindy Kane, translated by James Skofield, Dial, 1998

2000   *The Baboon King* by Anton Quintana, translated by John Nieuwenhuizer, Walker, 1999

2001   *Samir and Yonaton* by Daniella Carmi, translated by Yael Lotan, Scholastic, 2000

2002   *How I Became an American* by Karin Gündisch, translated by James Scofield, Cricket/Carus, 2001

2003   *The Thief Lord* by Cornelia Funke, translated by Oliver Latsch, Scholastic, 2002

2004   *Run, Boy, Run* by Uri Orlev, translated by Hillel Halkin, Houghton Mifflin, 2003

2005   *The Shadows of Ghadames* by Joëlle Stolz, translated by Catherine Temerson, Delacorte, 2004

2006   *An Innocent Soldier* by Josef Holub, translated by Michael Hofmann, Arthur Levine Books, 2005

2007   *The Pull of the Ocean* by Jean-Claude Mourlevat, translated by Y. Maudet, Delacorte, 2005

2008   *Brave Story* by Miyuki Miyabe, translated by Alexander O. Smith, VIZ Media, 2006

2009   *Moribito: Guardian of the Spirit* by Nahoko Uehashi, translated by Cathy Hirano, Scholastic, 2007

2010   *A Faraway Island* by Annika Thor, translated by Linda Schenc, Delacorte Press, 2008

2011   *A Time of Miracles* by Anne-Laure Bondoux, translated by Y. Maudet, Delacorte, 2010

2012   *Soldier Bear* by Bibi Dumon Tak, illustrated by Philip Hopman, translated by Laura Watkinson, Eerdmans, 2011

2013   *My Family for the War* by Anne C. Voorhoeve, translated by Tammi Reichel, Dial, 2012

The Laura Ingalls Wilder Award

This award is named in honor of the beloved author of the Little House books, who was also its first recipient. The Association for Library Service to Children of the American Library Association presents this award to the individual, either author or illustrator, whose work has over the years proved to be a significant contribution to children's literature. Originally awarded every five years, it was awarded every three years from 1980 to 2001. It is now awarded every two years.

1954   Laura Ingalls Wilder
1960   Clara Ingram Judson
1965   Ruth Sawyer
1970   E. B. White
1975   Beverly Cleary
1980   Theodore Geisel (Dr. Seuss)
1983   Maurice Sendak
1986   Jean Fritz
1989   Elizabeth George Speare
1992   Marcia Brown
1995   Virginia Hamilton
1998   Russell Freedman
2001   Milton Meltzer
2003   Eric Carle
2005   Laurence Yep
2007   James Marshall
2009   Ashley Bryan
2011   Tomie dePaola
2013   Katherine Paterson

The Coretta Scott King Award

Presented annually by the Social Responsibilities Round Table of the American Library Association, this award recognizes an African American author and, from 1974, an illustrator who have made an outstanding contribution to literature for children in the preceding year. The award is named for the widow of civil rights leader and Nobel Peace Prize winner Dr. Martin Luther King, Jr., and it acknowledges the humanitarian work of both Dr. and Mrs. King.

1970   *Martin Luther King, Jr., Man of Peace* by Lillie Patterson, Garrard

1971   *Black Troubadour: Langston Hughes* by Charlemae Rollins, Rand

1972   *17 Black Artists* by Elton C. Fax, Dodd

1973   *I Never Had It Made* by Jackie Robinson and Alfred Duckett, Putnam

1974   Author: *Ray Charles* by Sharon Bell Mathis, Crowell
         Illustrator: *Ray Charles* by Sharon Bell Mathis, illustrated by George Ford, Crowell

1975   Author: *The Legend of Africana* by Dorothy Robinson, Johnson
         Illustrator: *The Legend of Africana* by Dorothy Robinson, illustrated by Herbert Temple, Johnson

1976   Author: *Duey's Tale* by Pearl Bailey, Harcourt
         Illustrator: No award given

1977   Author: *The Story of Stevie Wonder* by James Haskins, Lothrop
         Illustrator: No award given

1978   Author: *Africa Dream* by Eloise Greenfield, Day/Crowell
         Illustrator: *Africa Dream* by Eloise Greenfield, illustrated by Carole Bayard, Day/Crowell

1979   Author: *Escape to Freedom* by Ossie Davis, Viking
         Illustrator: *Something on My Mind* by Nikki Grimes, illustrated by Tom Feelings, Dial

1980   Author: *The Young Landlords* by Walter Dean Myers, Viking
         Illustrator: *Cornrows* by Camille Yarbrough, illustrated by Carole Bayard, Coward

1981   Author: *This Life* by Sidney Poitier, Knopf
         Illustrator: *Beat the Story-Drum, Pum-Pum* by Ashley Bryan, Atheneum

1982   Author: *Let the Circle Be Unbroken* by Mildred Taylor, Dial
         Illustrator: *Mother Crocodile: An Uncle Amadou Tale from Senegal* adapted by Rosa Guy, illustrated by John Steptoe, Delacorte

1983   Author: *Sweet Whispers, Brother Rush* by Virginia Hamilton, Philomel
         Illustrator: *Black Child* by Peter Mugabane, Knopf

1984   Author: *Everett Anderson's Good-Bye* by Lucile Clifton, Holt
         Illustrator: *My Mama Needs Me* by Mildred Pitts Walter, illustrated by Pat Cummings, Lothrop

1985   Author: *Motown and Didi* by Walter Dean Myers, Viking
         Illustrator: No award given

1986   Author: *The People Could Fly: American Black Folktales* by Virginia Hamilton, Knopf
         Illustrator: *Patchwork Quilt* by Valerie Flournoy, illustrated by Jerry Pinkney, Dial

1987   Author: *Justin and the Best Biscuits in the World* by Mildred Pitts Walter, Lothrop
         Illustrator: *Half Moon and One Whole Star* by Crescent Dragonwagon, illustrated by Jerry Pinkney, Macmillan

1988   Author: *The Friendship* by Mildred D. Taylor, Dial
         Illustrator: *Mufaro's Beautiful Daughters: An African Tale* retold and illustrated by John Steptoe, Lothrop

1989   Author: *Fallen Angels* by Walter Dean Myers, Scholastic
         Illustrator: *Mirandy and Brother Wind* by Patricia McKissack, illustrated by Jerry Pinkney, Knopf

1990   Author: *A Long Hard Journey* by Patricia and Fredrick McKissack, Walker
         Illustrator: *Nathaniel Talking* by Eloise Greenfield, illustrated by Jan Spivey Gilchrist, Black Butterfly Press

1991   Author: *Road to Memphis* by Mildred D. Taylor, Dial
         Illustrator: *Aida* retold by Leontyne Price, illustrated by Leo and Diane Dillon, Harcourt

1992   Author: *Now Is Your Time! The African-American Struggle for Freedom* by Walter Dean Myers, HarperCollins
         Illustrator: *Tar Beach* by Faith Ringgold, Crown

1993   Author: *The Dark-Thirty: Southern Tales of the Supernatural* by Patricia McKissack, Knopf
         Illustrator: *Origins of Life on Earth: An African Creation Myth* by David A. Anderson, illustrated by Kathleen Atkins Smith, Sight Productions

1994   Author: *Toning the Sweep* by Angela Johnson, Orchard
         Illustrator: *Soul Looks Back in Wonder* compiled and illustrated by Tom Feelings, Dial

1995   Author: *Christmas in the Big House, Christmas in the Quarters* by Patricia and Fredrick McKissack, illustrated by John Thompson, Scholastic
         Illustrator: *The Creation* by James Weldon Johnson, illustrated by James E. Ransom, Holiday

1996   Author: *Her Stories* by Virginia Hamilton, illustrated by Leo and Diane Dillon, Scholastic
         Illustrator: *The Middle Passage: White Ships, Black Cargo* by Tom Feelings, Dial

1997   Author: *SLAM!* by Walter Dean Myers, Scholastic
         Illustrator: *Minty: A Story of Young Harriet Tubman* by Alan Schroeder, illustrated by Jerry Pinkney, Dial

1998   Author: *Forged by Fire* by Sharon M. Draper, Atheneum
         Illustrator: *In Daddy's Arms I Am Tall: African Americans Celebrating Fathers* by Javaka Steptoe, Lee & Low

1999   Author: *Heaven* by Angela Johnson, Simon & Schuster
         Illustrator: *I See The Rhythm* by Michele Wood, Children's Book Press

2000   *Bud, Not Buddy* by Christopher Paul Curtis, Delacorte
         Illustrator: *In the Time of the Drums* by Kim L. Siegelson, illustrated by Brian Pinkney, Hyperion

2001   Author: *Miracle's Boys* by Jacqueline Woodson, Putnam
         Illustrator: *Uptown* by Brian Collier, Holt

2002   Author: *The Land* by Mildred D. Taylor, Penguin
         Illustrator: *Goin' Someplace Special* by Patricia McKissack, illustrated by Jerry Pinkney, Atheneum

2003   Author: *Bronx Masquerade* by Nikki Grimes, Dial
         Illustrator: *Talkin about Bessie* by E. B. Lewis, Scholastic

2004   Author: *The First Last Part* by Angela Johnson, Simon & Schuster
         Illustrator: *Beautiful Blackbird* by Ashley Bryan, Atheneum

2005   Author: *Remember: The Journey to School Integration* by Toni Morrison, Houghton Mifflin
         Illustrator: *Ellington Was Not a Street* by Ntozake Shange, illustrated by Nadir Nelson, Simon & Schuster

2006   Author: *Day of Tears: A Novel in Dialogue* by Julius Lester, Hyperion
         Illustrator: *Rosa* by Bryan Collier, Holt

2007   Author: *Copper Sun* by Sharon Draper, Simon & Schuster
         Illustrator: *Moses: When Harriet Tubman Led Her People to Freedom* by Kadir Nelson, Hyperion

2008   Author: *Elijah of Buxton* by Christopher Paul Curtis, Scholastic
         Illustrator: *Let It Shine* by Ashley Bryan, Atheneum

2009   Author: *We Are the Ship: The Story of Negro League Baseball* by Kadir Nelson, Disney
         Illustrator: *The Blacker the Berry* by Joyce Carol Thomas, illustrated by Floyd Cooper, HarperCollins

2010   Author: *Bad News for Outlaws: The Remarkable Life of Bass Reeves, Deputy U.S. Marshal* by Vaunda Micheaux Nelson, Carolrhoda
         Illustrator: *My People* by Langston Hughes, illustrated by Charles R. Smith, Jr., Atheneum

2011   Author: *One Crazy Summer* by Rita Williams-Garcia, Amistad
         Illustrator: *Dave the Potter: Artist, Poet, Slave* by Laban Carrick Hill, illustrated by Bryan Collier, Little, Brown

2012   Author: *Heart and Soul: The Story of America and African Americans* by Kadir Nelson, Balzer + Bray
         Illustrator: *Underground: Finding the Light to Freedom* by Shane W. Evans, Roaring Book Press

National Council of Teachers of English Award for Excellence in Poetry for Children

This award is now presented biennially (from 1977 through 1982 it was awarded annually and until 2009, triennially) by the National Council of Teachers of English. The award was established to recognize a living poet's lifetime contribution to poetry for children.

1977	David McCord
1978	Aileen Fisher
1979	Karia Kuskin
1980	Myra Cohn Livingston
1981	Eve Merriam
1982	John Ciardi
1985	Lilian Moore
1988	Arnold Adoff
1991	Valerie Worth
1994	Barbara Juster Esbensen
1997	Eloise Greenfield
2000	X. J. Kennedy
2003	Mary Ann Hoberman
2006	Nikki Grimes
2009	Lee Bennett Hopkins
2011	J. Patrick Lewis
2013	Joyce Sidman

The Scott O'Dell Award for Historical Fiction

Established by the noted children's novelist Scott O'Dell and administered by the Advisory Committee of the Bulletin of the Center for Children's Books, this award is presented to the most distinguished work of historical fiction set in the New World and written by a citizen of the United States.

1984	*The Sign of the Beaver* by Elizabeth George Speare, Houghton Mifflin
1985	*The Fighting Ground* by Avi, Harper
1986	*Sarah, Plain and Tall* by Patricia MacLachlan, Harper
1987	*Streams to the River, River to the Sea: A Novel of Sacagawea* by Scott O'Dell, Houghton Mifflin
1988	*Charlie Skedaddle* by Patricia Beatty, Morrow
1989	*The Honorable Prison* by Lyll Becerra de Jenkins, Lodestar
1990	*Shades of Gray* by Carolyn Reeder, Macmillan
1991	*A Time of Troubles* by Pieter van Raven, Scribner's
1992	*Stepping on the Cracks* by Mary Downing Hahn, Clarion
1993	*Morning Girl* by Michael Dorris, Hyperion
1994	*Bull Run* by Paul Fleischman, Harper
1995	*Under the Blood Red Sun* by Graham Salisbury, Delacorte
1996	*The Bomb* by Theodore Taylor, Flare

1997   *Jip: His Story* by Katherine Paterson, Lodestar

1998   *Out of the Dust* by Karen Hesse, Scholastic

1999   *Forty Acres and Maybe a Mule* by Harriette Gillem Robinette, Atheneum

2000   *Two Suns in the Sky* by Miriam Bat-Ami, Front Street

2001   *The Art of Keeping Cool* by Janet Taylor Lisle, Atheneum

2002   *The Land* by Mildred Taylor, Dial

2003   *Trouble Don't Last* by Shelley Pearsall, Knopf

2004   *River between Us* by Richard Peck, Dial

2005   *Worth* by A. LaFaye, Simon & Schuster

2006   *The Game of Silence* by Louise Erdrich, HarperCollins

2007   *The Green Glass Sea* by Ellen Klages, Viking

2008   *Elijah of Buxton* by Christopher Paul Curtis, Scholastic

2009   *Chains* by Laurie Halse Anderson, Simon & Schuster

2010   *The Storm in the Barn* by Matt Phelan, Candlewick

2011   *One Crazy Summer* by Rita Williams-Garcia, Amistad

2012   *Dead End in Norvelt* by Jack Gantos, Farrar, Straus & Giroux

2013   *Chickadee* by Louise Erdrich, HarperCollins

NCTE Orbis Pictus Award for Outstanding Nonfiction for Children

This award is given annually by the National Council of Teachers of English to the best works of nonfiction published in the preceding year. The award is named for Johannes Amos Comenius's *Orbis Pictus—The World in Pictures,* an illustrated Latin vocabulary book published in 1657 and considered the first picture book actually intended for children. Although several honor books and recommended titles are included each year, only the winners are listed here. See the NCTE website for a complete list.

1990   *The Great Little Madison* by Jean Fritz, Putnam

1991   *Franklin Delano Roosevelt* by Russell Freedman, Clarion

1992   *Flight: The Journey of Charles Lindbergh* by Robert Burleigh, illustrated by Mike Wimmer, Philomel Books

1993   *Children in the Dust Bowl: The True Story of the School at Weedpatch Camp* by Jerry Stanley, Crown

1994   *Across America on an Emigrant Train* by Jim Murphy, Clarion

1995   *Safari Beneath the Sea: The Wonder World of the North Pacific Coast* by Diane Swanson, Sierra Club Books

1996   *The Great Fire* by Jim Murphy, Scholastic

1997   *Leonardo da Vinci* by Diane Stanley, Morrow Junior Books

1998   *An Extraordinary Life: The Story of a Monarch Butterfly* by Laurence Pringle, Orchard Books

1999   *Shipwreck at the Bottom of the World: The Extraordinary True Story of Shackleton and the Endurance* by Jennifer Armstrong, Crown

2000   *Through My Eyes* by Ruby Bridges and Margo Lundell, Scholastic

2001   *Hurry Freedom: African Americans in Gold Rush California* by Jerry Stanley, Crown

2002   *Black Potatoes: The Story of the Great Irish Famine, 1845–1850* by Susan Campbell Bartoletti, Houghton Mifflin

2003   *When Marian Sang: The True Recital of Marian Anderson: The Voice of a Century* by Pam Munoz Ryan, illustrated by Brian Selznick, Scholastic

2004   *An American Plague: The True and Terrifying Story of the Yellow Fever Epidemic of 1793* by Jim Murphy, Clarion

2005   *York's Adventures with Lewis and Clark: An African-American's Part in the Great Expedition* by Rhoda Blumberg, HarperCollins

2006   *Children of the Great Depression* by Russell Freedman, Clarion

2007   *Quest for the Tree Kangaroo: An Expedition to the Cloud Forest of New Guinea* by Sy Montgomery, photos by Nic Bishop, Houghton Mifflin

2008   *M.L.K.: Journey of a King* by Tonya Bolden, Abrams Books

2009   *Amelia Earhart: The Legend of the Lost Aviator* by Shelley Tanaka, illustrated by David Craig, Abrams Books

2010   *The Secret World of Walter Anderson* by Hester Bass, illustrated by E. B. Lewis, Candlewick

2011   *Ballet for Martha: Making Appalachian Spring* by Jan Greenberg and Sandra Jordan, illustrated by Brian Floca, Roaring Brook Press

2012   *Balloons over Broadway: The True Story of the Puppeteer of Macy's Parade* by Melissa Sweet, Houghton Mifflin

2013   *Monsieur Marceau: Actor without Words* by Leda Schubert, illustrated by Gérard DuBois, Roaring Brook Press

Robert F. Sibert Informational Book Award

This annual award was established by the American Library Association in 2001 to honor the most distinguished information book published in English in the preceding year. It is named for the one-time president of Bound to Stay Bound Books, Inc., of Jacksonville, Illinois, which sponsors the award.

2001   *Sir Walter Raleigh and the Quest for El Dorado* by Marc Aronson, Clarion

2002   *Black Potatoes: The Story of the Great Irish Famine, 1845–1850* by Susan Campbell Bartoletti, Houghton Mifflin

2003   *The Life and Death of Adolf Hitler* by James Cross Giblin, Clarion

2004   *An American Plague: The True and Terrifying Story of the Yellow Fever Epidemic of 1793* by Jim Murphy, Clarion

2005   *The Voice That Challenged a Nation: Marian Anderson and the Struggle for Equal Rights* by Russell Freedman, Clarion

2006   *Secrets of a Civil War Submarine: Solving the Mysteries of the H. L. Hunley* by Sally M. Walker, Carolrhoda

2007   *Team Moon: How 400,000 People Landed Apollo 11 on the Moon* by Catherine Thimmesh, Houghton

2008   *The Wall: Growing Up Behind the Iron Curtain* by Peter Sis, Farrar, Straus & Giroux

2009   *We Are the Ship: The Story of Negro League Baseball* by Kadir Nelson, Disney

2010   *Almost Astronauts: 13 Women Who Dared to Dream* by Tanya Lee Stone, Candlewick

2011   *Kakapo Rescue: Saving the World's Strangest Parrot* by Sy Montgomery, photographs by Nic Bishop, Houghton Mifflin

2012   *Balloons over Broadway: The True Story of the Puppeteer of Macy's Parade* by Melissa Sweet, Houghton Mifflin

2013   *Bomb: The Race to Build—and Steal—the World's Most Dangerous Weapon* by Steve Sheinkin, Roaring Brook Press

International Awards

The Carnegie Medal

Awarded by the British Library Association to an outstanding book first published in the United Kingdom, this medal has been awarded annually since it was established in 1937 (the first award being presented to a book published in the preceding year). The date given is the date of publication.

1936   *Pigeon Post* by Arthur Ransome, Cape

1937   *The Family from One End Street* by Eve Garnett, Muller

1938   *The Circus Is Coming* by Noel Streatfield, Dent

1939   *Radium Woman* by Eleanor Doorly, Heinemann

1940   *Visitors from London* by Kitty Barne, Dent

1941   *We Couldn't Leave Dinah* by Mary Treadgold, Penguin

1942   *The Little Grey Men* by B. B., Eyre & Spottiswoode

1943   No award given

1944   *The Wind on the Moon* by Eric Linklater, Macmillan

1945   No award given

1946   *The Little White Horse* by Elizabeth Goudge, Brockhampton Press

1947   *Collected Stories for Children* by Walter de la Mare, Faber

1948   *Sea Change* by Richard Armstrong, Dent

1949   *The Story of Your Home* by Agnes Allen, Transatlantic

1950   *The Lark on the Wind* by Elfrida Vipont Foulds, Oxford

1951   *The Woolpack* by Cynthia Harnett, Methuen

1952   *The Borrowers* by Mary Norton, Dent

1953   *A Valley Grows Up* by Edward Osmond, Oxford

1954   *Knight Crusader* by Ronald Welch, Oxford

1955   *The Little Bookroom* by Eleanor Farjeon, Oxford

1956   *The Last Battle* by C. S. Lewis, Bodley Head

1957   *A Grass Rope* by William Mayne, Oxford

1958   *Tom's Midnight Garden* by Philippa Pearce, Oxford

1959   *The Lantern Bearers* by Rosemary Sutcliff, Oxford

1960   *The Making of Man* by I. W. Cornwall, Phoenix

1961   *A Stranger at Green Knowe* by Lucy Boston, Faber

1962   *The Twelve and the Genii* by Pauline Clarke, Faber

1963   *Time of Trial* by Hester Burton, Oxford

1964   *Nordy Banks* by Sheena Porter, Oxford

1965   *The Grange at High Force* by Philip Turner, Oxford

1966   No award given

1967   *The Owl Service* by Alan Garner, Collins

1968   *The Moon in the Cloud* by Rosemary Harris, Faber

1969   *The Edge of the Cloud* by K. M. Peyton, Oxford

1970   *The God beneath the Sea* by Leon Garfield and Edward Blishen, Kestrel

1971   *Josh* by Ivan Southall, Angus & Robertson

1972   *Watership Down* by Richard Adams, Rex Collings

1973   *The Ghost of Thomas Kempe* by Penelope Lively, Heinemann

1974   *The Stronghold* by Mollie Hunter, Hamilton

1975   *The Machine Gunners* by Robert Westall, Macmillan

1976   *Thunder and Lightnings* by Jan Mark, Kestrel

1977   *The Turbulent Term of Tyke Tiler* by Gene Kemp, Faber

1978   *The ExeterBlitz* by David Rees, Hamish Hamilton

1979   *Tulku* by Peter Dickinson, Dutton

1980   *City of Gold* by Peter Dickinson, Gollancz

1981   *The Scarecrows* by Robert Westall, Chatto & Windus

1982   *The Haunting* by Margaret Mahy, Dent

1983   *Handles* by Jan Mark, Kestrel

1984   *The Changeover* by Margaret Mahy, Dent

1985   *Storm* by Kevin Crossley-Holland, Heinemann

1986   *Granny Was a Buffer Girl* by Berlie Doherty, Methuen

1987   *The Ghost Drum* by Susan Price, Faber

1988   *Pack of Lies* by Geraldine McCaughrean, Oxford

1989   *My War with Goggle-Eyes* by Anne Fine, Joy Street

1990   *Wolf* by Gillian Cross, Oxford

1991   *Dear Nobody* by Berlie Doherty, Hamish Hamilton

1992   *Flour Babies* by Anne Fine, Hamish Hamilton

1993   *Stone Cold* by Robert Swindells, Hamish Hamilton

1994   *Whispers in the Graveyard* by Theresa Breslin, Methuen

1995   *Northern Lights* by Philip Pullman, Doubleday (U.S. title: *The Golden Compass*)

1996   *Junk* by Melvin Burgess, Andersen/Penguin

1997   *River Boy* by Tim Bowler, Oxford

1998   *Skellig* by David Almond, Hodder

1999   *Postcards from No Man's Land* by Aidan Chambers, Bodley Head

2000   *The Other Side of Truth* by Beverley Naidoo, Puffin

2001   *The Amazing Maurice and His Educated Rodents* by Terry Pratchett, Doubleday

2002   *Ruby Holler* by Sharon Creech, Bloomsbury

2003   *A Gathering of Light* by Jennifer Donnelly, Bloomsbury

2004   *Millions* by Frank Cottrell Boyce, Macmillan

2005   *Tamar* by Mal Peet, Walker

2007   *Just in Case* by Meg Rosoff, Penguin

2008   *Here Lies Arthur* by Philip Reeve, Scholastic

2009   *Bog Child* by Siobhan Dowd, David Fickling

2010   *The Graveyard Book* by Neil Gaiman, Bloomsbury

2011   *Monsters of Men* by Patrick Ness, Walker

2012   *A Monster Calls* by Patrick Ness, Walker

2013   *Maggot Moon* by Sally Gardner, Hot Keys

The Kate Greenaway Medal

Named for the celebrated nineteenth-century children's illustrator, this medal is awarded annually by the British Library Association to the most distinguished illustrated work for children first published in the United Kingdom during the preceding year. (Unless otherwise noted, the author is also the illustrator. The date given is the year of publication.)

1956   *Tim All Alone* by Edward Ardizzone, Oxford

1957   *Mrs. Easter and the Storks* by V. H. Drummond, Faber

1958   No award given

1959   *Kashtanka and a Bundle of Ballads* by William Stobbs, Oxford

1960   *Old Winkle and the Seagulls* by Elizabeth Rose, illustrated by Gerald Rose, Faber

1961   *Mrs. Cockle's Cat* by Philippa Pearce, illustrated by Anthony Maitland, Kestrel

1962   *Brian Wildsmith's ABC* by Brian Wildsmith, Oxford

1963   *Borka* by John Burningham, Jonathan Cape

1964   *Shakespeare's Theatre* by C. W. Hodges, Oxford

1965   *Three Poor Tailors* by Victor Ambrus, Hamilton

1966   *Mother Goose Treasury* by Raymond Briggs, Hamilton

1967   *Charlie, Charlotte & the Golden Canary* by Charles Keeping, Oxford

1968   *Dictionary of Chivalry* by Grant Uden, illustrated by Pauline Baynes, Kestrel

1969   *The Quangle-Wangle's Hat and the Dragon of an Ordinary Family* by Helen Oxenbury, Heinemann

1970   *Mr. Gumpy's Outing* by John Burningham, Jonathan Cape

1971   *The Kingdom under the Sea* by Jan Pienkowski, Jonathan Cape

1972   *The Woodcutter's Duck* by Krystyna Turska, Hamilton

1973   *Father Christmas* by Raymond Briggs, Hamilton

1974   *The Wind Blew* by Pat Hutchins, Bodley Head

1975   *Horses in Battle* by Victor Ambrus, Oxford

1976   *The Post Office Cat* by Gail E. Haley, Bodley Head

1977   *Dogger* by Shirley Hughes, Bodley Head

1978   *Each Peach Pear Plum* by Janet and Allan Ahlberg, Kestrel

1979   *The Haunted House* by Jan Pienkowski, Dutton

1980   *Mr. Magnolia* by Quentin Blake, Jonathan Cape

1981   *The Highwayman* by Alfred Noyes, illustrated by Charles Keeping, Oxford

1982   *Long Neck and Thunder Foot* by Michael Foreman, Kestrel; *Sleeping Beauty and Other Favorite Fairy Tales* by Michael Foreman, Gollancz

1983   *Gorilla* by Anthony Browne, Julia McRae Books

1984   *Hiawatha's Childhood* by Errol LeCain, Faber

1985   *Sir Gawain and the Loathly Lady* by Selina Hastings, illustrated by Juan Wijngaard, Walker

1986   *Snow White in New York* by Fiona French, Oxford

1987   *Crafty Chameleon* by Adrienne Kennaway, Hodder & Stoughton

1988   *Can't You Sleep, Little Bear?* by Martin Waddell, illustrated by Adrienne Kennaway, Hodder & Stoughton

1989   *War Boy: A Country Childhood* by Michael Foreman, Arcade

1990   *The Whale's Song* by Dyan Sheldon, illustrated by Gary Blythe, Dial

1991   *The Jolly Christmas Postman* by Janet and Allan Ahlberg, Heinemann

1992   *Zoo* by Anthony Browne, Julie MacRae Books

1993   *Black Ships before Troy* retold by Rosemary Sutcliff, illustrated by Alan Lee, Frances Lincoln

1994   *Way Home* by Libby Hawthorne, Anderson

1995   *The Christmas Miracle of Jonathan Toomey* by Susan Wojciechowski, illustrated by P. J. Lynch, Candlewick

1996   *The Baby Who Wouldn't Go to Bed* by Helen Cooper, Doubleday

1997   *When Jessie Came across the Sea* by Amy Hest, illustrated by P. J. Lynch, Doubleday

1998   *Pumpkin Soup* by Helen Cooper, Doubleday

1999   *Alice's Adventures in Wonderland* by Lewis Carroll, illustrated by Helen Oxenbury, Walker

2000   *I Will Not Ever Eat a Tomato* by Lauren Child, Orchard

2001   *Pirate Diary* by Chris Riddell, Walker

2002   *Jethro Byrde: Fairy Child* by Bob Graham, Walker

2003   *Ella's Big Chance* by Shirley Hughes, Bodley Head

2004   *Jonathan Swift's "Gulliver"* by Marti Jenkins, illustrated by Chris Riddell

2005   *Wolves* by Emily Gravett, Macmillan

2007   *The Adventures of the Dish and the Spoon* by Mini Grey, Jonathan Cape

2008   *Little Mouse's Big Book of Fears* by Emily Gravett, Macmillan

2009   *Harris Finds His Feet* by Catherine Rayner, Little Tiger Press

2010   *Harry & Hooper* by Freya Blackwood, Scholastic

2011   *FArTHER* by Graham Baker-Smith, Templar

2012   *A Monster Calls* by Patrick Ness, illustrated by Jim Kay, Walker

2013   *Black Dog* by Levi Pinfold, Templar

The Hans Christian Andersen Award

This medal, named for the great Danish storyteller, is presented every two years by the International Board on Books for Young People to a living author and (since 1966) living illustrator whose works have made a significant international contribution to children's literature.

1956   Eleanor Farjeon (Great Britain)

1958   Astrid Lindgren (Sweden)

1960   Erich Kastner (Germany)

1962   Meindert DeJong (United States)

1964   René Guillot (France)

1966   Author: Tove Jansson (Finland)
        Illustrator: Alois Carigiet (Switzerland)

1968   Authors: James Krüss (Germany) and José Maria Sanchez-Silva (Spain)
        Illustrator: Jirí Trnka (Czechoslovakia)

1970   Author: Gianni Rodari (Italy)
        Illustrator: Maurice Sendak (United States)

1972   Author: Scott O'Dell (United States)
        Illustrator: Ib Spang Olsen (Denmark)

1974   Author: Maria Gripe (Sweden)
        Illustrator: Farsid Mesghali (Iran)

1976   Author: Cecil Bødker (Denmark)
        Illustrator: Tatjana Mawrina (U.S.S.R.)

1978   Author: Paula Fox (United States)
        Illustrator: Svend Otto S. (Denmark)

1980   Author: Bohumil Riha (Czechoslovakia)
        Illustrator: Suekichi Akaba (Japan)

1982   Author: Lygia Gojunga Nunes (Brazil)
        Illustrator: Zbigniew Rychlicki (Poland)

1984   Author: Christine Nostlinger (Austria)
        Illustrator: Mitsumasa Anno (Japan)

1986   Author: Patricia Wrightson (Australia)
           Illustrator: Robert Ingpen (Australia)

1988   Author: Annie M. G. Schmidt (the Netherlands)
           Illustrator: Dusan Kállay (Yugoslavia)

1990   Author: Tormod Haugen (Norway)
           Illustrator: Lisbeth Zwerger (Austria)

1992   Author: Virginia Hamilton (United States)
           Illustrator: Keveta Pacovská (Czechoslovakia)

1994   Author: Michio Mado (Japan)
           Illustrator: Jörg Müller (Switzerland)

1996   Author: Uri Orlev (Israel)
           Illustrator: Klaus Ensikat (Germany)

1998   Author: Katherine Paterson (United States)
           Illustrator: Tomi Ungerer (United States)

2000   Author: Ana Maria Machado (Brazil)
           Illustrator: Anthony Browne (Great Britain)

2002   Author: Aidan Chambers (Great Britain)
           Illustrator: Quentin Blake (Great Britain)

2004   Author: Martin Waddell (Ireland)
           Illustrator: Max Velthuijs (the Netherlands)

2006   Author: Margaret Mahy (New Zealand)
           Illustrator: Wolf Erlbruch (Germany)

2008   Author: Jürg Schubiger (Switzerland)
           Illustrator: Roberto Innocenti (Italy)

2010   Author: David Almond (Great Britain)
           Illustrator: Jutta Bauer (Germany)

2012   Author: Maria Teresa Andruetto (Argentina)
           Illustrator: Peter Sis (Czech Republic)

The Astrid Lindgren Memorial Award

Named in honor of the beloved author of *Pippi Longstocking,* this international award from the Swedish government carries a prize of 5 million Swedish crowns, second only to the Nobel Prize among literature prizes in the world. The award (one or two a year) may be given to an individual or organization whose work has promoted children's and youth literature.

2003   Christine Nöstlinger (Austria) and Maurice Sendak (United States)

2004   Lygia Bojunga (Brazil)

2005   Ryôji Arai (Japan) and Philip Pullman (United Kingdom)

2006   Katherine Paterson (United States)

2007   Banco del Libro (Venezuela)

2008   Sonya Harnett (Australia)

2009   The Tamer Institute for Community Education (Palestine)

2010   Kitty Crowther (Belgium)

2011   Shaun Tan (Australia)

2012   Guus Kuijer (the Netherlands)

2013   Isol (Argentina)

Glossary

Alliteration The repetition of similar sounds at the beginnings of words in close proximity, as in "Billy Button bought a buttered biscuit"

Anachronism In a historical novel, a feature that is out of place for the time period—e.g., telephone in the Civil War—either for humor or result of an author's carelessness

Anapest A poetic metrical foot consisting of two unstressed syllables followed by a stressed syllable, as in the phrase "in the still of the night"

Antagonist The character who is opposed to or works against the principal character in a literary work—often, though not always, the villain

Anthropomorphism Giving human qualities (such as speech or emotions) to something nonhuman—e.g., a talking animal, a plant, or a machine

Artistic medium The material an artist uses to produce an illustration—oil paints, watercolors, pencil, ink, and so on

Art Nouveau An artistic style developed in the late nineteenth century, characterized by fluid, sinuous lines and florid designs

Assonance The repetition of similar vowel sounds within words of close proximity—as the long *a* sounds in *slate* and *grey* and *lake* in this line: "The surface of a slate-grey lake is lit" (Seamus Heaney)

Autobiography The life story of an individual written by the individual himself or herself

Ballad A narrative poem typically of folk origin, in four-line stanzas, and intended to be sung (*see also* Narrative poem)

Bibliotherapy The treatment of psychological or emotional problems through the use of selected reading materials

Biography The life story of an individual written by another person

Border In book illustration, the framing element for a picture, usually consisting of white space, but sometimes decorated

Cartoon art An artistic style characterized by simple, grossly exaggerated figures, usually for humorous or satirical effect

Censorship The act of restricting the public's access—through speech or the written word—to what certain authorities deem to be objectionable ideas

Cinquain A poem consisting of five lines, usually containing two, four, six, eight, and two syllables, respectively, with the first and last lines often bearing some relationship

Climax The high point of a dramatic plot when all the threads come together—usually the turning point

Collage An artistic composition made up of a variety of materials, usually nonpainterly, such as fabric, paper, wood, and metal

Coming-of-age story A story in which the protagonist, through a variety of experiences, undergoes personal growth and development

Consonance The repetition of similar consonant sounds within words of close proximity—such as the *l* sounds in "Afternoon light falling beautifully into the room" (Richard Jones)

Cubism An artistic movement of the early twentieth century characterized by abstract drawings emphasizing the geometric shape and structure of an object rather than pictorial representation

Cumulative plot A story consisting of an accumulation of events, which, in its telling, repeats the entire sequence with each addition—used most commonly in folktales such as *The Gingerbread Man* and usually for comic effect

Dactyl A poetic metrical foot consisting of one stressed syllable followed by two unstressed syllables, as in the word *beautiful*

Dénouement Literally, the "unraveling" or "untying," applied to the final outcome of a dramatic plot

Dialogue The words spoken between two or more characters in a literary work

Didacticism Instruction or teaching; when applied to literature, it refers to stories whose purpose is to deliver a moral or ethical lesson

Digital art Art generated by a computer program

Dramatic plot A story consisting of a single major conflict, chronologically organized and leading up to a climax and a concluding dénouement

Dynamic character A fictional character—always a round one—who undergoes a significant change or emotional growth in the course of the action

Episodic plot A story, usually told in chapters, describing a series of adventures, tied together by characters, setting, or theme

Exposition The information provided in a literary work to supply needed background information to the audience

Expressionism In picture book art, a style that evokes the artist's emotional response to the subject rather than a realistic portrayal, characterized by unusual distortions (elongated figures, for example), unrealistic use of colors, shapes that only suggest objects, and so on

First-person narrator A storyteller who is a character in the story and who refers to himself or herself as *I*

Flashback In a narrative, a shift backward in time to reveal events that happened earlier, chiefly used as a means of explaining character motivation

Flat character A one-dimensional fictional character without depth or complexity, common among minor characters and always a static character

Foil character A fictional character whose personality traits sharply contrast with those of another character in the work

Folk art In picture book art, a style that is associated with a specific folk culture, usually identified by uncomplicated drawings and the use of cultural symbols and culturally specific colors, patterns, or designs

Foreshadowing In a narrative, hints of what is to come; a device used to create suspense and to avoid what might otherwise seem incredible.

Found poetry A poem created from an ordinary piece of prose—an advertisement or a passage from a book, newspaper, or magazine—that retains the original language but has the sentences rearranged to resemble a poetic form

Free verse Poetry that observes no strict rules about rhythm or rhyme or stanza length—but most free verse still uses such devices as simile, metaphor, personification, and so on

Functionary character A minor character whose role is to perform specific necessary functions—as a servant, for example, or an official

Graphic novel A book-length work that uses both text and art, usually in comic book format, to tell the story (*manga* refers specifically to Japanese graphic novels)

Graphic technique A method by which a graphic artist creates images through the use of blocks, plates, or type, including woodblocks, linocuts, and so on

Gutter In a book, the crease caused by the binding—an important consideration in picture books that use double-page spreads

Haiku A Japanese poetic form usually consisting of 17 syllables in three lines and reflecting on nature

Iamb A poetic metrical foot consisting of one unstressed syllable followed by one stressed syllable, as in the word *arise*

Illustrated book A book that uses illustrations to highlight or support specific points in the text—as opposed to a picture book, in which the pictures share equally with the text

Irony Literary incongruity—a difference between what is said and what is meant or between what happens and what we would normally expect to happen

Limerick A humorous five-line poem, with an *a-a-b-b-a* rhyme scheme and a regular rhythm

Limited narrator A third-person storyteller who is not a character in the story but tells the story from just one character's point of view

Lyric poem A poem that expresses the poet's personal feelings or thoughts about a subject (rather than telling a story), often following a verse pattern, sometimes intended to be sung; sonnets, odes, cinquains, and so on are examples

Metaphor An implied comparison, giving the attributes of one thing to another—for example, "All the world's a stage" (Shakespeare)

Meter A pattern of stressed and unstressed syllables (called metrical feet) in a line of poetry (*see also* "Anapest," "Dactyl," "Iamb," and "Trochee")

Montage An artistic composition created by artfully arranging graphic images, such as photographs, in contrast with a collage, which combines various non-painterly materials

Motif A recurring thematic or plot element in literature, such as the recurring plot devices found throughout folktales

Motivation In a fictional story, the reason(s) behind a character's actions, which causes a character to behave in a certain way or to do certain things

Naïve art An artistic style that is deliberately made to resemble childlike drawings, often disproportioned and without depth of perspective

Narrative poem A story, complete with characters, setting, and plot, told in verse

New realism A type of fiction begun in the 1960s, characterized by more realistic portrayal of social and personal issues confronting teenagers, including sexuality, drugs, gangs, and similar matters

Nonsense verse Comical verse featuring outlandish characters, absurd actions, and, often, made-up words and rollicking rhyme and rhythm

Omniscient narrator A third-person storyteller who is not a character in the story and is usually both all-seeing and all-knowing

Painterly technique A method by which an artist creates images by applying a medium (paint, ink, gouache, tempera, and so on) to a surface (usually paper), in contrast with digital art, or woodblocks, for example

Panel In a picture book, a framed illustration, usually combined with others, that permits the simultaneous depiction of varying perspectives or passing time on a single page

Parallel plot A story consisting of two or more dramatic plots, often interwoven, operating simultaneously

Parody A literary work (e.g., a story or a poem) that imitates another in order to poke fun

Personification Giving inanimate objects human qualities—"around us the trees full of night lean hushed in their dreams" (W. S. Merwin)

Picture book A book in which the illustrations share equally with the text in conveying the story or information

Playground poetry The traditional oral verses that children themselves both share and invent, including playground games, camp songs, and so on

Plot The interrelated sequence of events making up a story; *see also* "Cumulative plot," "Dramatic plot," "Episodic plot," and "Parallel plot"

Problem novel A type of realistic fiction, developed in the 1960s, that focuses on a specific psychological or social issue confronting the protagonist

Protagonist The principal sympathetic character in a literary work, the main character

Reader-response theory A reading theory (sometimes called "transactional analysis") which proposes that each reader derives something personal from reading a text, based on past experiences and knowledge, and that rereading a text will result in a still different response

Realism In picture book art, representational drawing or painting that attempts to give lifelike detail to objects

Renaissance In European history, the time period from about 1400 to1650 that experienced a flowering of art and culture, based on a revived interest in the civilizations of ancient Greece and Rome

Round character A fictional character with a fully developed personality that has numerous facets

Satire A literary work that pokes fun, often through the use of irony, at some human folly or vice

Scanimation Originally a term used to describe analog computer animation (which gave way to digital animation), now applied to a technique, developed by Rufus Seder Butler, by which scrambled images are passed behind a transparent film marked with thin stripes, giving the images the illusion of motion

Sentimentalism A literary tone that expresses excessive emotion—overly sweet, overly mournful, overly passionate—that seems disproportionate to the circumstances

Setting The time and place in which the action of a story occurs

Simile An explicit comparison that uses the word *like* or *as*—for example, "His breath hung in the air like a white balloon" (Baron Wormser)

Static character A fictional character—either flat or round—who does not undergo any significant change throughout the work

Stylized intensification In folk narratives, the exaggeration of a repeated plot element for dramatic purposes—for example, each of the three little pigs building a slightly sturdier house

Stock character A fictional character—always a flat one—who represents a type rather than an individual: the boor, the buffoon, the ingénue, the penny-pincher, the prude, and so on

Surrealism In picture book art, a style that is drawn with realistic detail but with unrealistic, even unsettling, subject matter, often with a nightmarish quality

Tabula rasa Latin for "blank slate," a term philosopher John Locke used to describe his notion of a child's intellectual capacity at birth; the idea helped spur a multitude of didactic children's books in the eighteenth century

Theme The controlling idea of a literary work, the fundamental concept the author is attempting to convey

Tone The author's attitude—comical, satirical, cynical, and so on—toward the subject of a literary work

Transactional analysis *See* "Reader-response theory"

Trochee A poetic metrical foot consisting of one stressed followed by one unstressed syllable, as in the word *happy*

Typography The way in which letters are designed (including size and shape) and their arrangement on a page

Urchin poetry Poetry that deliberately appeals to a young reader's fixation on the disgusting and gross, as in some of the poetry of Shel Silverstein

Verse novel A novel written in poetry rather than prose; popular in the nineteenth century adult fiction, the form has gained prominence in modern children's fiction. The poetry is typically free verse and often from a first-person narrator's viewpoint; *see* also "Free verse" and "First-person narrator."

Vignette In a picture book, a small picture integrated into a larger illustration to supply additional information or perhaps to add humor

Visual poem Also called concrete poem or shape poem, a poem in which the text is designed to resemble a shape on the page, usually illustrative of the poem's subject—for example, a poem about a butterfly shaped like a butterfly

Zone of proximal development (ZPD) A term created by the psychologist Vygotsky to refer to the difference between what a person can learn on his or her own and what the person can learn with the assistance of others

Children's Literature Resources

General Reference Works

These publications provide background information on a multitude of topics in children's literature and are excellent places to begin research. They can be found in large libraries and online.

Children's Literature Review (1976–). Detroit: Gale.
A series devoted to assembling critical commentary on children's authors, with each volume focusing on approximately 10 individuals. Excerpts are taken from scholarly journals, book reviews, and similar sources. A good place to find out what critics are saying about a specific work.

Dictionary of Literary Biography (1978–). Detroit: Gale.
A multivolume series that includes extensive scholarly essays on literary figures; each volume focuses on a specific type of writing, and several volumes deal with children's writers and illustrators. A good place to find biographical material as well as some in-depth critical commentary on an individual's work.

Oxford Encyclopedia of Children's Literature. Jack Zipes, ed. New York: Oxford University Press, 2006.
A four-volume set that includes articles on writers, illustrators, works, and topics important in the field of children's literature—all written by specialists in the field.

Something about the Author (1971–). Detroit: Gale.
A multivolume series that includes biographical entries on children's authors and illustrators. A good place to find an introductory overview of an individual's life and work.

Periodicals

Some of the many periodicals that publish articles on children's literature are listed here. Notice that some publications are devoted largely to book reviews and are most helpful for book selection. Other publications feature scholarly essays on topics in children's literature, which are most helpful for academic research.

ALAN Review—A publication of the Assembly on Literature for Adolescents of the National Council of Teachers of English that features articles on adolescent literature.

Bookbird—A quarterly publication of International Board on Books for Young People (IBBY) that is devoted to international children's literature.

Booklist—The review journal of the American Library Association; includes recommended books for both children and adults and reviews some 7,500 books a year.

Bulletin of the Center for Children's Books—A monthly publication featuring reviews of the latest books for children.

Children's Literature—An annual publication of the Children's Literature Association, with scholarly articles on the entire range of children's literature.

Children's Literature Association Quarterly—A quarterly publication of the Children's Literature Association that has scholarly articles on the entire range of children's literature and reviews of recent scholarly books on children's literature.

Children's Literature in Education—A quarterly publication featuring scholarly articles of special interest to educators, including both pedagogy and literary analysis.

The Horn Book Magazine—A bimonthly publication with informal articles on children's books and a lengthy section devoted to brief reviews of the most recently published children's books.

Language Arts—A bimonthly publication of the National Council of Teachers of English, featuring scholarly articles of particular interest to elementary and middle-school teachers, featuring current research on classroom theory and practice, and reviews of books for children.

The Lion and the Unicorn—A triennial publication featuring scholarly articles on the entire range of children's literature, also emphasizing international literature and reviews of recent scholarly books on children's literature; also awards the annual *The Lion and Unicorn Poetry Award* for the year's best poetry publication.

School Library Journal—A monthly publication of book reviews, intended, as the name implies, for libraries, but very helpful for educators as well.

Professional Organizations

Many professional organizations related to the field of children's literature exist, each with a slightly different focus. The following are only some of the most prominent. (Notice that professional associations are fond of acronyms.)

Children's Literature Association (ChLA)—For those interested in the scholarly pursuit of children's literature, especially educators and scholars.

International Board on Books for Young People (IBBY)—For those interested in international children's literature.

International Reading Association (IRA)—For those interested primarily in the instruction and scholarship of reading skills.

Modern Language Association (MLA)—For those interested in the scholarly pursuit of literature in general; MLA includes a children's literature section.

National Council of Teachers of English (NCTE)—For those interested in the profession of language arts education at all levels, from elementary through high school.

Popular Cultural Association—For those interested in the broader issues of popular culture, including music, art, and media.

Index

Abel's Island (Steig, W.), 207
Aboriginal legends, 16
Absolutely True Story of a Part-Time Indian, The (Sherman), 63–64
Across Five Aprils (Hunt), 225–226
Acrylics, 111
Adams, Richard, 208
Adler, David, 250–251
Adventures of Huckleberry Finn, The (Twain), 33, 44, 190, 229, 235–236
Adventures of Pinocchio, The (Collodi), 15, 44–45, 52, 208
Adventures of Tom Sawyer, The (Twain), 10, 227
Adventure stories, 10, 233–234
Aeneid (Virgil), 211
Aesop, 2, 161–162
African Americans
    bibliography about, 72–73
    depicted in literature, 59–61
Aguilar, David, 257
A Is for Always (Anglund), 88
Alcott, Louise May, 10, 225, 227, 229–230
Alexander, Lloyd, 14, 204, 211
Alexander and the Wind-up Mouse (Lionni), 209
Alger, Horatio, Jr., 10
Alice's Adventures in Wonderland (Carroll), 8, 10, 44–45, 93, 138– 139, 183, 202, 210
Aliki, 250, 260–261
Allard, Harry, 210
Alliteration, 130–131
Alphabatics (MacDonald, S.), 87
Alphabet books, 85
    bibliography of, 97–98
    content of, 87–88
Alphabet from Z to A (With Much Confusion on the Way) (Viorst), 88
Alternative families, 68
Amazing Crocodiles & Reptiles (Ling), 255
Amelia Bedelia series (Parish), 94
American Born Chinese (Yang), 120
American Plague: The True and Terrifying Story of the Yellow Fever Epidemic of 1793, An (Murphy), 43, 250, 260
Am I Blue?: Coming Out from the Silence (Bauer), 235
Anansi the Spider (McDermott), 113, 166–168
Anapest, 132
Andersen, Hans Christian, 8, 15, 295–296
Anderson, Laurie Halse, 235
Anglund, Joan Walsh, 88
Animal Alphabet (Kitchen), 87
Animalia (Base), 88
Animal Popposites: A Pop-up Book of Opposites (Reinhart), 93
Animal stories
    fantasy, 207–208
    folktales, 161–162
    realistic fiction, 237–238
Anna Karenina (Tolstoy), 229
Anne of Green Gables (Montgomery), 16, 232
Anno, Mitsumasa, 90–91

Anno's Journey (Anno), 90–91
Application questions, 46–47
Aquinas, Thomas, 192
Archetypal approach, to reading, 194–195
Are You There, God? It's Me Margaret (Blume), 26, 186, 192, 235
Arnold, Nick, 254, 257–258
Arnosky, Jim, 252
Aronson, Marc, 258
Art Attack: A Short Cultural History of the Avant-Garde (Aronson), 258
Arthur, for the Very First Time (MacLachlan), 228
Artistic experiences, 51–52
Artistic media, in picture books, 110–111
Artistic styles, in picture books, 112–114
Art nouveau, in illustration, 114
Asbjørnsen, Peter, 153
Ashanti to Zulu: African Traditions (Musgrove), 88
Ash Road (Southall), 16
Asian Americans, 14, 64–65
    bibliography about, 76–77
Assonance, 131
Astrid Lindgren Memorial Award, 15, 296
Athletic Shorts (Crutcher), 237
Australian Legendary Tales (Parker), 16
Autonomy versus doubt stage, 25
"Autumn" (Clare), 133
Avatar, 169
Avi, 226
Awards, book
    Astrid Lindgren Memorial Award, 15, 296
    Caldecott Medal, 12, 15, 282–284
    Carnegie Medal, 15, 291–293
    Coretta Scott King Award, 61, 287–288
    Hans Christian Andersen Award, 15, 295–296
    Kate Greenaway Medal, 15, 293–295
    Laura Ingalls Wilder Award, 15, 286
    Meggendorfer Prize, 93
    Michael Printz Award, 120
    Mildred L. Batchelder Award, 285–286
    National Council of Teachers of English Award for Excellence in Poetry for Children, 289
    NCTE Orbis Pictus Award for Outstanding Nonfiction for Children, 290–291
    Newbery Medal, 7, 15, 279–282
    Robert F. Sibert Informational Book Award, 291
    Scott O'Dell Award for Historical Fiction, 289–290

Babbitt, Natalie, 14, 47, 184, 187–188, 204
Babe, the Gallant Pig (King-Smith), 208
Baby (MacLachlan), 231
Baby-Sitters Club series, 228
Baby's Opera, The (Crane), 11
Bailey, Jacqui, 259
Ballads, 136–137
Ballantyne, R. M., 10, 227
Bambi (Salten), 16
Bang, Molly, 89

Bannerman, Helen, 59–61
"Barbara Allen," 136–137
Barrie, J. M., 12
Base, Graeme, 88
Baseball in April (Soto), 62
Bats (Bland), 253
Bauer, Marion Dane, 235
Baum, L. Frank, 10, 93, 183, 191, 204
Beardsley, Aubrey, 114
"Beauty and the Beast," 155, 162
Because of Winn-Dixie (DiCamillo), 233–234
Beck, Debra, 259
Bee, Clair, 237
Behavioral stereotypes, 67
Bemelmans, Ludwig, 51, 106, 109, 114, 116–117
Ben and Me (Lawson, R.), 262
Bennett, James, 227
Bentham, Jeremy, 141
Beowulf, 2
Beowulf (Morpurgo), 169
Beowulf (Rumford), 2
Berenstain, Jan, 32
Berenstain, Stan, 32
Berenstain Bears and the Bad Dream, The (Berenstain and Berenstain), 32
Berenstain Bears Go to the Doctor (Berenstain and Berenstain), 32
Bettelheim, Bruno, 196
Bianco, Margery Williams, 208
Biblical stories, 2
Bibliotherapy, 31–33
Biggest, Strongest, Fastest (Jenkins), 89–90, 254
Bildungsroman, 229
Biography
    autobiography, 260, 262–263
    collective, 261
    definition of, 260
    fictionalized, 261–262
    partial, 261
Birthday Basket for Tia, A (Mora), 62
Bishop, Claire Huchet, 64
Bishop, Rudine Sims, 58
Black Americans: A History in Their Own Word, The (Meltzer), 260
Black Arrow, The (Stevenson. R. L.), 223
Black Beauty: The Autobiography of a Horse (Sewell), 207
Black? White! Day? Night! (Seeger), 89
Bland, Celia, 253
Block, Francesca Lia, 15
Blogs, 54
Bloom, Valerie, 135
Blubber (Blume), 24, 228
Blueberries for Sal (McCloskey), 103–104, 110, 182
Blue Fairy Book, The (Lang), 8, 10
Blume, Judy, 14, 24, 26, 186, 192, 228, 235
Body Owner's Handbook, The (Arnold), 254, 258
Book creation, 52
Book of Common Prayer, The, 29
Book of Nonsense, A (Lear), 10, 15
Book of Nursery and Mother Goose Rhymes (de Angeli), 85
Book of Three, The (Alexander), 14

Book report alternatives, 48, 49
Book talks, 46–47
Borders (Mora), 62
Borders, in illustrations, 116–117
Borrowers, The (Norton), 14, 204, 211–212
Bosch, Hieronymus, 114
Boston, Lucy, 14, 212
Bowen, Abel, 9
Boy in the Striped Pajamas, The (Boyne), 226, 234
Boyne, John, 226, 234
Boy: Tales of Childhood (Dahl), 263
Brandenburg, Jim, 256
Bridge to Terabithia (Paterson), 47, 192, 236
Briggs, Raymond, 85
Bright, Robert, 212
Brink, Carol Ryrie, 13
Broker, Ignatia, 63
Brontë, Charlotte, 229
Brooke, L. Leslie, 81
Brooks, Walter R., 208
Brother Can You Spare a Dime? The Great Depression: 1929-1933 (Meltzer), 260
Brown, Marcia, 111
Brown, Margaret Wise, 24–25, 29, 92, 177
Browne, Anthony, 89
Browning, Robert, 136, 238
Bryan, Ashley, 15
Bud, Not Buddy (Curtis), 177
Bunyan, John, 3
Buried Onions (Soto), 62
Burnett, Frances Hodgson, 13, 44, 232, 234
Burningham, John, 15, 109–110, 113, 115, 119
Burton, Virginia Lee, 24, 104
Butler, Francelia, 84
Byars, Betsy, 237, 263

Caddie Woodlawn (Brink), 13
Caldecott, Randolph, 11–12, 282–284
Caldecott Medal, 12, 15, 282–284
Call Me Charley (Jackson, J.), 59–60
Call of the Wild, The (London), 233, 237
Cameron, James, 169
Canto Familia (Soto), 62
Can You Hear It? (Latch), 258
Captain Kidd's Cat (Lawson, R.), 262
Card, Orson Scott, 213
Carle, Eric, 92, 112
Carnegie Medal, 15, 291–293
Carroll, Lewis, 8, 10, 44–45, 93, 138–139, 142, 183, 202, 210, 214
Carry on, Mr. Bowditch (Latham, J. L.), 262
Carson, Rachel, 197–198
Cartoon art, 113
Castle (Macaulay), 258–259
Catcher in the Rye (Salinger), 14, 229
Cathedral (Macaulay), 254, 258–259
Cat in the Hat, The (Seuss), 93
Cat's Night Out (Stutson), 16
Caxton, William, 2
Censorship, 33–34
Chagall, Marc, 114

Chalk, in illustrations, 111
Chancy and the Grand Rascal (Fleischman), 210
Changeover, The (Mahy), 16
Changing You: A Guide to Body Changes and Sexuality (Saltz), 259
Chants (Mora), 62
Character(s), 59
   development, 180
   in folktales, 155–156
   in picture books, 104
   revelation, 180–181
   traits, 180
   types, 179–180
Charlie and the Chocolate Factory (Dahl), 44, 190
Charlotte's Web (White), 14, 24, 27, 44, 46–47, 177–178, 180–181, 184, 187, 192, 205, 208
Chat rooms, 54
Chemical Chaos (Arnold), 258
Chickens Aren't the Only Ones (Heller), 250
Child, Lauren, 15
Child development theories, 22–28
Children of Green Knowe, The (Boston), 14
Children's Homer, The (Colum), 1–2, 169
Childress, Alice, 60, 178, 184–186, 227
Child's Garden of Verses, A (Stevenson, R. L.), 10
China: Land of Dragons and Emperors (Mah), 260
Chocolate War, The (Cormier), 27, 191
Christmas Story, A (Dickens), 188
Christopher, Matt, 237
Christopher Columbus, Great Explorer (Adler), 250–251
Christopher Columbus and the World around Him (Meltzer), 250–251
Chronicles of Narnia series (Lewis), 14, 182, 201, 211
"Chronicles of Prydain" (Alexander), 204, 211
"Cinderella," 47, 143, 153–155, 160, 162, 170
Cinderella: A Pop-up Fairy Tale (Reinhart), 93
Cinquains, 138
Cisneros, Sandra, 62
Civil War for Kids, The (Herbert), 254
Clare, John, 133
Cleary, Beverly, 14, 26–27, 67, 228, 231
Cleaver, Bill, 231
Cleaver, Vera, 231
"Clever Gretel," 50
Click, Clack, Moo: Cows That Type (Cronin), 24
Clifton, Lucille, 32, 68–69
Cognitive theory of development, 23–25
Cole, Babette, 28, 253–254
Coleridge, Samuel Taylor, 129, 203
Collage, 112
Collier, Christopher, 236
Collier, John Lincoln, 236
Collins, Suzanne, 14, 201, 214, 229
Collodi, Carlo, 15, 44–45, 52, 208
Color/black and white, 109–110
Color of His Own, A (Lionni), 89
Color printing, 11
Colum, Padraic, 1–2, 169
Columbus (Parin d'Aulaire and Parin d'Aulaire), 250, 261
Come Away from the Water, Shirley (Burningham), 119
Comenius, John, 3, 5, 290–291

Comet in Moominland (Jansson), 16
Comic books, 120
Common Core Curriculum, 42–44
Common Sense Book of Baby and Child Care, The (Spock), 13–14
Communion (Mora), 62
Composition, in illustrations, 108–109
Conan Doyle, Arthur, 236
Concrete operations period, 24
Conflict, types of, 183–186
Confucius and the Golden Rule (Freedman), 260
Consonance, 131
Contemporary realism
   background of, 226–227
   bibliography of, 243–247
   definition of, 223, 226
Conventional level of development, 27
Cook, Eliza, 134
Coolies (Yin), 65
Cooney, Barbara, 15, 111, 113
Coraline (Gaimon), 212
Coral Island, The (Ballantyne), 10, 227
Corduroy (Freeman), 209
Coretta Scott King Award, 61, 287–288
Cormier, Robert, 27, 184, 191, 201
Counting books, 88–89
   bibliography of, 98–100
Cowboys of the Wild West (Freedman), 260
Crane, Walter, 11, 158–159
Crapsey, Adelaide, 138
Craven, Margaret, 63, 226–227
Crayon, in illustrations, 111
Creech, Sharon, 48–49
Cronin, Dorothy, 24
Crow Boy (Yashima), 69
Crutcher, Chris, 68, 237
Culturally diverse literature
   African Americans, 59–61
   Asian Americans, 64–65
   criteria for, 59
   definition of, 58–59
   Hinduism, 66
   Judaism, 65–66
   Latino/as, 62
   Muslims, 66
   Native Americans, 63–64
cummings, e. e., 192
Cumulative tales, 164–165
Curtis, Christopher Paul, 14, 60, 177, 225

Dactyl, 132
Daddy Is a Monster . . . Sometimes (Steptoe), 114
Daddy's Roommate (Willhoite), 14–15, 28–29
Dahl, Roald, 44, 183, 190, 263
Daily, Don, 2
Daisy Chain, The (Yonge), 10, 227
Daldry, Jeremy, 259
Danny and the Dinosaur (Hoff), 94
Darwin, Charles, 192
Dashner, James, 214
Dead Bird, The (Brown, M. W.), 29

de Angeli, Marguerite, 85
Dear Mr. Henshaw (Cleary), 14, 27, 67, 231
Death and dying, 29–31
Death and dying stories, 235–236
de Brunhoff, Jean, 15, 117, 207
Defoe, Daniel, 3–4, 227, 233
de laMare, Walter, 134
Deliver Us from Evie (Kerr, M. E.), 15, 235
Demi, 66
de Saint-Exupéry, Antoine, 15–16
Diary of a Young Girl (Frank), 33, 65, 234
DiCamillo, Kate, 233–234
Dickens, Charles, 188, 227–229
Dickinson, Terence, 256–257
Dick Whittington's Cat (Brown, Marcia), 111
Didacticism, 188–189
Digital art, 112
Discussion boards, 54
Diversity, 14, 17, 57
Divorce, 68
Doctor Dolittle books (Lofting), 208
Dodgson, Charles. *See* Carroll, Lewis
Döhl, Reinhard, 138
Donovan, John, 235
Don't Let the Pigeon Drive the Bus (Willem), 117, 207
Doorbell Rang, The (Hutchins), 89
Doré, Gustave, 154
Dowd, Siobhan, 192–193
Dragonwings (Yep), 65
Dramatic experiences, 50–51
Dr. Seuss's ABC (Seuss), 87
Duck, Death and the Tulip (Erlbruch), 30–31
Duffy and the Devil (Zemach), 111
Dystopias, 213–214

"Eagle, The " (Tennyson), 131
"Earthsea" cycle (Le Guin), 204, 229
East of the Sun West of the Moon, 51
Easy readers, 93–94
    bibliography of, 96–100
Eats, Shoots & Leaves: Why Commas Do Make a Difference (Truss), 259
Ecocriticism, 197–198
Edgeworth, Maria, 7
Educational theories, 39–42
Eggleston, Edward, 10
Eland, J. S., 230
Elementary Treatise on Mechanics, An (Whewell), 141
Elephant Prince: The Story of Ganesh (Novesky), 66
Elizabeth II (queen), 192
Elsie Dinsmore series (Finley), 189
Emerson, Ralph Waldo, 192
Emil and the Detectives (Kästen), 16
Emile (Rousseau), 7
Eminem, 130–131
Emotionally challenged children, 68–69
Enchanted journey fantasies, 210
Enchantress from the Stars (Engdahl), 213
Encyclopedia Brown series (Sobol), 237
Ender's Game (Card), 213

Engdahl, Sylvia, 204, 213
Engle, Margarita, 238
English Fairy Tales (Jacobs), 8, 10
Epic fantasy, 210–211
Epics, 169
Eric Carle's Opposites, 89
Erikson, Erik, 22–23, 25–26
Erlbruch, Wolf, 30–31
Estes, Eleanor, 13, 192, 229–230, 232–233
Evaluation questions, 47
Everett Anderson's 1, 2, 3 (Clifton), 32, 68
Everett Anderson's Good-bye (Clifton), 32
Exploring the Night Sky (Dickinson), 256–257
Expressionism, in illustration, 114

Fables, 161–162
Fables (Aesop), 2
Fables of Aesop, The (Caxton), 2
Fabulous Histories (Trimmer), 7–8
Face to Face with Wolves (Brandenburg), 256
Falconer, Ian, 67
Fama, Elizabeth, 66
Family Picture/Cuadros de Familia (Garza), 62
Family relationships in literature, 229–231
Fantasy
    bibliography of, 216–222
    characteristics of, 202–203
    characters in, 205–206
    definition of, 201
    journeys in, 210
    qualities of, 203–205
    rules in, 204–205
    types of, 205–214
    world of, 204
Farewell to Manzanar (Wakatsuki and Houston), 65
Far Side of Evil, The (Engdahl), 213
Fatal Forces (Arnold), 258
Feelings, Muriel, 89
Feelings, Tom, 89
Feminist approach, to reading, 197
Fictionalized biography, 261–262
Field, Rachel, 208
Finelli, Sara, 254
Finley, Martha, 189
Fire in My Hands, A (Soto), 62
First-person narrator, 177–178
Fitzhugh, Louise, 26, 67, 233–234
Five Children and It (Nesbit), 209
Five Chinese Brothers (Bishop, C. H.), 64
Fleischman, Sid, 210
Flynn, Benedict, 2–3
Folk art, 113
Folk literature/folktales
    American Indian, 63
    bibliography of, 171–176
    character in, 155–156
    classroom use of, 169–170
    elements of, 154–160
    images and symbols in, 157–159
    language and style in, 156–157

motifs in, 157, 160
plot in, 155
setting in, 154–155
taboos in, 160
types of, 161–168
Follow That Map! A First Book of Mapping Skills (Ritchie), 254
Ford, H. J., 163
Foreman, Michael, 2–3, 15
Foreshadowing, 187–188
Forever (Blume), 228
Formal operations period, 24–25
Forster, E. M., 181
Fortune Cookie Fortunes (Lin), 64–65
Found poetry, 140–141
Found Poetry Review, 141
Fox, Mem, 16
Fox Steals Home, The (Christopher), 237
Francisco Manzano, Juan, 238
Frank, Anne, 33, 65, 234
Frankenstein (Shelley), 213
Freddy Goes to Florida (Brooks), 208
Frederick (Lionni), 112
Freedman, Russell, 43, 250, 253, 260–262
Freeman, Don, 209
Free verse, 138
Freud, Sigmund, 196
Friedrich (Richter), 226
Friends, The (Guy), 66
Friendship in literature, 231
Fritz, Jean, 263
Frog and Toad Are Friends (Lobel), 94
Frog and Toad series (Lobel), 93–94
Frog and Toad Together (Lobel), 94
Frog He Would A-Wooing Go, The (Caldecott), 12
"Frog King, The," 153
Froman, Robert, 140
From Seed to Plant (Gibbons), 256
Frost, Robert, 129
Frye, Northrop, 194

Gág, Wanda, 110, 117
Gaimon, Neil, 212
Gallaz, Christophe, 31
Gallop! (Seder), 93
Gammage Cup, The (Kendall), 212
Ganesha's Sweet Tooth (Patel and Haynes), 66
Garne, S. T., 89
Garner, Alan, 212
Garza, Carmen Lomas, 62
Gashlycrumb Tinies, The (Gorey), 88, 190
Gates, Henry Louis, Jr., 58
Geisel, Theodore, 13
Gender, 23
Gender awareness, 67–68
George, Jean Craighead, 4, 179, 185, 234
George Washington: Young Leader (Stevenson, A.), 261
Georgie and the Robbers (Bright), 212
Ghost in the Noonday Sun, The (Fleischman), 210
Ghost of Thomas Kempe, The (Lively), 212
Ghost stories, 165–166

Gibbons, Gail, 256
Giblin, James Cross, 260
Gift from Zeus: Sixteen Favorite Myths, A (Steig, J.), 1–2
"Gingerbread Man, The," 155, 157
Giver, The (Lowry), 213–214
Golden Fleece and the Heroes Who Lived before Achilles, The (Colum), 169
Golding, William, 229
Gone with the Wind (Mitchell, M.), 224
Goodnight Moon (Brown, M. W.), 25, 92, 177
Gorey, Edward, 88, 190
Gouache, in illustrations, 111
Graham, Bob, 16
Grahame, Kenneth, 12, 204, 207–208
Grandfather's Journey (Say), 64
Graphic art, 51–52
Graphic novels, 120–121
Graphic techniques, in illustrations, 111–112
Gravett, Emily, 15
Great Expectations (Dickens), 229
Great Gilly Hopkins, The (Paterson), 68, 228, 234
Greek myths, 1–2
Greek Myths (Williams), 1–2
Green, John, 236
Greenaway, Kate, 11, 82, 293–295
"Green Knowe" books (Boston), 212
Grimm, Jacob, 8, 153
Grimm, Wilhelm, 8, 153
Grollman, Earl A., 259
Gulliver's Travels (Swift), 4, 211, 214
Gutenberg, Johannes, 3
Gutter, in illustrations, 117
Guy, Rosa, 60, 66

Haiku, 137
Hailstones and Halibut Bones (O'Neill), 145
Hale, Lucretia, 210
Halinka (Pressler), 68, 227
Hall, Donald, 111, 113
Hamilton, Virginia, 14, 60, 69, 227
Handford, Martin, 91
Hans Christian Andersen Award, 15, 295–296
"Hansel and Gretel," 48, 50, 153, 155–157, 170, 194–198
Hardy Boys series, 237
Harold and the Purple Crayon (Johnson), 25
Harriet the Spy (Fitzhugh), 26, 67, 233–234
Harris, Robie, 28
Harry Potter and the Sorcerer's Stone (Rowling), 14
Harry Potter series (Rowling), 203, 211
Hastings, Selina, 2–3
Haunting, The (Mahy), 16
Have Space Suit Will Travel (Heinlein), 213
Haynes, Emily, 66
Heart and the Bottle, The (Jeffers), 29–30
Heather Has Two Mommies (Newman and Souza), 29
Heinlein, Robert, 213
Heller, Ruth, 250–251, 256
"Hello," I Lied (Kerr, M. E.), 227
"Henny Penny," 161, 164
Henry, Marguerite, 237–238

Henry and Mudge series (Rylant), 94
Henry Huggins (Cleary), 26
Herbert, Janis, 254
Herculeah Jones series (Byars), 237
Hero Ain't Nothin' but a Sandwich, A (Childress), 60, 178, 184–186, 227
Heroes of Olympus, The (Riordan), 2
Heroic epics, 169
Herron, Carolivia, 61, 117
Hesse, Karen, 225, 238
Hiaasen, Carl, 238
Hidden Animals (Selsam), 252
Higher Power of Lucky, The (Patron), 33, 231
High-Rise Private Eyes series (Rylant), 237
"Highwayman, The " (Noyes), 136
Hinduism, 66
Hinton, S. E., 228
Hiroshima No Pika (Maruki), 31
His Dark Materials series (Pullman), 201, 211, 229
Historical approach, to reading, 195–196
Historical novels, 10
Historical realism
    anachronisms and, 226
    bibliography of, 240–243
    definition of, 223–225
    language in, 225–226
History of Little Goody Two-Shoes, The, 188–189
Hitty: Her First Hundred Years (Field), 208
Hoban, Russell, 209
Hobbit; or, There and Back Again, The (Tolkien), 13, 204
Hoff, Syd, 94
Hoffman, Heinrich, 16
Holes (Sachar), 201
Homecoming (Voigt), 68, 231
Homecoming: My Own Story (Fritz), 263
Homer, 1–2, 153, 169, 211
Hoosier Schoolmaster, The (Eggleston), 10
Hoot (Hiaasen), 238
Hornbooks, 3–4
Horrible Science series (Arnold), 257–258
House at Pooh Corner, The (Milne), 208–209
House on Mango Street, The (Cisneros), 62
Houston, James D., 65
Howe, James, 68
How I Came to Be a Writer (Naylor), 263
How I Live Now (Rosoff), 214
Hughes, Thomas, 10, 227
Humor, 189–190
Hundred Dresses, The (Estes), 232–233
Hunger Games, The (Collins), 14
"Hunger Games" trilogy (Collins), 201, 214, 229
Hunt, Irene, 11, 225–226
Hunter, Mollie, 236
Hutchins, Pat, 89, 116

Iamb, 132
I Am the Cheese (Cormier), 184, 191, 201
Ibatoulline, Bagram, 260
I Can Hear the Mourning Dove (Bennett), 227
Ice Is Coming, The (Wrightson), 16

Identity versus role confusion stage, 26
I Discover Columbus (Lawson, R.), 262
I Heard the Owl Call My Name (Craven), 63, 226–227
Iliad, The (Homer), 1–2, 153, 211
I'll Get There. It Better Be Worth the Trip (Donovan), 235
Illustrated books, 11, 15, 81
    culturally diverse literature, 59, 61, 64
    unsavories in, 80, 82–83
    wood engravings, 4–6, 80
Industry versus inferiority stage, 26
Initiative versus guilt stage, 25–26
Ink, in illustrations, 111
Innocenti, Roberto, 31
Intellectual freedom, 33–34
Intellectually challenged children, 68–69
Interpretation questions, 46
In the Night Kitchen (Sendak), 33
Introduction to Children's Literature, An (Hunt), 11
Invention of Hugo Cabret, The (Selznick), 120
Irony, 191
Island Keeper, The (Mazer), 234
Island of the Blue Dolphins (O'Dell), 4, 44, 179, 185, 192, 201, 233–234
It Gets Better: Coming Out, Overcoming Bullying, and Creating a Life Worth Living (Savage), 259
It's Perfectly Normal: Changing Bodies, Growing Up, Sex, and Sexual Health (Harris), 28
Ivanhoe (Scott, W.), 223

"Jabberwocky, The" (Carroll), 142
"Jack and the Beanstalk," 153
Jackson, Jesse, 59–60
Jackson, Peter, 169
"Jack Sprat," 80–81
Jacobs, Joseph, 8, 10, 153
James and the Giant Peach (Dahl), 183
Jane Eyre (Brontë), 229
Jansson, Tove, 16, 183
Jay, Alison, 89
Jeffers, Oliver, 29–30
Jenkins, Steve, 89–90, 254
Jewish culture
    bibliography on, 77–78
    depiction of, 65–66
Johnny and the Dead (Pratchett), 212
Johnny Maxwell series (Pratchett), 212–213
Johnson, Crockett, 25
Johnston, Basil, 16
Journals, keeping, 48–49
Journeys, 3–4, 183
Julie of the Wolves (George), 4, 179, 185, 234
Jumanji (Van Allsburg), 105, 107–111, 114–115
Jump tales, 166
Jung, Carl Gustav, 21, 194, 215
Juxtaposition, in picture books, 115

Kandinsky, Wassily, 114
Kappas, Katharine, 189–190
Kästen, Erich, 16
Kate Greenaway Medal, 15, 293–295

Keats, Ezra Jack, 25–26, 32, 60–61, 89, 103–104, 112
Keats, John, 133–134
Kendall, Carol, 212
Kennedy, John F., 261
Kerr, Judith, 65, 103, 111, 114, 116, 234
Kerr, M. E., 15, 227, 235
Kidnapped (Stevenson, R. L.), 10, 233
Killing the Kudu (Meyer, C.), 69
Kilner, Dorothy, 207
King, Martin Luther, Jr., 287
King, Stephen, 214
King Arthur and the Knights of the Round Table (Flynn), 2–3
King-Smith, Dick, 208
Kitchen, Bert, 87
Kite Flying (Lin), 64–65
Klassen, Jon, 16
Klee, Paul, 114
Klein, Norma, 68
Knight, Eric, 237–238
Knoth, Maeve Visser, 32
"Kob Antelope," 134–135
Kohlberg, Lawrence, 22–23, 26–27
Konigsburg, E. L., 233
Kraus, Robert, 69
Kunhardt, Dorothy, 23, 92–93, 191

Lagerlöf, Selma, 16, 210
Lang, Andrew, 8, 10, 153
Language
    acquisition of, 22, 83–84
    in folktales, 156–157
    gender awareness, 67
    in historical realism, 225–226
    in picture books, 104
Language of Goldfish, The (Oneal), 234
Lassie Come Home (Knight), 237–238
Latch, William, 258
Latham, Dr., 249
Latham, Jean Lee, 262
Latinos/as
    bibliography on, 75–76
    depiction of, 62
Laura Ingalls Wilder Award, 15, 286
"Law and Order" Orientation, 27
Lawson, JoArno, 15
Lawson, Robert, 110, 113, 262
Layout, of picture books, 118–119
Leaf, Munro, 105, 107–108, 110
Lear, Edward, 10, 15, 132, 141–142
Lee, Harper, 229
Le Guin, Ursula, 14, 183, 204, 229
L'Engle, Madeleine, 213
Leo the Late Bloomer (Kraus), 69
Les Fauves, in illustrations, 114
Letter to Amy, A (Keats, E. J.), 32
Levine, Robert, 258
Lewis, C. S., 14, 44, 182, 201, 204, 211, 214
Life and Perambulations of a Mouse, The (Kilner), 207
Light beyond the Forest, The (Sutcliffe), 169
Light in the Attic, A (Silverstein), 33, 143

Limericks, 140
Limited narrator, 178
Lin, Grace, 14, 64–65, 228
Lincoln: A Photobiography (Freedman), 43, 250, 253, 261–262
Lindgren, Astrid, 15–16, 192, 201, 209–210, 296
Line, in illustrations, 105
Line, in picture books, 105
Ling, Mary, 255
Linocuts, in illustrations, 111
Lion, the Witch and the Wardrobe, The (Lewis), 14, 44, 204
Lionni, Leo, 89, 112, 209
Literature as Exploration (Rosenblatt), 41
Little Bear series (Minarik), 93–94
Little Black Sambo (Bannerman), 59–61
Little House in the Big Woods, The (Wilder), 13, 24, 178–179,
    181–182, 187
"Little Jack Horner," 80
"Little Miss Muffet," 82–83
Little Pretty Pocket Book, A (Newbery), 7
Little Prince, The (de Saint-Exupéry), 15–16
"Little Red RidingHood," 153–154, 157, 160, 170
Little Women (Alcott), 10, 225, 227, 229–230
Lively, Penelope, 212
Living Dead Girl (Scott, E.), 235
Livingston, Myra Cohn, 15
Lobel, Arnold, 2, 93–94
Local legends, 165
Locke, John, 7
Lofting, Hugh, 208
London, Jack, 233, 237
Long, Sylvia, 84
Longfellow, Henry Wadsworth, 130, 136
Long Way from Chicago, A (Peck), 177–178
Lon Po Po: A Red-Riding Hood Story from China (Young, E.), 64
Looking for Alaska (Green), 236
Lord of the Flies (Golding), 229
Lord of the Rings, The (Tolkien), 13
Lord of the Rings, The series (Tolkien), 169, 211
Lowry, Lois, 54, 179, 192, 213–214, 226, 236
Lucas, George, 169
Lyric poetry, 137–140
Lytle, Ruby, 137

Macaulay, David, 15, 117, 254, 258–259
MacCann, Donnarae, 64
MacDonald, George, 10
MacDonald, Suse, 87, 89
MacLachlan, Patricia, 228, 231
MacLeod, Anne Scott, 226
Madeline (Bemelmans), 51, 106, 109, 114, 116–117
Magical fantasy, 209–210
Mah, Adeline Yen, 260
Mahy, Margaret, 16
Make Lemonade (Wolf), 238
Make Way for Ducklings (McCloskey), 110, 112
Manzoni, Alessandro, 224
Mapping, 48
Marcellino, Fred, 59, 61
Märchen, 162
Marcus, Julie, 191

Markham, Edwin, 70
Mark Twain? What Kind of Name Is That? (Quackenbush), 262
Marshall, James, 210
Maruki, Toshi, 31
Mary Poppins (Travers), 13, 209
Mazel and Shlimazel (Singer), 65–66
Mazer, Harry, 234
Maze Runner, The (Dashner), 214
McCaughrean, Geraldine, 3
McCloskey, Robert, 103–104, 110, 112, 182
McCloud, Scott, 120
McCord, David, 15
McDermott, Gerald, 113, 166–168
Medieval Feast, A (Aliki), 250
Meggandorfer, Lothar, 93
Meggandorfer Prize, 93
Meltzer, Milton, 250–251, 260
Memory questions, 46
Merry tales, 162–164
"Messy Room" (Silverstein), 143
Metamorphoses (Ovid), 2
Metaphor, 135
Meyer, Carolyn, 69
Meyer, Michele Lee, 66
Meyer, Stephanie, 212
Michael Printz Award, 120
Middle Ages, literature of, 2–3
Midsummer Night's Dream, A (Shakespeare), 183
Mike Mulligan and His Steam Shovel (Burton), 24, 104
Mildred L. Batchelder Award, 285–286
Millions of Cats (Gág), 110, 117
Milne, A. A., 12, 208–209
Minarik, Else Holmelund, 93–94
Miniature fantasy, 211–212
Misty of Chincoteague (Henry), 237–238
Mitchell, Adrian, 2
Mitchell, Margaret, 224
Moe, Jørgen, 153
Moffats, The (Estes), 13, 192, 229–230
Moja Means One: A Swahili Counting Book (Feelings and Feelings), 89
Mom, the Wolfman, and Me (Klein), 68
Mommy Laid an Egg; Or, Where Do Babies Come From? (Cole), 28, 253–254
Monster Calls, A (Ness and Dowd), 192–193
Montessori, Maria, 13
Montgomery, Lucy Maud, 16, 232
Moominsummer Madness (Jansson), 183
"Moon, The" (Stevenson, R. L.), 131
Moon and I, The (Byars), 263
Mora, Pat, 62
Moral stories, 7–8
Morpurgo, Michael, 2–3, 169
Moss, Lloyd, 117–118
Mother Goose rhymes. *See* Nursery rhymes
Mother Goose's Melodies (Bowen), 9
Mother Goose Treasury, The (Briggs), 85
Mouse and His Child, The (Hoban), 209
"Mouse and the Cake, The" (Cook), 134
"Mouse's Tale, The" (Carroll), 138–139

Movable-type printing press, 3
Mr. Grumpy's Outing (Burningham), 109–110
Mr. Lunch Takes a Plane Ride (Walsh), 112
Mrs. Frisby and the Rats of NIMH (O'Brien), 208
Muhammad (Demi), 66
Mummies Made in Egypt (Aliki), 260
Murphy, Jim, 43, 250, 260
Musgrove, Margaret, 88
"Musicians of Bremen-Town, The," 161
Muslim culture depiction, 66
My Brother Sam Is Dead (Collier and Collier), 236
My Daddy Is Jewish and My Mommy Is Christian (Meyer, M. L.), 66
My Darling, My Hamburger (Zindel), 235
Myers, Walter Dean, 14, 227
My Feet Aren't Ugly! A Girl's Guide to Loving Herself from the Inside Out (Beck), 259
My Friend Flicka (O'Hara), 237–238
My Friend Jacob (Clifton), 69
My Friend Rabbit (Rohmann), 91–92, 107, 113
My Map Book (Finelli), 254
My Name in Asher Lev (Potok), 66
My Side of the Mountain (George), 234
Mystery stories, 235–236
Myths
    ancient Greek and Roman, 168–169
    Native American, 169
    Norse, 168–169

Na, An, 65
Naïve art, in illustrations, 114
Nancy Drew series, 237
Nappy Hair (Herron), 61, 117
Narrative poetry, 136
Narrative point of view, 177–179
Nasty Nature (Arnold), 258
National Council of Teachers of English Award for Excellence in Poetry for Children, 289
Native Americans
    bibliography about, 73–75
    depiction of, 63–64
Naylor, Phyllis Reynolds, 238, 263
NCTE Orbis Pictus Award for Outstanding Nonfiction for Children, 290–291
Nesbit, E., 209
Ness, Philip, 192–193
Newbery, Elizabeth, 8
Newbery, John, 7, 279–282
Newbery Medal, 7, 15, 279–282
New England Primer, 3, 6
Newman, Leslea, 29
New Realism, 14–15, 227–228
New Way Things Work, The (Macaulay), 117, 258
Nielsen, Kay, 51, 114–117
Night Flying Woman: An Ojibway Narrative (Broker), 63
No Child Left Behind Act of 2001, 42
Nodelman, Perry, 109, 116, 118–119
Nonfiction books
    arts and leisure, 258–259
    bibliography of, 266–278
    biography and autobiography, 260–263

characteristics of, 249–254
Common Core Curriculum and, 43, 263
definition of, 249, 252
factual information, 250–252
format of, 252–253
history, society, culture, 260
human growth and development, 259
illustrations in, 253–255
purpose and audience, 250
science and nature, 256–258
style of, 252
types of, 254–263
Nonsense verse, 141–142
Norton, Mary, 14, 204, 211–212
Novalis, 146
"November Night" (Crapsey), 138
Novesky, Amy, 66
Noyes, Alfred, 136
Number the Stars (Lowry), 54, 179, 192, 226
Nursery rhymes
aesthetic development and, 83–84
bibliography of, 96–97
child development and, 81–85
choices of, 85
cognitive development and, 81–83
definition and origin, 79–81
language acquisition from, 83–84
physical development and, 84
violent content in, 84

O'Brien, Robert, 208
O'Dell, Scott, 4, 44, 63, 179, 185, 192, 201, 233–234, 289–290
Odyssey, The (Homer), 1–2, 211
O'Hara, Mary, 237–238
Oil paint, in illustrations, 111
Old Testament, 153
Omniscient narrator, 178
1, 2, 3: A Child's First Counting Book (Jay), 89
Oneal, Zibby, 234
One Gorilla: A Counting Book (Browne), 89
O'Neill, Mary, 134, 145
One Morning in Maine (McCloskey), 103
One of the Problems of Everett Anderson (Clifton), 32
One White Sail (Garne), 89
One World, Many Religions: The Way We Worship (Osborne), 260
Only You Can Save Mankind (Pratchett), 213
Optic, Oliver, 10
Orbis Sensualium Pictus (Comenius), 3, 5, 290–291
Osborne, Mary Pope, 260
Otto of the Silver Hand (Pyle), 10, 223–224
Out of Sight: Pictures of Hidden Worlds (Simon), 254
Out of the Dust (Hesse), 225, 238
Outsiders (Hinton), 228
Outward Bound: or, Young America Afloat (Optic), 10
"Outwitted" (Markham), 70
Overboard (Fama), 66
"Over in the Meadow," 89
Ovid, 2
"Owl and the Pussy Cat, The" (Lear), 132

Owl Service (Garner), 212
Ox-Cart Man, The (Hall), 111, 113

Page layout, in illustrations, 116–117
Page size and shape, in picture books, 116
Painterly techniques, in illustrations, 110–111
Panels, in illustrations, 117
Parind'Aulaire, Edgar, 250, 261
Parind'Aulaire, Ingri, 250, 261
Parish, Peggy, 94
Parker, Kate Langloh, 16
Parody, 190–191
Pastels, in illustrations, 111
Patel, Sanjay, 66
Paterson, Katherine, 47, 68, 192, 228, 234, 236
Patron, Susan, 33, 231
"Pattern Poem with an Elusive Intruder" (Döhl), 138
Pat the Bunny (Kunhardt), 23, 92–93, 191
Pat the Politician (Marcus), 191
Pearce, Philippa, 204, 212
Peck, Richard, 177–178, 236
Pencil, in illustrations, 111
Perceptual concept books, 89–90
bibliography of, 98–100
Percy Jackson and the Olympians (Riordan), 2
Perrault, Charles, 8, 79
Personification, 136
Perspective, in illustrations, 109
Peterkin Papers, The (Hale), 210
Peter Pan (Barrie), 12
Peter's Chair (Keats, E. J.), 25–26, 32
Photography, 112
Physically challenged children, 68–69
Piaget, Jean, 15, 22–25
Picture books
art nouveau in, 114
bibliography of, 123–128
cartoon art, 113
characteristics, 101–103
characters in, 104
collage in, 112
color/black and white, 109–110
composition in, 108–109
digital art, 112
expressionism in, 114
folk art in, 113
graphic novels, 120–121
graphic techniques, 111–112
juxtaposition in, 115
language in, 104
layout of, 118–119
line in, 105
naïve art in, 114
page layout in, 116–117
page size and shape in, 116
painterly techniques, 110–111
perspective in, 109
photography, 112
plot in, 103–104
realism, 113

Picture books (*continued*)
  rhythm and movement in, 115–116
  shape in, 105
  space in, 105, 107
  stories, 103–104
  surrealism in, 114
  tension in, 116
  texture in, 107–108
  typography in, 117–118
  words in, 118–119
"Pied Piper of Hamelin, The" (Browning), 136
Pilgrim's Progress, The (Bunyan), 3
Pinckney, Jerry, 2
Pinker, Steven, 22
Pippi Longstocking (Lindgren), 16, 192, 201, 209–210, 296
Planet of Junior Brown, The (Hamilton), 60
Plastic art, 52
Plato, 213
Playground poetry, 143–144
Plot
  dramatic structure, 181
  episodic structure, 181–182
  in fiction, 181–183
  in folktales, 155
  journey, 183
  parallel structure, 182–183
  in picture books, 103–104
Poe, Edgar Allan, 133, 236
Poetry
  comparative description in, 134–136
  definition, 129–130
  kinds of, 136–144
  pictures in, 133–136
  sensory description in, 133–134
  sharing with children, 144–146
  sounds in, 130–132
Poet Slave of Cuba, The (Engle), 238
Pollyanna (Porter), 189
Porter, Eleanor, 189
Postconventional level of development, 27
Potok, Chaim, 66
Potter, Beatrix, 11, 26–27, 51, 103, 110–111, 113, 116–117, 188, 207
Pourquoi tales, 167–168
PowerPoint, 53
Pratchett, Terry, 212, 213
Preconventional level of development, 26–27
Prelutsky, Jack, 15
Preoperational period, 23–24
Pressler, Mirjam, 68, 227
Priceman, Marjorie, 117–118
Princess and the Goblin, The (MacDonald, G.), 10
Principles Conscience Orientation, 27
Problem novels, 227–228
Professional stereotypes, 67
Profiles in Courage (Kennedy), 261
Psychoanalytical approach, to reading, 196
Psychology, 13–14
Pullman, Phillip, 201, 211, 229
Punishment/Obedience Orientation, 26–27

Puppet theater, 51
Puritanism, influence of, 3, 6
Puzzler stories, 235–236
Pyle, Howard, 10, 223–224
Pyramid (Macaulay), 258–259

Quackenbush, Robert, 262
Quest fantasy. *See* Epic fantasy

Rackham, Arthur, 83
Ragged Dick: or, Street Life in New York (Alger), 10
Rain Forests (Vogt), 256
Ramayana, 153
Ramona books (Cleary), 228
Ramona the Pest (Cleary), 26
Rapunzel, 103, 108–111, 113, 116, 157
"Rapunzel," 153, 162–163
"Raven, The" (Poe), 133
Rawlings, Marjorie Kinnan, 236, 238
Rawls, Wilson, 236, 238
Reader, the Text, the Poem: The Transactional Theory of the Literary Work, The (Rosenblatt), 41
Reader-response theory, 41–42
Reader's theater, 50–51
Reader's Theater Editions, 170
Reading
  archetypal approach to, 194–195
  ecocriticism in, 197–198
  feminist approach to, 197
  formal approach to, 193–194
  historical approach to, 195–196
  psychoanalytical approach to, 196
  reading aloud, 44–45
Realism
  contemporary, 223
  historical, 223
  in illustrations, 113
Realistic fiction
  bibliography of, 240–247
  contemporary realism in, 226–228
  historical realism in, 223–226
  topics in, 228–238
Real Mother Goose, The (Wright), 85–86
Reason for a Flower, The (Heller), 250–251, 256
Red Fairy Book, The (Lang), 8
Red Fox (Roberts), 16, 237
Reinhart, Matthew, 93
Reinventing Comics (McCloud), 120
Remembering the Good Times (Peck), 236
Renaissance in Europe, 3–6
Republic (Plato), 213
Rhyme
  in aesthetic development, 83–84
  in child development, 81–83
  in poetry, 130–131
  violence in, 84–85
Rhythm, 115–116, 131–132
Richards, Laura, 142
Richter, Hans, 226
Ring and the Boo, The (Browning), 238

Riordan, Rick, 2
Ritchie, Scot, 254
Robert F. Sibert Informational Book Award, 291
Roberts, Charles G. D., 16, 237
Robinson, Charles, 232
Robinson Crusoe (Defoe), 3–4, 227, 233
Rohmann, Eric, 91–92, 107, 113
Rojankovsky, Feodor, 89
Roll of Thunder, Hear My Cry (Taylor), 27, 60, 67, 184, 201
Roman myths and legends, 2
Rose Blanche (Innocenti and Gallaz), 31
Rosenblatt, Louise, 41–42
Rosie's Walk (Hutchins), 116
Rosoff, Meg, 214
Rousseau, Jean-Jacques, 7
Rowling, J. K., 14, 33, 203, 211–212
Ruby (Guy), 60, 66
Rumford, James, 2
Rumpelstiltskin (Zelinsky), 115
"Rumpelstiltskin," 41–42, 153, 155, 160
Runaway Bunny, The (Brown, M. W.), 24, 92
Rylant, Cynthia, 94, 237

Sabuda, Robert, 93
Sachar, Louis, 201
Salinger, J. D., 14, 229
Salten, Felix, 16
Saltz, Gail, 259
Sanchez, Alex, 15
"Sarah Cynthia Sylvia Stout" (Silverstein), 143
Savage, Dan, 259
Say, Allen, 64
School stories, 10
Science fiction, 213
Scieszka, John, 170, 190
Scorpions (Myers), 227
Scott, Elizabeth, 235
Scott, Walter, 223
Scott O'Dell Award for Historical Fiction, 289–290
Secret Garden, The (Burnett), 13, 44, 232, 234
Secrets of the Sphinx (Giblin), 260
Seder, Rufus Butler, 93
Seeger, Laura Vacaro, 89
"Seeing Poem, A" (Froman), 140
Seibold, J.otto, 112
Self-interest Orientation, 27
Selsam Millicent, 252
Selznick, Brian, 120
Sendak, Maurice, 15, 33, 93–94, 103, 111, 118–119, 185–186
Sensorimotor period, 23
Sentimentalism, 189
Series books, 10
Sesame Street, 91
Seton, Ernest Thompson, 16, 237
Setting
    definition, 179
    in fiction, 179
    in folktales, 154–155
Seuss, Dr., 13, 15, 87, 93, 113
Sewell, Anna, 207

Sex, Puberty, and All That Stuff: A Guide to Growing Up (Bailey), 259
Sexuality, 14–15
Sexuality stories, 235
Shadows of Ghadames, The (Stoltz), 66
Shakespeare, William, 131–132, 183
Shape, in illustrations, 105
Shape by Shape (MacDonald, S.), 89
Shapeshifters: Tales from Ovid's Metamorphoses (Mitchell, A.), 2
Shelley, Mary, 213
Shepard, Ernest H., 207
Sherman, Alexie, 63–64
Sherwood, Mrs., 8
Shiloh (Naylor), 238
Shlemiel Went to Warsaw and Other Stories (Singer), 65–66
Siegal, Aranka, 65
Sight, in poetry, 133
Silent Spring (Carson), 197–198
Silverstein, Shel, 15, 33, 143
Simile, 134–135
Simon, Seymour, 43, 254
Simple Susan (Edgeworth), 7
Sing Down the Moon (O'Dell), 63
Singer, Isaac Bashevis, 65–66
Sir Gawain and the Green Knight (Morpurgo), 2–3
Sir Gawain and the Loathly Lady (Hastings), 2–3
Skipping Around the World (Butler), 84
Sleeping Bear Dune, in folktales, 167–168
"Sleeping Beauty, The," 155, 159–160, 162
Smell, in poetry, 133–134
Sneed, Brad, 2
Snowbound (Mazer), 234
"Snow White," 155, 157–158
Snowy Day, The (Keats, E. J.), 32, 60–61, 103–104, 112
Snyder, Zilpha, 204–205
Sobol, Donald, 237
Social Contract Orientation, 27
Social diversity
    alternative families, 68
    gender awareness, 67–68
    physically, emotionally, and intellectually challenges, 68–69
    types of, 66–69
Social outcast stories, 234
Socrates, 39
"Song of Hiawatha, The" (Longfellow), 136
Soto, Gary, 62
Sound, in poetry, 133
Sound of Chariots, A (Hunter), 236
Southall, Ivan, 16
Souza, Diana, 29
Space, in illustrations, 105, 107
Speak (Anderson), 235
Special needs children, 68–69
Speculative fiction, 213
Spock, Benjamin, 13–14
Sports stories, 237
Star Wars series, 169, 213
Staying Fat for Sarah Byrnes (Crutcher), 68
Steig, Jeanne, 1–2
Steig, William, 207, 209

Step from Heaven, A (Na), 65
Steptoe, John, 114–115
Stevenson, Augusta, 261
Stevenson, Robert Louis, 10, 44, 131, 136, 179–180, 223, 233
Stevenson, Suçie, 94
Stewig, John Warren, 115
Stine, R. L., 214
Stoltz, Joelle, 66
Stone lithography, in illustrations, 112
Story circle, 50
Story of Babar, the Little Elephant, The (de Brunhoff), 15, 117, 207
Story of Ferdinand, The (Leaf), 105, 107–108, 110
Story of Johnny Appleseed, The (Aliki), 261
Story of Little Babaji (Marcellino and Bannerman), 59, 61
Story of Mankind, The (van Loon), 249
Story of the Orchestra (Levine), 258
Story of the Robins, The (Trimmer), 7–8, 207
Storytelling, 45–46
Story theater, 50
Straight Talk about Death for Teenagers: How to Cope with Losing Someone You Love (Grollman), 259
Struwwelpeter (Hoffman), 16
Stupids Die, The (Allard), 210
Stupids Have a Ball, The (Allard), 210
Stutson, Carolyn, 16
Style, literary
    dialogue, 187
    exposition, 187
    flashback, 188
    in folktales, 156–157
    foreshadowing, 187–188
    of nonfiction books, 252
Stylized intensification, 164–165
Summer to Die, A (Lowry), 236
Supernatural fantasy, 212
Surrealism, in illustrations, 114
Survival stories, 233–234
Sutcliff, Rosemary, 169
Sweet Valley High series, 228
Sweet Whispers, Brother Rush (Hamilton), 69
Swift, Jonathan, 4, 211, 214
Sylvester and the Magic Pebble (Steig, W.), 207, 209
Sylvia Long's Mother Goose (Long), 84

Tabula rasa, 7
Tactile and movable books, 23, 92–93, 98–100
Tale of Benjamin Bunny (Potter), 207
Tale of Peter Rabbit, The (Potter), 11, 26–27, 51, 103, 110–111, 113, 116–117, 188, 207
Tales from Mother Goose (Perrault), 79
Tales from the Arabian Nights, 8
Tales of a Fourth Grade Nothing (Blume), 24
Tales of Mother Goose (Perrault), 8
Tales the Elders Told: Ojibway Legends (Johnston), 16
Talking animal tales, 161
Tall tales, 165, 210
Taste, in poetry, 134
Taylor, Mildred, 14, 27, 60, 67, 184, 201, 227
Technology, 52–54

Teenage Guy's Survival Guide: The Real Deal on Girls, Growing Up and Other Guy Stuff, The (Daldry), 259
Tell, William, 165
Tempera, in illustrations, 111
Ten, Nine, Eight (Bang), 89
Tenniel, John, 202
Tennyson, Alfred, Lord, 131
Tension, in picture books, 116
Texture, 107–108
Theme
    definition, 191–192
    in fiction, 192–193
13 Planets: The Latest View of the Solar System (Aguilar), 257
This History of the Fairchild Family (Sherwood), 8
This Is Not My Hat (Klassen), 16
Thomas, Joseph T., Jr., 142
Thoughts Concerning Education (Locke), 7
"Three Billy Goats Gruff, The," 153, 161, 164–165
Three Little Wolves and the Big Bad Pig, The (Trivizas), 170, 190–191
Three Pigs, The (Wiesner), 119, 170, 191
"Three Pigs, The," 157, 161, 165, 170
"Three Wishes, The," 163–164
Through the Looking-Glass and What Alice Found There (Carroll), 8, 10, 142
Tiger Eyes (Blume), 228
Tiger Who Came to Tea, The (Kerr, J.), 103, 111, 114, 116
"Time's a Bird" (Bloom), 135
Time-shift fantasy, 212
"To Autumn" (Keats, J.), 133
To Kill a Mockingbird (Lee), 229
Tolkien, J. R. R., 13, 169, 204, 211
Tolstoy, Leo, 229
Tom Brown's School Days (Hughes), 10, 227
Tom's Midnight Garden (Pearce), 204, 212
Tone, literary, 188–191
Touchdown Pass (Bee), 237
Toy fantasy, 208–209
Transactional analysis, 41
Travers, P. L., 13, 209
Treasure Island (Stevenson, R. L.), 44, 179–180, 233
Trickster tales, 166–167
Trimmer, Sarah, 7–8, 207
Trivizas, Eugene, 170, 190–191
Trochee, 132
True Confessions of Charlotte Doyle (Avi), 226
True Story of the Three Little Pigs, The (Scieszka), 170, 190
Truss, Lynn, 259
Trust versus mistrust stage, 25
Tuchman, Barbara, 195
Tuck Everlasting (Babbitt), 14, 47, 184, 187–188, 204
Tuesday (Wiesner), 92, 103, 109–110
"Turnip, The," 155, 165
Tutu, Desmond, 192
Twain, Mark, 10, 33, 44, 190, 227, 229, 235–236, 262
"Twelve Dancing Princesses, The," 103, 110, 115
Twenty Thousand Leagues under the Sea (Verne), 213
Twilight (Meyer, S.), 212
Typography, 117–118

Unbuilding (Macaulay), 258–259
Understanding Comics (McCloud), 120
Universal Declaration of Human Rights, 69
Upon the Head of a Goat: A Childhood in Hungary, 1939-1944 (Siegal), 65
Urchin poetry, 142–143
Uses of Enchantment, The (Bettelheim), 196

Van Allsburg, Chris, 15, 87, 105, 107–111, 114–115
van Loon, Henkrik, 249
Velveteen Rabbit (Bianco), 208
Verne, Jules, 213
Verse (Crapsey), 138
Verse novels, 238
Very Hungry Caterpillar, The (Carle), 112
Victorian Golden Age, 8–12
View from Saturday, The (Konigsburg), 233
Vignette, in illustrations, 117
Violence, 31
Viorst, Judith, 88
Virgil, 211
Visual poetry, 138–140
Vogt, Richard C., 256
Voigt, Cynthia, 68, 227, 231
Voyage of the Dawn Treader, The (Lewis), 182
Vygotsky, Lev, 22, 40–41

Wakatsuki, Jeanne, 65
Walk Two Moons (Creech), 48–49
Walsh, Vivian, 112
War, 31
War Dances (Sherman), 63–64
War of the Worlds, The (Wells), 213
Watcher, The (Howe), 68
Watching Desert Wildlife (Arnosky), 252
Watercolors, in illustrations, 111
Watership Down (Adams), 208
Watsons Go to Birmingham, The (Curtis), 225
Waverley (Scott, W.), 223
Wayne, John, 192
Way Things Work, The (Macaulay), 258
Webbing, 47–48
WebQuest.org, 54
Websites, 53–54
Wells, H. G., 213
When Hitler Stole Pink Rabbit (Kerr, J.), 65, 234
When She Hollers (Voigt), 227
Where's Wally? series (Handford), 91
Where the Lilies Bloom (Cleaver and Cleaver), 231
Where the Mountain Meets the Moon (Lin), 65
Where the Red Fern Grows (Rawls), 236, 238
Where the Sidewalk Ends (Silverstein), 143
Where the Wild Things Are (Sendak), 103, 111, 118–119, 185–186
Whewell, William, 141

White, E. B., 14, 24, 27, 44, 46–47, 177–178, 180–181, 184, 187, 192, 205, 208
Whitman, Walt, 133–134
Wiese, Kurt, 64
Wiesner, David, 15, 92, 103, 109–110, 119, 170, 191
Wild Animals I Have Known (Seton), 16, 237
Wilder, Laura Ingalls, 13, 15, 24, 178–179, 181–182, 187, 286
Willems, Mo, 117, 207
Willhoite, Michael, 14–15, 28–29
Williams, Marcia, 1–2
Wilson, August, 58
Wilson, Edward O., 57
Wilson, Woodrow, 140
Wind in the Willows, The (Grahame), 12, 204, 207–208
Winnie-the-Pooh (Milne), 12, 208–209
Winter's Tale (Sabuda), 93
"Winter-Time" (Stevenson, R. L.), 136
Wizard of Earthsea, A (Le Guin), 14, 183
Wolf, Virginia Euwer, 238
Wonderful Adventures of Nils, The (Lagerlöf), 16, 210
Wonderful Wizard of Oz, The (Baum), 10, 93, 179–180, 183, 191, 204–206
Wonder tales, 162
Woodblocks, in illustrations, 111
Woodson, Jacqueline, 60
Wordless picture books, 90–92
Words, in picture books, 118–119
Wordsworth, Dorothy, 141
Wordsworth, William, 129
World literature, 15–16
Worth, Valerie, 15
Wreck of the Zephyr, The (Van Allsburg), 111
Wright, Blanche Fisher, 85–86
Wrightson, Patricia, 16
Wrinkle in Time, A (L'Engle), 213
Writing experiences, 47–49
Wyeth, N. C., 3–4

Yang, Gene Luen, 120
Yashima, Taro, 69
Yearling, The (Rawlings), 236, 238
Year of the Dog, The (Lin), 14, 65, 228
Yep, Laurence, 65
Yin, Rosanna, 65
Yonge, Charlotte, 10, 227
Young, Ed, 64
Young, Jerry, 255

Zelinsky, Paul, 110–111, 113–117
Zemach, Margot, 15, 111
Zindel, Paul, 235
Zin! Zin! Zin! A Violin (Moss), 117–118
Zlateh the Goat and Other Stories (Singer), 65–66
Zone of proximal development, 40
Z Was Zapped (Van Allsburg), 87

Credits

Image Credits

Page 4, By permission of the Folger Shakespeare Library. *Page 5,* Illustration from "Orbis Sensualium Pictus" (1659), John Comenius. Woodcut. *Page 6,* Illustrations from the "New England Primer" (1727). *Page 9,* "The Man in the Moon" from "Mother Goose's Melodies" (1833), Abel Bowen. Woodcut. *Page 11,* "Jack and Jill" from "The Baby's Opera" (1877), Walter Crane. *Page 12,* Illustration from "The Frog He Would A-Wooing Go" (1883), Randolph Caldecott. *Page 30,* "Duck, Death and the Tulip" by Wolf Erlbruch. Copyright © 2001 by Wolf Erlbruch. Reprinted with the permission of Gecko Press, distributed by Lerner Publishing Group, Inc. All rights reserved. No part of this illustration excerpt may be used or reproduced in any manner whatsoever without the prior written permission of Gecko Press. *Page 62,* Used by permission of HarperCollins Publishers. *Page 63,* Illustrations copyright © 2013 Fred Marcellino. First published in 1899. Used by permission of HarperCollins Publishers. *Page 82,* Illustration from "Mother Goose's Melodies" (1833). Wood engraving. Munroe & Francis, Boston. *Page 83,* Illustration from "The Nursery Rhyme Book" (ca. 1897), by Andrew Lang. Illustrated by L. Leslie Brooke. *Page 84,* Illustration from "Mother Goose or the Old Nursery Rhymes" (ca. 1881), Kate Greenaway. *Page 85,* "Little Miss Muffet" (1913), Arthur Rackham. *Page 88,* Illustration from "The Real Mother Goose" (1916), Blanche Fisher Wright. *Page 92,* Illustration from "Biggest, Strongest, Fastest" by Steve Jenkins. Copyright © 1995 by Steve Jenkins. Reprinted by permission of Houghton Mifflin Harcourt Publishing Company. All rights reserved. *Page 93,* From "My Friend Rabbit" copyright © 1999 by Eric Rohmann. Reprinted by permission of Henry Holt & Company, LLC. All Rights Reserved. *Page 104,* "The Tiger Who Came to Tea" copyright © 1968 by Kerr-Kneale Productions Ltd. Reproduced by permission of the publishers, Candlewick Press, Somerville, MA and HarperCollins Publishers Ltd. *Page 108,* From "Madeline" by Ludwig Bemelmans, copyright © 1939 by Ludwig Bemelmans, renewed copyright © 1967 by Madeline Bemelmans and Barbara Bemelmans Marciano. Used by permission of Viking Penguin, a division of Penguin Group (USA) LLC. *Page 109,* From "The Story of Ferdinand" by Munro Leaf, illustrated by Robert Lawson, copyright © 1936 by Munro Leaf and Robert Lawson, renewed copyright © 1964 by Munro Leaf and John W. Boyd. Used by permission of Viking Penguin, a division of Penguin Group (USA) LLC. *Page 110,* Illustration from "Jumanji" by Chris Van Allsburg. Copyright © 1981 by Chris Van Allsburg. Reprinted by permission of Houghton Mifflin Harcourt Publishing Company. All rights reserved. *Page 156,* From "Perrault's Fairy Tales" (1867), illustrated by Gustave Doré. *Page 160,* From "Household Stories by the Brothers Grimm" (1886), translated by Lucy Crane, illustrated by Walter Crane. *Page 161,* From "Household Stories by the Brothers Grimm" (1886), translated by Lucy Crane, illustrated by Walter Crane. *Page 165,* From "The Red Fairy Book" (1890), edited by Andrew Lang, illustrated by H. J. Ford. *Page 169,* From "Anansi the Spider" copyright © 1987 by Gerald McDermott. Reprinted by permission of Henry Holt & Company, LLC. All Rights Reserved. *Page 204,* From "Alice's Adventures in Wonderland" (1865), by Lewis Carroll, illustrated by Sir John Tenniel. *Page 208,* From "The Wonderful Wizard of Oz" (1900), by L. Frank Baum, illustrated by W. W. Denslow. *Page 209,* From "The Wind in the Willows" (1931), by Kenneth Grahame, illustrated by Ernest H. Shepard. *Page 226,* From "Otto of the Silver Hand" (1888), written and illustrated by Howard Pyle. *Page 232,* From "Little Women" (ca. 1900), by Louisa May Alcott, illustrated by J. S. Eland. *Page 253,* From "The Reason for a Flower" by Ruth Heller, copyright © 1983 by Ruth Heller. Used by permission of Grosset & Dunlap, Inc., a division of Penguin Group (USA) LLC. *Page 257,* "Hatching out" from "Amazing Worlds: Crocodiles and Reptiles" by Mary Ling, photographs by Jerry Young. Copyright © 1991 Dorling Kindersley. Reproduced by permission of Dorling Kindersley Ltd. *Page 259,* David A. Aguilar/Aspen Skies LLC.

Color Plate Credits

Plate A, Illustration from "The Tale of Peter Rabbit" (1901), Beatrix Potter. *Plate B,* From "Mr. Grumpy's Outing" copyright © 1971 by John Burningham. Reprinted by permission of Henry Holt & Company, LLC. All Rights Reserved. *Plate C,* From "In Powder and Crinoline, Fairy Tales Retold by Sir Arthur Quiller-Couch" illustrated by Kay Nielsen. London: Hodder & Stoughton, 1913. *Plate D,* Illustration from "Tuesday" by David Wiesner. Copyright © 1991 by David Wiesner. Reprinted by permission of Clarion Books, an imprint of Houghton Mifflin Harcourt Publishing Company. All rights reserved. *Plate E,* From "Rapunzel" by Paul O. Zelinksy, copyright © 1997 by Paul O. Zelinsky. Used by permission of Dutton Children's Books, a division of Penguin Group (USA) LLC.